THE GLOBALIZATION
OF RACISM

Series in Critical Narrative
Edited by Donaldo Macedo
University of Massachusetts Boston

Now in print

The Hegemony of English
  by Donaldo Macedo, Bessie Dendrinos, and
  Panayota Gounari (2003)
Letters from Lexington: Reflections on Propaganda
  New Updated Edition
  by Noam Chomsky (2004)
Pedogogy of Indignation
  by Paulo Freire (2004)
Howard Zinn on Democratic Education
  by Howard Zinn with Donaldo Macedo (2005)
How Children Learn: Getting Beyond the Deficit Myth
  by Terese Fayden (2005)
The Globalization of Racism
  edited by Donaldo Macedo and Panayota Gounari (2006)

Forthcoming in the series

Science, Truth, and Ideology
  by Stanley Aronowitz (2006)
Pedogogy of Dreaming
  by Paulo Freire (2006)
Dear Paulo: Letters from Teachers
  by Sonia Nieto (2006)

THE GLOBALIZATION OF RACISM

EDITED BY

DONALDO MACEDO

AND

PANAYOTA GOUNARI

Paradigm Publishers
Boulder • London

To those willing to rupture from the racist form of "charitable racism" and who are reborn with the conviction to struggle to recapture our endangered humanity.

Copyright © 2006 by Paradigm Publishers

Published in the United States by Paradigm Publishers, 3360 Mitchell Lane, Suite E, Boulder, Colorado 80301 USA.

Paradigm Publishers is the trade name of Birkenkamp & Company, LLC, Dean Birkenkamp, President and Publisher.

Library of Congress Cataloging-in-Publication Data

Macedo, Donaldo P. (Donaldo Pereira), 1950-
The globalization of racism / edited by Donaldo Macedo and Panayota Gounari.
p. cm. — (Series in critical narrative)
Includes bibliographical references and index.
ISBN 1-59451-076-8 (hardcover : alk. paper) — ISBN 1-59451-077-6
(paperback : alk. paper)
1. Racism.   2. Xenophobia.   3. Globalization.   I. Gounari, Panayota.
II. Title.   III. Series.
HT1521.M225 2005
305.8—dc22

2005016133

Printed and bound in the United States of America on acid-free paper that meets the standards of the American National Standard for Permanence of Paper for Printed Library Materials.

Designed and Typeset by Straight Creek Bookmakers.

10   09   08   07   06
1   2   3   4   5   6

CONTENTS

Contents

THE GLOBALIZATION
OF RACISM

1
GLOBALIZATION AND THE UNLEASHING OF NEW RACISM: AN INTRODUCTION

Donaldo Macedo and Panayota Gounari

⊷

Through the process of dehistoricizing race and, by implication, racism, the dominant ideology gives rise to a fertile terrain that confuses the meaning of race and enables conservatives as well as some liberal scholars to claim the "end of racism." By dominant ideology we refer to the organizing principles that generate, shape, and sustain white supremacy designed to exclude other human beings by virtue of their race, language, culture, and ethnicity so they can be exploited. In the United States, for example, writers such as Dinesh D'Souza who falsely claim the end of racism, despite overwhelming evidence to the contrary, are handsomely rewarded. This evidence ranges from the growing number of racial incidents on college campuses to the burning of synagogues and black churches to the proliferation of racist radio talk shows, whose hosts advocate killing Muslims in the name of patriotism.

The proposition that we have achieved "the end of racism" attempts to close down any space in which to question racism and the structures that produce and sustain it. In addition, this false proposition is intended to block all forms of interrogation concerning our understanding of race and racism while impeding clear analyses of these categories. The closing-down of the field of interpretation for racism has the consequence of dehistoricizing the term and its discourses and material practices. Through this dehistoricizing, racism is often disarticulated from politics and the ensuing political projects that crystallize subjectivities, agency and democratization. Individuals who embrace a dehistoricization process in their treatment of racism fail to recognize that racism is always historically specific and that it manifests itself differently in terms of geographical, cultural, ideological and material location, as accurately demonstrated by Loïc Wacquant's analysis of racism in the United States in chapter 6 of this volume. These factors invariably shape and define racism and its manifestations to a large degree. And while "historicality" usually conveys the raciological rationalization of history in

3

that it has been, according to Paul Gilroy, associated with "attempts to differentiate the status of peoples, their cultures, fates, destinies and different racial and national spirits," historicizing the race debate is crucial to our understanding of the racialization of discourses and the ensuing racist practices.[1]

Gilroy correctly observes that "'historicality' is a modern notion in that it presupposes a politics of time: making connections between ontology, nationality and theories of racial difference. It is associated with not only the idea of authenticity and the national principle but also, the elevation of 'race' to a determining position in theories of history, especially those that pronounce on war and conflict, naturalizing them in the convenient idea of specifically race-based imperial conflict."[2] Since historicality plays a fundamental role in the construction of the reality of race in the first place, we must look at the ways in which racism has and is currently manifested. Through a historical framework, it becomes much easier to adhere to David Theo Goldberg's notion that "if race is a conception, then racism is a condition; or more precisely, where race is a set of conceptions, racisms are sets of conditions," and conditions are never realized outside of history.[3] It is through history that we can more accurately identify the structures that shape and promote "the dominant feature of racist expression," which is, according to Goldberg, exclusion.[4] Hence racisms invariably involve promoting exclusions; consequently, any rigorous analysis must view racisms as phenomena of exclusion articulated on different levels and loci that either complement or clash with each other, constructing an arena where the diverse geographic, material, ideological and discursive elements coexist and are open to interpretation and analysis. Again, Goldberg's insights are illuminating: "racisms assume their particular characters, they are exacerbated, and they have different entailments and ramifications in relation to specific considerations of class constitution, gender, national identity, region and political structure."[5] By dehistoricizing the spaces that racism has occupied and is still occupying both imaginatively and materially, we are forced to embrace a depoliticized notion of race while remaining trapped in a field in which political interaction has been banished. "The end of racism" inaugurates a depoliticized space devoid of debate over meanings and institutions—a space where entailments and ramifications are simply terminated so as not to awaken dangerous memories or provoke uncomfortable discussions. That is why the topic of racism is usually labeled controversial, a characterization that discourages debate or discussion. Meanwhile, racial antagonisms remain present in shaping and reproducing the racialized discourses and practices.

Racism includes a set of ideologies, discourses, discursive practices, institutions and vocabularies. However, we take racism to be not simply an ideological construction, since, as Goldberg points out, this view "leaves unexplained the fact that racist expressions may at times define and promote rather than merely rationalize social arrangements and institutions."[6] As an academic designation it encompasses scholars in multiple disciplines who are preoccupied by the question of race and exclusion. As an object of scholarly research and study it produces theoretical and social discourses. This production of knowledge defines and shapes our understanding of racism as it is also shaped by its discourses and practices. The knowledge about racism as exclusion situates inclusions and exclusions that function as a false dichotomy whereby "us" is juxtaposed with "them" (as is the case with the clash of civilizations myth) in a way that "them" is always understood as a negative value. This dichotomy has been astutely used by the Bush administration to conduct its war on terror and expand its imperial ambitions unimpeded by a domestic opposition. By constructing a terrorist enemy that encompassed all Muslims (a "group" that amounts roughly to 1.2 billion people worldwide and comprises numerous countries, societies, traditions, languages and lived experiences), the Bush administration, aided by a compliant media, exacerbated the racism present in U.S. society so that all Muslims became suspected terrorists. And it legitimized racist treatment of Muslims, as when "Muslim-looking" individuals are deplaned by major airlines because white folks express fear of flying in their company. However, the same racial profiling was never applied to white males resembling Timothy McVeigh after the terrorist bombing of the federal building in Oklahoma City, where more than one hundred fifty people died, including women and children.

The us-versus-them dichotomy is constructed on both an academic and an imaginative level, and it produces the "reality" of what it means to have different races. It is the constructed knowledge around race that produces a racialized discourse. Furthermore, race as an "identity" marker has also been used to "reckon with the patterns of inclusion and exclusion that it cannot help creating."[7] Following Edward Said's line of thinking, racism is something historically and materially defined. We need to examine racism as a discourse or else we cannot possibly understand the enormous systematic discipline by which exclusions based on race, ethnicity, culture and other markers of "otherness" are able to produce racism materially, discursively, politically, sociologically, ideologically, scientifically and imaginatively. It is the work and dissemination of a powerful discourse through an acquiescent media, institutions for cultural reproduction, along with material practices, that produces racialized appearances.

Arguably radio hosts and television commentators who implicitly or explicitly advocate racist practices against Muslims are on the fringe and are not part of mainstream America. Unfortunately, the dehumanization of Muslims in the current fight on terror often blurs the boundaries between fringe and mainstream, as exemplified by the comments of Lieutenant General James N. Mattis: "You go into Afghanistan, you got guys who slap women around for five years because they didn't wear a veil. You know, guys like that ain't got no manhood left anyway. So it's a hell of a lot fun to shoot them."[8] Mattis was speaking as part of a panel sponsored by the Armed Forces Communications and Electronics Association, where his comments "were met with laughter and applause from the audience."[9] His comments also received no censure from his superior, General Mike Hagee, who remarked that "Lieutenant General Mattis often speaks with great deal of candor. I have counseled him concerning his remarks and he agrees he will choose his words more carefully."[10]

The current assault on Muslims worldwide and in the United States in particular points to the fact that "race is irreducibly a political category . . . and there is no generic racism, only historically specific racisms each with their own sociotemporally specific causes."[11] According to Goldberg, "There is no single (set of) transcendental determinant(s) that inevitably causes the occurrence of racism—be it nature, or drive, or mode of production, or class formation. There are only the minutiae that make up the fabric of daily life and specific interests and values, the cultures out of which racialized discourse and expressions arise. Racist expressions become normalized in and through the prevailing categories of modernity's epistemes and institutionalized in modernity's various modes of social articulations and power."[12] If Goldberg is correct, and we think he is, then the facile proposition claiming the end of racism not only ignores the historical specificities that give rise to racist practices but also reconstitutes itself as a racist expression to the degree that the very denial of racism is a racist act. Further, such a proposition relies on specific determinants that sustain the end of racism claim—determinants that remain disarticulated from a constellation of historical factors that give rise to and maintain multiple forms of racism. In addition, we want to argue that a thorough comprehension of a racist reality can be achieved only through a convergent model of analysis that gives proper weight to each historical factor and its relationship with other factors that serve as the root cause of a particular racist manifestation. In other words, no single factor provides enough basis for a thorough understanding of racism. Hence the apprehension of racism as an object of knowledge depends most of all on the articulation of multiple factors of history such as the interdependence of race and class, which in turn produces specific forms of racism as a fact of history.

The main goal of *The Globalization of Racism* is to denude the ideological manipulation inherent in the false proposition "the end of racism" while calling attention to new forms of racism that are manifesting globally and are exacerbated by the commonsense discourse of neoliberalism and its theological embrace of the market as a panacea for all world problems. The chapters in this volume are designed to provide readers with an understanding of the historical conditions that produce specific manifestations of racism—a theoretical posture that moves away from the rigidity of a particular model of racist analysis by showing that

> The claim that racism is nothing more than ideological is confusing or delimiting in a different way. It misleadingly leaves the deleterious effects of racist practices and institutions to be captured by some other term like racialism or racist dis-

crimination. Alternatively, by insisting that the raison d'être of the racist ideological structure is to hide some underlying form of economic, social, or political oppression, this widely shared claim refuses to acknowledge the materiality of racially defined effects in their own right. It fails to acknowledge, and so leaves unexplained, the fact that racist expressions may at times define and promote rather than merely rationalize social arrangements and institutions. Sepulveda's characterization of Mexican Indians as fit only for slavery enabled their enslavement to be conceived rather than simply serving to rationalize their exploitation *ex post facto*.[13]

By going beyond a model of analysis that merely serves to "rationalize social arrangements and institutions," the case study chapters for each country demonstrate how "racist expressions may at times define and promote" conditions that make it easier to exploit other human beings through the establishment of racial differences that invariably lead to exclusion. For example, in chapter 12, "Greece: Xenophobia of the Weak and Racism of the Progressive," by Georgios Tsiakalos, the analysis of racism is predicated not exclusively on racial differences per se but on exclusionary practices that target Albanians who belong to the white race. *The Globalization of Racism* also points out the impossibility of "the end of racism" in light of the exponential increase of xenophobia throughout the world, which has been caused in large measure by neoliberal policies producing economic dislocation that has impelled millions of the world's poor to seek economic relief by migrating from rural to urban areas and from poor to rich countries. This massive migration has, more often than not, heightened racism that has manifested itself differently in other contexts.

The United States is not alone in facing a dramatic increase in racism and xenophobia. In France the ultraright National Front Party headed by Jean-Marie Le Pen has mounted an incessant attack on immigrants, particularly Muslims from the former French colonies. In the past decade or so the National Front was able to elect four mayors in the south of France. In turn, these ultra right-wing politicians implemented racist policies in, for example, the town of Vitrolles near Marseilles, where French families with children were given $833 as a birth allowance, while foreign immigrant families received no allowance. In Germany there has been a significant increase in the number of neo-Nazi groups; they have been responsible for a number of house bombings against Turks and Greeks. In London racism has reached outrageous levels, prompting serious investigation concerning the widespread institutionalized racism at all levels of life in Britain. Similar xenophobia has been seen in Spain, particularly toward North African immigrants and Romani. For example, in the town of El Ejido, "thousands of people were armed with sticks and iron bars tearing down immigrant stores, bars that were frequented by [immigrants] . . . They burned down shacks, they destroyed archives, files . . . Spaniards were heard shouting at the immigrants: 'You will have to leave and we will stay here. We are going to kill you all.'. . . Among the thousands of people one could hear 'let's throw poison in the water they drink.'"[14] For years Portugal prided itself on creating a haven of racial harmony by disingenuously keeping out African immigrants. Now that the end of its colonialism has propelled massive numbers of Africans to Portugal, racist practices are as visible as the shanty-towns around Lisbon populated by those dispossessed Africans, who are excluded from full participation in the country's civic life. According to Josephine Ocloo,

> Racist and fascist activity has also been on the increase in many other European countries such as Belgium, Denmark, Sweden and the Czech Republic to name a few, with the election of Jorg Haider's Freedom Party setting a particularly worrying precedent with its capture of 27.2% of the vote in the Austrian elections in 1999. The move by the Conservative party to bring the Freedom Party into a coalition government provoked hostile and widespread international condemnation. Belgium's anti-immigration party (*Vlaamse Volk*) also emerged as the biggest political force in the country's second city in October 2000. The party increased its share of the vote in the local elections in Antwerp from 28% of the vote in 1994, to 33% of the vote in 2000. In places like Russia the *Anti-Fascist Centre* and the Helsinki based *Human Rights Watch* in 1998 pointed to a number of worrying incidents of racism. The former pointed to growing attacks on foreigners, blacks and Asians and the latter highlighted a dossier of accounts exposing beatings and torture of black citizens by the Moscow police. In Britain, racial violence exploded—literally—onto the agenda in April 1999, with the planting of a number of nail bombs deliberately targeting Black and gay communities. This left more than a hundred people injured and three dead. In the same year the press reported a 75% increase in incidents of racial violence (Guardian, 1999), and we saw the long awaited publication of the Stephen Lawrence Inquiry report by Lord MacPherson.[15]

In some countries anti-Semitism is also on the rise. A retired general and former Communist Party official, Albert Makashov, delivered a virulently anti-Semitic speech, and a leading Russian newspaper was led to alert the citizens about the increase in racial intolerance in a front-page headline. Serious concerns about anti-Semitism also became evident in Argentina, where the interior minister had begun an investigation concerning the suspicion that law enforcement officials were involved in the bombing of the Israeli embassy. A significant increase in anti-Semitism has also been observed in Austria and other European countries. At the same time, the Israeli treatment of Palestinians cannot be understood without taking a detour through an analysis of determinants that give rise to racism, as discussed in chapter 3 by Edward Said and chapter 7 by Kathleen and Bill Christison.

Against a landscape of growing racism and xenophobia worldwide, and particularly in the United States, the argument that the end of racism has been achieved holds water only if we engage once again in denying the ideological construction of racism. Although, as we have noted, that ideology is not the only lens through which racism can be viewed, it has often been used by the dominant group to promote racist relations while refusing to acknowledge the central role of ideology in the production and reproduction of a web of lies that robs individuals of the critical tools needed to understand that we cannot have reached the end of racism when white murderers deliberately attempt to frame young black men for their crimes.

In Boston, John Stuart killed his pregnant wife, drove to a black neighborhood, and then reported to police that a black man had murdered his wife and shot him in the stomach. The Boston police responded by putting the neighborhood under siege; every black man was a suspect and an innocent black man was sent to jail. Months later the attorney general's office, embarrassed, had to release the suspect when it became clear that Stuart himself had killed his wife. The same scenario occurred when Susan Smith drowned her two children by strapping them into their car seats and plunging the car into a lake. She claimed that a black man had hijacked her car at a stoplight and driven off with her two children in the back.

If in fact we have reached the end of racism, why do white murderers bank on their probable escape by scapegoating black men? If in fact we have ended racism in the United States, why did President Clinton feel the need to call for a national dialogue on race? If racism is a thing of the past, why are people of color routinely followed when they enter a department store and seldom given the benefit of the doubt accorded to most white people? If we now live in a colorblind society, why is it that for black people "there can also be an eerie risk to walking in one's own predominantly white neighborhood, or getting in one's car where one might commit the common, unofficial vehicular offense dubbed DWB—driving while Black"?[16]

How can intellectuals proclaim the end of racism in the United States when James Byrd Jr., a black man, was dragged to death by John William King in Jasper, Texas, until his head was torn off? It takes tremendous effort not to acknowledge that lynching of blacks and other racial and ethnic minorities is not a thing of the past. How can we honestly relegate lynching to the past when two white police officers in New York City brutally sodomized a Haitian immigrant, Abner Louima, with a toilet plunger? How can we deny that lynching is alive in our institutions of law and order when officers from the same New York police department pumped forty-one bullets into the body of an innocent African immigrant, Amadou Diallo, whose only crime, in the officers' eyes, was that he was a black man?

What ideological blinders are worn by Dinesh D'Souza and the other cultural commissars proclaiming the end of racism that they do not see such evidence as described by the Institute of Medicine, which contends that blacks, Hispanics and other minorities in the United States "tend to get lower quality health care than whites, even when income, age and whether they have insurance is factored in" and concludes that "significantly these differences are associated with greater mortality among African-American patients"?[17]

It is obvious that institutional racism is not a thing of the past, nor is it a problem unique to the New York Police Department. Throughout the United States racial profiling is as ubiquitous as McDonald's. Cornel West's fame as an intellectual and a professor of religion did not insulate him from the DWB vehicular offense: "Years ago, while driving from New York to teach at Williams College, I was stopped on fake charges of trafficking cocaine. When I told the police officer I was a professor of religion, he replied, 'Yeah, and I'm the Flying Nun. Let's go, nigger!' I was stopped three times in my first ten days in Princeton for driving too slow on a residential street with a speed limit of twenty-five miles per hour."[18]

By refusing to acknowledge the construction of racism that constitutes the very fabric of Western civilization, those who proclaim the end of racism and other Western cultural commissars fail "to understand that racism has always flourished as part and parcel of a system of power. Europeans did not encounter other cultures as tourists or disinterested scientific investigators. Racism arose not simply to explain difference but to justify conquest, colonization, enslavement, and economic domination."[19] Racism endures in the United States and, for that matter, all over the world, as the chapters in this volume convincingly demonstrate. Even though Jim Crow laws have been eradicated and racialized discourses have been somewhat cleansed, racism manifests in more subtle forms, such as blaming blacks in the United States for seeking federal protection, which according to D'Souza "cripples black efforts at advancement and has spawned the illegitimacy, criminality and hostility to hard work and educational advancement that characterize black America."[20] This systematic demonization and dehumanization of blacks and other subordinate groups along racial and ethnic lines represents a continuation of a colonial legacy through which "almost always, the colonialist also devotes himself to a systematic devaluation of the colonized."[21]

NEOLIBERALISM, GLOBALIZATION AND THE PRODUCTION OF RACISM

It is neither a coincidence nor a natural phenomenon that although neoliberal policies have been directly or indirectly detrimental to the lives of millions of people, neoliberalism still remains in people's minds an important currency and a viable, "successful" doctrine, even for many of those who have suffered its most catastrophic effects. For example, neoliberal policies have created economic havoc leading to economic collapse in Argentina and unseen hardship and economic dislocation in Bolivia, Mexico and other so-called third world countries. Nonetheless, the United States, right after invading Iraq, implemented draconian neoliberal policies, selling off national assets mostly to foreign bidders and undemocratically imposing a form of "democracy" that equates free market and fraudulent "free" elections with democratic practices—a form of democracy celebrated by the Western media that has the function of legitimizing U.S. occupation, leading many dissenters to label it "democratic occupation." While the compliant corporate media in the United States and in many European countries blindly celebrated elections in Iraq in an attempt to rewrite the illegality of the U.S. invasion, the same corporate media fail to acknowledge that "free election of masters does not abolish the masters or the slaves. Free choice among a wide variety of goods and services does not signify freedom if these goods and services sustain social controls over a life of toil and fear—that is if they sustain alienation."[22]

This willful not seeing happens largely because the neoliberal order has presented itself as the inevitable effect of an economic doctrine theologically guarded by economic institutions such as the World Bank, the International Monetary Fund and the World Trade Organization—institutions that largely promote and protect the economic interests of the developed world against those of the rest of the world population. The people of the so-called undeveloped countries (the appropriate term would be exploited countries) are condemned to poverty, exploitation and, as Jean-Paul Sartre once noted with respect to colonial exploitation, subhumanity. For example, while neoliberal policies forced an agreement between the Bolivian government and Sempra Energy of California to exploit natural gas, the Indians in Villa Ingenio "were freezing at 13,000 feet without gas hookups."[23] The gas line project was being funded by a $7 billion World Bank loan that was suspended when indigenous people protested the blatant exploitation of the nation's natural resources, which would provide outrageous profits to Sempra Energy and the minuscule Bolivian upper class while the vast majority of Indians would fall deeper into poverty and despair. This uprising of the indigenous people in Bolivia against neoliberal policies worried the U.S. military when in "Congressional testimony [in June 2004] Gen. James Hill, head of the Southern Command, warned that 'if radicals continue to hijack the indigenous movement, we could find ourselves faced with a narco-state that supports the uncontrollable cultivation of coca.'"[24] Interestingly, the U.S. military seems oblivious to the cultivation of opium in Afghanistan, which is now the chief exporter of this drug to Europe. The U.S. military is just as unconcerned by the exploitation of the Bolivian indigenous people who had to endure the hardship imposed by Bechtel Corporation when it jacked up the water rate beyond the means of the people after privatization.

Similar exploitation has taken place in India, where neoliberal policies have led to a "process of barbaric dispossession on a scale that has few parallels in history."[25] For example, the privatization of electricity in India guaranteed Enron exorbitant profits while "the power that the Enron plant produces is twice as expensive as its nearest competitor and seven times as expensive as the cheapest electricity available in Maharashtra."[26] When in January 2001 "the Maharashtra government . . . announced that it did not have the money to pay Enron's bills . . . Enron had decided to invoke the counterguarantee and that if the government did not come with cash, it would have to auction the government properties named as collateral security in the contract."[27] According to Arundhati Roy, "U.S. government officials warned India about vitiating the 'investment climate' and running the risk of frightening away future investors. In other words: Allow us to rob you blind or else we'll go away."[28] While U.S. officials are preoccupied with guaranteeing U.S. corporations maximum profit even if it means military intervention when indigenous people protest their ensuing impoverishment, U.S. officials remain callously unconcerned that the neoliberal policies they impose through globalization constitute "a mutant variety of colonialism, remote-controlled and digitally operated."[29] In fact, the underlying objective of neoliberalism is to truncate development of already impoverished countries, as when the U.S. Congress recommended that the World Bank stop loans to India that were designed to subsidize education for people who are too poor to afford any form of schooling. Clearly neoliberal policies produce unimaginable economic dislocation, widening the already obnoxious gap between the tiny group of developed nations and the majority of undeveloped countries. Neoliberal policies are predicated on the wholesale exclusion of most of the world population from partaking equitably in the world's resources, including education and health care, accelerating a downward shift toward unconscionable poverty and human misery. This form of blatant exclusion cannot be viewed as anything other than poster racism.

The permanent status of underdevelopment affects mostly countries that the dominant racialized discourse characterizes as "nonwhite" and "other." In addition to the characterization of otherness in order to devalue other human beings, neoliberal policies implement racist practices by largely excluding millions of people from equal participation in the economic world (dis)order it imposes. Such exclusionary practices are usually legitimized through a network of diffusion that has functioned to establish neoliberal ideologies along the lines of what Terry Eagleton calls "strategies of legitimization."[30] In this sense, the neoliberal framework has been promoting "beliefs and values congenial to it," and it has been naturalizing and universalizing such beliefs, producing thus the discourse of self-evidence and inevitability. It has been denigrating ideas that might challenge it, as it has done with the World Social Forum started in Porto Alegre, Brazil, and excluding rival forms of thought by relentlessly attacking leaders who dare to criticize neoliberalism, as has been the case with President Hugo Chavez in Venezuela, where the United States even supported a failed coup d'état against him even though he was democratically elected. Finally, it has been obscuring social reality by "suppressing social conflicts, from which arises the conception of [neoliberal] ideology as an imaginary resolution of real contradictions."[31] The new global disorder produced by neoliberalism has promoted more exclusion and human misery, as clearly demonstrated by Henry Giroux in chapter 5.

Against this neoliberal backdrop, the debate should be understood within the framework of advanced capitalism and the current neoliberal (dis)order. The neoliberal commonsense mechanisms not only trivialize and distort public discourses as part of their depoliticizing function, but they also generate and legitimize their own "transparent" and "natural" discourse that serves as a vehicle for circulating their myths and ideologies.[32] In this process, linguistic mediations are lost and, according to Herbert Marcuse, language "tends to express and promote the immediate identification of reason and fact, truth and established truth, essence and existence, the thing and its function."[33] At this juncture, the commodified language becomes both the tool and the end of neoliberal ideologies that operate in order to "guarantee" their aggressive and often inhumane practices. Their effects include the erasure of the welfare state, the shrinking of the public sector, the increasing inequalities and exclusions, the transfer of public wealth to private hands and the minimalization of the functions of the state, a process that jeopardizes its civilizing and helping functions.[34] Under neoliberalism the state gives up its social functions to undertake a surveillance and policing role, a logic that suggests a borderless world for capital but not for labor.[35]

Henry Giroux's work is instrumental on this point, especially his claim that what is lost in this perspective are "important questions about the varied sites, practices and forms of power that give meaning to how politics is shaped, deployed and played out on a daily basis." He concludes along these lines that "politics imitates the market to the degree that it highlights the importance of struggle but ignores the ethical implications of such struggles."[36] It is necessary to make these links between economic events and the human consequences because there is a clear dichotomy in neoliberal ideologies between economy and policies. In other words, neoliberalism presents itself as an economic doctrine that professes free markets, deregulation and freedom from government restrictions and trade controls, disguised in a positivistic economist discourse of "naturalness" and "inevitability." At the same time, it neglects to talk about the effects of this economic theory on real people or the social costs of implementing such an economic order. The separation between the economic and the social is very much part of a neoliberal agenda whereby increasing social inequalities, the widening gap between the rich and the poor and human suffering are perceived as individual problems or issues of character. Discussion centers around transactions, interested parties and agreements, or around skills, competition and choices, and these topics are largely presented as if they happen in a vacuum. Absent from this discussion are questions about who is affected by these transactions (certainly the so-called interested parties do not include the unemployed, welfare recipients or minimum wage workers) or what these transactions or policies are costing in terms of jobs, unemployment, sickness, suicide, alcoholism, drug addiction and other forms of human suffering. By using terms such as "interested parties" or "consumers," instead of "people" or maybe "citizens," neoliberalism positions individuals in an absolute apathy and inertia regarding any political project.

The neoliberal economic challenge, which supposedly invites everybody to drink from a fountain of equal opportunity, ignores the lines of class, race, gender, education, age, disability and so forth. It also pigeonholes people as skilled or unskilled workers, educated or uneducated, successful or unsuccessful, while leaving unchallenged the inequality inherent in the system designed to build skills. It obscures the fact that choices may not be the same for people who do not have the resources to realize these choices, in a society that largely promotes injustice and unequal opportunities and resources. In the current global disorder people are "free to be excluded" without anybody feeling the moral and ethical responsibility to intervene to change this reality.

The agenda for political choices today can hardly be politically constructed, as there is an ongoing separation of power from politics.[37] Power is no longer tied to any geographical location and is not contained within nation-states. On the contrary, power is extraterritorial; it flows. This extraterritorial conception reverses the logic of the traditional understanding of power, violence and authority. Capital is exported and circulated in international markets; contrary to neoliberal claims that there is no source of power, capital and the market become the sole sources of power. The difference is that the locus of this power cannot necessarily be set geographically, since as Beck argues, "the economy has broken out of the cage of territorially and nationally organized power conflict and has acquired new power moves in digital space."[38] Consequently the market is more mobile; it is not tied to a specific place and therefore can be disposed globally as it is controlled and managed by transnational corporate powers. The extraterritoriality of power necessarily affects our understanding, as the source of decision making and policy implementation become invisible and its effects become inevitable.

THE "END OF RACISM" TRAP: THE FOSSILIZATION OF A DEFERRED REVOLUTION

The false proposition "the end of racism" functions not only to dehistoricize the historical determinants that generate, shape and maintain racist practices, but it also naturalizes the backlash that is currently taking place against the gains achieved during the 1960s and 1970s. Even those who benefited greatly from, for example, the civil rights movement in the United States now argue vehemently against policies that enabled subordinated groups to begin to break down the walls of exclusion that marginalized them. Although the civil rights movement in the United States opened up opportunities for many subordinated groups, it was in many ways a reformist movement that lacked a revolutionary pedagogy. Such a pedagogy would have, on the one hand, embraced a societal transformation whereby all people would partake in more radical democracy and, on the other, prevented the present gulf between the relatively small number of subordinated individuals who gained access to the middle class and the vast majority who, by virtue of their race, culture, language and ethnicity, remain marginalized. A revolutionary pedagogy would also have prevented the emergence of intellectuals from these subordinated groups whose main task is to represent the oppressed majority left behind. By their role as representatives of the oppressed majority, these intellectuals generally become populists who are often eager to protect their new middle-class status, as they are beholden to the very system that sustains that status. As a result, they never became what Edward Said characterized as "an independent, autonomously functioning intellectual, one who is not beholden to, and therefore constrained by, his or her affiliations with universities that pay salaries, political parties that demand loyalty to party line, think tanks that while they offer freedom to do research perhaps more subtly compromise judgments and restrain the critical voice."[39] In essence, many of these representative intellectuals fail to see that the reformist agenda of the civil rights movement could only produce a deferred revolution—one that is fast becoming fossilized as we witness a retrenchment from the progressive causes and democratic ideals that served as bedrock for the movement during the 1960s and 1970s. Although there were exceptions, many leaders and intellectuals who helped shape the civil rights movement fall outside of Said's vision of an intellectual—a secular being, an "amateur foray" into the public sphere who is "advancing human freedom and knowledge" with his or her ideals deeply rooted in the belief that "all human beings are entitled to expect decent standards of behavior concerning freedom and justice from worldly powers or nations, and that deliberate or inadvertent violations of these standards need to be testified and fought against courageously."[40] This role should by no means be seen as a profession; Said warns against "intellectuals thinking of their work as something they do for a living, making themselves marketable and above all presentable, hence uncontroversial and apolitical and 'objective.'"[41] These professional intellectuals are accurately captured by Noam Chomsky when he refers to them as "commissars" who "are performing a service that is expected of them by the institutions for which they work, and they willingly, perhaps unconsciously, fulfill the requirements of the doctrinal system."[42]

Against a legacy of professional intellectuals who often sacrifice their principles to serve the dominant power structure through a form of accommodation, Said embraces a form of intellectualism that guarantees not only a spirit of critique but also a necessary independence of thinking. In other words, Said, like Paulo Freire, believes that an intellectual must always have the courage, the ethical posture, to denounce so as to be able to announce a world informed by a language of critique as well as a language of possibility. Amateurism means refusing to support academic professionalization of social criticism and taking the risk to expose oneself and one's ideas to the public sphere through lectures, books or articles; it means to speak truth to power. It also means activism and intellectual militancy in order to overthrow all forms of oppression by any means necessary, as Malcolm X so courageously put it. And it means not to align oneself with the interests of the powerful elite and not to submit to a system that constantly rewards individuals for obedience and their contributions to the reproduction of an inherently discriminatory and undemocratic reality. As Said argued, "being in that sort of professional position, where you are principally serving and winning rewards from power, is not at all conducive to the exercise of that critical and relatively independent spirit of analysis and judgment that, from my point of view, ought to be the intellectual's contribution."[43]

Again, the issue of space/terrain emerges as a critical factor in the intellectual's function. At this point the question is how to inhabit a public space where the constraints are a given (the universities pay the professors' salaries) and yet resist one's own accommodation, as well as how to redefine a fixed space as a democratic public sphere. This question is particularly timely given the rise of a new class of "public intellectuals" from subordinated groups who are commodified as stars. These new populist intellectuals have largely compromised the spirit of oppositional discourse while at the same time maintaining the image of respected figures who have something to say about "public life." Absent from their discourse is the very "public," which has been co-opted and in many respects serves the interests of the dominant ideologies against the public they are charged to represent and speak for. Within the commodification of intellectualism, populist intellectuals have been commodified by the system and are rewarded for the services they provide as professionals. In some real sense, the commodification of the mind invariably reduces the populist intellectual to the status of a clerk of the empire. In other words, by providing an intellectual service that legitimizes the ideological order of a particular society, the populist intellectual reaps tremendous rewards from the system, becoming what Adorno calls "the miser of our time . . . the man who considers nothing too expensive for himself, and everything for others. He thinks in equivalents, subjecting his whole private life to the law that one gives less than one receives in return, yet enough to ensure that one receives something. Every good deed is accompanied by an evident 'is it necessary?', 'do I have to?'"[44]

Along the same lines, commodification of the mind can be seen, for example, in the manufacturing of intellectuals as celebrities. The situation gets even more problematic when intellectuals coming from groups that have been historically oppressed, as is the case with black intellectuals, eagerly don the "stardom" badge and act as spokespeople for an entire social or ethnic group, while most members of that group are never allowed to be present in history as full citizens. This is obvious in the case of Henry Louis Gates and Cornel West, undoubtedly the two most prominent and popular black public intellectuals. As Giroux suggests, they "both exemplify the dangers that public intellectuals face when they take on the responsibility of speaking for an entire generation of black intellectuals. In the current work of both West and Gates there are indications that the spirit of oppositional discourse that keeps alive the radical thrust of being a public intellectual is being compromised."[45] That compromising process is part and parcel of what it means to be commodified. That is, the system initially buys dissent as a piece of knowledge that has a specific exchange value, and in turn the individual gets rewarded for giving up his or her principles and embracing a new order in which he or she is rewarded for speaking for the oppressed other. Safely protected in their elite institutions and living the "life of the mind," both West and Gates have little in common with the black people who are still relegated to subhumanity in the ghettoes. In a sense, they are promoted as embodying equal opportunity and diversity at institutions whose policies are in compliance with the very ideology that perpetuates white supremacy and functions to exclude minority students or students from low-income backgrounds. In numerous media appearances, cover stories (Gates in *Boston* magazine) and highly promoted publications, both West and Gates are less concerned with intervening in the public spheres where blacks are experiencing blatant racism and discrimination and more concerned with developing a public image that promotes them as spokespeople for the black community. Goldberg correctly argues that black intellectuals need to be vigorously engaged rather than simply dismissed or uncritically celebrated as Cornel West demanded. West and Gates, like most prominent public intellectuals, need to be measured against their own critical standards.

Goldberg also points out that when intellectuals intervene at the level of civic debate and speak to large audiences, they face enormous constraints regarding what they can say and how they represent themselves. While membership in a group that has been historically oppressed does not automatically make them critical and dissident, black public intellectuals should always assume a posture of dissent instead of accommodating so as to reproduce the values required by a capitalist order and the very ideology that created the need for representatives of oppressed groups. Giroux remarks that what is missing from the work of both Gates and West is a model of leadership embraced by W. E. B. Du Bois, who recognized that the best-educated people are not necessarily those who are most enlightened ethically or politically.

By becoming professional populist intellectuals, these representatives of the oppressed often lack the intellectual militancy and the revolutionary yearning to transform rather than merely reform oppressive conditions. As a result, the terrain becomes more fertile for a lack of ethical enlightenment and politically clear individuals—a lack of political clarity that is often glossed over by a euphemistic discourse that becomes part of an ideological straitjacket that binds people into thinking ideology is found only in the discourse of others. This euphemistic discourse enables the dominant ideologies to foster, even in so-called democratic societies, a form of historical amnesia that leads to the willful social construction of not seeing. They are prevented from acknowledging discriminatory practices against people who, because of their race, ethnicity, class or gender, are not treated with the dignity and respect called for by the democratic principles of a "free" society. We are often victims of our historical amnesia. For instance, the fault line of racism was exposed during O. J. Simpson's trial and in the Los Angeles uprising that followed the acquittal of the police officers who beat Rodney

King, which is referred to in the dominant discourse as the "Los Angeles riot." Even the choice of nomenclature is not ideologically neutral. For example, *uprising* and *riot* evoke different realities that call for very different social responses. By calling the uprising of blacks and Latinos a riot, the dominant ideology creates a justification for force. The social order that had been broken by the "rioting" individuals had to be forcibly restored. In the process, we are prevented from discussing and understanding the root causes of the "uprising" or appreciating attempts by individuals to correct a social wrong. Thus the dominant discourse does not permit the use of the word *uprising*.

Insofar as we use words as a sign to make meaning, we are deliberately attaching ideological values to the process of meaning making. As V. N. Volosinov so brilliantly argued, "a sign does not simply exist as part of reality, it reflects and refracts another reality. Therefore, it may distort that reality or be true to it, or may perceive it from a special point of view and so forth. Every sign is subject to the criteria of ideological evaluation (i.e. whether it is true, false, correct, fair, good, etc.). The domain of ideology coincides with the domain of signs. They equate with one another. Whenever a sign is present, ideology is present too."[46] Accordingly, Volosinov contends, it is impossible to speak of meaning making outside of ideology. Our word choices are determined by an ideological predisposition; they are never neutral or innocent. Let's look again at the terms *riot* and *uprising*. If Volosinov is correct, and we believe he is, these terms do not exist merely as a part of the reality characterized by public disturbances. Rather, they also reflect another reality, one necessarily linked to the criteria of ideological evaluation. Consider these two statements:

A: "Rioting blacks in Los Angeles were summarily arrested and beaten by the police."
B: "Uprising blacks in Los Angeles were summarily arrested and beaten by the police."

Note that reading the word *rioting* impels us to blindly support the law-and-order establishment, which in fact planted the seeds that ultimately gave rise to the disturbance. We are also persuaded to support the police, who, we are led to believe, are protecting us from violent public disorder led by blacks and Latinos without cause or foundation. On the other hand, the word *uprising* implies a cause, a struggle for social justice, which presupposes the denial of justice and the existence of oppressive conditions that need to be corrected. An uprising often inspires empathy with those who set out to correct such injustices. In example A the reality is distorted so as to prevent people from understanding the root causes that led blacks and Latinos in Los Angeles to take their frustration to the streets. An ideological space is created that makes it easy to blame the victims while absolving the perpetrators of oppression. In example B the reflection and refraction of reality coincide with material conditions that justify the act of the uprising itself; the statement itself induces both sympathy and support for the participants in the uprising. In this respect uprising as "an ideological sign is not only a reflection, a shadow of reality, but is also itself a material segment of that very reality."[47]

Given the complexity of the ideological manipulation inherent in proclaiming the end of racism, which we consider the use of language to obfuscate the material conditions that characterize a racist reality, we should denude this false proposition in order to avoid falling into a self-congratulatory mode in which even some blacks apologetically rationalize that "things are not as bad as they used to be"; affirmative action has outlived its purpose, reaching a point of diminishing returns and leading the African American professor Shelby Steele to argue that "preferential treatment 'no matter how justified in the light of day, subjects blacks to a midnight of self-doubt, and so often transforms their advantage into a revolving door.'"[48] In fact, conservatives and reactionary cultural commissars argue that affirmative action "is too clumsy a tool" and that persistent racism "is a myth invented by the black civil rights establishment. What discrimination takes place today is a 'rational response to black group traits'—illegitimacy, criminality and a desire to live off the government rather than work."[49] The apologists revel in announcing the end of racism and expect blacks to be grateful to white society that "things are not as bad as they used to be." This expectation of thankfulness was profoundly understood by Malcolm X, who responded that "if you stick a knife in my back, if you put it in nine inches and pull it out six inches, you haven't done me any favor. If you pull it all the way out, you haven't done me any favor."[50]

Even when progressive scholars devote considerable energy to denouncing, for example, the racialist practices of a given democracy, they often tend to compartmentalize race by separating it from the ideological construct that produced the racist structure of a particular "democratic" society in the first place—and we put "democracy" in quotation marks to signal that it is an oxymoron to claim democracy in a society that remains as fundamentally racist as the United States and most other Western "democracies."

The compartmentalization of those factors responsible for the production and reproduction of racism is part of the ideological construction that prevents the development of critical thinking that would enable one to read the world critically and to understand the reasons and linkages behind the facts in the construction of racism. Thus the study of racism should not be separated from an awareness of the ideology and other factors that produce it. In addition, by placing our analysis of racism in its historicity, we begin to understand that racism is part of a colonialist ideology, in which, as Albert Memmi reminds us:

All the efforts of the colonialist are directed toward maintaining this social immobility, and racism is the surest weapon for this aim. In effect, change becomes impossible, and any revolt could be absurd.

Racism appears then, not as an incidental detail, but as a consubstantial part of colonialism. It is the highest expression of the colonial system and one of the

most significant features of the colonialist. Not only does it establish a fundamental discrimination between colonizer and colonized, a sine qua non of colonial life, but it also lays the foundation for the immutability of this life.[51]

What is often missing from the analysis of racism in contemporary Western democracies, particularly in the United States, is the linkage between a
de facto colonial legacy and the racist expressions of that legacy. Thus, even
when many white progressives assume an antiracist posture within the society, they often direct their efforts toward the symptoms of racism and not
its root cause. It is this fragmentation of the social reality concerning racism
that has produced a very small but highly visible liberal movement that
condemns the perpetuation of overtly racist discrimination, exploitation and
oppression of black people and other subordinate groups. However, this
condemnation masks how all-pervasive white supremacy is in this society,
both as ideology and as behavior, and white supremacy structures remain
beyond analysis. In reality, any condemnation of racism that leaves the white
supremacy structures unexamined (and this is the case in most instances)
constitutes a more insidious form of racism to the extent that, by not
interrogating the white supremacy structures, the white liberal pseudo-anti-
racists continue to enjoy the white privileges inherently provided to them by
these structures.

This is not entirely surprising given the liberals' paradoxical posture with
respect to race issues. On the one hand, liberals progressively idealize "principles of liberty, equality and fraternity [while insisting] upon the moral
irrelevance of race. Race is irrelevant, but all is race."[52] On the other hand,
some liberals accept the notion of difference and call for the toleration of
difference. For example, there is a rapid growth of textbooks ostensibly
designed to teach racial and multicultural tolerance. But what these texts in
fact do is hide the asymmetrical distribution of power and cultural capital
through a form of paternalism that promises to the other a dose of tolerance. In other words, they say, "Since we coexist and must find ways to get
along, I will tolerate you." Missing from this posture is the ethical position
that calls for mutual respect and even racial and cultural solidarity. According to Goldberg, tolerance "presupposes that its object is morally repugnant, that it really needs to be reformed, that is, altered."[53] Consequently
racial and cultural "tolerance," as practiced by the dominant sectors in U.S.
society, permits the different "other" to think, or at least hope, that through
this so-called tolerance the intolerable features that characterize the different other will be eliminated or repressed. Thus Goldberg is correct in
pointing out that

> liberals are moved to overcome the racial differences they tolerate and have been
> so instrumental in fabricating by diluting them, by bleaching them out through
> assimilation or integration. The liberal would assume away the difference in
> otherness, maintaining thereby the dominance of a presumed sameness, the

universally imposed similarity in identity. The paradox is perpetrated: The commitment to tolerance turns only on modernity's natural inclination to intolerance; acceptance of otherness presupposes as it at once necessitates delegitimization of the other.[54]

Tolerance for different racial and ethnic groups as proposed by some white liberals does not just constitute a veil behind which they hide their racism; it also puts them in a compromising racial position. While calling for "racial tolerance," a paternalistic term, they often retain the white privilege that is complicit with the dominant ideology. That is, the call for tolerance never questions the asymmetrical power relations that give them their privilege. Thus many white liberals willingly call and work for cultural tolerance but are reluctant to confront issues of inequality, power, ethics, race, or ethnicity in a way that could actually make society more democratic and humane and less racist and discriminatory. This form of racism is readily understood by its victims. As Carol Swain, an African American professor at Princeton University, observed, "White liberals are among the most racist people I know; they're so patronizing towards blacks."[55] The contradictions inherent in the white liberals' patronizing antiracist stance were not lost in Malcolm X's analysis of race relations; he pointedly stated:

> the type of white person who perpetuates the problem is the one who poses as a liberal and pretends that the Negro should be integrated, as long as he integrates someone else's neighborhood. But all these whites that you see running around here talking about how liberal they are, and we believe everybody should have what they want, as soon as a Negro moves into that white liberal's neighborhood, that white liberal is—well he moves faster than the white bigot from Mississippi, Alabama, and from someplace else.[56]

This reminds us of a liberal professor who loves to wear her antiracist badge on her sleeve by telling anyone who would listen how her daughter prefers to travel from the suburbs to the inner city to play basketball in the "hood" where black players are so much better. While boasting about her daughter's love for playing basketball in the "hood" as an example of her antiracist posture, she would aggressively work against any perceived independent and powerful blacks and other minorities at the university. As the acting dean of a college in the university, she refused to offer tenure to a well-known and well-published African American woman as part of the provost's recruitment efforts to diversify a college, in an urban university, that was over 90 percent white. She would routinely undermine minority professors who are independent critical thinkers and established scholars. At the same time, her vaunted antiracism was always evident in her paternalistic "mentorship" of minority untenured assistant professors who represented the "right" type of minority: powerless and willing to never question the white supremacy structures that would reward the glaring contradictions in this professor's pseudo-antiracism.

By deconstructing the ideological conditions that, on the one hand, proclaim the end of racism and, on the other, give rise to the present violent assault on undocumented immigrants, African Americans and other racial and ethnic groups, we are able to single out those ideological factors that enable even highly educated individuals to embrace the false notion that racism has ended. Such deconstruction would also illustrate why the avowed antiracist liberal seldom links racism with the very racist structure of capitalism. In fact, in the United States it is taboo to attempt to link racism and capitalism. That is why many people believe that the assassination of Martin Luther King Jr. was precipitated by his shift from a denunciation of racism to a more critical posture that began to interrogate issues of class and economic oppression. Because a rigorous and aggressive denunciation of capitalism never really materialized, the civil rights movement became a deferred revolution to the extent that there can be no real revolution for racial and economic justice without some type of land reform and a substantial democratization of control over the means of production. In the absence of these changes, the aspirations to freedom and democracy by oppressed people are invariably truncated. In the end the civil rights movement sought only the *reform* of an immensely unjust social order when the entire exploitative and discriminatory structure needed to be *transformed*, including, obviously, the creation of equity in the control of the means of production. In addition, a transformation leading to economic and racial equity must invariably interrogate the role of capitalism in the creation of such inequitable structures to begin with.

As Paulo Freire often argued, "Revolution, by its very nature, must be a critical process. It is unrealizable without reflection and a deep communion with the marginalized masses." According to him, "In the midst of reflective action on the world to be transformed, the masses come to recognize that the world is indeed being transformed, not reformed. The world in transformation is the mediator of the dialogue between the masses, at one pole of the act of knowing, and the revolutionary leadership, at the other."[57] With all due respect for the great virtues of Martin Luther King Jr., he was a product of middle-class values and thus was constrained in the earlier stages of the movement from engaging in the required reflective critical dialogue with the vast majority of oppressed African Americans, who were and still are cut off from a social (dis)order that mostly benefits whites and a small percentage of middle-class African Americans and other subordinated groups. Although such communion cannot always be possible given historical and political circumstances, the leadership should constantly strive to maintain a dialogue with the masses in order to push forward the aspirations and needs of those for whom a revolution is taking place. Such witness began to come to the fore when Martin Luther King Jr., because of his conviction that poverty is a wrong created by humans and not an act of God, began to denounce the economic injustice perpetrated against the poor by the U.S. capitalistic democracy. For that, he paid with his life.

Although Western capitalistic democracies demonized Che Guevara, he remains the exemplar of the unceasing revolutionary leadership that gives primacy to dialogue with the masses. Incidentally, Malcolm X understood this revolutionary requirement very well, and it is not surprising that he too was assassinated. According to Freire, "Guevara did not hesitate to recognize the capacity to love as an indispensable condition for authentic revolutionaries. While he constantly noted the failure of the peasants to participate in the guerrilla movement, his references to them in the *Bolivian Diary* did not express disaffection. He never lost hope of ultimately being able to count on their participation."[58] In essence, for Guevara, as Freire often suggested, an authentic revolution must be a utopian revolution. An authentic revolutionary cannot allow his or her hope to be compromised by the entrapment of reform or the selective benefits received by a handful of pseudorevolutionaries who are often incorporated into the plantation and whose role in representing the masses is never at odds with the dominant ideological orientations. In consequence, an authentic revolutionary process is full of hope for a utopian society, and, according to Freire, "to be utopian is not to be merely idealistic or impractical but, rather, to engage in denunciation and annunciation."[59]

Unfortunately the pseudorevolutionary who in reality has been assimilated into the system that he or she pretends to denounce is almost always tongue-tied and unable to announce a more just and democratic society based on equality and racial harmony. Compare Guevara's posture of communion with the masses with the present black leadership in the United States, including in the academy, and their relationship with the masses left in the hopelessness of ghetto life. Think about the handful of academic stars who owe their stardom to their role as representing the community and the degree to which they remain subservient to the system that remunerates them for serving in that role. Think about most of them embracing Freire's pronouncement that "an authentic revolution cannot exist without a vision of men and women of the world. It formulates a scientific humanistic conception that finds its expression in a dialogical praxis in which leaders and masses come together in the act of analyzing a dehumanizing reality and denounce it while announcing its transformation in the name of liberation of men and women of the world."[60] This revolutionary posture is diametrically opposed to the existence of a "dream team" of handpicked African American academics at Harvard University. To continue to be rewarded by Harvard, they must fracture their communion with the community, as President Lawrence Summers made clear to Cornel West, who he said was veering from "scholarly work."

Think about the handful of black academic stars who charge $15,000 to $20,000 per lecture strategizing, analyzing, and developing plans for a radical democratic and utopian transformation of ghetto life where every man and woman, elder and child would be treated with dignity and respect. Think about what the oppressed community would have to go through to get these intellectuals to give lectures in the community about the oppression experienced in the ghetto. Think about the handful of black academic stars who are hired by universities to speak for the millions of African Americans who remain largely imprisoned in poverty and despair. Henry Louis Gates Jr. of Harvard University, for example, proclaimed on TV that his "community is Martha's Vineyard and Harvard Square." This comment was made to highlight the class differences among African Americans. While one can agree with and even demand a class analysis as a way to understand the class wedge that continues to partially account for the human misery that characterizes ghetto life, Gates's comments not only exemplify the moral burden that should accompany those selected to speak for the millions who remain chained in oppressive, racist conditions but also shed light on the reformist civil rights aftermath.

The reformist nature of the civil rights movement, with its unwillingness to demand broad land reform and a more equitable distribution of goods in the society, is in marked opposition to the spirit of communion that enabled Guevara to use the guerrilla encampment as the "theoretical context" in which he, his companions and the people together analyzed the concrete events they were living and planned the strategy of their action. In this sense, revolution must be also pedagogical—a pedagogy that remains faithful to the needs of the people as exemplified by Guevara, who "did not create dichotomies between the methods, the content and the objectives of his projects. In spite of the risks to his and his companions' lives, he justified guerrilla warfare as an introduction to freedom, as a call to life to those who are the living dead. Guevara did not become a guerrilla out of desperation. He became a guerrilla because as a lover of men and women he dreamed of a new man and woman being born in the experience of liberation."[61] In this respect Guevara incarnated the authentic revolutionary utopia. He was and continues to be one of the great prophets of the dehumanized oppressed of the third world and of the oppressed within first world reality euphemistically called "people of color" or "minority."

Even though the historical contexts in which Guevara engaged in revolutionary practices were markedly different from what U.S. civil rights movement leaders faced, his principles of coherence and communion with the masses cannot be dismissed if a gulf between leaders and the masses is to be avoided. In essence, leaders need to remain focused in their communion with the masses and, as Freire often insisted, must be "patiently impatient" in our struggle to transform the ugliness of our dehumanized world. We say "dehumanized" for we cannot conceive of humanity in which racism, classism, sexism and xenophobia are the social order of the day. We cannot reconcile the posture of many professional intellectuals and leaders with the requirements of an authentic revolution where communion with the masses provides the context for evaluating the revolution's gains against the needs of the people, whose humanity is often denied by the mass hunger and unemployment that exist side by side with opulence. To be in communion with the masses is to announce that hunger and human misery are not the result of destiny. A true communion with the masses requires us to transcend our paralysis and deepen our awareness that the ugliness of our world—its human misery, discrimination and human exploitation—are as Freire often suggested conditions of human violence rather than the dictates of a destiny.

Paraphrasing Freire, communion with the masses is—only to those with a utopian vision—one of the fundamental characteristics of cultural action for freedom where "authentic communion implies communication between men [and women], mediated by the world. Only praxis in the context of communion makes 'conscientization' a viable revolutionary project."[62] According to Freire, "conscientization is a joint project: It takes place in a person among other people, united by their action and by their reflection upon that action and upon the world."[63] It is this necessary praxis in the context of communion that was missing from the civil rights movement. Consequently the leadership could be content with their partial incorporation into a middle-class reality, and the gulf between the leadership and the vast majority of oppressed blacks and other minorities grew ever wider. This gulf is illustrated by the following episode.

When Donaldo Macedo participated in a major African American conference years ago, he noted the different referents used by the African American speakers to name their condition. When it was Donaldo's turn to speak, he began his speech with the following question: "Could the audience tell me what the previous speakers mean by 'economically marginal,' 'minority,' 'people of color,' 'disadvantaged,' 'marginalized,' 'at-risk youth,' 'underrepresented,' and 'disenfranchised'?" His question was followed by a long silence that was broken by an African American woman at the back of the conference hall. She got up and said, "Right on, brother! They are all talking about the oppressed but they are afraid to name it." After the conference Donaldo was invited by one of the speakers to join a group of colleagues for dinner. The successful professional who invited Donaldo had been a close personal friend of Martin Luther King Jr. and had fought by his side against the oppression of blacks during the 1960s. He had even been jailed with King on one occasion. Now he lived in a gated community where, by his own account, he was frequently stopped by police officers who demanded that he produce proper identification. During dinner, in a reflective tone, the host thanked Donaldo for "keeping him and his colleagues honest" and said that the struggle was far from over. He ended his comments by saying, "The language that one uses makes it easier not to think of our brothers and sisters as oppressed. I sit on many corporate boards and I am often asked to represent the community and, in all honesty, sometimes I feel uncomfortable doing so. I haven't been in the community for twenty-five years."

This story points nakedly to the gulf between most of the oppressed population and the small group of African Americans and other subordinat-

ed peoples who have been incorporated into the white middle-class plantation. And they have been incorporated with the charge to represent the rest
and, in some cases, sadly, to affirm that the system is working and that the
"underrepresented" groups are being fairly represented. This story also highlights the problem inherent in the politics of representation, a problem that
more often than not paralyzes the process of conscientization of both the
leaders and the masses they represent. The lack of conscientization of many
leaders in the civil rights movement not only deferred a utopian revolutionary vision, but it also created spaces whereby the white supremacist ideology
could recast its oppressive and dehumanizing mechanisms, making it much
harder for the oppressed to unveil the reality sustained by false slogans and
empty clichés. These false slogans and clichés find their legitimacy among
angry white males who opportunistically attempt to rationalize their economic insecurity by blaming affirmative action programs and "by proposing
to cut lunch programs for poor children, take away cash assistance to unwed
mothers with dependent children, tighten fuel assistance to the elderly,
abolish the food stamp program, and crack down on illegal immigrants
while denying social benefits to legal immigrants."[64]

An authentic revolution based on "cultural action for freedom" differs
radically from a reform based on cultural action for the domestication of the
masses. According to Freire, "the former problematizes, and the latter slo-
ganizes."[65] Since the civil rights movement in the United States was mostly
a reformist movement based on cultural action for domestication (there
were many exceptions to the reformist mode, but their expressions were
summarily suppressed by assassination and other coercive methods), the
dominant ideology would inevitably conceive ways to enlarge the gulf between the civil rights leaders and the sea of miserable humanity they left
behind and for whom they were spokespeople. This was abundantly clear
when the former head of the NAACP, Julian Bond, declared on television
that he had more in common with folks in his middle-class reality than with
folks in the community. As a reformist movement, civil rights had no pedagogical space in which an ongoing dialogue between the leadership and
the oppressed masses could occur and through which both the leadership
and the masses would expose myths and ideologies contrary to the oppressed class interests. For instance, the myth that the United States is a
classless society was never exposed or analyzed in a systematic and rigorous
manner, and the interplay between class and race never really achieved
prominence in the civil rights debate.

Regrettably the civil rights movement, as a mere reformist movement, by
and large failed to expose and interrogate the dominant capitalist ideology
and so failed to show that racism is an inherent feature of a capitalist
ideology. No antiracist struggle can succeed without a full understanding of
this relation. Many civil rights leaders failed to understand the fundamental
role of those committed to cultural action that leads to conscientization,
and those who understood the importance of concientization during the

early years of the struggle were silenced. Furthermore, many of these leaders failed to understand, paraphrasing Freire, that conscientization should not be reduced to banal phraseology designed to spout liberating ideas but should invite people to think together in order to uncover the truth of their reality. And that truth would require people "to reject decidedly any and every form of discrimination. Preconceptions of race, class, or sex offend the essence of human dignity and constitute a radical negation of democracy. How far from these values we are when we tolerate the impunity of those who kill a street child; those who murder peasants who struggle for a minimum justice; those who discriminate on the basis of color, burning churches where blacks pray because prayer," according to them, should be for whites only.[66] By understanding the internal mechanisms of the dominant capitalist ideology, oppressed people would soon come to realize that the oppressive mechanisms that relegated them to "subhumanity" are part of the structure that needs to be transformed. This would necessarily implicate the capitalist structure that also gave rise to white supremacy.

The lack of substantial land reform in the Civil Rights Act is a continuation of a history that has always denied blacks total freedom. Even with the abolition of slavery, attempts to give land to the landless freed slaves were rapidly crushed by the invocation of racist principles. President Andrew Jackson, for example, announced that "this is a country for white men, and, by God, so long as I am president, it shall be a government for white men."[67] Because Andrew Jackson's white supremacist posture rationalized the denial of land to blacks on the Sea Islands, the white owners easily regained control of the land as well as the means of production, which in turn kept the freed blacks in a state of semislavery. As this historical narrative illustrates, there is in principle a striking similarity between the backlash after the abolition of slavery—in which the small amount of land granted to former slaves was quickly reappropriated—and the present assault on civil rights benefits. For example, black farmers are fast losing their land through open government discrimination in lending practices and subsidies that favor large agribusiness corporations, forcing them to turn to "Congress to get compensation for years of being denied federal loans and access to training provided to white farmers, particularly the agri-business corporate farms."[68] Other subordinate groups find themselves assaulted in the media, for example, being characterized as "welfare queens" who lack moral values. David Duke, a former presidential candidate, unapologetically concluded: "It's them! They're what's wrong with America! They're taking your job, soaking up your tax dollars, living off food stamps, drinking cheap wine and making baby at your own expense."[69] Although the racist mechanisms for rationalizing the exploitation of blacks are different from those in Andrew Jackson's time, we cannot ignore the fact that racism (albeit in a less violent form) very much informs the ideology unleashed by former president Ronald Reagan's attempt to turn the clock back on what he viewed as the excess largesse of the civil rights legislation and social programs of the 1960s.

In order to justify violent discrimination and the economic exploitation of other human beings—through cheap labor and other forms of servitude (such as the almost permanent status of second class citizens)—the dominant white ideology must always portray the oppressed in a negative light. The majority members of the society, who claim to have a conscience, then see the oppressed as unworthy. This is achieved through a process of distinguishing between the oppressor and the oppressed. In fact, the distinction that devalues and dehumanizes is not very different from the "colonial racism [that] is built from three major ideological components: one, the gulf between the culture of the colonialist and the colonized; two, the exploitation of these differences for the benefit of the colonialist; three, the use of these supposed differences as standards of absolute fact."[70] Like the colonialists, the neocolonialists in democratic societies such as the United States remove "the factor from history, time, and therefore possible evolution. What is actually a sociological point becomes labeled as being biological."[71] Thus the material conditions that inform the oppressive and racist conditions under which the majority of U.S. blacks live are often devoid of their historicity, making it easy for cultural commissars like Charles Murray and Richard J. Herrnstein to construct arguments in their book *The Bell Curve* that transform what is actually sociological into a biological referent that portrays blacks in general as genetically inferior to whites. The pseudo-scientific social construction of biological traits to legitimize rejecting the humanity of the oppressed is part of a colonial ideology that has "at the basis of the entire construction, a common motive; the colonizer's economic and basic needs, which he substitutes for logic, and which shape and explain each of the traits he assigns to the colonized."[72]

It becomes dangerous and threatening to situate the analysis of racism within a theoretical framework that links it to both colonialist ideology and capitalism. However, if we analyze the colonial apparatus that informs present-day democracies, we soon realize that the mechanisms of racism and oppression remain in force. For example, the colonial mechanism of depersonalization, which Albert Memmi called the "mark of the plural," is still very useful in the dehumanization of those who have been targeted by our contemporary democracies to be exploited and oppressed. As Memmi argues, the "colonized is never characterized in an individual manner; he is entitled only to drown in an anonymous collectivity ('they are this,' 'they are all the same')."[73]

Even though colonialism is technically over, African Americans, Mexican Americans and other ethnic Americans still "drown in an anonymous collectivity," as demonstrated by David Duke's angry denunciation: "It's them! They're what's wrong with America." In fact, this colonial legacy of drowning the oppressed in an anonymous collectivity continues to be very much part of mainstream white America, as the current demonization of Muslims attests.

Just as racism summed up and symbolized "the fundamental relation which linked colonialist and colonized,"[74] so racism continues to sum up and symbolize the fundamental relation that informs the asymmetrical coexistence between the neocolonialist racists in contemporary "democratic" societies and the victims of racist and economic oppression.

Like the colonized, the racially and economically oppressed in contemporary democratic societies remain subjugated to cultural domination. Either that domination reduces them to the fatalistic acceptance of their own subjugation as they become cultural zombies in a world of human misery defined by a ghetto existence, or the dominant ideology succeeds, as Amilcar Cabral put it, "in imposing itself without damage to the culture of the dominated people—that is, to harmonize economic and political domination of these people with their cultural personality."[75] The latter strategy provides the basis for the assimilation theory that has informed the incorporation of the subjugated people in contemporary "democracies" and differs little "from the imperialist colonial domination [that] tried to create theories which, in fact, are only gross formulations of racism, and which, in practice, are translated into a permanent state of siege of the indigenous population."[76] Thus, for example, the civil rights movement in the United States, as a deferred revolution, represented a progressive but selective and partial assimilation of blacks, Latinos and other subjugated ethnic groups into a middle-class status that represents a process through which the profiled other is required to stop being in order to be. This can be seen in the enormous outcry that arose when Oakland, California, schools proposed incorporating Ebonics in the education of African American youngsters. Unfortunately, even middle-class blacks, including Jesse Jackson, joined the chorus denouncing Ebonics, ignoring the role of language in the construction of human subjectivities. It is the same need to accommodate that perhaps led Jesse Jackson, who had been practically dismissed as a black leader during Bill Clinton's first presidential campaign, to join the president in prayers in the White House during the turbulence surrounding Clinton's sexual escapades with Monica Lewinsky. The violent denial of the cultural manifestations of the subjugated people is also seen in the constant cultural assault against subjugated racial and ethnic groups by such cultural commissars as Pat Buchanan and Robert Bork.

While the assimilation process allows a small percentage of the dominated people to enter the gates of middle-class life, they are simultaneously denied the option to return to their cultural source. This became clear when Lawrence Summers, the president of Harvard University, chastised Cornel West, one of a handful of African American University Professors (the highest rank professors can achieve at Harvard) for what he categorized as lax scholarship and questionable political participation, as well as for making a rap CD. What Summers failed to realize is that a public intellectual of West's stature should not restrict his or her participation to the confines of the ivory tower and should be able to address and connect with multiple audiences, including issues related to the community that he or she claims to represent. Making a rap CD that denounces racism and white supremacy resonates with millions of oppressed African Americans, even though it may make those complicit with the human misery generated by racism uncomfortable. It is precisely because of the power inherent in a return to the cultural source that apologists such as Arthur Schlesinger Jr. become concerned that the "cult of ethnicity has arisen both among non-Anglo whites and among non-white minorities to denounce the idea of a melting pot, to challenge the concept of 'one-people' and to protect, promote and perpetuate separate ethnic and racial communities."[77] Schlesinger's position is not only dishonest but also serves to alarm the population against the "multiethnic dogma [that] abandons historic purposes, replacing assimilation by fragmentation, integration for separatism. It belittles unum and glorifies pluribus."[78] A more honest account of history would highlight the fact that African Americans did not create laws so they could be enslaved, did not promulgate legislation that made it a crime for them to be educated and did not create redlining policies that sentenced them to ghettos and segregated neighborhoods. Unless Schlesinger and other cultural commissars are willing to confront the historical truth, their concern for the disuniting of America is yet another ideological veil to mask the white supremacist values that put discriminatory policies in the United States beyond analysis and thus beyond scrutiny.

What also remains beyond scrutiny is the dominant ideology's unspoken but real requirement of greater and greater investment in the doctrinal system as a sine qua non of any type of reward from the system. As a result, liberation within the assimilationist model operative in the deferred revolution of the civil rights movement required blacks, for instance, to engage in systematic cultural denial as the price of admission to the middle class. It also required the members of the newly formed black middle class to distance themselves more and more from the disposable masses abandoned in ghettos. They are also required to forsake more and more the principles of social and economic justice for all people if they expect to continue to enjoy certain privileges as clerks of the empire. The irony inherent in this colonial assimilationist model is that while it requires the dominated people to emulate the dominant values, traits and behaviors, it simultaneously rejects attempts by the colonized to become full members of the club. Albert Memmi points out that "the major impossibility is not negating one's [cultural] existence, for [one] soon discovers that, even if [one] agrees to everything, [one] would not be saved. In order to be assimilated, it is not enough to leave one's group, but one must enter another; now he meets with colonizer's rejection . . . [and] the shrewder the ape, the better he imitates, and the more the colonizer becomes irritated."[79] The quintessential irony of the civil rights success story is found in the creation of the "dream team" of black intellectuals at Harvard, coordinated by Henry Louis Gates Jr. Although he may be considered the most important black man in the United States, he has not been spared invective from the dominant white supremacist ideology: *Boston* magazine some years ago characterized him on its cover as the "Head Negro in Charge." This characterization was a nasty reminder that racism is still very much alive. In some respects, the more successful blacks become, the more the white supremacist ideology will be inclined to remind them of their proper place. What is interesting in this unfortunate episode is that while black leaders in the community protested vigorously against the Negro invective, demanding an apology from *Boston* magazine, the one person who remained curiously silent throughout this episode was the victim himself. Gates—who is known not to miss a beat in manipulating the media over issues affecting the black community, ranging from AIDS to black racism against Jews—said little against *Boston,* nor did he take advantage of his privileged position at Harvard to let white America know that racism has not ended and that the economic subjugation of most blacks is getting worse rather than better. One could only assume that for Gates, remaining a member of the Martha's Vineyard and Harvard Square communities is more important than the aggressive denunciation of *Boston* magazine's glaring racism.

Harvard University, a bastion of white supremacist ideology, proudly points to Gates's dream team as the example par excellence of its newly formed antiracist sentiments. However, Harvard fails to acknowledge the dangers that black "public intellectuals face when they take on the responsibility of speaking for an entire generation of blacks," particularly when in most cases they are no longer part of the very community they are charged to represent and particularly when they are only rewarded as long they maintain what Michel Foucault calls a "double body."[80] The administrations of Harvard and other Ivy League schools say little about the compromises that the dominant ideology expects and demands from minority hires if they are to be rewarded. According to Henry Giroux,

> In the current work of both [Cornel] West and [Henry Louis] Gates, Jr. there are indications that the spirit of opposition discourse that keeps alive the radical thrust of being a public intellectual is being compromised. For example, while it might be too much to expect Henry Gates to act like a democratic socialist, it is disheartening to witness his increasing allegiance to a centrist politics made manifest in numerous media appearances, hastily written publications, and commentaries in which he seems less concerned with social justice and the dwindling state of democracy in this country than he does in recruiting a number of high profile African-American intellectuals to Harvard.[81]

Perhaps Gates's curious silence about the blatant racism demonstrated by *Boston* magazine represents his rapid shift from an oppositional and ethical discourse to a more accommodating and compromised posture toward the dominant ideology that has so rewarded him. However, it remains clear that while Gates is busy assembling his dream team at Harvard, the vast majority of blacks continue to experience what Malcolm X called the "American nightmare." It is also clear that the creation of the mythical dream team is no more than a Pyrrhic victory. The situation is intrinsically colonial. While a small percentage of blacks may enjoy the rewards of an American middle-class reality, for the vast majority the deferred civil rights revolution "has not taken even half a step forward; for the young [black] man, it is an internal catastrophe. He will remain glued to that [colonial] family which offers him warmth and tenderness but which simultaneously absorbs, clutches and emasculates him."[82]

Against this racist colonial paradox many white liberals (and some black liberals as well) fail to understand how they can embody white supremacist values and beliefs, even though they may not embrace racism as prejudice or domination (especially domination that involves coercive control). They cannot recognize how their actions support and affirm the very structure of racist domination and oppression they profess to wish to see eradicated. bell hooks is correct in urging us to look beyond the simple wish to see racism eradicated. For her, the real issue is not a facile denunciation of oppressive racist conditions but the critical understanding of many white liberals' complicity with "white supremacy" as a racist ideology that is all the more insidious to the extent that it keeps itself invisible.

By not understanding their complicity with white supremacist ideology, many white liberals reproduce a colonialist and assimilationist value system that gives rise to a form of tokenism parading under the rubric of diversity. As bell hooks has so eloquently argued, for example, "many English Professors . . . want very much to have 'a' black person in 'their' department, as long as that person thinks and acts like them, shares their values and beliefs, is in no way different."[83] That is why many white liberals prefer to promote "diversity" to the extent that diversity as a cultural model not only fails to interrogate the white privilege extracted from a white supremacist ideology but also allows white liberals to have blacks and other oppressed cultural groups as mascots in their Benneton color scheme of diversity. This form of diversity promoted through multicultural programs, for example, represents a mere reorganization of knowledge through which diversity is presented as a naturalization process whereby different ethnic and cultural groups (white groups are never associated with ethnicity, even though their ethnicity provides the yardstick against which all other groups are measured) are represented and their asymmetrical power relations with the dominant white group are never interrogated. An antiracist approach would forcibly interrogate the white supremacist ideology as a process and would denounce it so as to create conditions where more democratic human relations could be forged, relations in which the color of one's ideology would be more visible than the color of one's skin. Instead, by adopting the empty cliché of diversity, many white liberals attempt to utilize diversity in order to manage "difference" and discrimination. The process pretends to include everyone, so no one is really included. In short, the diversity movement is satisfied with a simple denunciation of myths and errors of the system. It refrains from undertaking a rational, rigorous critique of the capitalist ideology that breeds the very race, gender, class and economic inequities against which many white liberals purport to fight.

The quest for a truly racial and cultural democracy cannot be met by a skewed assimilationist approach that pretends to fit everyone into a white middle classness. Leaders in dialogue with the subordinated groups need to understand that racial and cultural equality cannot be achieved outside the class ideology that guides, shapes and maintains racial and cultural antagonisms. A true understanding of how class, race, gender and culture intersect to produce asymmetrical power relations would require that the struggle for cultural democracy be revolutionary and pedagogical in its orientation rather than assimilationist in its objectives. Hence, given its assimilationist and reformist nature, the civil rights movement precluded a revolutionary praxis based on a "form of cultural action [for freedom] that would bring about conscientization . . . [and] there can be no conscientization of the people without radical denunciation of dehumanizing structures, accompanied by the proclamation of a new reality to be created by men [and women]."[84]

Conscientization, according to Freire, involves a deep understanding of the reality and reasons behind facts achieved through a pedagogical revolutionary praxis designed to liberate men and women. In his words, a pedagogical revolutionary praxis is not merely a dream or impracticability; a pedagogical revolutionary praxis engages in denunciation and annunciation. Freire's notion of revolution is radically different from a revolutionary pedagogy of accommodation that restricts denunciation so as to preclude annunciation. Because a reformist practice rejects transformation, it cannot aspire to be more than a mere deferred revolution in that "the place upon which a new rebellion should be built is not the ethics of the marketplace with its crass insensitivity [through globalization and its insidious neoliberal policies] to the voice of genuine humanity but the ethics of universal human aspiration. The ethics of human solidarity."[85]

NOTES

1. Paul Gilroy, *Against Race: Imagining Political Culture beyond the Color Line* (Cambridge, MA: Harvard University Press, 2000), 64.

2. Gilroy, *Against Race*, 64.

3. David Theo Goldberg, *Racist Culture: Philosophy and the Politics of Meaning* (Oxford: Blackwell, 1993), 97.

4. Goldberg, *Racist Culture*, 100.

5. Goldberg, *Racist Culture*, 9.

6. Goldberg, *Racist Culture*, 95.

7. Gilroy, *Against Race*, 98.

8. John J. Lumpkin, "Marine General Says It's 'Fun' to Shoot Some People in Combat," *Boston Globe*, February 4, 2005, A3.

9. Lumpkin, "Marine General Says," A3.

10. Lumpkin, "Marine General Says," A3.

11. Goldberg, *Racist Culture*, 90.

12. Goldberg, *Racist Culture*, 90.

13. Goldberg, *Racist Culture*, 94.

14. *Diario El Mundo* (Madrid, Spain), February 7, 1997.

15. Josephine Ocloo, "Racism in Europe: A Rising Tide," *Social Work in Europe* 8, no. 2 (2001): 45–49.

16. Cited in Donaldo Macedo and Lilia I. Bartolome, *Dancing with Bigotry: Beyond the Politics of Tolerance* (New York: Palgrave, 1999).

17. "Report: Minorities Shortchanged in Health Care," Reuters, March 20, 2002.

18. Cornel West, *Race Matters* (Boston: Beacon Press, 1993), p. x.

19. Albert Memmi, *The Colonizer and the Colonized* (Boston: Beacon, 1991).

20. Cited in Macedo and Bartolome, *Dancing with Bigotry.*

21. Memmi, *The Colonizer and the Colonized,* 69–70.

22. Herbert Marcuse, *One-Dimensional Man* (Boston: Beacon, 1991), 7–8.

23. Tom Hayden, "Bolivia's Indian Revolt," *The Nation,* June 2, 2004, 18.

24. Hayden, "Bolivia's Indian Revolt," 18.

25. Arundhati Roy, "Shall We Leave It to the Experts?" *The Nation,* February 18, 2002, 16.

26. Roy, "Shall We Leave It to the Experts?" 17.

27. Roy, "Shall We Leave It to the Experts?" 17.

28. Roy, "Shall We Leave It to the Experts?" 18.

29. Roy, "Shall We Leave It to the Experts?" 16.

30. Terry Eagleton, *Ideology: An Introduction* (London: Verso, 1991), 28–30.

31. Eagleton, *Ideology,* 28–30.

32. Carl Boggs, *The End of Politics* (New York: Guilford, 2000).

33. Marcuse, *One-Dimensional Man,* 85.

34. Zsuzsa Ferge, "What Are the State Functions That Neoliberalism Wants to Eliminate?" in *Not for Sale: In Defense of Public Goods,* ed. Anatole Anton, Milton Fisk, and Nancy Holmstrom (Boulder, CO: Westview, 2000), 182.

35. Ulrich Beck, "Redefining Power in the Global Age: Eight Theses," *Dissent,* Fall 2001, 86.

36. Henry A. Giroux, *Public Spaces, Private Lives: Beyond the Culture of Cynicism* (Lanham, MD: Rowman & Littlefield, 2001), 118.

37. Zygmunt Bauman, *In Search of Politics* (Stanford, CA: Stanford University Press, 1999), 74.

38. Beck, "Redefining Power in the Global Age," 83.

39. Edward Said, *Representations of the Intellectual* (New York: Vintage, 1994), 11.

40. Said, *Representations of the Intellectual,* 11.

41. Said, *Representations of the Intellectual,* 74.

42. Noam Chomsky, *Chomsky on (Mis)education,* ed. Donaldo Macedo (Lanham, MD: Rowman & Littlefield, 2000), 17.

43. Said, *Representations of the Intellectual,* 74.

44. Theodor Adorno, *Minima Moralia* (London: Verso, 1974), 35.

45. Henry A. Giroux, "Black, Bruised, and Read All Over: Public Intellectuals and the Politics of Race," in *Class Issues: Pedagogy, Cultural Studies, and the Public Sphere,* ed. Amitava Kumar (New York: New York University Press, 1997).

46. V. N. Volosinov, *Marxism and the Philosophy of Language* (New York: Dominar Press, 1973), 9.

47. Volosinov, *Marxism and the Philosophy of Language,* 11.

48. Cited in Bill Turque with Bob Cohn, "Black Conservatives Quarrel over Quotas," *Newsweek,* December 24, 1990, 20.

49. Eric Foner, "Race and the Conservatives," in *Dissent,* Winter 1996.

50. Bruce Perry, ed., *Malcolm X: The Last Speeches* (New York: Pathfinder Press, 1989), 41.

51. Memmi, *The Colonizer and the Colonized,* 74.

52. Goldberg, *Racist Culture,* 6.

53. Goldberg, *Racist Culture,* 6.

54. Goldberg, *Racist Culture,* 6.

55. Quoted in Peter Applebone, "Goals Unmet, Duke Reveals the Perils in Effort to Increase Black Faculty," *New York Times,* September 19, 1993, 1.

56. Perry, *Malcolm X,* 33.

57. Paulo Freire, *The Politics of Education: Culture, Power, and Liberation* (New York: Bergin & Garvey, 1985), 84.

58. Freire, *The Politics of Education,* 84.

59. Freire, *Politics of Education,* 168.

60. Freire, *Politics of Education,* 57.

61. Freire, *Politics of Education,* 84.

62. Freire, *Politics of Education,* 84.

63. Freire, *Politics of Education,* 85.

64. Macedo and Bartolome, *Dancing with Bigotry,* 14–15.

65. Freire, *Politics of Education,* 85.

66. Freire, *Pedagogy of Freedom,* 41.

67. Cited in Donaldo Macedo, *Literacies of Power: What Americans Are Not Allowed to Know* (Boulder, CO: Westview, 1994).

68. *Boston Globe,* February 28, 2005, A2.

69. David Nyhan, "David Duke Sent 'em a Scare But Now He Faces the Old Pro," *Boston Globe,* October 24, 1991, 13.

70. Memmi, *The Colonizer and the Colonized,* 78.

71. Memmi, *The Colonizer and the Colonized,* 71.

72. Memmi, *The Colonizer and the Colonized,* 66.

73. Memmi, *The Colonizer and the Colonized,* 85.

74. Memmi, *The Colonizer and the Colonized,* 70.

75. Amilcar Cabral, *Return to the Source: Selected Speeches of Amilcar Cabral* (New York: Monthly Review Press, 1973), 40.

76. Cabral, *Return to the Source,* 40.

77. Arthur M. Schlesinger Jr., *The Disuniting of America: Reflections on a Multicultural Society* (New York: Norton, 1992), 13.

78. Schlesinger, *Disuniting of America,* 13.

79. Memmi, *The Colonizer and the Colonized,* 124.

80. Henry A. Giroux, *Channel Surfing: Racism, the Media, and the Destruction of Today's Youth* (New York: St. Martin's, 1998), 164–65.

81. Giroux, *Channel Surfing,* 164–65.

82. Memmi, *The Colonizer and the Colonized,* 99.

83. bell hooks, *Teaching to Transgress* (New York: Routledge, 1998).

84. Freire, *The Politics of Education,* 85.

85. Freire, *Pedagogy of Freedom,* 116.

2
THE CRISIS OF THE HUMAN WASTE DISPOSAL INDUSTRY

Zygmunt Bauman

⤎

A specter hovers over the planet—the specter of xenophobia. Old and new, never extinguished or freshly unfrozen, lit up tribal suspicions and animosities have mixed and blended with the brand-new fear for safety that has been distilled from the old and new uncertainties and insecurities of our liquid modern existence.

People worn-out and dead-tired by forever inconclusive tests of adequacy, frightened to the raw by the mysterious, inexplicable precariousness of their fortunes and by the global mists hiding their prospects from view, desperately seek the culprits of their trials and tribulations. They find them, unsurprisingly, under the nearest lamp post—in the only spot obligingly illuminated by the forces of law and order: "It is criminals who make us insecure, and it is outsiders who cause crime" we are told, and so "we must round up, incarcerate and deport the outsiders to restore our lost or stolen security."

Throughout the world ruled by democratically elected governments, it's the "I'll be tough on crime" card that has turned out to trump all others; the winning hand is almost invariably a combination of a promise of "more prisons, more policemen, longer sentences," often tied to an oath that there will be "no immigration, no asylum rights, no naturalization." As Donald G. McNeil put it, "Politicians across Europe use the 'outsiders cause crime' stereotype to link ethnic hatred, which is unfashionable, to the more palatable fear for one's own safety."

This past spring, the Chirac versus Jospin presidential duel in France degenerated in its preliminary stages into a public auction. Both competitors vied for electoral support by offering ever harsher measures against

Originally published in *Tikkun: A Bimonthly Jewish and Interfaith Critique of Politics, Culture & Society* 17, no. 5 (September–October 2002), 41–42, 47. Accessed on-line at www.tikkun.org. Reprinted by permission.

criminals and immigrants, but above all against immigrants who breed crime and against the criminality bred by immigrants (as recorded in a piece on Jospin by Nathaniel Herzberg and Cécile Prieur in *Le Monde*, May 5–6, 2002). First of all, though, the candidates did their best to refocus the anxiety stemming from the electors' ambient sense of *precarité* (the infuriating insecurity of social position intertwined with the acute uncertainty about the future of livelihood) onto their fear for personal safety (the integrity of their bodies, personal possessions, homes, and neighborhoods). On July 14, 2001, Chirac set the infernal machine in motion, announcing the need to fight the "growing threats to safety" in view of an almost 10 percent increase in recorded crime in the first half of the year; he declared he would ensure that a "zero tolerance" policy became law once he was reelected.

The tune of the presidential campaign had been set, and Jospin was quick to join in, elaborating his own variations on the shared motif (though, unexpectedly to the main soloists, but certainly not to the sociologically wise observers, it was Le Pen's voice that came on the top as the purest and so the most audible in this anticrime chorus). On August 28, 2002, Jospin proclaimed "the battle against insecurity," vowing "no laxity," while on September 6, 2002, Daniel Vaillant and Marylise Lebranchu, his ministers of, respectively, internal affairs and justice, swore that they wouldn't show any tolerance for crime in any form. Vaillant's immediate reaction to September 11 was to increase the powers of the police principally against the juveniles of the "ethnically alien" *banlieues,* where the devilish concoction of uncertainty and insecurity poisoning the Frenchmen's lives was, according to the official version, being brewed. Jospin himself went on castigating and reviling, in ever more vitriolic terms, the "angelic school" of the soft approach, to which he swore never to have belonged in the past and never to join in the future. The auction went on, and the bids climbed skyward. Chirac promised to create a ministry of internal security, to which Jospin responded with a commitment to a ministry "charged with public security" and the "coordination of police operations." When Chirac brandished the idea of a locked center to confine juvenile delinquents, Jospin echoed the promise with a vision of "locked structures" for juvenile offenders, outbidding his opponent with the prospect of "sentencing on the spot."

Moving south: A mere three decades ago, Portugal was (alongside Turkey) the main supplier of the *Gastarbeiter* feared by the German *Bürger* to despoil his homely townscapes and undercut the German social compact, the foundation of his security and comfort. Today, thanks to its sharply improved fortune, Portugal has turned from a labor-exporting into a labor-importing country. The hardships and humiliations suffered when earning bread in foreign countries having been promptly forgotten, 27 percent of Portuguese have now declared that crime- and foreigner-infested neighborhoods are their main worry. The newcomer politician Paulo Portas, by playing a single, fiercely anti-immigration card, helped the new right-wing coalition into power (just as Pia Kiersgaard's Danish People's Party did in Denmark, Umberto Bossi's Northern League in Italy, and the radically anti-immigrant Progress Party did in Norway—all countries that not so long ago sent their children to faraway lands to seek the bread which their homelands were too poor to offer).

All such news made it easily to the first page headlines (in Britain, the *Guardian* headlined the "UK plan for asylum crackdown" on June 13, 2002, and there's no need to mention tabloid first-page banners . . .). The main bulk of the immigrant phobia, however, stays hidden from Western Europe's attention (indeed, knowledge,) and never makes it to the surface. "Blaming the immigrants"—the strangers, the newcomers, and particularly the newcomers among the strangers—for all aspects of social malaise (and most of all for the nauseating, disempowering feeling of *Unsicherheit, in-certezza, precarité,* insecurity) is fast becoming a global habit. As Heather Grabbe, research director for the Centre for European Reform, put it, "the Germans blame the Poles, the Poles blame the Ukrainians, the Ukrainians blame the Kirghiz and Uzbeks"—while countries too poor to attract any neighbors desperately seeking a livelihood, like Romania, Bulgaria, Hungary, or Slovakia, turn their wrath against the usual suspects and standby culprits: the local but drifting, fixed-addresses shunning, and therefore "newcomers" and outsiders, always and everywhere—the Gypsies.

When it comes to setting global trends, the United States has undisputed priority rights and most of the time holds the initiative. But joining the global trend of immigrant bashing presents America with a rather difficult problem. The United States is an admittedly immigrant country; denigration of immigrants, throwing suspicion on the immigrants' noble calling, would go against the grain of American identity and perhaps deliver a mortal blow to the American Dream, its undisputed foundation and cement. Still, efforts are made, by trial and error, to square the circle. . . .

On June 10, the highest-ranking U.S. officials (FBI Director Robert Mueller, U.S. Deputy Attorney General Larry Thompson, and Deputy Defense Secretary Paul Wolfowitz among others) announced the arrest of a suspected al-Qaeda terrorist on his return to Chicago from a training trip to Pakistan. As the official version of the affair claimed, an American citizen, Jose Padilla (the name suggests Hispanic roots—the latest, relatively poorly settled addition to the long list of immigrant ethnic affiliations), converted to Islam, took the name of Abdullah al-Mujahir, and promptly went to his new Muslim brethren for instructions on how to harm his homeland. He was instructed in the artless art of patching together "dirty bombs"—"frighteningly easy to assemble" out of the few ounces of widely available conventional explosives and "virtually any type of radioactive material" that the would-be terrorists "can get their hands on" (it was not clear why sophisticated training was needed to assemble weapons "frighteningly easy to assemble"—but when it comes to sowing the seeds of fear for the grapes of wrath to grow, logic is neither here nor there). "A new phrase entered the post–Sept. 11 vocabulary of many average Americans: dirty bomb"—announced the *USA Today* reporters Nichols, Hall, and Eisler.

The affair was a master stroke: the trap of the American Dream had been skillfully bypassed since Jose Padilla was a stranger and an alien by his own free American's *free choice*. The terrorism was vividly depicted as simultaneously of foreign origin yet ubiquitous at home, lurking just beyond the corner and spreading over every neighborhood—just like "the Reds under the beds" scare of yore. It was an impeccable metaphor and a fully credible outlet for the equally ubiquitous fears and apprehensions of precarious life.

And yet this particular expedient proved to be an error. When watched from the other offices of the federal administration, the assets of the case looked more like liabilities. A "frighteningly easy to assemble" dirty bomb would expose the folly of a multi-billion dollar "antimissile shield," since the threat was at home, not abroad. The native credentials of al-Mujahir likewise could fix a huge question mark on the planned anti-Iraq crusade and all its yet unnamed sequels—why plan raids abroad if the danger comes from our own citizens? What was meat to some federal departments smacked of poison to some others. For the moment, those others seemed to get the upper hand, since the neck of the promising affair has promptly, swiftly, and expeditiously been wrung. But not for the lack of trying on the part of its authors and actors.

Modernity turned out, and kept turning out, from the start, huge volumes of human waste. The production of human waste was particularly profuse in two (still fully operative and working to capacity) branches of modern industry.

The manifest function of the first of the two branches is the production and reproduction of social order. Any model of order is selective and requires cutting off, trimming, segregating, separating, or excising of such parts of the human raw material as are unfit for the new order—unable or not allowed to fill any of its niches. At the other end of the order-building process, such parts emerge as "waste," as distinct from the "useful," because intended, product.

The second branch of modern industry known to turn out continuously vast volumes of human waste is economic progress—which requires the incapacitation, dismantling, and eventual annihilation of a certain number of ways and means of eking out human existence; such livelihoods as cannot and would not meet the constantly rising standards of productivity and profitability. Practitioners of these devalued forms of life cannot, as a rule, be accommodated en masse by the new, slimmer, and smarter arrangements for economic activity. They are denied access to such means of livelihood as the new arrangements have made legitimate/obligatory, while the orthodox means, now devalued, no longer offer survival. They are, for that reason, the waste of economic progress.

The potentially disastrous consequences of the accumulation of human waste were, for a better part of modern history, defused, neutralized, or at least mitigated thanks to another modern innovation: the waste disposal industry. That industry thrived thanks to the turning of large parts of the globe into dumping grounds to which all "surplus of humanity," the human waste turned out by the modernizing sectors of the planet, could be transported, disposed off, and decontaminated—thereby staving off the danger of self-combustion and explosion.

Today, however, the planet has run out of such dumping grounds, in large part due to the spectacular success—the planetary spread—of the modern form of life (since at least Rosa Luxemburg, modernity was suspected of an ultimately suicidal "snake eating its own tail" tendency). Dumping grounds are in ever shorter supply. While the production of human waste goes on unabated (if anything, rising in volume due to the globalization processes), the waste disposal industry has found itself in dire straits. The old ways of tackling human waste are no longer feasible, and new ways have not been invented, let alone put in operation. Along the fault lines of the world disorder piles of human waste are rising, and the first signs of this waste's tendency toward self-inflagration and imminent explosion multiply.

The crisis of the human waste disposal industry stands behind the present-day confusion, revealed by the desperate, though largely irrational and off-the-mark crisis management bustle triggered by the September 11 spectacle.

3
RACISM AND MIDDLE EAST POLITICS

Edward Said

‑‑‑‑‑

Despite Israel's effort to restrict coverage of its destructive invasion of the West Bank's Palestinian towns and refugee camps, information and images have nevertheless seeped through. The Internet has provided hundreds of verbal as well as pictorial eyewitness reports, as have Arab and European TV coverage, most of it unavailable or blocked or spun out of existence from the mainstream US media. That evidence provides stunning proof of what Israel's campaign has actually—has always—been about: the irreversible conquest of Palestinian land and society. The official line (which Washington has basically supported, along with nearly every US media commentator) is that Israel has been defending itself by retaliating against the suicide bombings that have undermined its security and even threatened its existence. That claim has gained the status of an absolute truth, moderated neither by what Israel has done nor by what in fact has been done to it.

Phrases such as "plucking out the terrorist network," "destroying the terrorist infrastructure" and "attacking terrorist nests" (note the total dehumanization involved) are repeated so often and so unthinkingly that they have given Israel the right to destroy Palestinian civil life, with a shocking degree of sheer wanton destruction, killing, humiliation and vandalism.

There are signs, however, that Israel's amazing, not to say grotesque, claim to be fighting for its existence is slowly being eroded by the devastation wrought by the Jewish state and its homicidal prime minister, Ariel Sharon. Take this front-page *New York Times* report, "Attacks Turn Palestinian Plans Into Bent Metal and Piles of Dust," by Serge Schmemann (no Palestinian propagandist) on April 11: "There is no way to assess the full extent of the damage to the cities and towns—Ramallah, Bethlehem, Tulkarm,

Originally published as "What Israel Has Done" in *The Nation*, May 6, 2002. Reprinted by permission.

Qalqilya, Nablus and Jenin—while they remain under a tight siege, with patrols and snipers firing in the streets. But it is safe to say that the infrastructure of life itself and of any future Palestinian state—roads, schools, electricity pylons, water pipes, telephone lines—has been devastated."

By what inhuman calculus did Israel's army, using dozens of tanks and armored personnel carriers, along with hundreds of missile strikes from US-supplied Apache helicopter gunships, besiege Jenin's refugee camp for over a week, a one-square-kilometer patch of shacks housing 15,000 refugees and a few dozen men armed with automatic rifles and no missiles or tanks, and call it a response to terrorist violence and a threat to Israel's survival? There are reported to be hundreds buried in the rubble, which Israeli bulldozers began heaping over the camp's ruins after the fighting ended. Are Palestinian civilian men, women and children no more than rats or cockroaches that can be attacked and killed in the thousands without so much as a word of compassion or in their defense? And what about the capture of thousands of men who have been taken off by Israeli soldiers, the destitution and homelessness of so many ordinary people trying to survive in the ruins created by Israeli bulldozers all over the West Bank, the siege that has now gone on for months and months, the cutting off of electricity and water in Palestinian towns, the long days of total curfew, the shortage of food and medicine, the wounded who have bled to death, the systematic attacks on ambulances and aid workers that even the mild-mannered Kofi Annan has decried as outrageous? Those actions will not be pushed so easily into the memory hole. Its friends must ask Israel how its suicidal policies can possibly gain it peace, acceptance and security.

The monstrous transformation of an entire people by a formidable and feared propaganda machine into little more than militants and terrorists has allowed not just Israel's military but its fleet of writers and defenders to efface a terrible history of injustice, suffering and abuse in order to destroy the civil existence of the Palestinian people with impunity. Gone from public memory are the destruction of Palestinian society in 1948 and the creation of a dispossessed people; the conquest of the West Bank and Gaza and their military occupation since 1967; the invasion of Lebanon in 1982, with its 17,500 Lebanese and Palestinian dead and the Sabra and Shatila massacres; the continuous assault on Palestinian schools, refugee camps, hospitals, civil installations of every kind. What antiterrorist purpose is served by destroying the building and then removing the records of the ministry of education; the Ramallah municipality; the Central Bureau of Statistics; various institutes specializing in civil rights, health, culture and economic development; hospitals, radio and TV stations? Isn't it clear that Sharon is bent not only on breaking the Palestinians but on trying to eliminate them as a people with national institutions?

In such a context of disparity and asymmetrical power it seems deranged to keep asking the Palestinians, who have no army, air force, tanks or functioning leadership, to renounce violence, and to require no comparable limitation on Israel's actions. It certainly obscures Israel's systematic use of lethal force against unarmed civilians, copiously documented by all the major human rights organizations. Even the matter of suicide bombers, which I have always opposed, cannot be examined from a viewpoint that permits a hidden racist standard to value Israeli lives over the many more Palestinian lives that have been lost, maimed, distorted and foreshortened by longstanding military occupation and the systematic barbarity openly used by Sharon against Palestinians since the beginning of his career.

There can be no conceivable peace that doesn't tackle the real issue, which is Israel's utter refusal to accept the sovereign existence of a Palestinian people that is entitled to rights over what Sharon and most of his supporters consider to be the land of Greater Israel, i.e., the West Bank and Gaza. A profile of Sharon in the April 5 *Financial Times* concluded with this telling extract from his autobiography, which the *FT* prefaced with, "He has written with pride of his parents' belief that Jews and Arabs could be citizens side by side." Then the relevant passage from Sharon's book: "But they believed without question that only they had rights over the land. And no one was going to force them out, regardless of terror or anything else. When the land belongs to you physically . . . that is when you have power, not just physical power but spiritual power."

In 1988 the PLO made the concession of accepting partition of Palestine into two states. This was reaffirmed on numerous occasions, and certainly in the Oslo documents. *But only the Palestinians explicitly recognized the notion of partition.* Israel never has. This is why there are now more than 170 settlements on Palestinian land, why there is a 300–mile road network connecting them to each other and totally impeding Palestinian movement (according to Jeff Halper of the Israeli Committee Against House Demolitions, it costs $3 billion and has been funded by the United States), and why no Israeli prime minister has ever conceded any real sovereignty to the Palestinians, and why the settlements have grown on an annual basis. The merest glance at the accompanying map reveals what Israel has been doing throughout the peace process, and what the consequent geographical discontinuity and shrinkage in Palestinian life has been. In effect, Israel considers itself and the Jewish people to own all of Palestine. There are land ownership laws in Israel itself guaranteeing this, but in the West Bank and Gaza the settlements, roads and refusal to concede sovereign land rights to the Palestinians serve the same function.

What boggles the mind is that no official—no US, no Palestinian, no Arab, no UN, no European, or anyone else—has challenged Israel on this point, which has been threaded through all of the Oslo agreements. Which is why, after nearly ten years of peace negotiations, Israel still controls the West Bank and Gaza. They are more directly controlled by more than 1,000 Israeli tanks and thousands of soldiers today, but the underlying principle is the same. No Israeli leader (and certainly not Sharon and his Land of Israel supporters, who are the majority in his government) has either officially recognized the occupied territories as occupied or gone on to recognize that Palestinians could or might theoretically have sovereign rights—that is, without Israeli control over borders, water, air or security—to what most of the world considers Palestinian land. So to speak about the vision of a Palestinian state, as has become fashionable, is a mere vision unless the question of land ownership and sovereignty is openly and officially conceded by the Israeli government. None ever has and, if I am right, none will in the near future. It should be remembered that Israel is the only state in the world today that has never had internationally declared borders; the only state not the state of its citizens but of the whole Jewish people; the only state where more than 90 percent of the land is held in trust for the use only of the Jewish people. That Israel has systematically flouted international law . . . suggests the depth and structural knottiness of the absolute rejectionism that Palestinians have had to face.

This is why I have been skeptical about discussions and meetings about peace, which is a lovely word but in the present context usually means Palestinians are told to stop resisting Israeli control over their land. It is among the many deficiencies of Arafat's terrible leadership (to say nothing of the even more lamentable Arab leaders in general) that he neither made the decade-long Oslo negotiations ever focus on land ownership, thus never putting the onus on Israel to declare itself willing to give up title to Palestinian land, nor asked that Israel be required to deal with any of its responsibility for the sufferings of his people. Now I worry that he may simply be trying to save himself again, whereas what we really need are international monitors to protect us, as well as new elections to assure a real political future for the Palestinian people.

The profound question facing Israel and its people is this: Is it willing to assume the rights and obligations of being a country like any other, and forswear the kind of impossible colonial assertions for which Sharon and his parents and soldiers have been fighting since day one? In 1948 Palestinians lost 78 percent of Palestine. In 1967 they lost the remaining 22 percent. Now the international community must lay upon Israel the obligation to accept the principle of real, as opposed to fictional, partition, and to accept the principle of limiting Israel's extraterritorial claims, those absurd, biblically based pretensions and laws that have so far allowed it to override another people. Why is that kind of fundamentalism unquestioningly tolerated? But so far all we hear is that Palestinians must give up violence and condemn terror. Is nothing substantive ever demanded of Israel, and can it go on doing what it has without a thought for the consequences? That is the real question of its existence, whether it can exist as a state like all others, or must always be above the constraints and duties of other states. The record is not reassuring.

4
THE GLOBAL REACH OF RACELESS STATES

David Theo Goldberg

ϖ

Racelessness took hold of the political imagination in modern state formation following World War II, assuming dominance at least discursively with
the waning of the twentieth century. I am concerned in this chapter with
why this occurred, what interests the discourse of racelessness represents
and speaks to, what shaping of the state it offers in the face of racial
histories. Instead of considering whether racelessness is normatively justifi-
able, I am focusing on why, for instance, color-blindness in the United
States became explicit initially in the late nineteenth century seemingly as a
countervoice to bald segregationism (witness Harlan's famous dissent at the
close of the century in *Plessy*) (Carr 1997). To what, as Reva Siegel asks, did
that commitment to color-blindness amount, and how has it served to
articulate rather than erase racial commitments (Siegel 1998)? How, by way
of comparison, has a "raced racelessness" emerged and become elaborated
in Brazil as racial democracy, or more recently in Europe in the expression
of ethnic pluralism, in Australia or Canada as state multiculturalism, and in
South Africa as nonracialism? What are the connections between various
assertions of state racelessness and the coterminous emergence of postracial
and "postracist racisms" (Comaroff and Comaroff 2000)?

I have argued elsewhere that the most significant distinction between racial
presuppositions and the patterns of racial theorizing and rule they prompt is
that between what I call racial naturalism and racial historicism. Racial naturalism, the view that most consider to exhaust historical views on race, is the
claim that those neither European nor more or less fully of European descent,
in some biological sense, are inherently or naturally inferior to those who are.
This is a very long and thick tradition in racial thinking and theorizing, running from the likes of Sepulveda in the mid-sixteenth century, through

Adapted from chapter 8 of David Theo Goldberg, *The Racial State* (Basil Blackwell, 2001).

Voltaire and Blumenbach, Kant and Hume, Carlyle and Spencer, the eugenicists and social Darwinists to the likes of Murray and Herrnstein, Coon and Rushton. Racial historicism, by contrast, consists of the set of claims that those other than European or descended from Europeans are not inherently inferior but historically immature or less developed. This is a tradition that runs arguably from Locke through the likes of John Stuart Mill and Auguste Comte, mid-nineteenth-century English political economists such as Merivale and Marx, to formal colonial policies of assimilationism, developmentalism and progressivism (Goldberg 2001).

Now historicism took hold, increasingly assertively, as a countervoice to naturalist racial presumptions from roughly the mid-nineteenth century on. For a century or so, these two paradigms of racial rule were in more or less sharp and explicit contest with each other, both between and within racially conceived and ordered regimes. Where naturalism underpinned the institution of slavery, historicist racial presuppositions mostly fueled abolitionist movements, proliferating as common sense in the wake of slavery's formal demise, promoted as civilized moral conscience in the face of insistent and persistent naturalist regimes. Sometimes, however, historicist assumptions were internalized, though never without conflict (see Balibar 1991, 18; Memmi 1965, 90–118), even by those marked as less developed by such assumptions and in the name of resistance: witness, for instance, Alexander Crummel, *The Progress of Civilization Along the West Coast of Africa* (1861). By the close of the nineteenth century, naturalism found itself on the defensive before increasingly heterogeneous urban arrangements, intensified migrations between colonies and metropoles, and an emergent shift from biologically driven to culturalist conceptions of race. As (a set of) conceptual commitment(s), naturalism thus was challenged explicitly to defend—to rationalize—its claims in ways it had not hitherto faced. In short, by the mid-twentieth century, naturalism had shifted explicitly from the given of racial rule to the anomaly, from the safely presumed to the protested, from the standard of social sophistication to the vestige of vulgarity.

Naturalism increasingly gave way to the common sense of historicism, the violence of an imposed physical repression to the infuriating subtleties of a legally fashioned racial order. In modern constitutional terms, the law is committed to the formal equality of treating like alike (and by extension the unlike differently). This abstract(ed) commitment to formal equality, in turn, entails the color-blinding constitutionalism of racelessness as the teleological narrative of modernization and racial progress. Racelessness is the logical implication of racial historicism. It is the perfect blending of modernist rationality and the maintenance of de facto, if deraced, racial domination juridically ordered and exercised.

CENTRALIZING STATE RACELESSNESS

The formalized commitment to racelessness, I am suggesting, grows out of the modern state's self-promotion in the name of rationality and the recognition of ethno-racially heterogeneous states. Modern states assumed their modernity in and through their racial elaboration. After abolition, in the face of growing self-assertion and the call for self-governance by the "despised races" in the late nineteenth century and alongside the shift from biology to culture in racial articulation, racial historicism increasingly challenged naturalism as the presumptive form of states of whiteness. Against this background, the modern state in the twentieth century came to promote its claims to modernization more and more through its insistence on racelessness—its insistence on rendering invisible the racial sinews of the body politic and modes of rule and regulation. As colonialism gave way to postcolonial forms of world making and the hegemony of globalized neoliberalism, racelessness came to represent state rationality, regarding race.

The displacement from naturalist to historicist discursive dominance as the prevailing common sense of racial presumption would take almost another century of racist brutality and bestiality. I do not mean to suggest, however, that naturalism disappeared as a commitment of rule within and across all (or indeed any) racial states. Naturalist commitments, while representing now the extremes of racist expression, nevertheless continue to circulate at the social margins and beneath the surface, as exemplified by slips of the tongue by public figures. Similarly, the persistent climb to power in Europe of the likes of Haider or Le Pen, of the National Front in France, Freedom Party in Austria, Northern League in Italy, or the Vlaamse Blok in Belgium reveals the circumspect circulation of naturalism just beneath the surface of contemporary historicist discursive dominance. So the argument at play here does not rest on a claim to "progression" from less to more enlightened views, though historicism certainly has proclaimed itself in those terms. And it certainly does not follow that naturalism has withered and deceased. A rearticulated naturalism has asserted itself as the social position of marginalized "conscience" and "critic" of hegemony, the object of state repression while bearing the burden of social progress.

Like historicist regimes, then, naturalism also would claim to promote state modernization. If naturalists have sought state modernization in the past on the backs of racial exploitation and dehumanization, they now seek it through racial separation and restrictions on "racial" immigration. Historicists, by contrast, have sought modernization through "humanization" and the denial of the effects of racial significance (cf. Balibar 1991, 21–3, and esp. note 6). Thus, where naturalists continue to see *race* as deeply significant, historicists insist on its *historical effects* as ultimately insignificant. Clearly the increasing ideological and administrative dominance of historicism in state modernization has displaced naturalism for the most part to the extreme, the antique, or the anomaly (cf. Essed 1996, 20–29). Witness the recent marginalization of white supremacist militias—in South Africa as in the United States, in Germany as in France, in the Netherlands as in Belgium—as extremist or terrorist. They are groups that define themselves precisely as dismissive of the contemporary state seen as representative of the racial interests of those not white or European at the expense of those who are. Naturalism and historicism accordingly remain dialectically definitive, as they have been from the outset of their formulation, of each other's respective parameters of possible articulation.

If colonial empires were established for the sake of raw materials and minerals, space and land, profits and the exercise of power, slave labor made (materially) possible their initiation and the maximization of their operability. As the implications of abolition and metropolitan industrialization were being realized, state modernization became the abiding concern. Toward the close of the nineteenth century, state modernization entailed and was promoted by centralization of administrative technologies and the nationalizing coherence of state identity. States sought to extend to themselves the coordinates of this centralizing coherence through national narratives. A common administrative apparatus promised the rationalizing efficiencies, in cost and effort, of expansive problem-solving capacities. Confidence in state administration "consisted (at least in part) in solving big national problems, through large-scale interventions, coordinated from the center. And the agent of social transformation was a much bigger, more powerful, more knowledgeable, state" (Posel 2000, 13). As states committed to the project of modernization, so state-ordered and state-ordained data collection expanded and intensified.

Since the 1930s race increasingly has been dismissed as a premodern marking, an ancient hangover. Nevertheless, it is evident from a string of examples—the Nazi Reich, postwar America, apartheid South Africa, Israel/ Palestine, repeated "race riots" in contemporary urban Britain and so on— how central race has remained, in a wide range of more or less deadly variations, to the modernizing state. States have sought through race to mediate and manage the tensions between economy and society, to maintain white privilege and power, to massage costs and controls. There is a marked distinction, however, between the kinds of modernization different racial regimes promoted. States sought to modernize themselves according to their existing needs and available resources, invoking varying forms of racial configuration in the process. Naturalist states modernized through expulsion and exclusion, denial and in the extreme the production of death of those defined as inherently inferior, as "naturally" not qualifying for citizenship. Historicist states sought to modernize by claiming to educate those regarded as less developed or lacking in progress, those historically less endowed with the capacities and rationalities of civilization, the mores and manners, values and virtues of democracy, most notably, the means to self-determination. And to marginalize surplus populations, intra- or internationally, by warehousing or willing them away.

In their purest form, naturalist racial regimes entail the teleology of (a) uniracial state(s), the state of whiteness (under some more or less specific interpretation) as final solution (on states of whiteness, see Goldberg 2001, chap. 7). So naturalism aims for the racelessness, the racial hygiene, of white self-elevation through the spatial and ultimately physical removal of those considered nonwhite. No further need for racial definition where the state has been reduced to uniracial formation through eviction or obliteration. Historicists seek the racelessness of absorption and transmogrification of the racially differentiated into a state of values and rationality defined by white standards and norms, ways of knowing and being, thinking and doing. This is a state characterized in the final analysis as racelessness. It is achievable only by the presumptive elevation of whiteness silently as (setting) the desirable standards, the teleological norms of civilized social life, even as it seeks to erase the traces of exclusions necessary to its achievement along the way.

Racelessness, then, offers the conditions either for global force and power (the "thousand-year Reich") or for the globalizing circulation of untethered corporate capital (the likes of the World Bank and International Monetary Fund). Racelessness, it might be said, is predicated on the reduction of all to the color of money. And as a matter of historical logic, money, as the Brazilian characterization has long had it, *whitens*. Race becomes not so much reduced to class as rearticulated through it. The popularity in the 1980s of *The Cosby Show*, in the United States and South Africa alike, hints at the redefinition of race through class mobility.

By the mid-nineteenth century racial naturalism had helped to effect a global capitalism the conditions for the sustenance of which it conceptually contradicted. Naturalism thus gave way in the end to the insistence of and upon racial historicism by the contingent logic of historical "necessity." Modernization promoted the proliferation and intensification of global flows of human, social and finance capital, both spatially and temporally. The artifice of national borders was rendered increasingly porous if not altogether archaic, replaced or really displaced by the latter quarter of the twentieth century more and more to their local reinscription. These products of colonial conditions, but also the cause of their demise, have called for(th) novel racial dispensations in the name of a new racelessness. The Cold War closed with not only the constriction of communism but the death of formal apartheid. In the wake of these emergent shifts in global capital and cultural formations—from the colonial to the postcolonial, segregationist to desegregationist, apartheid to postapartheid, nationalized to globalized—naturalism's intensely raced racelessness gave way almost hegemonically to the state of whitened color-blinding. The color-blinding state can be understood in this scheme of things as the ultimate victory of states of whiteness purged of their guilt and self-doubt, the language of race giving way to the lexicon of a bland corporate multiculturalism and ethnic pluralism.

To recapitulate: naturalist racial regimes, modernizing states with (lingering) naturalist commitments, tended in their twentieth-century modernizing drive to segregationist racial formations (and their apartheid successors) (Posel 2000, 7). Historicist regimes on the other hand opted for racelessness as the mark of modernizing global commitment, burying the threads

49

of their own racial articulation beneath the more or less vocal dismissals of naturalism as modernizing prehistory.

Segregationism, almost by definition, was a *regional* design seeking global reach. Regions were to be purged of racial distinction, conceiving states as racially discrete (at least in the purist fantasy if not quite the pragmatic version). Centralization in states predicated on purist assumptions of racial naturalism were committed to racist intensification, to forced racial removal for the sake of the artifice—the dangerous fantasy—of racial purity. The pragmatics of racial rule nevertheless sought to nuance what was possible in the wake of radical resistance and liberal caution to implement and effect. An intense struggle erupted, for instance, between the ideologues of a purist apartheid state (separation of races at all costs) and apartheid "realists" or pragmatists (a step-by-step implementation of apartheid policies determined by judgments of what could be achieved economically and politically). The struggle was won ultimately—as it likely only could be—by the pragmatists, led ironically by Verwoerd: "While on the one hand the policy of Apartheid has to be implemented at the same time it has to be done step for step in such a way that the country can bear the implementation of that policy" (House of Assembly Debates 1955, vol. 88, col. 3760; Posel 2000, 14–15).

Like segregation, apartheid in the end was about the attempt to merge white supremacy (as ideology, as commitment, as enactment in all domains) with maintenance of elevated and intensified white economic prosperity. And white supremacy, premised on the demands and imaginaries of white domination, realistically meant not complete absence of those defined as not white from the social formation but their controlled presence, their service of and obeisance to white order and oversight. White prosperity, like white supremacy, depended on it. They depended not on the absence of "nonwhites" from white space but their structured exploitation within it. After all, whites could measure their superiority and sense of racial self-worth only in the controlled presence of those not-white. Hence the strong surge of a qualified pragmatic racist "realism" (on "racial realism," cf. Balibar 1991, 23). The assumption of power in the late 1980s of the "pragmatic" W. F. De Klerk was not so much an anomaly to Afrikaner political power as the logical resolution of its internal ideological struggles (against the background of "raceless" global capital and intensified internal urban ungovernability).

Segregationism and its apartheid aftermath proved in the end radically incapable, whether in South Africa or the United States or Israel, of coping with the dynamics of rapid and intense ethno-racially diverse urbanization. Urbanization in the first three decades of the twentieth century was fueled by a shrinking rural sector and expansive industrialization, and so by migration and immigration. It was prompted by a rapidly transforming mode of production, labor demands and desires, requirements and hopes, needs and fantasies as well as by political and legal shifts. The issues emerging as a result were considered much too complex for "local, uneven, ad hoc interventions" (Posel 2000, 11), and so were deemed to require more centralized, rationalized, national responses. Initiated by the fantasized fears flowing from urbanized social mobilities, segregationist and apartheid regionalisms actually conjured the very possibility of black self-determination naturalism was committed to denying. Exacerbated by the duplicate costs of segregationist maintenance and declining profitability, this implosion of the logic of naturalism thus devolved into historicist assumptions, more muted and less assertive, to be sure, but an emergent and ultimately pervasive common sense in any case. Here lies the foundation for the expression of racelessness as "a given" of racial resolution—as a way, the least invasive way, logically—out of the apparent impasse.

This implosion of naturalist logic and its racial regimes prompted two primary effects. The first was not the "progressivist" demise or denouement of racist expression so readily proclaimed. There was rather, as I have insisted, an emergent shift to (an emphasis on) racial historicism, and at most a laborious meliorism committed to addressing racial "problems" in a piecemeal and mostly ambiguous manner. The second, relatedly, concerned the deflection of charges of racism from historicist presupposition. Racism, on this account, can be predicated only on naturalist assumption. It is deemed nothing other than the (irrational) claim of inherent, immutable, and so timeless racial (biological or moral) inferiority. Historicist racial meliorism—the claimed historical immaturity of those deemed racially undeveloped, and so admission of their developmental possibility—supposedly escapes the charge of racism by naturalist comparison. Racial historicism evades racism by definitional deflection. And in doing so it becomes the default position regarding late modern racial states.

That the distinction between naturalism and historicism regarding racism is overlooked, the latter camouflaged for the most part behind the former, explains also how liberals and conservatives alike (can) assert that racism is alleviated once naturalist articulation of it fades from view. Those committed to historicist conception accordingly can claim they are not racist but racial realists, sufficiently courageous "to call a spade a spade" (cf. D'Souza 1995). Thus racism persists behind the facade of a historicism parading itself as uncommitted to racist expression *in its traditional sense.*

STYLES OF STATE RACELESSNESS

Retrospectively, World War II can be read as the ultimate contestation between competing visions of and conditions for racial globalization: the naturalist and historicist, white supremacist and white developmentalist or progressivist, the Aryan Reich and Anglo-American capital, millenarian colonialism and flexible postcolonial accumulability. The Global War accordingly represents the moment of acute social crisis, racially conceived. That the forces of Good won out over those of Evil was taken (in the spirit of

ideology's demise) to promote the "end of racism," the limits of its irrational extremism (Malik 1996, 124; Barkan 1992, 1), thus at once camouflag-
ing the shift in racial configuration and representation. Racial historicism
could claim victory in the name of racelessness, sewing the assumptions of
(now historicized) racial advancement silently into the seams of postwar
and postcolonial reconstruction. Three-world theory, emerging as it did in
the early 1950s, simply structured the tapestry in more precise terms. If
apartheid was the ultimately doomed naturalist response to this crisis in
racial representation, naturalism's seemingly last gasp (Derrida 1985), color-blindness furnished the historicist form of crisis management and containment, maintenance of racial configuration and control.

World War II was a moment of radical uprooting. It exacerbated existing
population movements and gave rise to a wide range of new ones. Surviv-
ing Jews moved within and out of Europe in increasing numbers. East
Europeans moved West in the face of creeping communism. Colonial subjects served without much fanfare in the Allied forces, settling in the wake
of the war in Britain and France (Hesse 2000; Furedi 1998). It should
come as no surprise, for example, that the Pan-Africanist Congress would
hold its fourth international meeting in Manchester in 1945. In reitera-
tions of the black Atlantic, black Americans, Africans and Caribbeans moved
in search of work from South to North, or from lower northern cities to
more industrialized ones, and from East to West (as of course in another
sense was the experience of Asians), fueling the war economy (Halsey
1946; Smith 1949). They gravitated in the wake of the war also, though in
smaller numbers, from the likes of New York or Dakar, Bombay or King-
ston, Lagos or Accra to London, Paris, Amsterdam and Berlin to leave
behind them the weight of American racial degradation or to seek higher
education, as cultural producers or political critics. The anticolonial independence movements soon manifested in a series of heady successes: India
in 1947, China in 1949, Ghana in 1956, Algeria in 1961 and so on.
Postwar reconstruction and economic boom in the North pulled postcolonial subjects into European and North American metropoles, as the United
Nations condemned a naturalistic conception of racism as scientifically vac-
uous, and anti-Semitism became the dominant intellectual measure of racial
prejudice.

There emerged out of this increasingly heterogeneous worldly mobility
of people numerous contrasting, often competing, conceptions of racelessness taking root in different sociopolitical and cultural milieus. In the
United States color-blindness was crafted and codified in the contrast between desegregationism and integrationism; in South Africa nonracialism
became the dominant counter to apartheid, most notably articulated in the
Freedom Charter in 1956. In Europe especially, emphasis on ethnic pluralism has occluded racial reference and displaced charges of racism to the
margins of the "loony left," while in Brazil public advocacy of racial democracy swept any attempted political organization around racial injustice

behind a romanticized projection of racial—and so really a deracialized—peace.

Racelessness in its various explicit and implicit expressions thus gathered steam in the wake of World War II[1] and came to dominate public commitment in a variety of transnational settings from the 1960s onward. Seen in this light, the expressed commitment to racelessness was really about re-shaping the state in the face of civil rights, integrationist and demographic challenges to privilege and power. Justice Harlan, himself a former slave owner, had already recognized this challenge color-blindness posed as the appropriate reaction a half century earlier: "The white race deems itself to be the dominant race in this country. And so it is, in prestige, in achievements, in education, in wealth, and in power. So, I doubt not, it will continue to be for all time, if it remains true to its great heritage and holds fast to the principles of constitutional liberty" (*Plessy v. Ferguson* 1896). Thus, having established through racial governance and racist exclusion the indomitable superiority of whites—in prestige, achievements, education, wealth, and power—not as a natural phenomenon but as historical outcome, the best way to maintain it, as Harlan insisted, is to treat those de facto unlike as de jure *alike* (Crenshaw 1998, 285). The reproduction of white supremacy, Harlan's historicism makes clear, requires labor, a fact obscured by naturalists. Illegitimate inequalities—historical injustices in acquisition or transfer, as Nozick (1974) would have it—are to be legitimized by laundering them through the white wash with the detergent of color-blindness. Color-blindness enables as acceptable, as a principle of historical justice, the perpetuation of the inequities already established. Harlan outstripped his peers by half a century in recognizing that color-blindness would maintain—should maintain, as he conceived it—white supremacy, as well as in being able openly to admit it (cf. Carr 1997, 1–16).

While speaking to their sociospatial and sociotemporal specificities, often as critical commitments, the appeals to "racial democracy" in Brazil, "non-racialism" in South Africa, "ethnic pluralism" in Europe, and state "multiculturalism" in the likes of Australia and Canada each served to extend the racial status quo in and of those states. These various commitments to racelessness, fueled as they often were by a mix of guilt and moral enlightenment but also by a "racial realism" (Bell 1995; Balibar 1991, 23) and realpolitik, served nevertheless to renew white social control and to promote white power and privilege in the face of emerging challenges. In all these variations, racelessness was as much a refusal to address, let alone redress, deeply etched historical inequities and inequalities racially fashioned as it was an expressed embrace of principles of a race-ignoring fairness and equal opportunity. Racial configuration anywhere is shored up by forms of racial configuration everywhere; and racial conditions everywhere are maintained of course by their reproduction in particular places.

Racial democracy became the public expression of choice in Brazil from roughly the late 1930s onward. This banner of racial democratization through the processes of *mestizaje* and *blanqueamiento,* of whitening through mixing, has been waved more widely throughout Latin America, most notably in Colombia and Venezuela (Whitten and Torres 1998, vols. 1–2; Taussig 1980; Taussig 1997; Ware 1993). Associated most insistently[2] with the work of Gilberto Freyre, racial democracy denied the deeply marked racist past of Brazilian society, ideologically and materially (Schwarcz 1999; Fiola 1990; Levine and Crocitti 1999; Mitchell 1998; Fernandes 1998). Freyre had studied in the early 1920s with Franz Boas at Columbia University. From Boas he inherited a conception of the relation between race and culture (see author's introduction to Freyre 1946). This influence indicated a shift from presumptions of naturalism that had marked much of Brazilian thinking around race—medically and legally, socially and politically—throughout slavery more or less until abolition in 1888 (Schwarcz 1999) to culturalist assumptions consistent with historicism. From this culturalist commitment Freyre drew the central raceless implication that Brazil in the 1930s and 1940s was marked by no "racial problem." This racelessness, in turn, was bound up with Freyre's deeply questionable revisionist historical assumptions. These included claims of "soft slavery" *(escravidão suave)* and benign or "good masters" *(o bom senhor),* humane Portuguese colonialism and "marvelous accommodationism" of "slave to master, black to white," a "luso-tropical gentleness and carefreeness" among the Portuguese colonizers.

Following abolition by the Golden Law in 1888 and the declaration of the Republic a little over a year later, Brazil was reconstructed discursively as a tropical racial paradise. It projected itself as the laboratory of racial modernity and democracy through miscegenizing mixture, most notably, as a result of Portuguese men's sexual attraction to "hot black women" (Fiola 1990, 4–7). Metissage was supposed to result in a sort of racelessness through *blanqueamiento*—genetic, economic and sociocultural "elevation" following from the whitening of the body politic. The importation from Europe of those with superior and stronger "white blood" would eugenically purge Brazil of the less desirable African and Amerindian presence, producing in their place a "Latin" race (Fry 2000, 87). These "Law(s) of White Magic," as Antonio Collado has properly put it (Nascimento in Levine and Crocitti 1999, 380), fashioned the fairy tale of a raceless Brazilian, a new race beyond classical racial conceptions, a raceless race each individual member of which uniquely melded European, African and Amerindian biological and cultural heritage (Fry 2000, 90).

By the time of the various Vargas regimes from the 1930s through the 1950s, racial reference and politics, race-based organizations and mobilization had been outlawed in the name of a racial—really a race-denying and white-elevating—democracy. Thus immediately following abolition official documents pertaining to slavery were destroyed, and in the first century of the Republic census counts included "color" questions just three times. Indeed, by 1969 all studies documenting racial discrimination in Brazil were outlawed as subversive of national security (Fiola 1990, 17–19). Swept behind the veil of racelessness, the reification of deep historical inequalities, racially conceived and shaped with racial materials, had become untouchable and unspeakable. Marked by the interface of race and class, black people in Brazil today consequently live considerably shorter, less healthy and poorer lives, are less educated, face considerable employment discrimination in hiring and promotion including explicit racial restrictions on hiring in the private sector as well as extensive police harassment and violence. White infant mortality in 1980 was 25 percent lower than that for nonwhite babies, and whites would live almost seven years longer. Four times as many whites had completed high school in 1990 and their income averaged twice as much as that of blacks and mestizos. The percentage of people of color in the prisons of large cities such as Rio and São Paulo was roughly double their respective ratios in the demographic compositions of those cities, and about half as many whites charged with crimes await trial on bail than do similarly charged blacks (Fry 2000, 92–93). Racist stereotypes have pervaded the population, reinforced by images in school textbooks and popular culture (Fiola 1990, 22–36). Racelessness in Brazil has fixed racial effects in place, rendering its material conditions seemingly inevitable and their historical causes largely invisible and virtually causeless (cf. Hanchard 1994; Fry 2000, 99–100).

It is important to emphasize that Brazilian commitment to racelessness historically, while intellectually initiated, has been for the most part extended through state commitment. I do not mean by this to ignore the relative surge in Brazilian race consciousness over the past decade or so, prompted by a self-conscious campaign by activists to fashion a black racial identity in Brazil. This campaign has resulted in the modest introduction of some race-based policies, laws and programs (Fry 2000, 99–100). All this notwithstanding, recent surveys in São Paulo and Rio de Janeiro reveal that while almost 90 percent acknowledged racial discrimination in Brazil, most respondents remained vehemently committed to the prevailing conception of racial democracy and declared themselves personally free of prejudice (Fry 2000, 94). These knotted considerations trouble deeply the claims made of late by Pierre Bourdieu and Loïc Wacquant in a series of articles that globalization has generalized to the rest of the world through a form of pernicious cultural imperialism the prevailing structures of binary racial definition, (mis)comprehension, and order manifested in the United States (Bourdieu and Wacquant 1998, 1999).

Although nonracialism in South Africa was prompted by a different, if not unrelated, set of circumstances, it has come to represent similar effects. Nonracialism emerged as the prevailing expression of antiracism in the early 1950s, a seemingly reasoned if not radical response to the increasing institutionalization of formalized apartheid in policy and law, economy and society. If the state was being codified in the lexicon of race, if racially conceived and ordered culture was unavoidable and inevitable, its raison d'être rule by division, then resistance seemed to require at least the principled commitment to racelessness, to social arrangements that insisted on making no reference to race. The Freedom Charter of 1956, a document deemed by the apartheid state to be too subversive to be allowed to circulate, was fashioned through a remarkable coalition of the major liberal and socialist resistance groups united through their common opposition to apartheid. The coalition recognized, to its credit, that simple oppositionality would be insufficient to sustain the principled differences between them. Nonracialism became a coalitional cement, the common denominator between those committed to intensive land redistribution and nationalization of the mode of production at one end and the forces of a progressive liberalism based on a naively benign capitalism at the other.[3] The "Freedom Charter's terms," boasted Adam and Moodley (1986, 213–14), "resemble the old-fashioned values of liberal democracies. They lack the ideological zeal of the classless society and the fascist rule of the master race. The Freedom Charter is a pluralist document: 'national groups coexisting in equality with mutual tolerance. . . .' In the liberal modesty of the nonracial opposition lies its justness and moral promise."

And yet, in the name of "national groups coexisting in equality," the Freedom Charter inevitably presupposes and reinstates the very racial configurations it is expressly committed to challenging. By extension, once sewn into the postapartheid constitution nonracialism effectively reinstates prevailing racially figured class and in large part gendered formation as the status quo. Racelessness renders the material conditions of historically reified racial, and through them gendered formations unreachable. Indeed, while opening up a window of opportunity to a small sector of black women at the elite end, it has done nothing to make significantly less-privileged black women less vulnerable either to employment or sexual exploitation. Thus unemployment, rape and the incidence of AIDS among poor black women have risen dramatically in the past decade. The structural conditions of apartheid have been displaced to the realm of private individuated experiences under postapartheid. By the same token, the Truth and Reconciliation Commission, while importantly revealing how widespread were routine governmental abuses of black people throughout the era of apartheid, at once has had virtually nothing to say formally about widespread everyday racist expression in the same period. This everyday expression was structured and made possible by state racist formation. The unintended implication has been to render apartheid the effect almost wholly of a governmentality run amuck, an anomaly somehow silently disconnected from the otherwise human decency of the general white populace.

The claimed commitment to color-blindness in the United States, the rhetoric of racial democracy in Brazil, and the principled policy of nonracialism in South Africa each has had a triple effect. First, each has effected the relative silencing of public analysis or serious discussion of everyday racisms in the respective societies. Second, each has made it more or less impossible to connect historical configurations to contemporary racial formations.

Margaret Halsey explicitly ties the prospect of integrative color-blindness to historical denial when she writes, "So far as white people are concerned, there is one simple rule for interracial projects: don't try to atone for the past. Forget the past and build for the future" (Halsey 1946, 156). Witness also the explicit denial of such connection on the U.S. Supreme Court, with dramatic implications for the constitutionality of affirmative action.[4] And third, each instance of racelessness has displaced the tensions of contemporary racially charged relations to the relative invisibility of private spheres, seemingly out of reach of public policy intervention. As Reva Siegel (1998, 31) notes more narrowly in respect of color-blind constitutionalism in the United States, racelessness is the state strategy to institutionalize prevailing racial privilege and power by protecting "historical race" (Gotanda 1995) from state intervention or interference (cf. Posner 1974, 25 for evidence).

Now the European shift to the language of ethnic pluralism and the recent widening state invocation of multiculturalism over that of racial reference has had a triple effect too. For one, it has led to the relative disappearance from public debate of reference to European colonialism, its extensions, and its contemporary implications, thus reshaping the narrative of European history and memory (Werbner 1997, 261; Goldberg 2001). As racial reference has given way to the insistent silences as a result of the shift to racelessness, ethnic subjectification has become more characteristic, or at least more noticeable (and noted), at Europe's historical edges: Bosnia, Kosovo, Chechnya, Somalia, Rwanda, East Timor, Fiji, the Moluccas, Quebec. Second, the ethnic (re)turn has rendered relatively awkward, if not impossible, direct critical reference to contemporary racism in European or even in settler societies. Witness, for instance, the persistence of the rule of "German blood" in defining German citizenship; and while Haider's anti-Semitic expression in Austria has been roundly condemned, the recent repeated beatings of people of color in Viennese subways by or with the collusion of the police has barely warranted a mention.

The third effect of this shift to the framework of an ethnic pluralism identified with state multiculturalism has been to make more difficult the drawing of causal connections between colonial legacies and contemporary racial conditions in European or settler societies. The new managed multicultural Europe or Canada or Australia is taken to be the function of a new (neoliberal) world order that promotes immigration and refugees, criminalization and job competition, a world somehow connected, if at all, only marginally to their colonial histories.

As in Brazil, public institutions throughout Europe and European settler societies recently have been careful to espouse broadly explicit policies against racial discrimination with the view to being able to distance themselves from the phenomenon. But the effect of the World War II experience has been to narrow the concern over racism to its supposedly irrational and stereotyping expressions predicated on biological claims and so for the most part to limit contemporary racist expression to the extremes of neo-Nazi outbursts. Every-day racisms in private spheres proliferate behind the veil of their public disavowal in the name of ethnic pluralist and multicultural decency, on one hand, and the substitution of racial reference by the coded terms of policy concerns over immigration, criminalization, and the integrity of national culture, on the other (Essed 1996; Werbner and Modood 1997).

If nonracialism has left the materialities of racial distinction beyond reach, then critical multiculturalism has certainly prompted a radical rethinking of the exclusionary histories of racial structure. Nevertheless, the socially dom-inant conservative, liberal and corporate versions of multiculturalism that have informed state practice—in Canada, Australia, the United States and Europe, to name but the leading formulations—have extended the *effects* of racelessness even if not quite so readily its refusal of any and all racial reference. In 1993, then Australian Prime Minister P. J. Keating claimed that the "new socially just multicultural society could be painlessly achieved with no serious costs or losses for . . . 'we' non-Aboriginal Australians. It would not challenge, threaten, or set into crisis the basic values of Austra-lians (including 'our' right to enjoy beaches and other recreation areas, including national parks)" (Povinelli 1998, 589). Under colonial assimila-tion colonizers sought to eclipse, if not erase, indigenous colonized cul-tures; under the managed multiculturalist turn, by contrast, the project has been to put to economic and political work the value of cultural distinction silently ascribed to racial difference. Think of the decade-long commercials for Benetton or Budweiser, Gatorade or Gap, Cisco Systems or Nike Sports.

The foregoing line of analysis should not be taken to suggest that there are no relevant distinctions among American claims to color-blindness, Bra-zilian racial democracy, South African nonracialism, European ethno-plural-ist and Australian or Canadian multicultural maintenance. Each form of racelessness has been fashioned in the crucible of the conditions specific to their social, political, legal and cultural conditions peculiar to their historical contexts of articulation.

One broad distinction, however, is worth noting. Color-blindness and racial democracy are distinct from nonracialism and multiculturalism, at least under one set of interpretations. The former were each fashioned explicitly as forms of political and social evasion, at least initially, while the latter grew out of critical commitments even as they quickly assumed more accommo-dating and so pacifying expression. It is true that invocation of both color-blindness and racial democracy could be read as attempts at a compromising social reconstruction, projects of reconciliatory nation making or rebuilding in the wake of racially destructive histories. And indeed the codes of color-blindness in particular were taken up in the civil rights movement of the 1950s and 1960s as a coalescing of antiracist forces. In the latter case, the investment in eliminationism was not first and foremost about conceptual erasure but a commitment to eliminating the material conditions racial charac-terization historically has referenced (Guinier and Torres 2002, chap. 1). Yet the accommodating compromises in the name of national reconciliation signaled both by color-blindness in the United States and racial democracy in Brazil (and Latin America more broadly) exactly privileged, and in privileging reinforced, the relatively powerful and already privileged at the expense of the traditionally excluded. In short, they reinscribed a refurbished whiteness as the privileged, powerful and propertied to the ongoing exclusions of those considered or classified not white. The legacies of nonracialism and multiculturalism, because fashioned in some sense to bring down "the house that race built," even as they have ended up as forms of redecoration, have perhaps been more checkered in their particular institutional effects.

CONDITIONS AND CODES OF RACELESSNESS

Racelessness is the neoliberal attempt to go beyond—without (fully) coming to terms with—racial histories and their accompanying racist inequities and iniquities; to mediate the racially classed and gendered distinctions to which those histories have given rise without reference to the racial terms of those distinctions; to transform, via the negating dialectic of denial and ignoring, racially marked social orders into racially erased ones. In rubbing out the possibilities of racial cognition and recognition in those societies historically marked by race—and which modern society has somehow not been so marked?—the classing marks of racist derogation and debilitation are rendered relatively invisible, histories reduced to pasts happily placed beneath the focus of memory, conveniently repackaged for commercial consumption and nostalgic renarration purged of historical responsibility (Goldberg 2001). Proponents no doubt point to the virtues of this transcendence and forgetting, to the prospective leaving bygones behind and to the sort of optimistic hybridity reflected in Benetton's united colors. But those colors of commercial unification linger with the now unaddressed (and perhaps unaddressable) presumptions of stereotypical distinction: those long characterized as nonwhites whitened by the classed color of money nevertheless bearing the distinctive birthmarks of unaddressed because unaddressable inferiorized pasts ("never quite" white, always "not yet," as Françoise Verges [2001], riffing on Homi Bhabha, has reminded us).

Expressly committed to race blindness, that is, to a standard of justice protective of individual rights and not group results, raceless racism informally identifies racial groups so long as the recognition in question is no longer state formulated or fashioned. The possibility of racelessness publicly, and by extension of racial reference privately, trades exactly on an implicit and informal invocation of the sorts of massaged historical racial referents now denied in the public sphere. This in turn makes possible the devaluation of any individuals considered not white, or whitelike, the trashing or trampling of their rights and possibilities, for the sake of preserving the right to *private* "rational discrimination" of whites. If the raceless *state* ought not to discriminate, it remains open to its citizens to restrict rental of their "private white apartments" to their self-defined kind.[5] Such rational discriminators rationalize their avoidance of those not like themselves by appealing to statistical generalizations about groups intersectionally raced, gendered and classed. By rational discrimination is intended that the discrimination is instrumentally valuable: "It is efficient, it makes economic sense," as D'Souza notoriously has put it (D'Souza 1995, 277). If discrimination in hiring, mortgage leasing, education, criminal justice and consumption possibilities is mostly rational, the implication is that it ceases to be racist (Goldberg 1993, 14–40). The logical entailment of racelessness is the end not of racism but of its charge, its accusation and the bearing of its compensatory cost.

"Rational discrimination" is the handmaiden of racelessness. The values of efficiency and economy, the fundamentalist foundations of rational choice reason, assume the status of empirically established truth, the force of which is unquestionable and thus incontestable. Discrimination devolves, if not dissolves, into discretion. The disvalue of racist discrimination is discounted in the calculus of maximizing personal preference schemes. Not only are such preference-based racist exclusions, privileges, or distributions deemed acceptable in the private sphere, those racist configurations "that arise from differences in tastes or talents among racial groups" (Siegel 1998, 48) are rendered immune from state intervention. As Siegel points out, the concern of a raceless state agency shifts accordingly from redressing past and present racist exclusion to protecting the expression of private racial preference in the "racial marketplace" (Crenshaw 1998, 283) from state restriction.

I do not mean by this line of critique to say there has been no "racial progress." A commitment to a meliorism and progressivism that produced none after all would be too crass an ideological subterfuge to rise to the claims of legitimation. But every form of racial progress thus predicated on white normativity is laden with ambiguity and ambivalence, is undercut, qualified and discounted, by the tinge of special treatment or exceptionalism, overcoming the odds despite one's birth(right) and so on. Thus I am emphatically not denying that throughout much of the world marked historically by colonial conditions, liberation struggles and postcolonial transformation, racially predicated situations for peoples of color have markedly improved, de jure and de facto. But the necessity of such acknowledgment at once troubles the claim to progress itself by questioning the standards of judgment and the standpoint from which both those standards and the judgments presupposing those standards are made. Progress for whom, measured against what? Sure, some things have improved, but determined against a yardstick already so debased it would be difficult not to demonstrate progress once that commitment was proclaimed. The measure of improvement has been the historical conditions colonially and racially established, not the presumptively elevated conditions of the privileged. That the privileges were racially predicated in the first place is already silently denied in the privileging of the standard of measurement to begin with. The standards are deemed objective, the standard bearers deserving of their achievements on their own merits, the standard of progress neutrally determined as rational judgments. Naturalistically racist assumptions give way via racial historicism to the neutral judgments of objective assessment, the racial codes for which are nevertheless rendered imperceptible. Social seams remain sewn with racial threads now purged of all responsibility for their (re)production. Autogenerated, they are simply the way things are; social subjects abrogate responsibility for all but their own subjective expression, guiltlessly enjoying the benefits of social positioning or suffering the slights of social subjection "historistically" fashioned.

This latter point must be complemented by pointing out nevertheless that the sort of social or judicial standards represented here hold out the possibility that they can be invaded, and at least sometimes and to some degree infused with new meaning. Consider, for example, the most effective instances of the civil rights movement. Even in their most extreme racist manifestations, racial states do not fully determine or structure states of being, opportunity and possibility for state agents and objects of state structure. Rather, as extensions of racial states, raceless states set social agendas to which resistance is by definition a reaction. This is not to say that resistance is reactionary, but only to point out that agenda determination likely delimits the possibilities of conjuring, and certainly enacting, creative alternatives. These are concerns to which I will return in conclusion.

Racial states and their raceless extensions have maintained firm control over social resources by setting agendas for a wide range of social concerns. These include the shape of immigration and so the demographic profile of the nation; where people can live, and labor and under what sorts of social conditions; educational resources and access, that determine who gets educated and how, and who in turn is socially and politically mobile; and what counts as crime, who is marked as criminal, where criminal acts largely take place, and how they are punished. Raceless states thus silently extend the structure of social arrangements historically fashioned through race. The structure of racially skewed conditions are "diluted" through racelessness into class configurations (Takagi 1993, 1995). Liberal morality has long deemed class distinction more socially palatable precisely because one supposedly can be considered personally responsible for one's class position in ways one cannot be for racial determination, at least not on naturalistic assumption.

It is revealing, therefore, that in the conceptual collapse of race almost wholly into class that has accompanied the rise of that form of racial historicism I have identified as racelessness, apologists for color-blindness like Thomas Sowell have invoked the language of personal responsibility in charging African Americans with cultural poverty (Sowell 1995). Racelessness, as I have said, is the logical implication of racial historicism. Not only does it supposedly sweeten racial structure by diluting it in the substance of class formation; it renders individuals personally responsible—and so the agents of state-fashioned social structure literally irresponsible—for whatever racial distinctions linger. The politics of racelessness is bifurcated. It is not a politics of recognition but one of reconciliation and defensiveness, tolerance and dismissal (personal and positional) at the middle and upper ends of the social scale, and of desperate survival and reconstruction, but also sometimes of resentment and recrimination at the lower-class ends. As such, racelessness is the war not on racism but on racial reference, not on the conditions for the reproduction of racially predicated exclusion and discrimination but on the characterization of their effects and implications in racial terms.

RACELESS WORLDS

It follows that conditions referenced as "racial" are always displaced elsewhere.[6] The racial conditions at the heart of raceless states are the most illustrative example. The problems characterized as "racial" are "inevitably" somewhere else: in the South for the North, the East for the West; in the cities for the suburbs, in the inner cities for the central business district, or in the suburbs for the cities; in the colonies for the metropoles, in Africa for Europe; in Muslims for Serbs, Romas for Central Europeans, or migrants for Western Europe; in Central America for the United States, or in Chiapas for the PRI (Institutional Revolutionary Party); on the West Bank for Israel or in the aboriginal outback for white Australia. The "absent center of late modern life," its point of comparative reference, is the present place of race that we constantly displace to the stench of the not so well placed or appointed or *resourced backyard*. It is the sense of race as there but not, to which we are blind but which we conveniently find always visible. In that sense, racial displacement is to an elsewhere "that just happens to be" the dumping ground of history but is actually someone's place of belonging.[7] Our endless curiosity about the racial conditions racelessness seeks magically to have disappear reveals that, far from being a harbinger of some lost history, those conditions remain all about us, at the heart of defining or refining who we are and the states in which we live.

Racelessness thus represents a double displacement. It is first that guilt-shedding displacement from historical racial definition and conditions I have argued are central to modern state formation and states of being. But it is emblematic also of a displacement, a retreat from, a center modernity claimed to occupy but never quite did because its centeredness was always of its own fabrication. Greenwich is about as central an example as one could conjure. It is this latter displacement one might reference as the postcolonial condition. In the wake of its postcolonial fading, not only has Greenwich's meticulous timekeeping been tinkered with globally but its identity has shifted from the administrative heart of the British admiralty to tourist entertainment and recreational space, the home of the millennial dome. From one point of view, the postcolonial condition is experienced as a displacement circulating in the generalized politics of fear and ambiguity, ambivalence and sense of loss. These insecurities manifest in the tensions between terror and nostalgic longing in a world not so much out of control as one in which those formerly thinking they controlled the world of materiality or meaning no longer so clearly or firmly do.

Posed thus, issues of patriotism and patriarchy get raised anew. They too are about holding on to privileges and preferences in the face of insecurities over loss of old opportunities and control. But they are also about operating in those slippery spaces between lost securities and new possibilities, faded places and polities, hard-nosed rational choice calculations and feelings, persistent moralities and reinvented nostalgias whose holds nevertheless have become ever so tentative.

All this suggests that there is another form of displacement effected through racelessness, namely, from the state itself. The recent insistence on racelessness is at once commensurate and coterminous with the insistence on less government, on less state incursion into civil society. In the wake of civil rights and anticolonial struggles of the 1960s, states as such were seen by those once thinking themselves in political control no longer as states of whiteness but as being for the racially identified poor and marginalized. States were seen to side for the most part with undoing racial privilege, most notably through affirmative action programs and antidiscrimination legislation and hate crime and hate speech codes.

Thus the attack on the state and the arguments for racelessness are of a piece. If state intervention is dramatically curtailed, the state of being will "naturally" carry forward those racial privileges historically reproduced by restricting active delimitation against racial privileges by the state order. This informal racial reproduction will be achieved in the name of protecting exactly those liberties that states have been willing to erode, namely, the liberty to associate with whom one will, to accumulate the wealth merited by one's talents and relatives, in short, in the name of the freedom to discriminate as one chooses. If we "naturally prefer our own kind"—and some "racial kinds" are inherently, naturally, better at some practices than others and these practices just happen to be the ones identified with social privilege, power and accumulation of property—well, so be it. That's just the way the world "naturally" is, and a state that presumes to stand in the way of the state of nature is likely in the scheme of fitness to survive to find itself destined for the dustbin of history. Witness communist states. Indeed, so the argument might run to its logical conclusion, witness political states per se, as we have come to know them. Time for the private sphere and unregulated globalization to dictate terms to state formation. In racial terms, historicism returns to its naturalistic roots, though purged of explicit state implication.

This latter displacement from the state reveals moreover that racelessness and globalization are mutually implicated. The lunge to globalized frames of reference promotes the retreat from explicit racial reference; and the pull of racelessness disposes subjects to evacuate local racial terms. The more or less painless insistence on ending explicit formal racial reference in any place nevertheless is possible in the end precisely because of the ready circulation of racial states of being and informal, implicit racial reference in every (modern) place. Racial routinization and familiarity in the everyday breeds the possibility of formal racelessness in administrative and political ways.

Thus racelessness implies not the end of racial consciousness but its ultimate elevation to the given. The constantly moving, flowing racial images on the screen of representation are irreducible to any configuration of individuated raceless pixels the intersecting combinations of which manifest those images. The morphing liquidities of racial eliminativism, far from terminating the effects of the racial, assume racially invested identities and reproduce racially exclusive and exclusionary outcomes upon demand. Race, in and for the raceless state, is nowhere and everywhere at once, usable and discardable to whatever "productive" purpose those in command of production and the circulation of signification can sustain. At once sweated labor in Indonesia or Vietnam, the maquiladoras or Monterey and faceless fiscal facilitators not to mention consumers in New York, London, Tokyo, or Chicago; diamond traders fuelling wars in Sierra Leone and not quite faceless traders on the diamond exchanges of Antwerp or Amsterdam or Tel Aviv; natives of Europe and immigrants to Europe formerly identified as natives of Africa or Asia or Latin America; purveyors of war in the Balkans or the South Pacific, the Caucasus or Central Africa and arms manufacturers and brokers in the United States; "drug lords" in the South and East and "drug victims" in the North and West. Racial images supposedly rendered raceless in global circulation; racelessly consumed as racially produced. Racial historicism naturalized as the world turns from modern racisms to the postracist varieties, from racial configurations and racist exclusions state fashioned and facilitated to raceless extensions and meta-manifestations of racist configuration indelibly marking states of being. Worldly traces of modern racial states from which both state and race alchemically have been absented. We might call this globalization's will to the power of racelessness, and the late modern will to a superficially raceless and historically amnesiac power.

NOTES

1. "British governmental thinking in the early 1940s came increasingly to emphasize the color-blind nature both of British colonial policy and public attitudes in Britain in general" (Rich 1986, 149; cf. Wolton 2000).

2. Racism in Colombia, Peter Ware writes, lies just beneath the surface, "often subtle, not systematic or thoroughgoing, but pervasive and occasionally blatant. To avoid the stigma to which blackness and black culture . . . are subject by the dominant nonblack world of whites and mestizos, black people may adopt the mores of that world. Alternatively, they may retrench for protection or due to

rejection by the nonblack world. This is not simply a matter of choice about ethnic identity: the possibilities for either alternative are heavily structured, mainly by economic and political processes that circumscribe and indeed constitute the parameters of choice" (Ware 1993, 6). On the modern history of race in Peru, see De la Cadena 2000; in Guatemala, see Grandin 2000; and in Mexico, see Gall 1998.

3. It was exactly over this question of nonracialism and the principle of race-transcending coalitions that black nationalist essentialists broke from the ANC in the late 1950s to form the Pan African Congress (Unterhalter 1995).

4. "While there is no doubt that the sorry history of both private and public discrimination in this country has contributed to a lack of opportunities for black entrepreneurs, this observation, standing alone, cannot justify a rigid racial quota in the awarding of public contracts. . . ." Sandra Day O'Connor's majority opinion denying the constitutionality of the affirmative action plan in Richmond, Virginia. City of *Richmond v. Croson* 109 S. Ct 706, 724.

5. A 1970 advertisement, not untypical, in *The Courier* (Maryland), January 8, read: "FOR RENT: Furnished basement apartment. In private white home."

6. I am grateful to Ann Stoler for a set of exchanges in light of which the following points became elaborated. See also Van Dijk 2002.

7. Consider Supreme Court Justice Sandra Day O'Connor's choice words in *Shaw v. Reno* (1993), a reapportionment case concerning a majority black voting district in North Carolina: "Racial classifications of any sort pose the risk of lasting harm to our society. . . . Racial gerrymandering . . . may *balkanize* us into competing racial factions" (my emphasis).

REFERENCES

Adam, Heribert, and Kogila Moodley. 1986. *South Africa without Apartheid: Dismantling Racial Domination.* Berkeley: University of California Press.

Balibar, Etienne. 1991. "Is There a Neo-Racism?" In *Race, Nation, Class: Ambiguous Identities,* ed. Etienne Balibar and Immanuel Wallerstein, 17–28. London: Verso.

Barkan, Elazar. 1992. *The Retreat of Scientific Racism: Changing Concepts of Race in Britain and the United States between the World Wars.* Cambridge: Cambridge University Press.

Bell, Derrick. 1995. "Racial Realism." In *Critical Race Theory: The Key Writings That Formed the Movement,* ed. K. Crenshaw et al., 302–12. New York: New Press.

Bourdieu, Pierre, and Loïc Wacquant. 1999. "On the Cunning of Imperialist Reason." *Theory, Culture and Society* 16, no. 1: 41–58.

———. 1998. "Les ruses de la raison imperialiste." *Actes de la Recherche Sciences Sociale,* 121–22.

Carr, Leslie. 1997. *Color-Blind Racism.* Thousand Oaks, CA: Sage.

Comaroff, Jean, and John L. Comaroff. 2000. "Naturing the Nation: Aliens, Apocalypse, and the Postcolonial State." *HAGGAR: International Social Science Review* 1, no. 1: 7–40.

Crenshaw, Kimberle. 1998. "Color Blindness, History, and the Law." In *The House That Race Built,* ed. Wahneema Lubiano, 288. New York: Vintage.

Crummel, Alexander. 1861. "The Progress of Civilization along the West Coast of Africa." In *Classical Black Nationalism: From the American Revolution to Marcus*

Garvey, ed. Wilson Moses, 169–87. New York: New York University Press, 1996.

De la Cadena, Marisol. 2000. *Indigenous Mestizos: The Politics of Race and Culture in Cuzco, Peru, 1919–1991*. Durham, NC: Duke University Press.

Derrida, Jacques. 1985. "Racism's Last Word." *Critical Inquiry* 12, no. 1: 290–99.

D'Souza, Dinesh. 1995. *The End of Racism*. New York: Free Press.

Essed, Philomena. 1996. *Diversity: Gender, Color, and Culture*. Amherst: University of Massachusetts Press.

Fernandes, Florestan. 1998. "The Negro Problem in Class Society, 1951–1960." In *Blackness in Latin America and the Caribbean*, vol. 2, ed. Victor Whitten and Arlene Torres, 99–145. Bloomington: Indiana University Press.

Fiola, Jan. 1990. *Race Relations in Brazil: A Reassessment of the "Racial Democracy" Thesis*. Amherst: Latin American Studies Program, University of Massachusetts.

Freyre, Gilberto. 1946. *The Masters and the Slaves: A Study in the Development of Brazilian Civilization*. New York: Knopf.

Fry, Peter. 2000. "Politics, Nationality, and the Meanings of "Race" in Brazil." *Daedalus*, Spring, 83–118.

Furedi, Frank. 1998. *The Silent War: Imperialism and the Changing Perception of Race*. London: Pluto.

Gall, Olivia. 1998. "The Historical Structure of Racism in Chiapas." *Social Identities* 4, no. 2: 235–62.

Goldberg, David Theo. 2001. *The Racial State*. Oxford: Basil Blackwell.

———. 1993. *Racist Culture: Philosophy and the Politics of Meaning*. Oxford: Basil Blackwell.

Gotanda, Neil. 1995. "A Critique of 'Our Constitution Is Colorblind.'" In *Critical Race Theory: The Key Writings That Formed the Movement*, ed. K. Crenshaw et al., 257–75. New York: New Press.

Grantin, Greg. 2000. *The Blood of Guatemala: The History of Race and Nation*. Durham, NC: Duke University Press.

Guinier, Lani, and Gerald Torres. 2002. *The Miner's Canary: Enlisting Race, Resisting Power, Transforming Democracy*. Cambridge, MA: Harvard University Press.

Halsey, Margaret. 1946. *Color Blind: A White Woman Looks at the Negro*. New York: Simon & Schuster.

Hanchard, Michael. 1994. *Orpheus and Power: The Movimento Negro of Rio de Janeiro and São Paulo, Brazil, 1945–1988*. Princeton: Princeton University Press.

Hesse, Barnor, ed. 2000. *Un/Settled Multicultural isms: Diasporas, Entanglements, Transruptions*. London: Zed.

Levine, Robert, and John Crocitti, eds. 1999. *The Brazil Reader: History, Culture, Politics*. Durham, NC: Duke University Press.

Malik, Kenan. 1996. *The Meaning of Race: Race, History, and Culture in Western Society*. London: Macmillan.

Memmi, Albert. 1965. *The Colonizer and the Colonized*. New York: Orion.

Mitchell, Michael. 1998. "Blacks and the *Abertura Democratica*." In *Blackness in Latin America and the Caribbean*, vol. 2, ed. Victor Whitten and Arlene Torres, 75–98. Bloomington: Indiana University Press.

Nozick, Robert. 1974. *Anarchy, State, Utopia*. New York: Random House.

Posel, Deborah. 2000. "Modernity and Measurement: Further Thoughts on the Apartheid State." In *Science and Society in Southern Africa*, ed. Saul Dubow. Manchester, UK: Manchester University Press.

Posner, Richard. 1974. "The DeFunis Case and the Constitutionality of Preferential Treatment of Racial Minorities." *Superior Court Review* 12.

Povinelli, Elizabeth. 1998. "The State of Shame: Australian Multiculturalism and the Crisis of Indigenous Citizenship." *Critical Inquiry* 24, no. 2: 575–610.

Rich, Paul. 1986. *Race and Empire in British Politics*. Cambridge, UK: Cambridge University Press.

Schwarcz, Lilia Moritz. 1999. *The Spectacle of the Races: Scientists, Institutions, and the Race Question in Brazil, 1870–1930*. New York: Hill & Wang.

Siegel, Reva. 1998. "The Racial Rhetorics of Colorblind Constitutionalism: The Case of *Hopwood v. Texas*." In *Race and Representation: Affirmative Action*, ed. Robert Post and Michael Rogin, 29–72. New York: Zone.

Smith, Lillian. 1949. *Killers of the Dream*. New York: Norton.

Sowell, Thomas. 1995. *Race and Culture: A World View*. New York: Basic.

Takagi, Dana. 1995. "We Should Not Make Class a Proxy for Race." *Chronicle of Higher Education*, A25.

———. 1993. *The Retreat from Race: Asian Admissions and Racial Politics*. Berkeley: University of California Press.

Taussig, Michael. 1997. *The Magic of the State*. New York: Routledge.

———. 1980. *The Devil and Commodity Fetishism in South America*. Chapel Hill: University of North Carolina Press.

Van Dijk, Teun A. 2002. "Denying Racism: Elite Discourse and Racism." In *Race Critical Theories: Text and Context*, ed. Philomena Essed and David Theo Goldberg. Cambridge, MA: Basil Blackwell.

Verges, Francoise. 2001. "Post-Scriptum." In *Relocating Postcolonialism*, ed. Ato Quayson and Davis Theo Goldberg, 349–58. Oxford: Basil Blackwell.

Ware, Peter. 1993. *Blackness and Race Mixture: The Dynamics of Racial Identity in Colombia*. Baltimore: Johns Hopkins University Press.

Werbner, Pnina. 1997. "Afterword: Writing Multiculturalism and Politics in the New Europe." In *The Politics of Multiculturalism in the New Europe: Racism, Identity, and Community*, ed. Tariq Modood and Pnina Werbner, 261–65. London: Zed.

Werbner, Pnina, and Tariq Modood. 1997. *Debating Cultural Hybridity: Multicultural Identities and the Politics of Anti-racism*. London: Zed.

Whitten, Norman, and Arlene Torres, eds. 1998. *Blackness in Latin America and the Caribbean*. Vols. 1–2. Bloomington: Indiana University Press.

Wolton, Suke. 2000. *Lord Hailey, the Colonial Office, and the Politics of Race and Empire in the Second World War: The Loss of White Prestige*. London: Macmillan.

5
SPECTACLES OF RACE AND PEDAGOGIES OF DENIAL: ANTIBLACK RACIST PEDAGOGY

Henry A. Giroux

⤝

Race relations in the United States have changed considerably since W.E.B. Du Bois famously predicted in *The Souls of Black Folk* that "the problem of the 20th century is the problem of the color line."[1] This is not to suggest that race has declined in significance, or that the racial conditions, ideologies, and practices that provided the context for Du Bois' prophecy have been overcome; rather, the point is that they have been transformed, mutated, and recycled and have taken on new and in many instances more covert modes of expression.[2] Du Bois recognized that the color line was not fixed—its forms of expression changed over time, as a response to different contexts and struggles—and that one of the great challenges facing future generations would be not only to engage the complex structural legacy of race but also to take note of the plethora of forms in which it was expressed and experienced in everyday life. For Du Bois, race fused power and ideology and was deeply woven into both the public pedagogy of American culture and its geography, economics, politics, and institutions.

The great challenge Du Bois presents to this generation of students, educators, and citizens is to acknowledge that the future of democracy in the United States is inextricably linked "to the outcomes of racial politics and policies, as they develop both in various national societies and the world at large."[3] In part, this observation implies that how we experience democracy in the future will depend on how we name, think about, experience, and transform the interrelated modalities of race, racism, and social justice. It also suggests that the meaning of race and the challenges of racism change for each generation, and that the new challenges we face demand a new language for understanding how the symbolic power of race as a ped-

This chapter is reprinted with permission from Henry A. Giroux, "Spectacles of Race and Pedagogies of Denial," *Communication Education* 52, nos. 3–4 (2003): 19–21.

agogical force as well as a structural and materialist practice redefines the relationship between the self and the other, the private and the public. It is this latter challenge in particular that needs to be more fully addressed if racism is not to be reduced to an utterly privatized discourse that erases any trace of racial injustice by denying the very notion of the social and the operations of power through which racial politics are organized and legitimated.

When Du Bois wrote *The Souls of Black Folk,* racism was a visible and endemic part of the American political, cultural, and economic landscape. The racial divide was impossible to ignore, irrespective of one's politics. As we move into the new millennium, the politics of the color line and representations of race have become far more subtle and complicated than they were in the Jim Crow era when Du Bois made his famous pronouncement. And though far from invisible, the complicated nature of race relations in American society no longer appears to be marked by the specter of Jim Crow. A majority of Americans now believe that anti-black racism is a thing of the past, since it is assumed that formal institutions of segregation no longer exist. Yet, surveys done by the National Opinion Research Center at the University of Chicago have consistently found "that most Americans still believe blacks are less intelligent than whites, lazier than whites, and more likely than whites to prefer living on welfare over being self-support-ing."[4] Contradictions aside, conservatives and liberals alike now view America's racial hierarchy as an unfortunate historical fact that has no bearing on contemporary society. Pointing to the destruction of the Southern caste system, the problematizing of whiteness as a racial category, the passing of civil rights laws, a number of successful lawsuits alleging racial discrimination against companies such as Texaco and Denny's, and the emergence of people of color into all aspects of public life, the color line now seems in disarray, a remnant of another era that Americans have fortunately moved beyond. Best-selling books such as Dinesh D'Souza's *The End of Racism,* Jim Sleeper's *Liberal Racism,* and Stephan and Abigail Thernstrom's *America in Black and White: One Nation, Indivisible* all proclaim racism as an obsolete ideology and practice.[5] And a large number of white Americans seem to agree. In fact, poll after poll reveals that a majority of white Americans believe that people of color no longer face racial discrimination in American life. For example, a recent Gallup Poll on "Black-White Relations" observes that "7 out of 10 whites believe that blacks are treated equally in their communities. . . . Eight in ten whites say blacks receive equal educational opportunities, and 83% say blacks receive equal housing opportunities in their communities. Only a third of whites believe blacks face racial bias from police in their areas."[6] For many conservative and liberal intellectuals, the only remaining remnant of racist categorization and policy in an otherwise color-blind society is affirmative action, which is ironically alleged to provide blacks with an unfair advantage in higher education, the labor force, "entitlement programs," and "even summer scholarship programs."[7]

The importance of race and the enduring fact of racism are relegated to the dustbin of history at a time in American life when the discourses of race and the spectacle of racial representations saturate the dominant media and public life. The color line is now mined for exotic commodities that can be sold to white youth in the form of rap music, hip-hop clothing, and sports gear. African-American celebrities such as Michael Jordan, Etta James, and George Foreman are used to give market legitimacy to everything from gas grills to high-end luxury cars to clothes. Black public intellectuals such as Patricia Williams, Cornel West, Michael Dyson, and Henry Louis Gates command the attention of the *New York Times* and other eye-catching media. African-Americans now occupy powerful positions on the Supreme Court and at the highest levels of political life. The alleged collapse, if not transformation, of the color line can also be seen in the emergence of the black elite, prominently on display in television sitcoms, fashion magazines, Hollywood movies, and music videos. On the political scene, however, the supposedly race-transcendent public policy is complicated by ongoing public debates over affirmative action, welfare, crime, and the prison-industrial complex. All of which suggests that whereas the color line has been modified and dismantled in places, race and racial hierarchies still exercise a profound influence on how most people in the United States experience their daily lives.[8] Popular sentiment aside, race—rather than disappearing—has retained its power as a key signifier in structuring all aspects of American life. As Michael Omi keenly observes: "Despite legal guarantees of formal equality and access, race continues to be a fundamental organizing principle of individual identity and collective action. I would argue that, far from declining in significance (as William Julius Wilson would have us believe), the racial dimensions of politics and culture have proliferated."[9]

Representations of race and difference are everywhere in American society, and yet racism as both a symbol and a condition of American life is either ignored or relegated to an utterly privatized discourse, typified in references to individual prejudices or to psychological dispositions such as expressions of "hate." As politics becomes more racialized, the discourse about race becomes more privatized. While the realities of race permeate public life, they are engaged less as discourses and sites where differences are produced within iniquitous relations of power than as either unobjectionable cultural signifiers or desirable commodities. The public morality of the marketplace works its magic in widening the gap between political control and economic power while simultaneously reducing political agency to the act of consuming. One result is a growing cynicism and powerlessness among the general population as the political impotence of public institutions is reinforced through the disparaging of any reference to ethics, equity, justice, or other normative principles that prioritize democratic values over market considerations. Similarly, as corporate power undermines all notions of the public good and increasingly privatizes public space, it obliterates those public spheres in which there might emerge criticism that acknowledges the tensions wrought by a pervasive racism that "functions as one of the deep, abiding currents in everyday life, in both the simplest and the most complex interactions of whites and blacks."[10] Indifference and cynicism breed contempt and resentment as racial hierarchies now collapse into power-evasive strategies such as blaming minorities of class and color for not working hard enough, refusing to exercise individual initiative, or practicing reverse-racism. In short, marketplace ideologies now work to erase the social from the language of public life so as to reduce all racial problems to private issues such as individual character and cultural depravity.

Black public intellectuals such as Shelby Steele and John McWhorter garner national attention by asserting that the subject and object of racism have been reversed. For Steele, racism has nothing to do with soaring black unemployment, failing and segregated schools for black children, a criminal justice system that resembles the old plantation system of the South, or police brutality that takes its toll largely on blacks in urban cities such as Cincinnati and New York. On the contrary, according to Steele, racism has produced white guilt, a burden that white people have to carry as part of the legacy of the civil rights movement. To remove this burden from white shoulders, blacks now have to free themselves from their victim status and act responsibly by proving to whites that *their* suffering is unnecessary.[11] They can do so through the spirit of principled entrepreneurialism—allowing themselves to be judged on the basis of hard work, individual effort, a secure family life, decent values, and property ownership.[12] It gets worse. John McWhorter, largely relying on anecdotes from his own limited experience in the academy at UCLA–Berkeley, argues that higher education is filled with African-American students who are either mediocre or simply lazy, victims of affirmative action programs that coddle them because of their race while allowing them to "dumb down" rather than work as competitively as their white classmates. The lesson here is that the color line now benefits blacks rather than whites and that, in the end, for McWhorter, diversity rather than bigotry is the enemy of a quality education and functions largely to "condemn black students to mediocrity."[13]

Within this discourse, there is a glimmer of a new kind of racial reference, one that can imagine public issues only as private concerns. This is a racism that refuses to "translate private sufferings into public issues,"[14] a racism that works hard to remove issues of power and equity from broader social concerns. Ultimately, it imagines human agency as simply a matter of individualized choices, the only obstacle to effective citizenship and agency being the lack of principled self-help and moral responsibility. In what follows, I want to examine briefly the changing nature of the new racism by analyzing how some of its central assumptions evade notions of race, racial justice, equity, and democracy altogether. In the process, I analyze some elements of the new racism, particularly the discourse of color-blindness and neoliberal racism. I then address the ways in which the controversial Trent Lott affair demonstrated neoliberal racism as well as the racism of denial. I will conclude by offering some suggestions about how the new racism, particularly its neoliberal version, can be addressed as both a pedagogical and a political issue.

NEOLIBERALISM AND THE CULTURE OF PRIVATIZATION

The public morality of American life and social policy regarding matters of racial justice are increasingly subject to a politics of denial. Denial in this case is not merely about the failure of public memory or the refusal to know, but an active ongoing attempt on the part of many conservatives, liberals, and politicians to rewrite the discourse of race so as to deny its valence as a force for discrimination and exclusion either by translating it as a threat to American culture or relegating it to the language of the private sphere. The idea of race and the conditions of racism have real political effects, and eliding them only makes those effects harder to recognize. And yet, the urgency to recognize how language is used to name, organize, order, and categorize matters of race not only has academic value, it also provides a location from which to engage difference and the relationship between the self and the other and between the public and private. In addition, the language of race is important because it strongly affects political and policy agendas as well. One only has to think about the effects of Charles Murray's book *Losing Ground* on American welfare policies in the 1980s.[15] But language is more than a mode of communication or a symbolic practice that produces real effects; it is also a site of contestation and struggle. Since the mid-1970s, race relations have undergone a significant shift and acquired a new character as the forces of neoliberalism have begun to shape how Americans understand notions of agency, identity, freedom, and politics itself.[16]

Part of this shift has to be understood within the emerging forces of transnational capitalism and a global restructuring in which the economy is separated from politics and corporate power is largely removed from the control of nation-states. Within the neoliberal register, globalization "represents the triumph of the economy over politics and culture . . . and the hegemony of capital over all other domains of life."[17] Under neoliberal globalization, capital removes itself from any viable form of state regulation, power is uncoupled from matters of ethics and social responsibility, and market freedoms replace long-standing social contracts that once provided a safety net for the poor, the elderly, workers, and the middle class. The result is that public issues and social concerns increasingly give way to a growing culture of insecurity and fear regarding the most basic issues of individual livelihood, safety, and survival. Increasingly, a concern with either the past or the future is replaced by uncertainty, and traditional human bonds rooted in compassion, justice, and a respect for others are now replaced by a revitalized social Darwinism, played out nightly in the celebration of reality-based television, in which rabid self-interest becomes the organizing principle for a winner-take-all society. As insecurity and fear grip public consciousness, society is no longer identified through its allegiance to democratic values but through a troubling freedom rooted in a disturbing emphasis on individualism and competitiveness as the only normative measures to distinguish between what is a right or wrong, just or unjust, proper or improper action. Zygmunt Bauman captures this deracinated notion of freedom and the insecurity it promotes in his observation that

> [s]ociety no longer guarantees, or even promises, a collective remedy for individual misfortunes. Individuals have been offered (or, rather, have been cast into) freedom of unprecedented proportions—but at the price of similarly unprecedented insecurity. And when there is insecurity, little time is left for caring for values that hover above the level of daily concerns—or, for that matter, for whatever lasts longer than the fleeting moment.[18]

Within this emerging neoliberal ethic, success is attributed to thriftiness and entrepreneurial genius while those who do not succeed are viewed either as failures or as utterly expendable. Indeed, neoliberalism's attachment to individualism, markets, and antistatism ranks human needs as less important than property rights and subordinates "the art of politics . . . to the science of economics."[19] Racial justice in the age of market-based freedoms and financially driven values loses its ethical imperative to a neoliberalism that embraces commercial rather than civic values, private rather than pubic interests, and financial incentives rather than ethical concerns. Neoliberalism negates racism as an ethical issue and democratic values as a basis for citizen-based action. Of course, neoliberalism takes many forms as it moves across the globe. In the United States, it has achieved a surprising degree of success but is increasingly being resisted by labor unions, students, and environmentalists. Major protests against economic policies promoted by the World Bank, International Monetary Fund, and World Trade Organization have taken place in Seattle, Prague, New York, Montreal, Genoa, and other cities around the world. In the United States, a rising generation of students is protesting trade agreements like GATT and NAFTA as well as sweat-shop labor practices at home and abroad and the corporatization of public and higher education. Unfortunately, anti-racist theorists have not said enough about either the link between the new racism and neoliberalism, on the one hand, or the rise of a race-based carceral state, on the other. Neither the rise of the new racism nor any viable politics of an anti-racist movement can be understood outside the power and grip of neoliberalism in the United States. Hence, at the risk of oversimplification and repetition within other chapters, I want to be a bit more specific about neoliberalism's central assumptions and how it frames some of the more prominent emerging racial discourses and practices.

NEOLIBERALISM AND THE POLITICS OF THE NEW RACISM

As mentioned in the introduction, under the reign of neoliberalism in the United States, society is largely defined through the privileging of market relations, deregulation, privatization, and consumerism. Central to neoliberalism is the assumption that profit-making be construed as the essence of democracy and consuming as the most cherished act of citizenship. Strictly aligning freedom with a narrow notion of individual interest, neoliberalism works hard to privatize all aspects of the public good and simultaneously narrow the role of the state as both a gatekeeper for capital and a policing force for maintaining social order and racial control. Unrestricted by social legislation or government regulation, market relations as they define the economy are viewed as a paradigm for democracy itself. Central to neoliberal philosophy is the claim that the development of all aspects of society should be left to the wisdom of the market. Similarly, neoliberal warriors argue that democratic values be subordinated to economic considerations, social issues be translated as private dilemmas, part-time labor replace full-time work, trade unions be weakened, and everybody be treated as a customer. Within this market-driven perspective, the exchange of capital takes precedence over social justice, the making of socially responsible citizens, and the building of democratic communities. There is no language here for recognizing anti-democratic forms of power, developing nonmarket values, or fighting against substantive injustices in a society founded on deep inequalities, particularly those based on race and class. Hence, it is not surprising that under neoliberalism, language is often stripped of its critical and social possibilities as it becomes increasingly difficult to imagine a social order in which all problems are not personal, in which social issues provide the conditions for understanding private considerations, critical reflection becomes the essence of politics, and matters of equity and justice become crucial to developing a democratic society.

It is under the reign of neoliberalism that the changing vocabulary about race and racial justice has to be understood and engaged. As freedom is increasingly abstracted from the power of individuals and groups to actively participate in shaping society, it is reduced to the right of the individual to be free from social constraints. In this view, freedom is no longer linked to a collective effort on the part of individuals to create a democratic society. Instead, freedom becomes an exercise in self-development rather than social responsibility, reducing politics to either the celebration of consumerism or the privileging of a market-based notion of agency and choice that appears quite indifferent to how power, equity, and justice offer the enabling conditions for real individual and collective choices to be both made and acted upon. Under such circumstances, neoliberalism undermines those public spaces where noncommercial values and crucial social issues can be discussed, debated, and engaged. As public space is privatized, power is disconnected from social obligations and it becomes more difficult for isolated individuals living in consumption-oriented spaces to construct an ethically engaged and power-sensitive language capable of accommodating the principles of ethics and racial justice as a common good rather than as a private affair. According to Bauman, the elimination of public space and the subordination of democratic values to commercial interests narrows the discursive possibilities for supporting notions of the public good and creates the conditions for "the suspicion against others, the intolerance of difference, the resentment of strangers, and the demands to separate and banish them, as well as the hysterical, paranoiac concern with 'law and order.'"[20] Positioned within the emergence of neoliberalism as the dominant economic and political philosophy of our times, neoracism can be understood as part of a broader attack not only on difference but on the value of public memory, public goods, and democracy itself.

The new racism represents both a shift in how race is defined and a symptom of the breakdown of a political culture in which individual freedom and solidarity maintain an uneasy equilibrium in the service of racial, social, and economic justice. Individual freedom is now disconnected from any sense of civic responsibility or justice, focusing instead on investor profits, consumer confidence, the downsizing of governments to police precincts, and a deregulated social order in which the winner takes all. Freedom is no longer about either making the powerful responsible for their actions or providing the essential political, economic, and social conditions for everyday people to intervene in and shape their future. Under the reign of neoliberalism, freedom is less about the act of intervention than about the process of withdrawing from the social and enacting one's sense of agency as an almost exclusively private endeavor. Freedom now cancels out civic courage and social responsibility while it simultaneously translates public issues and collective problems into tales of failed character, bad luck, or simply indifference. As Amy Elizabeth Ansell points out:

> The disproportionate failure of people of color to achieve social mobility speaks nothing of the injustice of present social arrangements, according to the New Right worldview, but rather reflects the lack of merit or ability of people of color themselves. In this way, attention is deflected away from the reality of institutional racism and towards, for example, the "culture of poverty," the "drug culture," or the lack of black self-development.[21]

Appeals to freedom, operating under the sway of market forces, offer no signposts theoretically or politically for engaging racism as an ethical and political issue that undermines the very basis of a substantive democracy. Freedom in this discourse collapses into self-interest and as such is more inclined to organize any sense of community around shared fears, insecurities, and an intolerance of those "others" who are marginalized by class and color. But freedom reduced to the ethos of self-preservation and brutal self-interest makes it difficult for individuals to recognize the forms that racism often takes when draped in the language of either denial, freedom, or individual rights. In what follows, I want to explore two prominent forms of the new racism—color-blindness and neoliberal racism—and their connection to the New Right, corporate power, and neoliberal ideologies.

Unlike the old racism, which defined racial difference in terms of fixed biological categories organized hierarchically, the new racism operates in various guises proclaiming among other things race-neutrality, asserting culture as a marker of racial difference, or marking race as a private matter. Unlike the crude racism with its biological referents and pseudo-scientific legitimations, buttressing its appeal to white racial superiority, the new racism cynically recodes itself within the vocabulary of the civil rights movement, invoking the language of Martin Luther King, Jr., to argue that individuals should be judged by the "content of their character" and not by the color of their skin. Ansell, a keen commentator on the new racism, notes both the recent shifts in racialized discourse away from more rabid and overt forms of racism and its appropriation particularly by the New Right in the United States and Britain:

> The new racism actively disavows racist intent and is cleansed of extremist intolerance, thus reinforcing the New Right's attempt to distance itself from racist organizations such as the John Birch Society in the United States and the National Front in Britain. It is a form of racism that utilizes themes related to culture and nation as a replacement for the now discredited biological referents of the old racism. It is concerned less with notions of racial superiority in the narrow sense than with the alleged "threat" people of color pose—either because of their mere presence or because of their demand for "special privileges"—to economic, sociopolitical, and cultural vitality of the dominant (white) society. It is, in short, a new form of racism that operates with the category of "race." It is a new form of exclusionary politics that operates indirectly and in stealth via the rhetorical inclusion of people of color and the sanitized nature of its racist appeal.[22]

What is crucial about the new racism is that it demands an updated analysis of how racist practices work through the changing nature of language and other modes of representation. One of the most sanitized and yet most pervasive forms of the new racism is evident in the language of color-blindness. Within this approach, it is argued that racial conflict and discrimination are things of the past and that race has no bearing on an individual's or group's location or standing in contemporary American society. Color-blindness does not deny the existence of race but the claim that race is responsible for alleged injustices that reproduce group inequalities, privilege whites, and negatively impact on economic mobility, the possession of social resources, and the acquisition of political power. Put differently, inherent in the logic of color-blindness is the central assumption that race has no valence as a marker of identity or power when factored into the social vocabulary of everyday life and the capacity for exercising individual and social agency. As Charles Gallagher observes, "Within the color-blind perspective it is not race per se which determines upward mobility but how much an individual chooses to pay attention to race that determines one's fate. Within this perspective race is only as important as you allow it to be."[23] As Jeff, one of Gallagher's interviewees, puts it, race is simply another choice: "[Y]ou know, there's music, rap music is no longer, it's not a black thing anymore. . . .[W]hen it first came out it was black music, but now it's just music. It's another choice, just like country music can be considered like white hick music, you know it's just a choice."[24]

Hence, in an era "free" of racism, race becomes a matter of taste, lifestyle, or heritage but has nothing to do with politics, legal rights, educational access, or economic opportunities. Veiled by a denial of how racial histories accrue political, economic, and cultural weight to the social power of whiteness, color-blindness deletes the relationship between racial differences and power. In doing so it reinforces whiteness as the arbiter of value for judging difference against a normative notion of homogeneity.[25] For advocates of color-blindness, race as a political signifier is conveniently denied or seen as something to be overcome, allowing whites to ignore racism as a corrosive force for expanding the dynamics of ideological and structural inequality throughout society.[26] Color-blindness, then, is a convenient ideology for enabling whites to disregard the degree to which race is tangled up with asymmetrical relations of power, functioning as a potent force for patterns of exclusion and discrimination including but not limited to housing, mortgage loans, health care, schools, and the criminal justice system. If one effect of color-blindness functions is to deny racial hierarchies, another is that it offers whites the belief not only that America is now a level playing field but also that the success that whites enjoy relative to minorities of color is largely due to individual determination, a strong work ethic, high moral values, and a sound investment in education. In short, color-blindness offers up a highly racialized (though paraded as race-transcendent) notion of agency, while also providing an ideological space free of guilt, self-reflection, and political responsibility, despite the fact that blacks have a disadvantage in almost all areas of social life: housing, jobs, education, income levels, mortgage lending, and basic everyday services.[27] In a society marked by profound racial and class inequalities, it is difficult to believe that character and merit—as color-blindness advocates would have us believe—are the prime determinants for social and economic mobility and a decent standard of living. The relegation of racism and its effects in the larger society to the realm of private beliefs, values, and behavior does little to explain a range of overwhelming realities—such as soaring black unemployment, decaying cities, and segregated schools. Paul Street puts the issue forcibly in a series of questions that register the primacy of and interconnections among politics, social issues, and race:

> Why are African-Americans twice as likely to be unemployed as whites? Why is the poverty rate for blacks more than twice the rate for whites? Why do nearly one out of every two blacks earn less than $25,000 while only one in three whites makes that little? Why is the median black household income ($27,000) less than two thirds of the median white household income ($42,000)? Why is the black family's median household net worth less than 10 percent that of

whites? Why are blacks much less likely to own their own homes than whites? Why do African-Americans make up roughly half of the United States' massive population of prisoners (2 million) and why are one in three young, black male adults in prison or on parole or otherwise under the supervision of the American criminal justice system? Why do African-Americans continue in severe geographic separation from mainstream society, still largely cordoned off into the nation's most disadvantaged communities thirty years after the passage of the civil rights fair housing legislation? Why do blacks suffer disproportionately from irregularities in the American electoral process, from problems with voter registration to the functioning of voting machinery? Why does black America effectively constitute a Third World enclave of sub-citizens within the world's richest and most powerful state?[28]

Add to this list the stepped-up resegregation of American schools and the growing militarization and lock-down status of public education through the widespread use of zero-tolerance policies.[29] Or the fact that African-American males live on average six years less than their white counterparts. It is worth noting that nothing challenges the myth that America has become a color-blind post-racist nation more than the racialization of the criminal justice system since the late 1980s. As the sociologist Loïc Wacquant has observed, the expansion of the prison-industrial complex represents a "de facto policy of 'carceral affirmative action' towards African-Americans."[30] This is borne out by the fact that while American prisons house over 2 million inmates, "roughly half of them are black even though African-Americans make up less than 13 percent of the nation's population. . . . According to the Justice Policy Institute there are now more black men behind bars than in college in the United States. One in ten of the world's prisoners is an African-American male."[31]

As one of the most powerful ideological and institutional factors for deciding how identities are categorized and power, material privileges, and resources distributed, race represents an essential political category for examining the relationship between justice and a democratic society. But color-blindness is about more than the denial of how power and politics operate to promote racial discrimination and exclusion; it is also an ideological and pedagogical weapon powerfully mobilized by conservatives and the Right for arguing that because of the success of the civil rights movement, racism has been eliminated as an institutional and ideological force, thus eradicating the need for government-based programs designed to dismantle the historical legacy and effects of racism in all dimensions of the social order.

Within the last twenty years, a more virulent form of the new racism has appeared that also affirms the basic principles of color-blindness; but instead of operating primarily as a discourse of denial regarding how power and politics promote racial discrimination and exclusion, neoliberal racism is about the privatization of racial discourse. It is also proactive, functioning aggressively in the public arena as an ideological and pedagogical weapon powerfully mobilized by various conservatives and right-wing groups. Neoliberal racism asserts the insignificance of race as a social force and aggressively roots out any vestige of race as a category at odds with an individualistic embrace of formal legal rights. Focusing on individuals rather than on groups, neoliberal racism either dismisses the concept of institutional racism or maintains that it has no merit. In this context, racism is primarily defined as a form of individual prejudice while appeals to equality are dismissed outright. For instance, racial ideologues Richard J. Herrnstein and Charles Murray write in *The Bell Curve:* "In everyday life, the ideology of equality censors and straitjackets everything from pedagogy to humor. The ideology of equality has stunted the range of moral dialogue to triviality. . . . It is time for America once again to try living with inequality, as life is lived."[32] Arguing that individual freedom is tarnished if not poisoned by the discourse of equality, right-wing legal advocacy groups such as the Center for Individual Rights (CIR) and the Foundation for Individual Rights in Education argue that identity politics and pluralism weaken rather than strengthen American democracy because they pose a threat to what it means for the United States "to remain recognizably American."[33] But such groups do more than define American culture in racist and retrograde terms; they also aggressively use their resources—generously provided by prominent right-wing conservative organizations such as the Lynde and Harry Bradley Foundation, the John M. Olin Foundation, the Adolph Coors Foundation, and the Scaife Family Foundation—to challenge racial preference policies that are not based on a "principle of state neutrality."[34] With ample resources at their disposal, advocates of neoliberal racism have successfully challenged a number of cases before the Supreme Court over the legality of affirmative action programs, campus speech codes, hiring practices, the Violence Against Women Act, and the elimination of men's sports teams in higher education.[35] Hence, neoliberal racism provides the ideological and legal framework for asserting that since American society is now a meritocracy, government should be race neutral, affirmative action programs dismantled, civil rights laws discarded, and the welfare state eliminated. As Nikhil Aziz observes, "The Right argues that, because racism has been dealt with as a result of the Civil Rights Movement, race should not be a consideration for hiring in employment or for admission to educational institutions, and group identities other than 'American' are immaterial."[36]

Neoliberal racism is unwilling to accept any concept of the state as a guardian of the public interest. Motivated by a passion for free markets that is matched only by an anti-government fervor, neoliberal racism calls for a hollowing out of the social welfare functions of the state, except for its role in safeguarding the interests of the privileged and the strengthening of its policing functions. Rejecting a notion of the public good for private interest, advocates of neoliberal racism want to limit the state's role in public investments and social programs as a constraint on both individual rights and the expression of individual freedom. In this view, individual interests override any notion of the public good, and individual freedom operates outside of any ethical responsibility for its social consequences. The results of this policy are evident in right-wing attacks on public education, health care, environmental regulations, public housing, race-based scholarships, and other public services that embrace notions of difference. Many of these programs benefit the general public, though they are relied on disproportionately by the poor and people of color. As Zsuza Ferge points out, what becomes clear about neoliberal racism is that "the attack on the big state has indeed become predominantly an attack on the welfare functions of the state. . . .The underlying motif is the conviction that the supreme value is economic growth to be attained by unfettered free trade equated with freedom *tout court*. . . .The extremely individualist approach that characterizes this ethic justifies the diagnosis of many that neoliberalism is about the 'individualization of the social.'"[37] By preventing the state from addressing or correcting the effects of racial discrimination, state agencies are silenced, thus displacing "the tensions of contemporary racially charged relations to the relative invisibility of private spheres, seemingly out of reach of public policy intervention."[38]

The relentless spirit of self-interest within neoliberal racism offers an apology for a narrow market-based notion of freedom in which individual rights and choices are removed from any viable notion of social responsibility, critical citizenship, and substantive democracy. By distancing itself from any notion of liberal egalitarianism, civic obligation, or a more positive notion of freedom, neoliberal racism does more than collapse the political into the personal—invoking character against institutional racism and individual rights against social wrongs. Indeed, it claims, as Jean and John Comaroff argue, that

[t]he personal is the only politics there is, the only politics with a tangible referent or emotional valence. It is in these privatized terms that action is organized, that the experience of inequity and antagonism takes meaningful shape. . . . [Neoliberalism] is a culture that . . . re-visions persons not as producers from a particular community, but as consumers in a planetary marketplace.[39]

Neoliberalism devitalizes democracy because it has no language for defending a politics in which citizenship becomes an investment in public life rather than an obligation to consume, relegated in this instance to an utterly privatized affair. The discourse of neoliberal racism has no way of talking about collective responsibility, social agency, or a defense of the public good. But the absences in its discourse are not innocent because they both ignore and perpetuate the stereotypes, structured violence, and massive inequalities produced by the racial state, the race-based attack on welfare, the destruction of social goods such as schools and health care, and the rise of the prison-industrial complex. And its attack on the principles of equality, liberty, economic democracy, and racial justice, in the final analysis, represents "a heartless indifference to the social contract, or any other civic-minded concern for the larger social good."[40] In fact, neoliberalism has played a defining role in transforming the social contract to the carceral contract, which substitutes punishment for social investment. Hence, it is not surprising how neoliberal arguments embracing the primacy of individual solutions to public issues such as poverty or the ongoing incarceration of black males are quick to defend public policies that are both punitive and overtly racist such as workfare for welfare recipients or the public shaming rituals of prison chain gangs, with an overabundance of black males always on display. Neoliberal racism's "heartless indifference" to the plight of the poor is often mirrored in an utter disdain for human suffering, as in Shelby Steele's nostalgic longing for a form of social Darwinism in which "failure and suffering are natural and necessary elements of success."[41]

It is interesting that whenever white racism is invoked by critics in response to the spectacle of racism, advocates of color-blindness and neoliberal racism often step outside of the privatizing language of rights and have little trouble appropriating victim status for whites while blaming people of color for the harsh conditions under which so many have to live in this country. And in some cases, this is done in the name of a civility that is used to hide both the legacy and the reality of racism and a commitment to equality as a cornerstone of racial progress. A classic example of the latter can be found in *The End of Racism* by Dinesh D'Souza. He writes:

> Nothing strengthens racism in this country more than the behavior of the African-American underclass which flagrantly violates and scandalizes basic codes of responsibility and civility. . . .[I]f blacks as a group can show that they are capable of performing competitively in schools and the workforce, and exercising both the rights and responsibilities of American citizenship, then racism will be deprived of its foundation in experience.[42]

SPECTACLES OF RACE

Scripted denials of racism coupled with the spectacle of racial discourse and representations have become a common occurrence in American life. Power-evasive strategies wrapped up in the language of individual choice and the virtues of self-reliance provide the dominant modes of framing through which the larger public can witness in our media-saturated culture what Patricia Williams calls "the unsaid filled by stereotypes and self-identifying illusion, the hierarchies of race and gender circulating unchallenged," enticing audiences who prefer "familiar drama to the risk of serious democratization."[43] In what follows, I want to address the controversy surrounding the racist remarks made by Trent Lott at Strom Thurmond's centennial birthday celebration and how the Lott affair functions as an example of how controversial issues often assume the status of both a national melodrama and a scripted spectacle. I also want to analyze how this event functioned largely to privatize matters of white racism while rendering invisible the endorsement of systemic and state-fashioned racism. The Lott affair functions as a public transcript in providing a context for examining the public pedagogy of racial representations in media and print culture that are often framed within the ideology of the new racism in order to displace any serious discussion of racial exclusion in the United States. Finally, I offer some suggestions about how to respond politically to neoliberal racism and what the implications might be for a critical pedagogical practice aimed at challenging and dismantling it.

While attending Strom Thurmond's 100th birthday party on December 5, 2002, the then Senate majority leader, Trent Lott, offered the following salute to one of the most legendary segregationists alive: "I want to say this about my state: When Strom Thurmond ran for President, we voted for him. We're proud of it. And if the rest of the country had followed our lead, we wouldn't have had all these problems over all these years, either."[44] Of course, for the historically aware, the meaning of the tribute was clear since Thurmond had run in 1948 on a racist Dixiecrat ticket whose official campaign slogan was "Segregation Forever!"

It took five days before the incident got any serious attention in the national media. But once the story broke, Lott offered an endless series of apologies that included everything from saying he was just "winging it"(until it was revealed that he made an almost identical remark as a congressman at a Reagan rally a few decades earlier), to having found "Jesus," to proclaiming he was now "an across the board" advocate of affirmative action.[45] The Lott story evoked a range of opinions in the media extending from a craven defense provided by conservative columnist Bob Novak (who argued that Lott's racist comments were just a slip of the tongue) to vociferous moral condemnation from all sides of the ideological spectrum. Once Lott's voting record on civil rights issues was made public, he became an embarrassment and liability to those politicians who denounced open racial bigotry but had little to say about structural, systemic, and institutional racism.[46] Under pressure from his Republican party colleagues, Lott eventually resigned as Senate majority leader, though he retained his Senate seat, and the story passed in the national media from revelation to spectacle to irrelevance. The shelf-life of the spectacle in the dominant culture is usually quite long—witness the Gary Condit affair—except when it offers the possibility for revealing how racist expressions privately license relations of power that reproduce a wide range of racial exclusions in the wider social order.

Lott's remarks cast him as a supporter of the old racism—bigoted, crude, and overtly racist. And, for the most part, the wrath his remarks engendered from the Republican Party and its media cheerleaders was mainly of the sort that allowed the critics to reposition themselves in keeping with the dictates of the logic of color-blindness and neoliberal racism. In doing so they distanced themselves from Lott's comments as a safe way to attest their disdain for the old racist bigotry and to provide a display of their moral superiority and civility while at the same time distancing themselves from what Robert Kuttner has called some "inconvenient truths" when it came to talking about race. As Kuttner observes, "His stated views made it more difficult for the Republican party to put on minstrel shows and offer speeches dripping with compassion, while appointing racist judges, battling affirmative action, resisting hate crimes legislation, and slashing social outlays that help minorities. Lott made it harder to hold down black voting in the name of 'ballot security' while courting black voters, and disguising attacks on public education as expanded 'choice' for black parents and stingy welfare reform as promoting self-sufficiency."[47] Of course, singling out Lott also suggested that he was, as an editorial in the *Wall Street Journal* claimed, a one-of-a-kind bad apple, an unfortunate holdover from the Jim Crow era that no longer exists in America. David Brooks, the editor of the conservative *National Review*, proclaimed with great indignation that Lott's views were not "normal Republican ideas" and, to prove the point, asserted that after hanging out with Republicans for two decades he had "never heard an overtly racist comment."[48]

Brooks, like many of his fellow commentators, seems to have allowed his ode to racial cleansing to cloud his sense of recent history. After all, it was only about a decade ago that Kirk Fordice, a right-wing Republican, ended his victorious campaign for governor—orchestrated largely as an attack on crime and welfare cheaters—with a "still photograph of a Black woman and her baby."[49] And of course this was just a few years after George H.W. Bush ran his famous Willie Horton ad and a short time before Dan Quayle in the 1992 presidential campaign used the racially coded category of welfare to attack a sitcom character, Murphy Brown. Maybe David Brooks was just unaware of the interview that John Ashcroft had given in 1999 to the neoconfederate magazine, *Southern Partisan*, "in which he 'vowed to do more' to defend the legacy of Jefferson Davis."[50] Or, as *New York Times* writer Frank Rich puts it in response to the apparent newfound historical amnesia about the overt racism displayed by the Republican Party in more recent times:

> Tell that to George W. Bush, who beat John McCain in the 2000 South Carolina primary after what *Newsweek* called "a smear campaign" of leaflets, e-mails and telephone calls calling attention to the McCains' "black child" (an adopted daughter from Bangladesh). Or to Sonny Perdue, the new Republican governor of Georgia, elected in part by demagoguing the sanctity of the confederate flag.[51]

One telling example of how the Trent Lott affair was removed from the historical record of racialized injustices, the realm of political contestation, and, indeed, any critical understanding of how racializing categories actually take hold in the culture can be found in the December 23, 2002, issue of

Newsweek, which was devoted in entirety to the public uproar surrounding Lott's racist remarks.[52] *Newsweek* featured a 1962 picture of Lott on its cover with the caption "The Past That Made Him—and May Undo Him: Race and the Rise of Trent Lott." The stories that appeared in the magazine portrayed Lott either as an odd and totally out-of-touch symbol of the past ("A Man Out of Time," as one story headline read) or as an unrepentant symbol of racism that was no longer acceptable in American public life or in national politics. *Newsweek* ended its series on Lott with a short piece called "Lessons of the Trent Lott Mess."[53] The author of the article, Ellis Cose, condemned Lott's long history of racist affiliations, as did many other writers, but said nothing about why they were ignored by either the major political party or the dominant media over the last decade, especially given Lott's important standing in national politics. It is interesting to note that Lott's affiliation with the Council of Conservative Citizens (CCC)—a neo-confederate group that succeeded the notorious white Citizens Council, once referred to as the "uptown Klan"—was revealed in a 1998 story by Stanley Crouch, a writer for the *New York Daily News.* Surprisingly, the article was ignored at the time both by prominent politicians and by the dominant media. At issue here is the recognition that the history of racism in which Trent Lott participated is not merely his personal history but the country's history and, hence, should raise far more serious considerations about how the legacy of racism works through its cultural, economic, and social fabric. While Lott has to be held accountable for his remarks, his actions cannot be understood strictly within the language of American individualism—that is, as a bad reminder that the legacy of racism lives on in some old-fashioned politicians who cannot escape their past. In fact, Lott's remarks as well as the silence that allowed his racist discourse to be viewed in strictly personal and idiosyncratic terms must be addressed as symptomatic of a larger set of racist historical, social, economic, and ideological influences that still hold sway over American society. Collapsing the political into the personal, and serious reporting into talk-show clichés, Cose argues that the reason a person like Lott is serving and will continue to serve in the Senate, sharing power with America's ruling elite, is that "Americans are very forgiving folks."[54] This response is more than simply inane; it is symptomatic of a culture of racism that has no language for or interest in understanding systemic racism, its history, or how it is embodied in most ruling political and economic institutions in the United States. Or, for that matter, why it has such a powerful grip on American culture. The Trent Lott affair is important not because it charts an influential senator's fall from grace and power in the wake of an unfortunate racist remark made in public, but because it is symptomatic of a new racism that offers no resources for translating private troubles into public considerations.

The public pedagogy underlying the popular response to Trent Lott's racist remarks reveals how powerful the educational force of the culture is in shaping dominant conventions about race. Mirroring the logic of neoliberalism, the overall response to Lott both privatized the discourse of racism and attributed a racist expression to an unfortunate slip of the tongue, a psychological disposition, or the emotive residue of a man who is out of step with both his political party and the spirit of the country. But such an expression is not simply the assertion of a prejudiced individual; it is also a mode of exclusion, rooted in forms of authority largely used to name, classify, order, and devalue people of color. As David Theo Goldberg observes:

> As a mode of exclusion, racist expression assumes authority and is vested with power, literally and symbolically, in bodily terms. They are human bodies that are classified, ordered, valorized, and devalued. . . .When this authority assumes state power, racialized discourse and its modes of exclusion become embedded in state institutions and normalized in the common business of everyday institutional life. . . . As expressions of exclusion, racism appeals either to inherent superiority or to differences. These putative differences and gradations may be strictly physical, intellectual, linguistic, or cultural. Each serves in two ways: They purport to furnish the basis for justifying differential distributions or treatment, and they represent the very relations of power that prompted them.[55]

As part of the discourse of denial, the Trent Lott episode reveals how racism is trivialized through a politics of racial management in which racism is consigned to an outdated past, a narrow psychologism, the private realm of bad judgment or personal indiscretion. But racial discourse is not simply about private speech acts or individualized modes of communication; it is also about contested histories, institutional relations of power, ideology, and the social gravity of effects. Racist discourses and expressions should alert us to the workings of power and the conditions that make particular forms of language possible and others seemingly impossible, as well as to the modes of agency they produce and legitimate—an issue almost completely ignored in the mainstream coverage of the Lott affair. What was missing from such coverage is captured by Teun A. Van Dijk in his analysis of elite discourse and racism:

> Racism, defined as a system of racial and ethnic inequality, can survive only when it is daily reproduced through multiple acts of exclusion, inferiorization, or marginalization. Such acts need to be sustained by an ideological system and by a set of attitudes that legitimate difference and dominance. Discourse is the principal means for the construction and reproduction of this sociocognitive framework.[56]

CONCLUSION

Any attempt to address the politics of the new racism in the United States must begin by reclaiming the language of the social and affirming the project of an inclusive and just democracy. This suggests addressing how the politics of the new racism is made invisible under the mantle of neoliberal ideology—that is, raising questions about how neoliberalism works to hide the effects of power, politics, and racial injustice. What is both troubling and must increasingly be made problematic is that neoliberalism wraps itself in what appears to be an unassailable appeal to common sense. As Jean and John Comaroff observe:

> [T]here is a strong argument to be made that neoliberal capitalism, in its millennial moment, portends the death of politics by hiding its own ideological underpinnings in the dictates of economic efficiency: in the fetishism of the free market, in the inexorable, expanding "needs" of business, in the imperatives of science and technology. Or, if it does not conduce to the death of politics, it tends to reduce them to the pursuit of pure interest, individual or collective.[57]

Defined as the paragon of all social relations, neoliberalism attempts to eliminate an engaged critique about its most basic principles and social consequences by embracing the "market as the arbiter of social destiny."[58] More is lost here than neoliberalism's willingness to make its own assumptions problematic. Also lost is the very viability of politics itself. Not only does neoliberalism in this instance empty the public treasury, hollow out public services, and limit the vocabulary and imagery available to recognize anti-democratic forms of power and narrow models of individual agency, it also undermines the socially discursive translating functions of any viable democracy by undercutting the ability of individuals to engage in the continuous translation between public considerations and private interests by collapsing the public into the realm of the private.[59] Divested of its political possibilities and social underpinnings, freedom finds few opportunities for rearticulating private worries into public concerns or individual discontent into collective struggle.[60] Hence, the first task in engaging neoliberalism is to reveal its claim to a bogus universalism and make clear how it functions as a historical and social construction. Neoliberalism hides the traces of its own ideology, politics, and history either by rhetorically asserting its triumphalism as part of the "end of history" or by proclaiming that capitalism and democracy are synonymous. What must be challenged is neoliberalism's "future-tense narrative of inevitability, demonstrating that the drama of world history remains wide open."[61]

But the history of the changing economic and ideological conditions that gave rise to neoliberalism must be understood in relation to the corresponding history of race relations in the United States and abroad. Most importantly, since the history of race is either left out or misrepresented by the official channels of power in the United States, it is crucial that the history of slavery, civil rights, racial politics, and ongoing modes of struggle at the level of everyday life be remembered and used pedagogically to challenge the historical amnesia that feeds neoliberalism's ahistorical claim to power and the continuity of its claims to common sense. The struggle against racial injustice cannot be separated from larger questions about what kind of culture and society is emerging under the imperatives of neoliberalism, what kind of history it ignores, and what alternatives might point to a substantive democratic future.

Second, under neoliberalism all levels of government have been hollowed out and largely reduced either to their policing functions or to maintaining the privileges of the rich and the interests of corporate power holders—both largely white. In this discourse, the state is not only absolved of its traditional social contract of upholding the public good and providing crucial social provisions and minimal guarantees for those who are in need of such services; it also embraces a notion of color-blind racelessness. State racelessness is built on the right-wing logic of "rational racists" such as D'Souza, who argues that "[w]hat we need is a separation of race and state."[62] As Goldberg points out, this means that the state is now held

> to a standard of justice protective of individual rights and not group results. . . . [T]his in turn makes possible the devaluation of any individuals considered not white, or white-like, the trashing or trampling of their rights and possibilities, for the sake of preserving the right to *private* "rational discrimination" of whites. . . . [Thus] racist discrimination becomes privatized, and in terms of liberal legality state protected in its privacy.[63]

Defined through the ideology of racelessness, the state removes itself from either addressing or correcting the effects of racial discrimination, reducing matters of racism to individual concerns to be largely solved through private negotiations between individuals, and adopting an entirely uncritical role in the way in which the racial state shapes racial policies and their effects throughout the economic, social, and cultural landscape. Lost here is any critical engagement with state power and how it imposes immigration policies, decides who gets resources and access to a quality education, defines what constitutes a crime, how people are punished, how and whether social problems are criminalized, who is worthy of citizenship, and who is responsible for addressing racial injustices. As the late Pierre Bourdieu argued, there is a political and pedagogical need, not only to protect the social gains, embodied in state policies, that have been the outcome of important collective struggles, but also "to invent another kind of state."[64] This means challenging the political irresponsibility and moral indifference that are the organizing principles at the heart of the neoliberal vision. As Bourdieu suggests, it is necessary to restore the sense of utopian possibility rooted in the struggle for a democratic state. The racial state and its neoliberal ideology need to be challenged as part of a viable anti-racist pedagogy and politics.

Anti-racist pedagogy also needs to move beyond the conundrums of a limited identity politics and begin to include in its analysis what it would mean to imagine the state as a vehicle for democratic values and a strong proponent of social and racial justice. In part, reclaiming the democratic and public responsibility of the state would mean arguing for a state in which tax cuts for the rich, rather than social spending, are seen as the problem; using the state to protect the public good rather than waging a war on all things public; engaging and resisting the use of state power to both protect and define the public sphere as utterly white; redefining the power and role of the state so as to minimize its policing functions and strengthen its accountability to the public interests of all citizens rather than to the wealthy and corporations. Removing the state from its subordination to market values means reclaiming the importance of social needs over commercial interests and democratic politics over corporate power; it also means addressing a host of urgent social problems that include but are not limited to the escalating costs of health care, housing, the schooling crisis, the growing gap between rich and poor, the environmental crisis, the rebuilding of the nation's cities and impoverished rural areas, the economic crisis facing most of the states, and the increasing assault on people of color. The struggle over the state must be linked to a struggle for a racially just, inclusive democracy. Crucial to any viable politics of anti-racism is the role the state will play as a guardian of the public interest and as a force in creating a multiracial democracy.

Third, it is crucial for any anti-racist pedagogy and politics to recognize that power does not just inhabit the realm of economics or state power, but is also intellectual, residing in the educational force of the culture and its enormous powers of persuasion. This means that any viable anti-racist pedagogy must make the political more pedagogical by recognizing how public pedagogy works to determine and secure the ways that racial identity, issues, and relations are produced in a wide variety of sites including schools, cable and television networks, newspapers and magazines, the Internet, advertising, churches, trade unions, and a host of other public spheres in which ideas are produced and distributed. This, in turn, means becoming mindful of how racial meanings and practices are created, mediated, reproduced, and challenged through a wide variety of "discourses, institutions, audiences, markets, and constituencies which help determine the forms and meaning of publicness in American society."[65] The crucial role that pedagogy plays in shaping racial issues reaffirms the centrality of a cultural politics that recognizes the relationship between issues of representation and the operations of power, the important role that intellectuals might play as engaged, public intellectuals, and the importance of critical knowledge in challenging neoliberalism's illusion of unanimity. But an anti-racist cultural pedagogy also suggests the need to develop a language of both critique and possibility and to wage individual and collective struggles in a wide variety of dominant public spheres and alternative counter-publics. Public pedagogy as a tool of anti-racist struggles understands racial politics, not only as a signifying activity through which subject positions are produced, identities inhabited, and desires mobilized, but also as the mobilization of material relations of power as a way of securing, enforcing, and challenging racial injustices. While cultural politics offers an opportunity to understand how race matters and racist practices take hold in everyday life, such a pedagogical and cultural politics must avoid collapsing into a romanticization of the symbolic, popular, or discursive. Culture matters as a rhetorical tool and mode of persuasion, especially in the realm of visual culture, which has to be taken seriously as a pedagogical force, but changing consciousness is only a precondition to changing society and should not be confused with what it means to actually transform institutional relations of power. In part, this means contesting the control of the media by a handful of transnational corporations.[66] The social gravity of racism as it works through the modalities of everyday language, relations, and cultural expressions has to be taken seriously in any anti-racist politics, but such a concern and mode of theorizing must also be accompanied by an equally serious interest in the rise of corporate power and "the role of state institutions and agencies in shaping contemporary forms of racial subjugation and inequality."[67] Racist ideologies, practices, state formations, and institutional relations can be exposed pedagogically and linguistically, but they cannot be resolved merely in the realm of the discursive. Hence, any viable anti-racist pedagogy needs to draw attention to the distinction between critique and social transformation, to critical modes of analysis, and to the responsibility of acting individually and collectively on one's beliefs.

Another important consideration that has to be included in any notion of anti-racist pedagogy and politics is the issue of connecting matters of racial justice to broader and more comprehensive political, cultural, and social agendas. Neoliberalism exerts a powerful force in American life because its influence and power are spread across a diverse range of political, economic, social, and cultural spheres. Its ubiquity is matched by its aggressive pedagogical attempts to reshape the totality of social life in the image of the market, reaching into and connecting a wide range of seemingly disparate factors that bear down on everyday life in the United States. Neoliberalism is persuasive because its language of commercialism, consumerism, privatization, freedom, and self-interest resonates with and saturates so many aspects of public life. Differences in this discourse are removed from matters of equity and power and reduced to market niches. Agency is privatized and social values are reduced to market-based interests. And, of course, a democracy of citizens is replaced by a democracy of consumers. Progressives, citizens, and other groups who are concerned about matters of race and difference need to maintain their concerns with particular forms of oppression and subordination; yet, at the same time, the limits of various approaches to identity politics must be recognized so as not to allow them to become either fixed or incapable of making alliances with other social movements as part of a broader struggle over not just particular freedoms but also the more generalized freedoms associated with an inclusive and radical democracy.

I have not attempted to be exhaustive in suggesting what it might mean to recognize and challenge the new racism that now reproduces more subtle forms of racial subordination, oppression, and exclusion, though I have tried to point to some pedagogical and political concerns that connect racism and neoliberal politics. The color line in America is neither fixed nor static. Racism as an expression of power and exclusion takes many meanings and forms under different historical conditions. The emphasis on its socially and historically constructed nature offers hope because it suggests that what can be produced by dominant relations of power, can also be challenged and transformed by those who imagine a more utopian and just world. The challenge of the color line is still with us today and needs to be recognized not only as a shameful example of racial injustice but also as a reprehensible attack on the very nature of democracy itself.

NOTES

1. W.E.B. Du Bois, *The Souls of Black Folk*, in *Three Negro Classics* (New York: Avon Books, 1965), p. 221.

2. It is important to note that while such covert modes of expression may be true of anti-black racism, they certainly do not characterize the racist policies being enacted by the United States against immigrants and nationals from the Middle East. The racial profiling, harassment, and outright use of unconstitutional means to intimidate, deport, and jail members of the Arab and Muslim populations in the United States represent a most shameful period in this country's ongoing history of state-sanctioned racist practices. Thus, while the focus of this chapter is on black-white relations, I am not suggesting that racism encompasses only the latter. Obviously, any full account of racism would have to be applied to the wide range of groups who constitute diverse peoples of color and ethnic origin.

3. Howard Winant, "Race in the Twenty-First Century," *Tikkun* 17:1 (2002), p. 33.

4. Cited in David Shipler, "Reflections on Race," *Tikkun* 13:1 (1998), p. 59.

5. Dinesh D'Souza, *The End of Racism* (New York: The Free Press, 1995); Jim Sleeper, *Liberal Racism: How Fixating on Race Subverts the American Dream* (Lanham, MD: Rowman and Littlefield, 2002); Stephan and Abigail Thernstrom, *America in Black and White: One Nation, Indivisible* (New York: Simon and Schuster, 1999).

6. Cited in Tim Wise, "See No Evil: Perception and Reality in Black and White," *ZNet Commentary* (August 2, 2002). Available online at www.znet commentary@tao.ca. The Gallup Poll on Black-White Relations in the United States— 2001 Update is available online at http://www.gallup.com/poll/specialReports/.

7. As Greg Winter points out, the Center for Equal Opportunity and the American Civil Rights Institute, two groups that oppose affirmative action, have launched a new offensive "against scholarships and summer programs intended to ease minority students into college life." See Winter, "Colleges See Broader Attack on Their Aid to Minorities," *New York Times* (March 30, 2003), p. A15.

8. Following is a representative sample of works that point to the pervasive racism at work in American life: Howard Winant, *The World Is a Ghetto: Race and Democracy Since World War II* (New York: Basic Books, 2001); Manning Marable, *The Great Wells of Democracy: The Meaning of Race in American Life* (New York: BasicCivitas Books, 2002); David Theo Goldberg, *The Racial State* (Malden, MA: Blackwell Books, 2002); Steve Martinot, *The Rule of Racialization: Class, Identity, Governance* (Philadelphia: Temple University Press, 2003).

9. Michael Omi, "Racialization in the Post-Civil Rights Era," in Avery Gor-

don and Christopher Newfield, eds., *Mapping Multiculturalism* (Minneapolis: University of Minnesota Press, 1996), p. 183.

10. Jack Geiger, "The Real World of Race," *The Nation* (December 1, 1997), p. 27.

11. See, for instance, Shelby Steele, "The Age of White Guilt," *Harper's Magazine* (November 2002), pp. 33–42.

12. This position is fully developed in Shelby Steele, *The Content of Our Character* (New York: Harper, 1990).

13. John McWhorter, "Don't Do Me Any Favors," *American Enterprise Magazine* (April/May 2003). Available online at www.theamericanenterprise.org/taeam03d.htm.

14. Zygmunt Bauman, *The Individualized Society* (London: Polity Press, 2001), p. 205.

15. Charles Murray, *Losing Ground: American Social Policy, 1950–1980* (New York: Basic Books, 1985).

16. For excellent analyses of this shift in race relations, see Eduardo Bonilla-Silva, *White Supremacy and Racism in the Post-Civil Rights Era* (Boulder: Lynne Rienner Publishers, 2001); and Amy Elizabeth Ansell, *New Right, New Racism: Race and Reaction in the United States and Britain* (New York: New York University Press, 1997).

17. Douglas Kellner, "Globalization and New Social Movements: Lessons for Critical Theory and Pedagogy," in Nicholas Burbules and Carlos Torres, eds., *Globalization and Education* (New York: Routledge/Falmer, 2000), p. 307.

18. Bauman, *The Individualized Society*, p. 159.

19. Lewis H. Lapham, "Res Publica," *Harper's Magazine* (December 2001), p. 8.

20. Zygmunt Bauman, *Globalization: The Human Consequences* (New York: Columbia University Press, 1998), p. 47.

21. Ansell, *New Right, New Racism*, p. 111.

22. Ibid., pp. 20–21.

23. Charles Gallagher, "Color-Blind Privilege: The Social and Political Functions of Erasing the Color Line in Post Race America," unpublished essay, p. 12.

24. Ibid., p. 11.

25. This issue is taken up brilliantly in David Theo Goldberg, *The Racial State* (Malden, MA: Blackwell Books, 2002), especially on pp. 200–238.

26. Manning Marable, "Beyond Color-Blindness," *The Nation* (December 14, 1998), p. 29.

27. For specific figures in all areas of life, see Bonilla-Silva, *White Supremacy and Racism in the Post-Civil Rights Era,* especially the chapter titled "White Supremacy in the Post–Civil Rights Era," pp. 89–120.

28. Paul Street, "A Whole Lott Missing: Rituals of Purification and Racism Denial," *Z Magazine* (December 22, 2002). Available online at www.zmag.org/content/print_article.cfm?itemID=2784&seciton.

29. I address these issues in detail in Henry A. Giroux, *Public Spaces, Private Lives: Democracy Beyond 9/11* (Lanham, MD: Rowman and Littlefield, 2002).

30. Loïc Wacquant, "From Slavery to Mass Incarceration: Rethinking the 'Race Question' in the U.S.," in *New Left Review* (January-February 2002), p. 44.

31. Paul Street, "Mass Incarceration and Racist State Priorities at Home and Abroad," *Dissident Voice* (March 11, 2003), pp. 6–7. Available online at http://www.dissidentvoice.org/Articles2/Street_MassIncarceration.htm.

32. Richard J. Herrnstein and Charles Murray, *The Bell Curve: Intelligence and Class Structure in American Life* (New York: The Free Press, 1994), pp. 533–534, 551.

33. Nikhil Aziz, "Moving Right On! Fairness, Family, and Faith," *The Public Eye* 16:2 (Summer 2002), p. 5.

34. See "Civil Rights" within the Mission section of the CIR's website, at http://www.cir-usa.org/civil_rights_theme.html.

35. For an excellent summary and analysis of many of these legal cases, see Aziz, "Moving Right On!"

36. Ibid., p. 15.

37. Zsuza Ferge, "What Are the State Functions That Neoliberalism Wants to Eliminate?" in Antole Anton, Milton Fisk, and Nancy Holmstrom, eds., *Not for Sale: In Defense of Public Goods* (Boulder: Westview Press, 2000), p. 183.

38. David Theo Goldberg, *The Racial State* (Malden, MA: Blackwell, 2002), p. 217. The ideas in the sentence prior to this quote are also taken from Goldberg's text.

39. Jean Comaroff and John L. Comaroff, "Millennial Capitalism: First Thoughts on a Second Coming," *Public Culture* 12:2 (2000), pp. 305–306.

40. Aziz, "Moving Right On!" p. 6.

41. Cited in Philip Klinker, "The 'Racial Realism' Hoax," *The Nation* (December 14, 1998), p. 37.

42. Dinesh D'Souza, *The End of Racism: Principles for a Multiracial Society* (New York: The Free Press, 1995), p. 268.

43. Patricia J. Williams, *Seeing a Color-Blind Future: The Paradox of Race* (New York: Noonday Press, 1997). pp. 18, 26.

44. John Meacham, "A Man Out of Time," *Newsweek* (December 23, 2003), p. 27.

45. Ibid.

46. On Trent Lott's voting record on matters of race, see Derrick Z. Jackson, "Brother Lott's Real Record," *Boston Globe* (December 18, 2002). Available online at www.commondreams.org/views02/1218-09.htm.

47. See Robert Kuttner, "A Candid Conversation About Race in America," *Boston Globe* (December 27, 2002). Available online at www.commondreams.org/views02/1225-02.htm.

48. David Brooks, "We Don't Talk This Way," *Newsweek* (December 23, 2002), p. 31.

49. Cited in David Roediger, *Toward the Abolition of Whiteness* (London: Verso Press, 1994), p. 8.

50. Frank Rich, "Bonfire of the Vanities," *New York Times* (Saturday, December 21, 2002), p. A35.

51. Ibid.

52. I have taken this idea from David Theo Goldberg, *Racial Subjects: Writing on Race in America* (New York: Routledge, 1997), pp. 17–26.

53. Ellis Cose, "Lessons of the Trent Lott Mess," *Newsweek* (December 23, 2002), p. 37.

54. Ibid.

55. David Theo Goldberg, "Racialized Discourse," in *Racist Culture* (Malden, MA: Blackwell, 1993), pp. 54, 55, 56.

56. Teun A. Van Dijk, "Denying Racism: Elite Discourse and Racism," in Philomena Essed and David Theo Goldberg, eds., *Race Critical Theories: Texts and Contexts* (Malden, MA: Blackwell, 2002), pp. 323–323.

57. Jean Comaroff and John L. Comaroff, "Millennial Capitalism: First Thoughts on a Second Coming," *Public Culture* 12:2 (Spring 2000), p. 322.

58. James Rule, "Markets, in Their Place," *Dissent* (Winter 1998), p. 31.

59. Bauman, *The Individualized Society*, p. 107.

60. Ibid.

61. Leerom Medovoi, "Globalization as Narrative and Its Three Critiques," *Review of Education/Pedagogy/Cultural Studies* 24:1–2 (2002), p. 66.

62. D'Souza, *The End of Racism*, p. 545.

63. David Theo Goldberg, *The Racial State* (Malden, MA: Blackwell, 2002), p. 229.

64. Pierre Bourdieu and Günter Grass, "The 'Progressive' Restoration: A Franco-German Dialogue," *New Left Review* 14 (March–April 2002), p. 71.

65. John Brenkman, "Race Publics: Civic Illiberalism, or Race After Reagan," *Transition* 5:2 (Summer 1995), p. 8.

66. On this subject, see Robert W. McChesney and John Nichols, *Our Media, Not Theirs* (New York: Seven Stories Press, 2002).

67. David Goldberg and John Solomos, "Introduction to Part III," in David Goldberg and John Solomos, eds., *A Companion to Ethnic and Racial Studies* (Malden, MA: Blackwell, 2002), p. 231.

6
FROM SLAVERY TO MASS INCARCERATION: RETHINKING THE "RACE QUESTION" IN THE UNITED STATES

Loïc Wacquant

⟣

Not one but several 'peculiar institutions' have successively operated to define, confine, and control African-Americans in the history of the United States. The first is *chattel slavery* as the pivot of the plantation economy and inceptive matrix of racial division from the colonial era to the Civil War. The second is the *Jim Crow system* of legally enforced discrimination and segregation from cradle to grave that anchored the predominantly agrarian society of the South from the close of Reconstruction to the Civil Rights revolution which toppled it a full century after abolition. America's third special device for containing the descendants of slaves in the Northern industrial metropolis is the *ghetto*, corresponding to the conjoint urbanization and proletarianization of African-Americans from the Great Migration of 1914–30 to the 1960s, when it was rendered partially obsolete by the concurrent transformation of economy and state and by the mounting protest of blacks against continued caste exclusion, climaxing with the explosive urban riots chronicled in the Kerner Commission Report.[1]

The fourth, I contend here, is the novel institutional complex formed by the *remnants of the dark ghetto and the carceral apparatus* with which it has become joined by a linked relationship of structural symbiosis and functional surrogacy. This suggests that slavery and mass imprisonment are genealogically linked and that one cannot understand the latter—its timing, composition, and smooth onset as well as the quiet ignorance or acceptance of its deleterious effects on those it affects—without returning to the former as historic starting point and functional analogue.

Viewed against the backdrop of the full historical trajectory of racial domination in the United States (summed up in Table 6.1), the glaring and

Originally published in *New Left Review* 13 (January–February 2002). Reprinted by permission.

Table 6.1. The four 'peculiar institutions' and their basis

Institution	Form of labour	Core of economy	Dominant social type
Slavery (1619–1865)	unfree fixed labour	Plantation	slave
Jim Crow (South, 1865–1965)	free fixed labour	Agrarian and extractive	sharecropper
Ghetto (North, 1915–1968)	free mobile labour	Segmented industrial manufacturing	menial worker
Hyperghetto & Prison (1968–)	fixed surplus labour	Polarized post-industrial services	welfare recipient & criminal

growing 'disproportionality' in incarceration that has afflicted African-Americans over the past three decades can be understood as the result of the 'extra-penological' functions that the prison system has come to shoulder in the wake of the crisis of the ghetto and of the continuing stigma that afflicts the descendants of slaves by virtue of their membership in a group constitutively deprived of ethnic honour (Max Weber's *Massehre*).

Not crime, but the need to shore up an eroding caste cleavage, along with buttressing the emergent regime of desocialized wage labour to which most blacks are fated by virtue of their lack of marketable cultural capital, and which the most deprived among them resist by escaping into the illegal street economy, is the main impetus behind the stupendous expansion of America's penal state in the post-Keynesian age and its de facto policy of 'carceral affirmative action' towards African-Americans.[2]

LABOUR EXTRACTION AND CASTE DIVISION

America's first three 'peculiar institutions', slavery, Jim Crow, and the ghetto, have this in common: they were all instruments for the conjoint *extraction of labour* and *social ostracization* of an outcast group deemed unassimilable by virtue of the indelible threefold stigma it carries. African-Americans arrived under bondage in the land of freedom. They were accordingly deprived of the right to vote in the self-appointed cradle of democracy (until 1965 for residents of the Southern states). And, for lack of a recognizable national affiliation, they were shorn of ethnic honour, which implies that, rather than simply standing at the bottom of the rank ordering of group prestige in American society, they were barred from it *ab initio*.[3]

1. *Slavery (1619–1865)*. Slavery is a highly malleable and versatile institution that can be harnessed to a variety of purposes, but in the Americas property-in-person was geared primarily to the provision and control of labour.[4] Its introduction in the Chesapeake, Middle Atlantic and Low Country regions of the United States in the 17th century served to recruit and regulate the unfree workforce forcibly imported from Africa and the West Indies to cater to their tobacco, rice and mixed-farming economy. (Indentured labourers

RACIAL DISPROPORTIONALITY IN US IMPRISONMENT

Three brute facts stand out and give a measure of the grotesquely dispro-portionate impact of mass incarceration on African-Americans. First, the ethnic composition of the inmate population of the United States has been virtually inverted in the last half century, going from about 70% (Anglo) white at the mid-century point to less than 30% today. Contrary to common perception, the predominance of blacks behind bars is not a long-standing pattern but a novel and recent phenomenon, with 1988 as the turning point: it is the year when then-Vice-President George Bush ran his infamous 'Willie Horton' advertisement during the presidential campaign, featuring sinister images of the black rapist of a white woman as emblematic of the contemporary 'crime problem,' as well as the year after which African-American men supply a majority of prison admissions for the country as a whole.[1]

Next, whereas the difference between arrest rates for whites and blacks has been stable, with the percentage of blacks oscillating between 29% and 33% of all arrestees for property crimes and between 44% and 47% for violent offences between 1976 and 1992,[2] the white-black incarcera-tion gap has grown rapidly in the past quarter-century, jumping from 1 for 5 in 1985 to about 1 for 8 today. This trend is all the more striking for occurring during a period when significant numbers of African-Amer-icans have entered into and risen through the ranks of the police, the courts, and the corrections administration and when the more overt forms of racial discrimination that were commonplace in them into the seventies have been greatly reduced, if not stamped out.[3]

Lastly, the lifelong cumulative probability of 'doing time' in a state or federal penitentiary based on the imprisonment rates of the early egos is 4% for whites, 16% for Latinos and a staggering 29% for blacks.[4] Given the class gradient of incarceration, this figure suggests that a majority of African-Americans of (sub) proletarian status are facing a prison term of one or several years (and in many cases several terms) at some point in their adult life, with all the family, occupational and legal disruptions this entails, including the curtailment of social entitlements and civil rights and the temporary or permanent loss of the right to vote. As of 1997, nearly one black man in six nationwide was excluded from the ballot box due to a felony conviction and more than one fifth of them were prohib-ited from casting a vote in Alabama, Connecticut, Florida, Iowa, Missis-sippi, New Mexico, Texas, Washington, and Wyoming.[5] A short thirty-five years after the Civil Rights movement finally gained African-Americans effective access to the voting booth, a full century after Abolition, this right is being taken back by the penal system via legal dispositions that are of dubious constitutional validity and violate in many cases (notably lifetime disenfranchisement) international conventions on human rights ratified by the United States.

NOTES

1. David Anderson, *Crime and the Politics of Hysteria,* New York 1995.
2. Michael Tonry, *Malign Neglect,* Oxford 1995, p. 64
3. Alfred Blumstein, 'Racial Disproportionality of US Prisons Revisited', *University of Colorado Law Review,* vol. 64, 1993, pp. 743–60; but see the powerful counter-argument offered by David Cole, *No Equal Justice,* New York 1999.
4. Thomas Bonczar and Allen Beck, 'Lifetime Likelihood of Going to State or Federal Prison', *Bureau of Justice Statistics Special Report,* Washington, BJS, March 1997, p. 1; for a state-by-state analysis, see Marc Mauer, 'Racial Disparities in Prison Getting Worse in the 1990s', *Overcrowded Times,* vol. 8, no. 1, February 1997, pp. 9–13
5. John Hagan and Ronit Dinowitzer, 'Collateral Consequences of Imprisonment for Children, Communities, and Prisoners', in Michael Tonry and Joan Petersilia, eds, *Prisons,* Chicago 1999, pp. 121–62; and Jamie Fellner and Marc Mauer, *Losing the Vote: the Impact of Felony Disenfranchisement in the US,* Washington 1998.

from Europe and native Indians were not enslaved because of their greater capacity to resist and because their servitude would have impeded future immigration as well as rapidly exhausted a limited supply of labour.) By the close of the 18th century, slavery had become self-reproducing and expanded to the fertile crescent of the Southern interior, running from South Carolina to Louisiana, where it supplied a highly profitable organization of labour for cotton production and the basis for a plantation society distinctive for its feudallike culture, politics, and psychology.[5]

An *unforeseen by-product* of the systematic enslavement and dehumanization of Africans and their descendants on North American soil was the creation of a racial caste line separating what would later become labelled 'blacks' and 'whites.' As Barbara Fields has shown, the American ideology of 'race', as putative biological division anchored by the inflexible application of the 'one-drop rule' together with the principle of hypodescent, crystallized to resolve the blatant contradiction between human bondage and democracy.[6] The religious and pseudo-scientific belief in racial difference reconciled the brute fact of unfree labor with the doctrine of liberty premised on natural rights by reducing the slave to live property—three-fifths of a man according the sacred scriptures of the Constitution.

2. Jim Crow (South, 1865–1965). Racial division was a consequence, not a precondition, of US slavery, but once it was instituted it became detached from its initial function and acquired a social potency of its own. Emancipation thus created a double dilemma for Southern white society: how to secure anew the labour of former slaves, without whom the region's economy would collapse, and how to sustain the cardinal status distinction between whites and 'persons of colour,' i.e, the social and symbolic distance needed to prevent the odium of 'amalgamation' with a group considered inferior, rootless and vile. After a protracted interregnum lasting into the 1890s, during which early white hysteria gave way to partial if inconsistent relaxation of ethnoracial strictures, when blacks were allowed to vote, to hold public office, and even to mix with whites to a degree in keeping with the intergroup intimacy fostered by slavery, the solution came in the form of the 'Jim Crow' regime.[7] It consisted of an ensemble of social and legal codes that prescribed the complete separation of the 'races' and sharply circumscribed the life chances of African-Americans while binding them to whites in a relation of suffusive submission backed by legal coercion and terroristic violence.

Imported from the North where it had been experimented within cities, this regime stipulated that blacks travel in separate trains, streetcars and waiting rooms; that they reside in the 'darktown' slums and be educated in separate schools (if at all); that they patronize separate service establishments and use their own bathrooms and water fountains; that they pray in separate churches, entertain themselves in separate clubs and sit in separate 'nigger galleries' in theatres; that they receive medical care in separate hospitals and exclusively from 'coloured' staff; and that they be incarcerated in separate cells and buried in separate cemeteries. Most crucial of all, laws joined mores in condemning the 'unspeakable crime' of interracial marriage, cohabitation or mere sexual congress so as to uphold the 'supreme law of self-preservation' of the races and the myth of innate white superiority. Through continued white ownership of the land and the generalization of sharecropping and debt peonage, the plantation system remained virtually untouched as former slaves became a 'dependent, propertyless peasantry, nominally free, but ensnared by poverty, ignorance, and the new servitude of tenantry'.[8] While sharecropping tied African-American labour to the farm, a rigid etiquette ensured that whites and blacks never interacted on a plane of equality, not even on the running track or in a boxing ring—a Birmingham ordinance of 1930 made it unlawful for them to play at checkers and dominoes with one another.[9] Whenever the 'colour line' was breached or even brushed, a torrent of violence was unleashed in the form of periodic pogroms, Ku Klux Klan and vigilante raids, public floggings, mob killings and lynchings, this ritual caste murder designed to keep 'uppity niggers' in their appointed place. All this was made possible by the swift and near-complete disenfranchisement of blacks as well as by the enforcement of 'Negro law' by courts which granted the latter fewer effective legal safeguards than slaves had enjoyed earlier by dint of being both property and persons.

3. *Ghetto (North, 1915–68).* The sheer brutality of caste oppression in the South, the decline of cotton agriculture due to floods and the boll weevil, and the pressing shortage of labour in Northern factories caused by the outbreak of World War I created the impetus for African-Americans to emigrate en masse to the booming industrial centers of the Midwest and

Northeast (over 1.5 million left in 1910–30, followed by another 3 million in 1940–60). But as migrants from Mississippi to the Carolinas flocked to the Northern metropolis, what they discovered there was not the 'promised land' of equality and full citizenship but another system of racial enclosure, the ghetto, which, though it was less rigid and fearsome than the one they had fled, was no less encompassing and constricting. To be sure, greater freedom to come and go in public places and to consume in regular commercial establishments, the disappearance of the humiliating signs pointing to 'Coloured' here and 'White' there, renewed access to the ballot box and protection from the courts, the possibility of limited economic advancement, release from personal subservience and from the dread of omnipresent white violence, all made life in the urban North incomparably preferable to continued peonage in the rural South: it was 'better to be a lamppost in Chicago than President of Dixie,' as migrants famously put it to Richard Wright. But restrictive covenants forced African-Americans to congregate in a 'Black Belt' which quickly became overcrowded, underserved and blighted by crime, disease, and dilapidation, while the 'job ceiling' restricted them to the most hazardous, menial, and underpaid occupations in both industry and personal services. As for 'social equality', understood as the possibility of 'becoming members of white cliques, churches and voluntary associations, or marrying into their families', it was firmly and definitively denied.[10]

Blacks had entered the Fordist industrial economy, to which they contributed a vital source of abundant and cheap labour willing to ride along its cycles of boom and bust. Yet they remained locked in a precarious position of structural economic marginality and consigned to a secluded and dependent microcosm, complete with its own internal division of labour, social stratification, and agencies of collective voice and symbolic representation: a 'city within the city' moored in a complexus of black churches and press, businesses and professional practices, fraternal lodges and communal associations that provided both a 'milieu for Negro Americans in which they [could] imbue their lives with meaning' and a bulwark 'to "protect" white America from "social contact" with Negroes'.[11] Continued caste hostility from without and renewed ethnic affinity from within converged to create the ghetto as the third vehicle to extract black labour while keeping black bodies at a safe distance, to the material and symbolic benefit of white society.

The era of the ghetto as paramount mechanism of ethnoracial domination had opened with the urban riots of 1917–19 (in East St. Louis, Chicago, Longview, Houston, etc.). It closed with a wave of clashes, looting and burning that rocked hundreds of American cities from coast to coast, from the Watts uprising of 1965 to the riots of rage and grief triggered by the assassination of Martin Luther King in the summer of 1968. Indeed, by the end of the sixties, the ghetto was well on its way to becoming functionally obsolete or, to be more precise, increasingly *unsuited* to accomplishing the twofold task historically entrusted to America's 'peculiar institutions.'

On the side of *labour extraction*, the shift from an urban industrial economy to a suburban service economy and the accompanying dualization of the occupational structure, along with the upsurge of working-class immigration from Mexico, the Caribbean and Asia, meant that large segments of the workforce contained in the 'Black Belts' of the Northern metropolis were simply no longer needed. On the side of *ethnoracial closure*, the decades-long mobilization of African-Americans against caste rule finally succeeded, in the propitious political conjuncture of crisis stemming from the Vietnam war and assorted social unrest, in forcing the federal state to dismantle the legal machinery of caste exclusion. Having secured voting and civil rights, blacks were at long last full citizens who would no longer brook being shunted off into the separate and inferior world of the ghetto.[12]

But while whites begrudgingly accepted 'integration' in principle, in practice they strove to maintain an unbridgeable social and symbolic gulf with their compatriots of African descent. They abandoned public schools, shunned public space, and fled to the suburbs in their millions to avoid mixing and ward off the spectre of 'social equality' in the city. They then turned against the welfare state and those social programmes upon which the collective advancement of blacks was most dependent. A *contrano*, they extended enthusiastic support for the 'law-and-order' policies that vowed to firmly repress urban disorders connately perceived as racial threats.[13] Such policies pointed to yet another special institution capable of confining and controlling if not the entire African-American community, at least its most disruptive, disreputable and dangerous members: the prison.

THE GHETTO AS PRISON, THE PRISON AS GHETTO

To grasp the deep kinship between ghetto and prison, which helps explain how the structural decline and functional redundancy of the one led to the unexpected ascent and astonishing growth of the other during the last quarter-century, it is necessary first to characterize accurately the ghetto.[14] But here we come upon the troublesome fact that the social sciences have failed to develop a robust analytic concept of the ghetto; instead they have been content to borrow the folk concept current in political and popular discourse at each epoch. This has caused a good deal of confusion, as the ghetto has been successively conflated with—and mistaken for—a segregated district, an ethnic neighbourhood, a territory of intense poverty or housing blight and even, with the rise of the policy myth of the 'underclass' in the more recent period, a mere accumulation of urban pathologies and antisocial behaviours.[15]

A comparative and historical sociology of the reserved Jewish quarters in the cities of Renaissance Europe and of America's 'Bronzeville' in the Fordist metropolis of the twentieth century reveals that a ghetto is essentially a sociospatial device that enables a dominant status group in an urban setting simultaneously to ostracize and exploit a subordinate group endowed with negative symbolic capital, that is, an incarnate property perceived to make its contact degrading by virtue of what Max Weber calls 'negative social estimation of honour.' Put differently, it is a relation of ethnoracial control and closure built out of four elements: (i) stigma; (ii) constraint; (iii) territorial confinement; and (iv) institutional encasement. The resulting formation is a distinct space, containing an ethnically homogeneous population, which finds itself forced to develop within it a set of interlinked institutions that duplicates the organizational framework of the broader society from which that group is banished and supplies the scaffoldings for the construction of its specific 'style of life' and social strategies. This parallel institutional nexus affords the subordinate group a measure of protection, autonomy and dignity, but at the cost of locking it in a relationship of structural subordination and dependency.

The ghetto, in short, operates as an *ethnoracial prison:* it encages a dishonoured category and severely curtails the life chances of its members in support of the 'monopolization of ideal and material goods or opportunities' by the dominant status group dwelling on its outskirts.[16] Recall that the ghettos of early modern Europe were typically delimited by high walls with one or more gates which were locked at night and within which Jews had to return before sunset on pain of severe punishment, and that their perimeter was subjected to continuous monitoring by external authorities.[17] Note next the structural and functional homologies with the prison conceptualized as a *judicial ghetto:* a jail or penitentiary is in effect a reserved *space* which serves to forcibly confine a legally denigrated *population* and wherein this latter evolves its distinctive *institutions,* culture and sullied identity. It is thus formed of the same four fundamental constituents—stigma, coercion, physical enclosure and organizational parallelism and insulation—that make up a ghetto, and for similar purposes.

Much as the ghetto protects the city's residents from the pollution of intercourse with the tainted but necessary bodies of an outcast group in the manner of an 'urban condom,' as Richard Sennett vividly put it in his depiction of the 'fear of touching' in sixteenth-century Venice,[18] the prison cleanses the social body from the temporary blemish of those of its members who have committed crimes, that is, following Durkheim, individuals who have violated the sociomoral integrity of the collectivity by infringing on 'definite and strong states of the collective conscience.' Students of the 'inmate society' from Donald Clemmer and Gresham Sykes to James Jacobs and John Irwin have noted time and again how the incarcerated develop their own argot roles, exchange systems and normative standards, whether as an adaptive response to the 'pains of imprisonment' or through selective importation of criminal and lower-class values from the outside, much like residents of the ghetto have elaborated or intensified a 'separate sub-culture' to counter their sociosymbolic immurement.[19] As for the secondary aim of the ghetto, to facilitate exploitation of the interned category, it was central to the 'house of correction' which is the direct historical predecessor of the modern prison and it has periodically played a major role in the evolution and operation of the latter.[20] Finally, both prison and ghetto are authority structures saddled with inherently dubious or problematic legitimacy whose maintenance is ensured by intermittent recourse to external force.

By the end of the seventies, then, as the racial and class backlash against the democratic advances won by the social movements of the preceding decade got into full swing, the prison abruptly returned to the forefront of American society and offered itself as the universal and simplex solution to all manners of social problems. Chief among these problems was the 'break-down' of social order in the 'inner city,' which is scholarly and policy euphemism for the patent incapacity of the dark ghetto to contain a dish-onoured and supernumerary population henceforth viewed not only as de-viant and devious but as downright dangerous in light of the violent urban upheavals of mid-sixties. As the walls of the ghetto shook and threatened to crumble, the walls of the prison were correspondingly extended, enlarged and fortified, and 'confinement of differentiation', aimed at keeping a group apart (the etymological meaning of *segregare)*, gained primacy over 'con-finement of safety' and 'confinement of authority'—to use the distinction proposed by French sociologist Claude Faugeron.[21] Soon the black ghetto, converted into an instrument of naked exclusion by the concurrent re-trenchment of wage labour and social protection, and further destabilized by the increasing penetration of the penal arm of the state, became bound to the jail and prison system by a triple relationship of functional equivalen-cy, structural homology and cultural syncretism, such that they now consti-tute a single *carceral continuum* which entraps a redundant population of younger black men (and increasingly women) who circulate in closed circuit between its two poles in a self-perpetuating cycle of social and legal margin-ality with devastating personal and social consequences.[22]

Now, the carceral system had already functioned as an ancillary institu-tion for caste preservation and labour control in America during one pre-vious transition between regimes of racial domination, that between slavery and Jim Crow in the South. On the morrow of Emancipation, Southern prisons turned black overnight as 'thousands of ex-slaves were being arrest-ed, tried, and convicted for acts that in the past had been dealt with by the master alone' and for refusing to behave as menials and follow the demean-ing rules of racial etiquette. Soon thereafter, the former Confederate states introduced 'convict leasing' as a response to the moral panic of 'Negro crime' that presented the double advantage of generating prodigious funds for the state coffers and furnishing abundant bound labour to till the fields, build the levees, lay down the railroads, clean the swamps, and dig the mines of the region under murderous conditions.[23] Indeed, penal labour, in the form of the convictlease and its heir, the chain gang, played a major role in the economic advancement of the New South during the Progres-sive era, as it 'reconciled modernization with the continuation of racial domination'.[24]

What makes the racial intercession of the carceral system different today is that, unlike slavery, Jim Crow and the ghetto of mid-century, it does not carry out a positive economic mission of recruitment and disciplining of the workforce: it serves only to warehouse the precarious and deproletarianized fractions of the black working class, be it that they cannot find employment owing to a combination of skills deficit, employer discrimination and competition from immigrants, or that they refuse to submit to the indignity of substandard work in the peripheral sectors of the service economy—what ghetto residents commonly label 'slave jobs.' But there is presently mounting financial and ideological pressure, as well as renewed political interest, to relax restrictions on penal labour so as to (re)introduce mass unskilled work in private enterprises inside American prisons: putting most inmates to work would help lower the country's 'carceral bill' as well as effectively extend to the inmate poor the workfare requirements now imposed upon the free poor as a requirement of citizenship.[25] The next decade will tell whether the prison remains an appendage to the dark ghetto or supersedes it to go it alone and become America's fourth 'peculiar institution.'

RACE MAKING AND SOCIAL DEATH

Slavery, the Jim Crow system and the ghetto are 'race making' institutions, which is to say that they do not simply process an ethnoracial division that would somehow exist outside of and independently from them. Rather, each *produces* (or co-produces) this division (anew) out of inherited demarcations and disparities of group power and inscribes it at every epoch in a distinctive constellation of material and symbolic forms. And all have consistently racialized the arbitrary boundary setting African-Americans apart from all others in the United States by actively denying its cultural origin in history, ascribing it instead to the fictitious necessity of biology.

The highly particular conception of 'race' that America has invented, virtually unique in the world for its rigidity and consequentiality, is a direct outcome of the momentous collision between slavery and democracy as modes of organization of social life *after* bondage had been established as the major form of labour conscription and control in a underpopulated colony home to a precapitalist system of production. The Jim Crow regime reworked the racialized boundary between slave and free into a rigid caste separation between 'whites' and 'Negros'—comprising all persons of known African ancestry, no matter how minimal—that infected every crevice of the postbellum social system in the South. The ghetto, in turn, imprinted this dichotomy onto the spatial makeup and institutional schemas of the industrial metropolis. So much so that, in the wake of the 'urban riots' of the sixties, which in truth were uprisings against intersecting caste and class subordination, 'urban' and black became near-synonymous in policy making as well as everyday parlance. And the 'crisis' of the city came to stand for the enduring contradiction between the individualistic and competitive tenor of

American life, on the one hand, and the continued seclusion of African-Americans from it, on the other.[26]

As a new century dawns, it is up to the fourth 'peculiar institution' born of the adjoining of the hyperghetto with the carceral system to remould the social meaning and significance of 'race' in accordance with the dictates of the deregulated economy and the post-Keynesian state. Now, the penal apparatus has long served as accessory to ethnoracial domination by helping to stabilize a regime under attack or bridge the hiatus between successive regimes: thus the 'Black Codes' of Reconstruction served to keep African-American labour in place following the demise of slavery while the criminalization of civil rights protests in the South in the 1950s aimed to retard the agony of Jim Crow. But the role of the carceral institution today is different in that, for the first time in US history, it has been elevated to the rank of main machine for 'race making.'

Among the manifold effects of the wedding of ghetto and prison into an extended carceral mesh, perhaps the most consequential is the practical revivification and *official solidification of the centuries-old association of blackness* within criminality and devious violence. Along with the return of Lombroso-style mythologies about criminal atavism and the wide diffusion of bestial metaphors in the journalistic and political field (where mentions of 'super-predators', 'wolf packs', 'animals' and the like are commonplace), the massive over-incarceration of blacks has supplied a powerful common-sense warrant for 'using colour as a proxy for dangerousness'.[27] In recent years, the courts have consistently authorized the police to employ race as 'a negative signal of increased risk of criminality' and legal scholars have rushed to endorse it as 'a rational adaptation to the demographics of crime', made salient and verified, as it were, by the blackening of the prison population, even though such practice entails major inconsistencies from the standpoint of constitutional law. Throughout the urban criminal justice system, the formula 'Young + Black + Male' is now openly equated with 'probable cause' justifying the arrest, questioning, bodily search and detention of millions of African-American males every year.

In the era of racially targeted 'law-and-order' policies and their sociological pendant, racially skewed mass imprisonment, the reigning public image of the criminal is not just that of 'a monstruum—a being whose features are inherently different from ours', but that of a black monster, as young African-American men from the 'inner city' have come to personify the explosive mix of moral degeneracy and mayhem. The conflation of blackness and crime in collective representation and government policy (the other side of this equation being the conflation of blackness and welfare) thus re-activates 'race' by giving a legitimate outlet to the expression of anti-black animus in the form of the public vituperation of criminals and prisoners. As writer John Edgar Wideman points out:

> It's respectable to tar and feather criminals, to advocate locking them up and throwing away the key. It's not racist to be against crime, even though the

archetypal criminal in the media and the public imagination almost always wears 'Willie' Horton's face. Gradually, 'urban' and 'ghetto' have become codewords for terrible places where only blacks reside. Prison is rapidly being re-lexified in the same segregated fashion.[28]

Indeed, when 'to be a man of colour of a certain economic class and milieu is equivalent in the public eye to being a criminal', being processed by the penal system is tantamount to being made black, and 'doing time' behind bars is at the same time 'marking race'.[29]

By assuming a central role in the post-Keynesian government of race and poverty, at the crossroads of the deregulated low-wage labour market, a revamped 'welfare-workfare' apparatus designed to support casual employment, and the vestiges of the ghetto, the overgrown carceral system of the United States has become a major engine of symbolic production in its own right. It is not only the pre-eminent institution for signifying and enforcing blackness, much as slavery was during the first three centuries of US history. Just as bondage effected the 'social death' of imported African captives and their descendants on American soil, mass incarceration also induces the civic death of those it ensnares by extruding them from the social compact.[30] Today's inmates are thus the target of a threefold movement of exclusionary closure:

1. Prisoners are denied access to valued cultural capital: just as university credentials are becoming a prerequisite for employment in the (semi)protected sector of the labour market, inmates have been expelled from higher education by being made ineligible for Pell Grants, starting with drug offenders in 1988, continuing with convicts sentenced to death or lifelong imprisonment without the possibility of parole in 1992, and ending with all remaining state and federal prisoners in 1994. This expulsion was voted by Congress for the sole purpose of accentuating the symbolic divide between criminals and 'law-abiding citizens' in spite of overwhelming evidence that prison educational programmes drastically cut recidivism as well as help to maintain carceral order.[31]

2. Prisoners are systematically excluded from social redistribution and public aid in an age when work insecurity makes access to such programmes more vital than ever for those dwelling in the lower regions of social space. Laws deny welfare payments, veterans' benefits and food stamps to anyone in detention for more than 60 days. The Work Opportunity and Personal Responsibility Act of 1996 further banishes most ex-convicts from Medicaid, public housing, Section 8 vouchers and related forms of assistance. In the spring of 1998, President Clinton denounced as intolerable 'fraud and abuse' perpetrated against 'working families' who 'play by the rules' the fact that some prisoners (or their households) continued to get public payments due to lax

bureaucratic enforcement of these prohibitions. And he proudly launched 'unprecedented federal, state, and local cooperation as well as new, innovative incentive programs' using the latest 'high-tech tools to weed out any inmate' who still received benefits (see opposite), including the disbursement of bounties to counties who promptly turn in identifying information on their jail detainees to the Social Security administration.

3. Convicts are banned from *political participation* via 'criminal disenfranchisement' practised on a scale and with a vigour unimagined in any other country. All but four members of the Union deny the vote to mentally competent adults held in detention facilities; 39 states forbid convicts placed on probation from exercising their political rights and 32 states also interdict parolees. In 14 states, ex-felons are barred from voting even when they are no longer under criminal justice supervision—for life in ten of these states. The result is that nearly 4 million Americans have temporarily or permanently lost the ability to cast a ballot, including 1.47 million who are not behind bars and another 1.39 million who served their sentence in full.[32] A mere quarter of a century after acceding to full voting rights, one black man in seven nationwide is banned from the electoral booth through penal disenfranchisement and seven states permanently deny the vote to more than one-fourth of their black male residents.

Through this *triple exclusion,* the prison and the criminal justice system more broadly contribute to the ongoing *reconstruction of the 'imagined community' of Amercans* around the polar opposition between praiseworthy 'working families'—implicitly white, suburban, and deserving—and the despicable 'underclass' of criminals, loafers, and leeches, a two-headed antisocial hydra personified by the dissolute teenage 'welfare mother' on the female side and the dangerous street 'gang banger' on the male side—by definition dark-skinned, urban and undeserving. The former are exalted as the living incarnation of genuine American values, self-control, deferred gratification, subservience of life to labour; the latter is vituperated as the loathsome embodiment of their abject desecration, the 'dark side' of the 'American dream' of affluence and opportunity for all, believed to flow from morality anchored in conjugality and work. And the line that divides them is increasingly being drawn, materially and symbolically, by the prison.

On the other side of that line lies an institutional setting unlike any other. Building on his celebrated analyses of Ancient Greece, classical historian Moses Finley has introduced a fruitful distinction between 'societies with slaves' and 'genuine slave societies'.[33] In the former, slavery is but one of several modes of labour control and the division between slave and free is neither impermeable nor axial to the entire social order. In the latter, enslaved labour is epicentral to both economic production and class structure, and the slave-master relation provides the pattern after which all other

CLINTON PROUDLY 'CRACKS DOWN' ON INMATE 'FRAUD AND ABUSE'

Good morning. This morning I'd like to talk to you about one way we are working to restore Americans' faith in our national government, in our efforts to shore up Social Security and other vital benefits by cracking down on fraud and abuse.

For 60 years, Social Security has meant more than just an ID number on a tax form, even more than a monthly check in the mail. It has reflected our deepest values, the duties we owe to our parents, to each other, to our children and grandchildren, to those who misfortune strikes, to those who deserve a decent old age, to our ideal of one America.

That's why I was so disturbed some time ago to discover that many prisoners who are, by law, barred from receiving most of these federal benefits, were actually collecting Social Security checks while locked up behind bars. Inmates were, in effect, under our law, getting away with fraud, primarily because it was so difficult to gather up-to-date information on criminals in our nation's more than 3,500 jails. But thanks to an unprecedented federal, state, and local cooperation, as well as new, innovative incentive programs, we're now finishing the job.

The Social Security Administration has produced a continually updated database that now covers more than 99 percent of all prisoners, the most comprehensive list of our inmate population in history. And more important, the Social Security Administration is using the list to great effect. By the end of last year we had suspended benefits to more than 70,000 prisoners. That means that over the next five years we will save taxpayers $2.5 billion—that's $2.5 billion—that will go toward serving our hard-working families.

Now we're going to build on the Social Security Administration's success in saving taxpayers from inmate fraud. In just a few moments I will sign an executive memorandum that directs the Departments of Labor, Veterans Affairs, Justice, Education and Agriculture to use the Security Administration's expertise and high-tech tools to enhance their own efforts to weed out any inmate who is receiving veteran's benefits, food stamps, or any other form of federal benefit denied by law.

We expect that these comprehensive sweeps by our agencies will save taxpayers millions upon millions of more dollars, in addition to the billions already saved from our crackdown on Social Security fraud. We will ensure that those who have committed crimes against society will not have an opportunity to commit crimes against taxpayers as well.

The American people have a right to expect that their national government is always on guard against every type of waste, fraud and abuse. It is our duty to use every power and every tool to eliminate that kind of fraud. We owe it to the American people to ensure that their Social Security contributions and other tax dollars are benefiting only those who worked hard, played by the rules, and are, by law, eligible to receive them. That's exactly what we're trying to do.

Thanks for listening.

President Clinton's Saturday Radio Address, 25 April 1998.
Available on the White House website.

social relations are built or distorted, such that no corner of culture, society and self is left untouched by it. The astronomical overrepresentation of blacks in houses of penal confinement and the increasingly tight meshing of the hyperghetto with the carceral system suggests that, owing to America's adoption of mass incarceration as a queer social policy designed to discipline the poor and contain the dishonoured, lower-class African-Americans now dwell, not in a society with prisons as their white compatriots do, but in the *first genuine prison society* in history.

NOTES

1. See, respectively: Kenneth Stampp, *The Peculiar Institution: Slavery in the AnteBellum South*, New York [1956] 1989; Ira Berlin, *Many Thousands Gone: The First Two Centuries of Slavery in North America*, Cambridge, MA 1998; C. Vann Woodward, *The Strange Career of Jim Crow*, Oxford [1957] 1989; Leon Litwack, *Trouble in Mind: Black Southerners in the Age of Jim Crow*, New York 1998; Allan Spear, *Black Chicago: The Making of a Negro Ghetto*, 1890–1920, Chicago 1968; Kerner Commission, 1968 *Report of the National Advisory Commission on Civil Disorders*, New York [1968] 1988.

2. See my 'Crime et chatiment en Amerique de Nixon a Clinton', *Archives de politique criminelle*, vol. 20, pp. 123–38; and *Les Prisons de la misère*, Paris 1999, pp. 71–94 (English trans. *Prisons of Poverty*, Minneapolis 2002).

3. 'Among the groups commonly considered unassimilable, the Negro people is by far the largest. The Negroes do not, like the Japanese and the Chinese, have a politically organized nation and an accepted culture of their own outside of America to fall back upon. Unlike the Oriental, there attaches to the Negro an historical memory of slavery and inferiority. It is more difficult for them to answer prejudice with prejudice and, as the Orientals may do, to consider themselves and their history superior to the white Americans and their recent cultural achievements. The Negroes do not have these fortifications of self-respect. They are more helplessly *imprisoned* as a subordinate caste, a caste of people deemed to be lacking a cultural past and assumed to be incapable of a cultural future.' Gunnar Myrdal, *An American Dilemma: The Negro Problem and Modern Democracy*, New York [1944] 1962, p. 54; emphasis added.

4. Seymour Drescher and Stanley Engerman, A *Historical Guide to World Slavery*, Oxford 1998.

5. Gavin Wright, *The Political Economy of the Cotton South*, New York 1978; Peter Kolchin, *American Slavery: 1619–1877*, New York 1993.

6. 'Slavery, Race and Ideology in the United States of America', NLR 1/181, May–June 1990.

7. The term comes from a song-and-dance routine, 'Jumping Jim Crow', first performed in 1828 by Thomas Dartmouth Rice, a popular travelling actor considered the father of the 'black-and-white' minstrel show; see Woodward, *Strange Career of Jim Crow.*

8. Neil McMillen, *Dark Journey: Black Mississippians in the Age of Jim Crow*, Urbana 1990.

9. The Mississippi legislature went so far as to outlaw the advocacy of social equality between blacks and whites. A law of 1920 subjected to a fine of 500 dollars

and 6 months' jail anyone 'found guilty of printing, publishing or circulating arguments in favour of social equality or intermarriage': McMillen, *Dark Journey*, pp. 8–9.

10. St. Clair Drake and Horace Cayton, *Black Metropolis: A Study of Negro Life in a Northern City*, New York [1945] 1962, vol. 1, pp. 112–28.

11. *Black Metropolis*, vol. 2, p. xiv.

12. This was the meaning of Martin Luther King's Freedom Campaign in the summer of 1966 in Chicago: it sought to apply to the ghetto the techniques of collective mobilization and civil disobedience successfully used in the attack on Jim Crow in the South, to reveal and protest against the life to which blacks were condemned in the Northern metropolis. The campaign to make Chicago an open city was swiftly crushed by formidable repression, spearheaded by 4,000 National Guardsmen. Stephen Oakes, *Let the Trumpet Sound: The Life of Martin Luther King*, New York 1982.

13. Thomas Byrne Edsall and Mary Edsall, *Chain Reaction: The Impact of Race, Rights and Taxes on American Politics*, New York 1i991; Jill Quadagno, *The Colour of Welfare: How Racism Undermined the War on Poverty*, Oxford 1994; Katherine Beckett and Theodore Sasson, *The Politics of Injustice*, Thousand Oaks 2000, pp. 49–74.

14. By 1975 the carceral population of the US had been steadily declining for nearly two decades to reach a low of 380,000 inmates. The leading analysts of the penal question, from David Rothman to Michel Foucault to Alfred Blumstein, were then unanimous in predicting the imminent marginalization of the prison as an institution of social control or, at worst, the stabilization of penal confinement at a historically moderate level. No one foresaw the runaway growth that has quadrupled that figure to over two million in 2000 even as crime levels remained stagnant.

15. See my 'Gutting the Ghetto' for a historical recapitulation of the meanings of 'ghetto' in American society and social science, leading to a diagnosis of the curious expurgation of race from a concept expressly forged to denote a mechanism of ethnoracial domination, which ties it to the changing concerns of state elites over the nexus of poverty and ethnicity in the metropolis. In Malcolm Cross and Robert Moore, eds, *Globalization and the New City*, Basingstoke 2000.

16. Max Weber, *Economy and Society*, Berkeley 1978, p. 935.

17. Louis Wirth, *The Ghetto*, Chicago 1928.

18. Richard Sennett, *Flesh and Stone: The Body and the City in Western Civilization*, New York 1994.

19. *Black Metropolis*, vol. 2, p. xiii.

20. Describing London's Bridewell, the *Zuchthaus* of Amsterdam and the Paris *Hôopital général*, Georg Rusche and Otto Kirschheimer show that the main aim of the house of correction was 'to make the labour power of the unwilling people socially useful' by forcing them to work under close supervision in the hope that, once released, 'they would voluntarily swell the labour market'. *Punishment and Social Structure*, New York 1939, p. 42; for the modern prison, see Pieter Spierenburg, *The Prison Experience*, New Brunswick, NJ 1991.

21. 'La dérive pénale', *Esprit* 215, October 1995.

22. A fuller discussion of this 'deadly symbiosis' between ghetto and prison in the post–Civil Rights era is provided in my 'Deadly Symbiosis', *Punishment and Society*, vol. 3, no. 1, pp. 95–134.

23. This is not a figure of speech: the annual mortality rate for convicts reached 16 per cent in Mississippi in the 1880s, where 'not a single leased convict ever lived

long enough to serve a sentence of ten years or more'. Hundreds of black children, many as young as six years old, were leased by the state for the benefit of planters, businessmen and financiers, to toil in conditions that even some patrician Southerners found shameful and 'a stain upon our manhood'. See David Oshinsky, *Worse Than Slavery: Parchman Farm and the Ordeal of Jim Crow Justice*, New York 1996, p. 45.

24. Alex Lichtenstein, *Twice the Work of Free Labour: The Political Economy of Convict Labour in the New South*, London and New York 1999, p. 195.

25. See my *Les Prisons de la misère*, Paris 1999, pp. 71–94. Expert testimony presented to the House Committees on the Judiciary and Crime during discussion of the Prison Industries Reform Act of 1998 explicitly linked welfare reform to the need to expand private prison labour.

26. Two indicators suffice to spotlight the enduring ostracization of African-Americans in US society. They are the only group to be 'hypersegregated', with spatial isolation shifting from the macro-level of state and county to the micro-level of municipality and neighbourhood so as to minimize contacts with whites throughout the century. See Douglas Massey and Nancy Denton, *American Apartheid*, Cambridge 1993; Douglas Massey and Zoltan Hajnal, 'The Changing Geographic Structure of Black-White Segregation in the United States', *Social Science Quarterly*, vol. 76, no. 3, September 1995, pp. 527–42. They remain barred from exogamy to a degree unknown to any other community, notwithstanding the recent growth of so-called multiracial families, with fewer than 3 per cent of black women marrying out compared to a majority of Hispanic and Asian women. Kim DaCosta, 'Remaking the Colour Line: Social Bases and Implications of the Multiracial Movement,' Berkeley, Ph.D. Dissertation.

27. Randall Kennedy, *Race, Crime and the Law*, New York 1997, pp. 136–67.

28. John Edgar Wideman, 'Doing Time, Marking Race', *The Nation*, October 30, 1995.

29. 'Doing Time, Marking Race'.

30. Orlando Patterson, *Slavery as Social Death*, Cambridge, MA 1982.

31. Josh Page, 'Eliminating the Enemy: A Cultural Analysis of the Exclusion of Prisoners from Higher Education', Master's thesis, Department of Sociology, University of California, Berkeley.

32. Jamie Fellner and Marc Mauer, *Losing the Vote*.

33. 'Slavery', *International Encyclopaedia of the Social Sciences*, New York 1968.

7
ZIONISM AS A RACIST IDEOLOGY: REVIVING AN OLD THEME TO PREVENT PALESTINIAN ETHNICIDE

Kathleen Christison and Bill Christison

༈

During a presentation on the Palestinian-Israeli situation in 2001, an American-Israeli acquaintance of ours began with a typical attack on the Palestinians. Taking the overused line that "Palestinians never miss an opportunity to miss an opportunity," he asserted snidely that, if only the Palestinians had had any decency and not been so all-fired interested in pushing the Jews into the sea in 1948, they would have accepted the UN partition of Palestine. Those Palestinians who became refugees would instead have remained peacefully in their homes, and the state of Palestine could in the year 2001 be celebrating the 53rd anniversary of its independence. Everything could have been sweetness and light, he contended, but here the Palestinians were, then a year into a deadly intifada, still stateless, still hostile, and still trying, he claimed, to push the Jews into the sea.

It was a common line but with a new and intriguing twist: what if the Palestinians had accepted partition; would they in fact have lived in a state at peace since 1948? It was enough to make the audience stop and think. But later in the talk, the speaker tripped himself up by claiming, in a tone of deep alarm, that Palestinian insistence on the right of return for Palestinian refugees displaced when Israel was created would spell the destruction of Israel as a Jewish state. He did not realize the inherent contradiction in his two assertions (until we later pointed it out to him, with no little glee). You cannot have it both ways, we told him: you cannot claim that, if Palestinians had not left the areas that became Israel in 1948, they would now be living peaceably, some inside and some alongside a Jewish-majority state, and then also claim that, if they returned now, Israel would lose its Jewish majority and its essential identity as a Jewish state.[1]

Originally published in *Counterpunch* (November 8–9, 2003), http://www.counter
punch.org/christison11082003.html. Reprinted by permission.

This exchange, and the massive propaganda effort by and on behalf of Israel to demonstrate the threat to Israel's Jewish character posed by the Palestinians' right of return, actually reveal the dirty little secret of Zionism. In its drive to establish and maintain a state in which Jews are always the majority, *Zionism absolutely required that Palestinians, as non-Jews, be made to leave in 1948 and never be allowed to return.* The dirty little secret is that this is blatant racism.

But didn't we finish with that old Zionism-is-racism issue over a decade ago, when in 1991 the UN repealed a 1975 General Assembly resolution that defined Zionism as "a form of racism or racial discrimination"? Hadn't we Americans always rejected this resolution as odious anti-Semitism, and didn't we, under the aegis of the first Bush administration, finally prevail on the rest of the world community to agree that it was not only inaccurate but downright evil to label Zionism as racist? Why bring it up again, now?

The UN General Assembly based its 1975 anti-Zionist resolution on the UN's own definition of racial discrimination, adopted in 1965. According to the International Convention on the Elimination of All Forms of Racial Discrimination, racial discrimination is "any distinction, exclusion, restriction or preference based on race, colour, descent, or national or ethnic origin which has the purpose or effect of nullifying or impairing the recognition, enjoyment or exercise, on an equal footing, of human rights and fundamental freedoms in the political, economic, social, cultural or any other field of public life." As a definition of racism and racial discrimination, this statement is unassailable and, if one is honest about what Zionism is and what it signifies, the statement is an accurate definition of Zionism. But in 1975, in the political atmosphere prevailing at the time, putting forth such a definition was utterly self-defeating.

So would a formal resolution be in today's political atmosphere. But enough has changed over the last decade or more that talk about Zionism as a system that either is inherently racist or at least fosters racism is increasingly possible and increasingly necessary. Despite the vehement knee-jerk opposition to any such discussion throughout the United States, serious scholars elsewhere and serious Israelis have begun increasingly to examine Zionism critically, and there is much greater receptivity to the notion that no real peace will be forged in Palestine-Israel unless the bases of Zionism are examined and in some way altered. It is for this reason that honestly labeling Zionism as a racist political philosophy is so necessary: unless the world's, and particularly the United States', blind support for Israel as an exclusivist Jewish state is undermined, unless the blind acceptance of Zionism as a noble ideology is undermined, and unless it is recognized that Israel's drive to maintain dominion over the occupied Palestinian territories is motivated by an exclusivist, racist ideology, no one will ever gain the political strength or the political will necessary to force Israel to relinquish territory and permit establishment of a truly sovereign and independent Palestinian state in a part of Palestine.

RECOGNIZING ZIONISM'S RACISM

A racist ideology need not always manifest itself as such, and, if the circumstances are right, it need not always actually practice racism to maintain itself. For decades after its creation, the circumstances were right for Israel. If one forgot, as most people did, the fact that 750,000 Palestinians (non-Jews) had left their homeland under duress, thus making room for a Jewish-majority state, everyone could accept Israel as a genuine democracy, even to a certain extent for that small minority of Palestinians who had remained after 1948. That minority was not large enough to threaten Israel's Jewish majority; it faced considerable discrimination, but because Israeli Arabs could vote, this discrimination was viewed not as institutional, state-mandated racism but as the kind of discrimination, deplorable but not institutionalized, faced by blacks in the United States. The occupation of the West Bank, Gaza, and East Jerusalem, with their two million (soon to become more than three million) Palestinian inhabitants, was seen to be temporary, its end awaiting only the Arabs' readiness to accept Israel's existence.

In these "right" circumstances, the issue of racism rarely arose, and the UN's labeling of Israel's fundamental ideology as racist came across to Americans and most Westerners as nasty and vindictive. Outside the third world, Israel had come to be regarded as the perpetual innocent, not aggressive, certainly not racist, and desirous of nothing more than a peace agreement that would allow it to mind its own business inside its original borders in a democratic state. By the time the Zionism-is-racism resolution was rescinded in 1991, even the PLO had officially recognized Israel's right to exist in peace inside its 1967 borders, with its Jewish majority uncontested. In fact, this very acceptance of Israel by its principal adversary played no small part in facilitating the U.S. effort to garner support for overturning the resolution. (The fact of U.S. global dominance in the wake of the first Gulf war and the collapse of the Soviet Union earlier in 1991, and the atmosphere of optimism about prospects for peace created by the Madrid peace conference in October also played a significant part in winning over a majority of the UN when the Zionism resolution was brought to a vote of the General Assembly in December.)

Realities are very different today, and a recognition of Zionism's racist bases, as well as an understanding of the racist policies being played out in the occupied territories are essential if there is to be any hope at all of achieving a peaceful, just, and stable resolution of the Palestinian-Israeli conflict. The egg of Palestine has been permanently scrambled, and it is now increasingly the case that, as Zionism is recognized as the driving force in the occupied territories as well as inside Israel proper, pre-1967 Israel can no longer be considered in isolation. It can no longer be allowed simply to go its own way as a Jewish-majority state, a state in which the circumstances are "right" for ignoring Zionism's fundamental racism.

As Israel increasingly inserts itself into the occupied territories, and as

Israeli settlers, Israeli settlements, and Israeli-only roads proliferate and a state infrastructure benefiting only Jews takes over more and more territory, it becomes no longer possible to ignore the racist underpinnings of the Zionist ideology that directs this enterprise. It is no longer possible today to wink at the permanence of Zionism's thrust beyond Israel's pre-1967 borders. It is now clear that Israel's control over the occupied territories is, and has all along been intended to be, a drive to assert exclusive Jewish control, taming the Palestinians into submission and squeezing them into ever smaller, more disconnected segments of land or, failing that, forcing them to leave Palestine altogether. It is totally obvious to anyone who spends time on the ground in Palestine-Israel that the animating force behind the policies of the present and all past Israeli governments in Israel and in the occupied West Bank, Gaza, and East Jerusalem has always been a determination to assure the predominance of Jews over Palestinians. Such policies can only be described as racist, and we should stop trying any longer to avoid the word.

When you are on the ground in Palestine, you can see Zionism physically imprinted on the landscape. Not only can you see that there are settlements, built on land confiscated from Palestinians, where Palestinians may not live. Not only can you see roads in the occupied territories, again built on land taken from Palestinians, where Palestinians may not drive. Not only can you observe that water in the occupied territories is allocated, by Israeli governmental authorities, so inequitably that Israeli settlers are allocated five times the amount per capita as are Palestinians and, in periods of drought, Palestinians stand in line for drinking water while Israeli settlements enjoy lush gardens and swimming pools. Not only can you stand and watch as Israeli bulldozers flatten Palestinian olive groves and other agricultural land, destroy Palestinian wells, and demolish Palestinian homes to make way for the separation wall that Israel is constructing across the length and breadth of the West Bank. The wall fences off Palestinians from Israelis, supposedly to provide greater security for Israelis but in fact in order to cage Palestinians, to define a border for Israel that will exclude a maximum number of Palestinians.

But, if this is not enough to demonstrate the inherent racism of Israel's occupation, you can also drive through Palestinian towns and Palestinian neighborhoods in and near Jerusalem and see what is perhaps the most cruelly racist policy in Zionism's arsenal: house demolitions, the preeminent symbol of Zionism's drive to maintain Jewish predominance. Virtually every street has a house or houses reduced to rubble, one floor pancaked onto another or simply a pile of broken concrete bulldozed into an incoherent heap. Jeff Halper, founder and head of the non-governmental Israeli Committee Against House Demolitions (ICAHD), an anthropologist and scholar of the occupation, has observed that Zionist and Israeli leaders going back 80 years have all conveyed what he calls "The Message" to Palestinians. The Message, Halper says, is "Submit. Only when you abandon your dreams for an independent state of your own, and accept that Palestine has become the Land of Israel, will we relent [i.e., stop attacking Palestinians]." The deeper meaning of The Message, as carried by the bulldozers so ubiquitous in targeted Palestinian neighborhoods today, is that "You [Palestinians] do not belong here. We uprooted you from your homes in 1948 and now we will uproot you from all of the Land of Israel."

In the end, Halper says, the advance of Zionism has been a process of displacement, and house demolitions have been "at the center of the Israeli struggle against the Palestinians" since 1948. Halper enumerates a steady history of destruction: in the first six years of Israel's existence, it systematically razed 418 Palestinian villages inside Israel, fully 85 percent of the villages existing before 1948; since the occupation began in 1967, Israel has demolished 11,000 Palestinian homes. More homes are now being demolished in the path of Israel's "separation wall." It is estimated that more than 4,000 homes have been destroyed in the last two years alone.

The vast majority of these house demolitions, 95 percent, have nothing whatever to do with fighting terrorism, but are designed specifically to displace non-Jews and assure the advance of Zionism. In Jerusalem, from the beginning of the occupation of the eastern sector of the city in 1967, Israeli authorities have designed zoning plans specifically to prevent the growth of the Palestinian population. Maintaining the "Jewish character" of the city at the level existing in 1967 (71 percent Jewish, 29 percent Palestinian) required that Israel draw zoning boundaries to prevent Palestinian expansion beyond existing neighborhoods, expropriate Palestinian-owned lands, confiscate the Jerusalem residency permits of any Palestinian who cannot prove that Jerusalem is his "center of life," limit city services to Palestinian areas, limit development in Palestinian neighborhoods, refuse to issue residential building permits to Palestinians, and demolish Palestinian homes that are built without permits. None of these strictures is imposed on Jews. According to ICAHD, the housing shortage in Palestinian neighborhoods in Jerusalem is approximately 25,000 units, and 2,000 demolition orders are pending.

Halper has written that the human suffering involved in the destruction of a family home is incalculable. A home "is one's symbolic center, the site of one's most intimate personal life and an expression of one's status. It is a refuge, it is the physical representation of the family, maintaining continuity on one's ancestral land." Land expropriation is "an attack on one's very being and identity." Zionist governments, past and present, have understood this well, although not with the compassion or empathy that Halper conveys, and this attack on the "very being and identity" of non-Jews has been precisely the animating force behind Zionism.

Zionism's racism has, of course, been fundamental to Israel itself since its establishment in 1948. The Israeli government pursues policies against its own Bedouin minority very similar to its actions in the occupied territories. The Bedouin population has been forcibly relocated and squeezed into small areas in the Negev, again with the intent of forcing an exodus, and half of the 140,000 Bedouin in the Negev live in villages that the Israeli government does not recognize and does not provide services for. Every Bedouin home in an unrecognized village is slated for demolition; all homes, and the very presence of Bedouin in them, are officially illegal.

The problem of the Bedouins' unrecognized villages is only the partial evidence of a racist policy that has prevailed since Israel's foundation. After Zionist/Israeli leaders assured that the non-Jews (i.e., the Palestinians) making up the majority of Palestine's population (a two-thirds majority at the time) departed the scene in 1948, Israeli governments institutionalized favoritism toward Jews by law. As a Zionist state, Israel has always identified itself as the state of the Jews: as a state not of its Jewish and Palestinian citizens, but of all Jews everywhere in the world. The institutions of state guarantee the rights of and provide benefits for Jews. The Law of Return gives automatic citizenship to Jews from anywhere in the world, but to no other people. Some 92 percent of the land of Israel is state land, held by the Jewish National Fund "in trust" for the Jewish people; Palestinians may not purchase this land, even though most of it was Palestinian land before 1948, and in most instances they may not even lease the land. Both the Jewish National Fund, which deals with land acquisition and development, and the Jewish Agency, which deals primarily with Jewish immigration and immigrant absorption, have existed since before the state's establishment and now perform their duties specifically for Jews under an official mandate from the Israeli government.

CREATING ENEMIES

Although few dare to give the reality of house demolitions and state institutions favoring Jews the label of racism, the phenomenon this reality describes is unmistakably racist. There is no other term for a process by which one people can achieve the essence of its political philosophy only by suppressing another people, by which one people guarantees its perpetual numerical superiority and its overwhelming predominance over another people through a deliberate process of repression and dispossession of those people. From the beginning, Zionism has been based on the supremacy of the Jewish people, whether this predominance was to be exercised in a full-fledged state or in some other kind of political entity, and Zionism could never have survived or certainly thrived in Palestine without ridding that land of most of its native population. The early Zionists themselves knew this (as did the Palestinians), even if naïve Americans have never quite gotten it. Theodore Herzl, father of Zionism, talked from the beginning of "spiriting" the native Palestinians out and across the border; discussion of "transfer" was common among the Zionist leadership in Palestine in the 1930s; talk of transfer is common today.

There has been a logical progression to the development of Zionism, leading inevitably to general acceptance of the sense that, because Jewish needs are paramount, Jews themselves are paramount. Zionism grew out of the sense that Jews needed a refuge from persecution, which led in turn to the belief that the refuge could be truly secure only if Jews guaranteed their own safety, which meant that the refuge must be exclusively or at least overwhelmingly Jewish, which meant in turn that Jews and their demands were superior, taking precedence over any other interests within that refuge. The mindset that in U.S. public discourse tends to view the Palestinian-Israeli conflict from a perspective almost exclusively focused on Israel arises out of this progression of Zionist thinking. By the very nature of a mindset, virtually no one examines the assumptions on which the Zionist mindset is based, and few recognize the racist base on which it rests.

Israeli governments through the decades have never been so innocent. Many officials in the current right-wing government are blatantly racist. Israel's outspoken education minister, Limor Livnat, spelled out the extreme right-wing defense of Zionism a year ago, when the government proposed to legalize the right of Jewish communities in Israel to exclude non-Jews. Livnat justified Israel's racism as a matter of Jewish self-preservation. "We're involved here," she said in a radio interview, "in a struggle for the existence of the State of Israel as the state of the Jews, as opposed to those who want to force us to be a state of all its citizens." Israel is not "just another state like all the other states," she protested. "We are not just a state of all its citizens."

Livnat cautioned that Israel must be very watchful lest it find in another few years that the Galilee and the Negev, two areas inside Israel with large Arab populations, are "filled with Arab communities." To emphasize the point, she reiterated that Israel's "special purpose is our character as a Jewish state, our desire to preserve a Jewish community and Jewish majority hereso that it does not become a state of all its citizens." Livnat was speaking of Jewish self-preservation not in terms of saving the Jews or Israel from a territorial threat of military invasion by a marauding neighbor state, but in terms of preserving Jews from the mere existence of another people within spitting distance.

Most Zionists of a more moderate stripe might shudder at the explicitness of Livnat's message and deny that Zionism is really like this. But in fact this properly defines the racism that necessarily underlies Zionism. Most centrist and leftist Zionists deny the reality of Zionism's racism by trying to portray Zionism as a democratic system and manufacturing enemies in order to be able to sustain the inherent contradiction and hide or excuse the racism behind Zionism's drive for predominance.

Indeed, the most pernicious aspect of a political philosophy like Zionism that masquerades as democratic is that it requires an enemy in order to survive and, where an enemy does not already exist, it requires that one be created. In order to justify racist repression and dispossession, particularly in a system purporting to be democratic, those being repressed and displaced must be portrayed as murderous and predatory. And in order to keep its own population in line, to prevent a humane people from objecting to their own government's repressive policies, it requires that fear be instilled in the population: fear of "the other," fear of the terrorist, fear of the Jew-hater. The Jews of Israel must always be made to believe that they are the preyed-upon. This justifies having forced these enemies to leave, it justifies discriminating against those who remained, it justifies denying democratic rights to those who later came under Israel's control in the occupied territories.

Needing an enemy has meant that Zionism has from the beginning had to create myths about Palestinians, painting Palestinians and all Arabs as immutably hostile and intransigent. Thus the myth that in 1948 Palestinians left Palestine so that Arab armies could throw the Jews into the sea; thus the continuing myth that Palestinians remain determined to destroy Israel. Needing an enemy means that Zionism, as one veteran Israeli peace activist recently put it, has removed the Palestinians from history. Thus the myths that there is no such thing as a Palestinian, or that Palestinians all immigrated in modern times from other Arab countries, or that Jordan is Palestine and Palestinians should find their state there.

Needing an enemy means that Zionism has had to make its negotiating partner into a terrorist. It means that, for its own preservation, Zionism has had to devise a need to ignore its partner/enemy or expel him or assassinate him. It means that Zionism has had to reject any conciliatory effort by the Palestinians and portray them as "never missing an opportunity to miss an opportunity" to make peace. This includes, in particular, rejecting that most conciliatory gesture, the PLO's decision in 1988 to recognize Israel's existence, relinquish Palestinian claims to the three-quarters of Palestine lying inside Israel's pre-1967 borders, and even recognize Israel's "right" to exist there.

Needing an enemy means, ultimately, that Zionism had to create the myth of the "generous offer" at the Camp David summit in July 2000. It was Zionist racism that painted the Palestinians as hopelessly intransigent for refusing Israel's supposedly generous offer, actually an impossible offer that would have maintained Zionism's hold on the occupied territories and left the Palestinians with a disconnected, indefensible, non-viable state. Then, when the intifada erupted (after Palestinian demonstrators threw stones at Israeli police and the police responded by shooting several demonstrators to death), it was Zionist racism speaking when Israel put out the line that it was under siege and in a battle for its very survival with Palestinians intent on destroying it. When a few months later the issue of Palestinian refugees and their "right of return" arose publicly, it was Zionist racism speaking when Israel and its defenders, ignoring the several ways in which Palestinian negotiators signaled their readiness to compromise this demand, propagated the view that this too was intended as a way to destroy Israel, by flooding it with non-Jews and destroying its Jewish character.

THE ZIONIST DILEMMA

The supposed threat from "the other" is the eternal refuge of the majority of Israelis and Israeli supporters in the United States. The common line is that "We Israelis and friends of Israel long for peace, we support Israeli withdrawal from the West Bank and Gaza, we have always supported giving the Palestinians self-government. But 'they' hate us, they want to destroy Israel. Wasn't this obvious when Arafat turned his back on Israel's generous offer? Wasn't this obvious when Arafat started the intifada? Wasn't this obvious when Arafat demanded that the Palestinians be given the right of return, which would destroy Israel as a Jewish state? We have already made concession after concession. How can we give them any further concessions when they would only fight for more and more until Israel is gone?" This line relieves Israel of any responsibility to make concessions or move toward serious negotiations; it relieves Israelis of any need to treat Palestinians as equals; it relieves Israelis and their defenders of any need to think; it justifies racism, while calling it something else.

Increasing numbers of Israelis themselves (some of whom have long been non-Zionists, some of whom are only now beginning to see the problem with Zionism) are recognizing the inherent racism of their nation's *raison d'être*. During the years of the peace process, and indeed for the last decade and a half since the PLO formally recognized Israel's existence, the Israeli left could ignore the problems of Zionism while pursuing efforts to promote the establishment of an independent Palestinian state in the West Bank and Gaza that would coexist with Israel. Zionism continued to be more or less a non-issue: Israel could organize itself in any way it chose inside its own borders, and the Palestinian state could fulfill Palestinian national aspirations inside its new borders.

Few of those nettlesome issues surrounding Zionism, such as how much democracy Zionism can allow to non-Jews without destroying its reason for being, would arise in a two-state situation. The issue of Zionism's responsibility for the Palestinians' dispossession could also be put aside. As Haim Hanegbi, a non-Zionist Israeli who recently went back to the fold of single-state binationalism (and who is a long-time cohort of Uri Avnery in the Gush Shalom movement), said in a recent interview with the Israeli newspaper *Ha'aretz*, the promise of mutual recognition offered by the Oslo peace process mesmerized him and others in the peace movement and so "in the mid-1990s I had second thoughts about my traditional [binational] approach. I didn't think it was my task to go to Ramallah and present the Palestinians with the list of Zionist wrongs and tell them not to forget what our fathers did to their fathers." Nor were the Palestinians themselves reminding Zionists of these wrongs at the time.

As new wrongs in the occupied territories increasingly recall old wrongs from half a century ago, however, and as Zionism finds that it cannot cope with end-of-conflict demands like the Palestinians' insistence that Israel accept their right of return by acknowledging its role in their dispossession, more and more Israelis are coming to accept the reality that Zionism can never escape its past. It is becoming increasingly clear to many Israelis that Israel has absorbed so much of the West Bank, Gaza, and East Jerusalem into itself that the Jewish and the Palestinian peoples can never be separated fairly. The separation wall, says Hanegbi, "is the great despairing solution of the Jewish-Zionist society. It is the last desperate act of those who cannot confront the Palestinian issue. Of those who are compelled to push the Palestinian issue out of their lives and out of their consciousness." For Hanegbi, born in Palestine before 1948, Palestinians "were always part of my landscape," and without them, "this is a barren country, a disabled country."

Old-line Zionist Meron Benvenisti, who has also moved to support for binationalism, used almost identical metaphors in a *Ha'aretz* interview run alongside Hanegbi's. Also Palestine-born and a contemporary of Hanegbi, Benvenisti believes "this is a country in which there were always Arabs. This is a country in which the Arabs are the landscape, the natives. I don't see myself living here without them. In my eyes, without Arabs this is a barren land."

Both men discuss the evolution of their thinking over the decades, and both describe a period in which, after the triumph of Zionism, they un-thinkingly accepted its dispossession of the Palestinians. Each man describes the Palestinians simply disappearing when he was an adolescent ("They just sort of evaporated," says Hanegbi), and Benvenisti recalls a long period in which the Palestinian "tragedy simply did not penetrate my consciousness." But both speak in very un-Zionist terms of equality. Benvenisti touches on the crux of the Zionist dilemma. "This is where I am different from my friends in the left," he says, "because I am truly a native son of immigrants, who is drawn to the Arab culture and the Arabic language because it is here. It is the land.Whereas the right, certainly, but the left too hates Arabs. The Arabs bother them; they complicate things. The subject generates moral questions and that generates cultural unease."

Hanegbi goes further. "I am not a psychologist," he says, "but I think that everyone who lives with the contradictions of Zionism condemns him-self to protracted madness. It's impossible to live like this. It's impossible to live with such a tremendous wrong. It's impossible to live with such con-flicting moral criteria. When I see not only the settlements and the occupa-tion and the suppression, but now also the insane wall that the Israelis are trying to hide behind, I have to conclude that there is something very deep here in our attitude to the indigenous people of this land that drives us out of our minds."

While some thoughtful Israelis like these men struggle with philosophical questions of existence and identity and the collective Jewish conscience, few American defenders of Israel seem troubled by such deep issues. Racism is often banal. Most of those who practice it, and most of those who support Israel as a Zionist state, would be horrified to be accused of racism, because their racist practices have become commonplace. They do not even think about what they do. We recently encountered a typical American supporter of Israel who would have argued vigorously if we had accused her of racism. During a presentation we were giving to a class, this (non-Jewish) woman rose to ask a question that went roughly like this: "I want to ask about the failure of the other Arabs to take care of the Palestinians. I must say I sympathize with Israel because Israel simply wants to have a secure state, but the other Arabs have refused to take the Palestinians in, and so they sit in camps and their hostility toward Israel just festers."

This is an extremely common American, and Israeli, perception, the idea being that if the Arab states would only absorb the Palestinians so that they became Lebanese or Syrians or Jordanians, they would forget about being Palestinian, forget that Israel had displaced and dispossessed them, and forget about "wanting to destroy Israel." Israel would then be able simply to go about its own business and live in peace, as it so desperately wants to do. This woman's assumption was that it is acceptable for Israel to have established itself as a Jewish state at the expense of (i.e., after the ethnic cleansing of) the land's non-Jewish inhabitants, that any Palestinian objection to this reality is illegitimate, and that all subsequent animosity toward Israel is ultimately the fault of neighboring Arab states who failed to smother the Palestinians' resistance by anesthetizing them to their plight and erasing their identity and their collective memory of Palestine.

When later in the class the subject arose of Israel ending the occupation, this same woman spoke up to object that, if Israel did give up control over the West Bank and Gaza, it would be economically disadvantaged, at least in the agricultural sector. "Wouldn't this leave Israel as just a desert?" she wondered. Apart from the fact that the answer is a clear "no" (Israel's agricultural capability inside its 1967 borders is quite high, and most of Israel is not desert), the woman's question was again based on the automatic assumption that Israel's interests take precedence over those of anyone else and that, in order to enhance its own agricultural economy (or, presumably, for any other perceived gain), Israel has the right to conquer and take permanent possession of another people's land.

The notion that the Jewish/Zionist state of Israel has a greater right to possess the land, or a greater right to security, or a greater right to a thriving economy, than the people who are native to that land is extremely racist, but this woman would probably object strenuously to having it pointed out that this is a Jewish supremacist viewpoint identical to past justifications for white South Africa's apartheid regime and to the rationale for all European colonial (racist) systems that exploited the human and natural resources of Africa, the Middle East, and Asia over the centuries for the sole benefit of the colonizers. Racism must necessarily be blind to its own immorality; the burden of conscience is otherwise too great. This is the banality of evil.

(Unconsciously, of course, many Americans also seem to believe that the shameful policies of the U.S. government toward Native Americans somehow make it acceptable for the government of Israel to pursue equally shameful policies toward the Palestinians. The U.S. needs to face its racist policies head on as much as it needs to confront the racism of its foremost partner, Israel.)

This woman's view is so very typical, something you hear constantly in casual conversation and casual encounters at social occasions, that it hardly seems significant. But this very banality is precisely the evil of it; what is evil is the very fact that it is "hardly significant" that Zionism by its nature is racist and that this reality goes unnoticed by decent people who count themselves defenders of Israel. The universal acceptability of a system that is at heart racist but proclaims itself to be benign, even noble, and the license this acceptability gives Israel to oppress another people, are striking testimony to the selectivity of the human conscience and its general disinterest in human questions of justice and human rights except when these are politically useful.

COUNTERING THE COUNTER-ARGUMENTS

To put some perspective on this issue, a few clarifying questions must be addressed. Many opponents of the occupation would argue that, although Israel's policies in the occupied territories are racist in practice, they are an abuse of Zionism and that racism is not inherent in it. This seems to be the position of several prominent commentators who have recently denounced Israel severely for what it does in the West Bank and Gaza but fail to recognize the racism in what Israel did upon its establishment in 1948. In a recent bitter denunciation of Zionist policies today, Avraham Burg, a former Knesset speaker, lamented that Zionism had become corrupted by ruling as an occupier over another people, and he longed for the days of Israel's youth when "our national destiny" was "as a light unto the nations and a society of peace, justice and equality." These are nice words, and it is heartening to hear credible mainstream Israelis so clearly denouncing the occupation, but Burg's assumption that before the occupation Zionism followed "a just path" and always had "an ethical leadership" ignores the unjust and unethical policy of ethnic cleansing that allowed Israel to become a so-called Jewish democracy in the first place.

Acknowledging the racist underpinnings of an ideology so long held up as the embodiment of justice and ethics appears to be impossible for many of the most intellectual of Israelis and Israeli defenders. Many who strongly oppose Israel's policies in the occupied territories still, despite their opposition, go through considerable contortions to "prove" that Israel itself is not racist. Rabbi Michael Lerner, editor of the Jewish magazine *Tikkun* and a long-time opponent of the occupation, rejects the notion that Zionism is racist on the narrow grounds that Jewishness is only a religious identity and that Israel welcomes Jews of all races and ethnicities and therefore cannot be called racist. But this confuses the point. Preference toward a particular religion, which is the only aspect of racism that Lerner has addressed and which he acknowledges occurs in Israel, is no more acceptable than preference on ethnic grounds.

But most important, racism has to do primarily with those discriminated against, not with those who do the discriminating. Using Lerner's reasoning, apartheid South Africa might also not be considered racist because it welcomed whites of all ethnicities. But its inherent evil lay in the fact that its very openness to whites discriminated against blacks. Discrimination *against* any people on the basis of "race, colour, descent, or national or ethnic origin" is the major characteristic of racism as the UN defines it. Discrimination against Palestinians and other non-Jews, simply because they are not Jews, is the basis on which Israel constitutes itself. Lerner seems to believe that, because the Palestinian citizens of Israel have the vote and are represented in the Knesset, there is no racial or ethnic discrimination in Israel. But, apart from skipping over the institutional racism that keeps Palestinian Israelis in perpetual second-class citizenship, this argument ignores the more essential reality that Israel reached its present ethnic balance, the point at which it could comfortably allow Palestinians to vote without endangering its Jewish character, only because in 1948 three-quarters of a million Palestinians were forced to leave what became the Jewish state of Israel.

More questions need to be addressed. Is every Israeli or every Jew a racist? Most assuredly not, as the examples of Jeff Halper, Haim Hanegbi, Meron Benvenisti, and many others like them strikingly illustrate. Is every Zionist a racist? Probably not, if one accepts ignorance as an exonerating factor. No doubt the vast majority of Israelis, most very good-hearted people, are not consciously racist but "go along" unquestioningly, having been born into or moved to an apparently democratic state and never examined the issue closely, and having bought into the line fed them by every Israeli government from the beginning, that Palestinians and other Arabs are enemies and that whatever actions Israel takes against Palestinians are necessary to guarantee the personal security of Israelis.

Is it anti-Semitic to say that Zionism is a racist system? Certainly not. Political criticism is not ethnic or religious hatred. Stating a reality about a government's political system or its political conduct says nothing about the qualities of its citizens or its friends. Racism is not a part of the genetic makeup of Jews, any more than it was a part of the genetic makeup of Germans when Hitler ran a racist regime. Nor do Zionism's claim to speak for all Jews everywhere and Israel's claim to be the state of all Jews everywhere make all Jews Zionists. Zionism did not ask for or receive the consent of universal Jewry to speak in its name; therefore labeling Zionism as racist does not label all Jews and cannot be called anti-Semitic.

WHY IT MATTERS

Are there other racist systems, and are there governing systems and political philosophies, racist or not, that are worse than Zionism? Of course, but this fact does not relieve Zionism of culpability. (Racism obviously exists in the United States and in times past was pervasive throughout the country, but, unlike Israel, the U.S. is not a racist governing system, based on racist foundations and depending for its *raison d'être* on a racist philosophy.)

Many defenders of Israel (Michael Lerner and columnist Thomas Friedman come to mind) contend that when Israel is "singled out" for criticism not also leveled at oppressive regimes elsewhere, the attackers are exhibiting a special hatred for Jews. Anyone who does not also criticize Saddam Hussein or Kim Jong Il or Bashar al-Assad for atrocities far greater than Israel's, they charge, is showing that he is less concerned to uphold absolute values than to tear down Israel because it is Jewish. But this charge ignores several factors that demand criticism of Zionist racism. First, because the U.S. government supports Zionism and its racist policy on a continuing basis and props up Zionism's military machine with massive amounts of military aid, it is wholly appropriate for Americans (indeed, it is incumbent on Americans) to call greater attention to Zionism's racism than, for instance, to North Korea's appalling cruelties. The United States does not assist in North Korea's atrocities, but it does underwrite Zionism's brutality.

There is also a strong moral reason for denouncing Zionism as racist. Zionism advertises itself, and actually congratulates itself, as a uniquely moral system that stands as a "light unto the nations," putting itself forward as in a real sense the very embodiment of the values Americans hold dear. Many Zionist friends of Israel would have us believe that Zionism is us, and in many ways it is: most Americans, seeing Israelis as "like us," have grown up with the notion that Israel is a noble enterprise and that the ideology that spawned it is of the highest moral order. Substantial numbers of Americans, non-Jews as well as Jews, feel an emotional and psychological bond with Israel and Zionism that goes far beyond the ties to any other foreign ally. One scholar, describing the U.S.-Israeli tie, refers to Israel as part of the "being" of the United States. Precisely because of the intimacy of the relationship, it is imperative that Zionism's hypocrisy be exposed, that Americans not give aid and comfort to, or even remain associated with, a morally repugnant system that uses racism to exalt one people over all others while masquerading as something better than it is. The United States can remain supportive of Israel as a nation without any longer associating itself with Israel's racism.

Finally, there are critical practical reasons for acknowledging Zionism's racism and enunciating a U.S. policy clearly opposed to racism everywhere and to the repressive Israeli policies that arise from Zionist racism. Now more than at any time since the United States positioned itself as an enthusiastic supporter of Zionism, U.S. endorsement, and indeed facilitation, of Israel's racist policies put this country at great risk for terrorism on a massive scale. Terrorism arises, not as President Bush would have us believe from "hatred of our liberties," but from hatred of our oppressive, killing policies throughout the Arab and Muslim worlds, and in a major way from our support for Israel's severe oppression of the Palestinians. Terrorism is never acceptable, but it is explainable, and it is usually avoidable. Supporting the oppression of Palestinians that arises from Israel's racism only encourages terrorism.

It is time to begin openly expressing revulsion at the racism against Palestinians that the United States has been supporting for decades. It is time to sound an alarm about the near irreversibility of Israel's absorption of the occupied territories into Israel, about the fact that this arises from a fundamentally racist ideology, about the fact that this racism is leading to the ethnicide of an entire nation of people, and about the fact that it is very likely to produce horrific terrorist retaliation against the U.S. because of its unquestioning support. Many who are intimately familiar with the situation on the ground are already sounding an alarm, usually without using the word racism but using other inflammatory terms. Israeli commentator Ran HaCohen recently observed that "Israel's atrocities have now intensified to an extent unimaginable in previous decades." Land confiscation, curfew, the "gradual pushing of Palestinians from areas designated for Jews" have accompanied the occupation all along, he wrote, but the level of oppression now "is quite another story. [This is] an eliminationist policy on the verge of genocide."

The Foundation for Middle East Peace, a Washington-based institution that has tracked Israeli settlement-building for decades, came to much the same conclusion, although using less attention-getting language, in its most recent bimonthly newsletter. Israel, it wrote, is "undertaking massive, unprecedented efforts beyond the construction of new settlement housing, which proceeds apace, to put the question of its control of these areas beyond the reach of diplomacy." Israel's actions, particularly the "relentless" increase in territorial control, the foundation concluded, have "compromised not only the prospect for genuine Palestinian independence but also, in ways not seen in Israel's 36-year occupation, the very sustainability of everyday Palestinian life."

It signals a remarkable change when Israeli commentators and normally staid foundations begin using terms like "unprecedented," "unimaginable in previous decades," "in ways not seen in Israel's 36-year occupation," even words like "eliminationist" and "genocide." While the Bush administration, every Democratic presidential candidate (including, to some degree, even the most progressive), Congress, and the mainstream U.S. media blithely ignore the extent of the destruction in Palestine, more and more voices outside the United States and outside the mainstream in the U.S. are finally coming to recognize that Israel is squeezing the life out of the Palestinian nation. Those who see this reality should begin to expose not only the reality but the racism that is at its root.

Some very thoughtful Israelis, including Haim Hanegbi, Meron Benvenisti, and activists like Jeff Halper, have come to the conclusion that Israel has absorbed so much of the occupied territories that a separate, truly independent Palestinian state can never be established in the West Bank and Gaza. They now regard a binational solution as the only way. In theory, this would mean an end to Zionism (and Zionist racism) by allowing the Jewish and the Palestinian peoples to form a single secular state in all of Palestine in which they live together in equality and democracy, in which neither people is superior, in which neither people identifies itself by its nationality or its religion but rather simply by its citizenship. Impossible? Idealized? Pie-in-the-sky? Probably so but maybe not.

Other Israeli and Jewish activists and thinkers, such as Israel's Uri Avnery and *CounterPunch* contributor Michael Neumann, have cogently challenged the wisdom and the realism of trying to pursue binationalism at the present time. But it is striking that their arguments center on what will best assure a decent outcome for Palestinians. In fact, what is most heartening about the newly emerging debate over the one- versus the two-state solution is the fact that intelligent, compassionate people have at long last been able to move beyond addressing Jewish victimhood and how best to assure a future for Jews, to begin debating how best to assure a future for both the Palestinian and the Jewish people. Progressives in the U.S., both supporters and opponents of present U.S. policies toward Israel, should encourage similar debate in this country. If this requires loudly attacking the American Israel Public Affairs Committee (AIPAC) and its intemperate charges of anti-Semitism, so be it.

We recently had occasion to raise the notion of Israeli racism, using the actual hated word, at a gathering of about 25 or 30 (mostly) progressive (mostly) Jews, and came away with two conclusions: 1) it is a hard concept to bring people to face, but 2) we were not run out of the room and, after the initial shock of hearing the word racist used in connection with Zionism, most people in the room, with only a few exceptions, took the idea aboard. Many specifically thanked us for what we had said. One man, raised as a Jew and now a Muslim, came up to us afterward to say that he thinks Zionism is nationalist rather than racist (to which we argued that nationalism was the motivation but racism is the resulting reality), but he acknowledged, with apparent approbation, that referring to racism had a certain shock effect. Shock effect is precisely what we wanted. The United States' complacent support for everything Israel does will not be altered without shock.

When a powerful state kills hundreds of civilians from another ethnic group; confiscates their land; builds vast housing complexes on that land for the exclusive use of its own nationals; builds roads on that land for the exclusive use of its own nationals; prevents expansion of the other people's neighborhoods and towns; demolishes on a massive scale houses belonging to the other people, in order either to prevent that people's population growth, to induce them "voluntarily" to leave their land altogether, or to provide "security" for its own nationals; imprisons the other people in their own land behind checkpoints, roadblocks, ditches, razor wire, electronic fences, and concrete walls; squeezes the other people into ever smaller, disconnected segments of land; cripples the productive capability of the other people by destroying or separating them from their agricultural land, destroying or confiscating their wells, preventing their industrial expansion, and destroying their businesses; imprisons the leadership of the other people and threatens to expel or assassinate that leadership; destroys the security forces and the governing infrastructure of the other people; destroys an entire population's census records, land registry records, and school records; vandalizes the cultural headquarters and the houses of worship of the other people by urinating, defecating, and drawing graffiti on cultural and religious artifacts and symbols when one people does these things to another, a logical person can draw only one conclusion: the powerful state is attempting to destroy the other people, to push them into the sea, to ethnically cleanse them.

These kinds of atrocities, and particularly the scale of the repression, did not spring full-blown out of some terrorist provocations by Palestinians. These atrocities grew out of a political philosophy that says whatever advances the interests of Jews is acceptable as policy. This is a racist philosophy.

What Israel is doing to the Palestinians is not genocide, it is not a holocaust, but it is, unmistakably, ethnicide. It is, unmistakably, racism. Israel worries constantly, and its American friends worry, about the destruction of Israel. We are all made to think always about the existential threat to Israel, to the Jewish people. But the nation in imminent danger of elimination today is not Israel but the Palestinians. Such a policy of national destruction must not be allowed to stand.

NOTE

1. Assuming, according to the scenario put forth by our Israeli-American friend, that Palestinians had accepted the UN-mandated establishment of a Jewish state in 1948, that no war had ensued, and that no Palestinians had left Palestine, Israel would today encompass only the 55 percent of Palestine allocated to it by the UN partition resolution, not the 78 percent it possessed after successfully prosecuting the 1948 war. It would have no sovereignty over Jerusalem, which was designated by the UN as a separate international entity not under the sovereignty of any nation. Its 5.4 million Jews (assuming the same magnitude of Jewish immigration and natural increase) would be sharing the state with approximately five million Palestinians (assuming the same nine-fold rate of growth among the 560,000 Palestinians who inhabited the area designated for the Jewish state as has occurred in the Palestinian population that actually remained in Israel in 1948). Needless to say, this small, severely overcrowded, binational state would not be the comfortable little Jewish democracy that our friend seems to have envisioned.

8
THE RACISM OF GLOBALIZATION

Anja Weiss

↬

Modern institutions are universalistic in principle but limited in practice. Democracy, for example, means that everyone who is affected by the results of a decision should participate in making that decision (Habermas 1996). As important political decisions may affect all of humankind, democracy should by now be a global institution. On the other hand, the practice of democracy presumes the existence of a public sphere, a Habermasian discourse, a decision-making procedure, and so on. Those preconditions depend on resources such as a common language and thus are limited—most often to the nation-state. The dilemma between universalism and particularist social closure is typical for modern institutions and it becomes more obvious due to globalization processes. Giddens's definition of globalization even emphasizes the problem of global effects: Globalization is "the intensification of worldwide social relations which link distant localities in such a way that local happenings are shaped by events occurring many miles away and vice versa" (Giddens 1990, 64).

In the field of international migration the contradictions of modern institutions are especially visible. Migration used to be a one-way process, and migrants could be conceptually included into their state of origin or destination. Today a significant percentage of migrants go back and forth between their countries of origin and destination. Their social ties link them to two or more countries, and in some cases a third (transnational) social space is developing (Glick Schiller et al. 1992; Pries 1999). Thus the classical assumption that every person clearly belongs to one territory that coincides with one administrative entity and one collective identity is challenged. The myth of a clear-cut national citizenship has become more difficult to uphold.

How can democracies determine the limits of participation in a world in which collective decisions may affect everyone? How can nation-states decide about citizenship, when many people live in transnational social spaces? These questions are related and describe a dilemma common to modern institutions: they follow universalistic norms and have acted as expansive agents of globalization processes. Yet borders are necessary for their functioning, and it is increasingly difficult to justify the selectivity of their inclusion practices.

I will argue that there are no convincing criteria for the closure of modern institutions. They have to close, but due to globalization processes they cannot distinguish clearly and legitimately between those who should and those who should not be included (part 1). This problem is solved by structural racism, which effectively creates barriers between people on the basis of illegitimate and arbitrary criteria. Veiled forms of structural racism have become a basic component of the social structure of modern societies (part 2). On the basis of the first part of the chapter we can distinguish analytically between side-effect exclusion, which is related in content to the border regulation of the national welfare state, and structural racism, which transforms contingent criteria into a basis for national closure (part 3).

In Germany structural racism has undergone enormous changes in content while continuing as a stable form of symbolic power. Structural racism in Germany has referred to varying criteria that are not limited to the black–white divide. Content-centered theories of race are criticized for confusing the contingent criteria of racist closure with the core of racial domination (part 4). The final part of the chapter exemplifies the stability of symbolic domination by analyzing a white German group that fights racism but cannot avoid reproducing its privileged position.

I. BORDER REGULATION OF THE NATIONAL WELFARE STATE

The empirical changes associated with "globalization" have not left traditional sociological concepts unscathed (Beck 2002). While the core of sociological thinking presumes the nation-state to be a self-evident, quasi-natural precondition of social formation (Urry 2000), world systems theory has started from a different perspective. "It was at this point that I abandoned the idea altogether of taking either the sovereign state or that vague concept, the national society, as the unit of analysis. I decided that neither one was a social system and that one could only speak of social change in social systems. The only social system in this scheme was the world-system" (Wallerstein 1974, 7).

The newer forms of systems theory (e.g., in the Luhmannian tradition), conceptually transcend the nation-state. They define social systems as networks of communications. Since communications by now span the globe, this automatically introduces a global perspective to sociology.

Luhmann distinguishes between segmented, stratified and functionally differentiated societies. In segmented and stratified societies persons are integrated into multifunctional entities such as families, households, monasteries, or castes and stratums respectively. Integration is understood as an adaptation of persons to the social norms and values relevant for their social position. In functionally differentiated societies, on the other hand, one person participates in many different subsystems of society. She is not integrated into society as a complete entity but *aspects of* her person are addressed by diverse *sub*systems of society (Nassehi 1997). For example, she may be included in the health system as a patient, in the economic system as an employee, in the financial system as a credit card holder and in the political system as a mayor. Since subsystems in modern societies operate independently from each other, the position of a complete person in a society is highly specific and individualized. Few persons will share exactly the same pattern of inclusions and exclusions.

One of the few exceptions to this argument concerns the relationship of persons to national welfare states. In contrast to the majority of the other subsystems, the political system is territorially (i.e., nationally) segmented. The political system has to address *complete* persons as citizens of the nation-state in order to produce loyalty to the state and legitimacy of decisions (Bommes 1999, 16). This exception to the rule of partial inclusion has far-reaching effects, as the exclusion of a complete person from a nation-state influences inclusion options into other subsystems. Persons who may not enter a national territory are automatically excluded from organizations that operate only in that territory and that require physical presence. Economic organizations presuppose a specific biography and career when they evaluate job applicants (Bommes 2000). As careers depend on nationally organized education systems, candidates from other nation-states typically lack the educational certificates expected by employers in a specific nation-state.[1] According to Bommes, the national welfare state establishes a "threshold of inequality" (see Bommes 1999, 147) that affects numerous functionally differentiated subsystems and the majority of organizations.

Bommes shows that the inclusion of complete persons into national welfare states is an anomaly in a globalized world. While most social systems reach across national borders and address only the *aspects* of persons that are relevant to a specific subsystem, the political system still attempts a clear-cut decision about citizenship referring to *complete* persons. Thereby Bommes offers a partial explanation for the position of migrants in national labor markets. Their disadvantaged position results from a lack of formal citizenship and from the fact that they offer resources that may not be compatible with the expectations of the nationally specific organizations to which they apply. As their career diverges from the national standards of the country of destination, they are treated by economic organizations like the large group of those with relatively low formal education and their cultural capital is not acknowledged. In comparison to local unqualified workers they can gain a favorable market position, however. As they have lower expectations and spend part of their wages in poorer states, the threshold of inequality creates employment niches for first-generation immigrants. In a world in which

wealth is unevenly distributed between nation-states and in which rich national welfare states offer better opportunities and protection to their inhabitants than weak states, international migration improves individual inclusion
options through geographic mobility.

Generally speaking, this argument is quite convincing. Taking a closer
look, the fit between resources and the expectations of organizations turns
into an interesting and contentious question. Staying with the example of
economic organizations, which are profit oriented, we can easily accept that
an organization will prefer applicants with the best individual performance.
This should result in selecting the candidates with the best track record
from as large a pool of applicants as possible thereby paying the lowest
necessary wages. On the other hand, economic organizations depend on
collective goods such as education, social welfare, and trust, which are
cheapest when monopolized by a limited group of people. Bourdieu and
numerous others have shown that organizations tend to prefer applicants
with high social and symbolic capital. As the value of these types of capital
is a matter of opinion, employment is limited to applicants who share the
predominant values in the organization or the field (Bourdieu 1984). Employers may also find it reasonable to reduce the conflicts that might result
from diversity.[2] Recruiting personnel through private networks is seen by
many as a means to avoid conflicts and save recruiting costs. Finally, most
national labor markets are limited to those with citizenship or a work permit. This also reduces the number of potential applicants.

At this point we again run into the problem of universalizing institutions
that cannot legitimize particularized closure. The goal of efficiency explains
why the economic subsystem selects applicants according to individual performance. It can also explain why the number of applicants should be
limited. However, it cannot decide according to which criteria the number
of applicants should be reduced. Similarly the political subsystem and its
most prominent institution—the nation-state—needs to limit its members
but cannot legitimately decide whom to exclude in a globalized world.[3]
Thus we encounter many contradictory and contentious compromises between universalist principles and particularist practice. Take the example of
an Iranian doctor moving to Europe. In Great Britain this doctor will be
incorporated into the public health system easily. In Germany legislation on
foreigners will keep her from working as a doctor. In some regions right-
wing extremists may limit her options in public space so much that she will
not even want to live there as a nurse.

The compatibility between applicants and organizations, between people
and nation-states respectively is not only organized by the needs of specific
systems. It is also mediated by barriers to mobility. Some of these barriers
can be rationalized easily. Most of them respond to the simple goal of
reducing the number of potential applicants and members—which by itself
can increase efficiency. If selection procedures mainly serve the goal of
limiting numbers, it will be impossible to legitimize the criteria according to

which selection takes place. As a result these selection processes are highly contentious, and often practices of social closure step in where formal exclusion fails. Racism can be seen as a part of these barriers to mobility. In the following discussion I will show how arbitrary criteria of social closure can be institutionalized as structural racism. As a result they appear as self-evident and legitimate even though intense political and normative struggles were necessary in order to introduce them.

2. A STRUCTURALIST MODEL OF RACISM

Pierre Bourdieu dealt with the problem of ascribed classifications in his work on male domination. His description of classifications turning into stable social structures can be generalized to other relations of domination. It was first developed with reference to the traditional Kabyle society.

> To account for the fact that women are, throughout most known societies, consigned to inferior social positions, it is necessary to take into account the asymmetry of status ascribed to each gender in the economics of symbolic exchanges. Whereas men are the *subjects* of matrimonial strategies through which they work to maintain or to increase their symbolic capital, women are always treated as *objects* of these exchanges in which they circulate as symbols fit for striking alliances. . . . Male domination is thus founded upon the logic of the economics of symbolic exchanges, that is, upon the fundamental asymmetry between men and women instituted in the social construction of kinship and marriage: that between subject and object, agent and instrument. (Bourdieu and Wacquant 1992, 173f.)

Male domination originates in the gendered classification, due to which men and women enter marriage markets with asymmetrical starting positions. Bourdieu then goes on to show that asymmetrical market positions gain importance by promoting divergent strategies of action. For example, "women can exercise some degree of power only by turning the strength of the strong against them or by accepting the need to efface themselves and, in any case, to deny a power that they can only exercise vicariously, as 'éminences grises'" (Bourdieu 2001, 32). They will appear as cunning, whereby the classification of women as the opposite of men is stabilized. "The androcentric view is thus continuously legitimated by the very practices that it determines. Because their dispositions are the product of embodiment of the *negative prejudice* against the female that is instituted in the order of things, women cannot but constantly confirm this prejudice" (Bourdieu 2001, 32).

As time goes by, both classifications and practices become habitualized and thus part of the accepted social order. Bourdieu speaks of symbolic violence or power (Bourdieu 1998, 209), if subjective structures, like the dichotomous and hierarchical classification of men and women, and objective structures, like the gendered division of labor, coincide without leaving room for doubt or criticism (Bourdieu 1977).[4] "Symbolic power is that invisible power which can be exercised only with the complicity of those who do not want to know that they are subject to it or even that they themselves exercise it" (Bourdieu 1991, 164).

According to Bourdieu, male domination is characterized by the fact that it regulates a specific market: the marriage market and the work of reproduction. Can the mechanism by which classifications develop into social structures also be applied to racialized situations? In this case we would have to generalize Bourdieu's argument from marriage markets to all markets or subsystems of a society.

Let us assume that some actors are delegitimized with reference to arbitrary criteria in a multiplicity of markets. Their right to participate in the markets is contested and they are asked to prove why they should be accepted as equals. In this case a similar process like the one described for male domination would take place. In order for classifications to affect practices, it is sufficient that the right to be included as equals is doubted. For example, an employer will feel some skepticism toward applicants who might have "visa problems." A landlady may anticipate hostility from "normal" tenants if she rents an apartment to "foreigners." Sartre has described the fear of assimilated Jews that someone at some time may start to research ancestry once more (Sartre 1965). Once the threat of delegitimation is generalized, it translates into divergent action strategies and finally into symbolic power.[5] Then delegitimation starts to become largely independent from individual situations. Racialized classifications develop into an objective structuration of society much in the way Bourdieu describes for male domination.

Following and extending Bourdieu's lead, I suggest that the stable forms of racist delegitimation be treated as a specific type of symbolic capital (see Weiss 2001a,b).[6] Racialized symbolic capital is an asymmetrically distributed resource with considerable influence on the life chances of its owners. Physical features such as light skin and an "angelic face" have turned into symbolic goods signifying equal standing. Racialized symbolic capital is similar to cultural capital, since it has to be acquired through lengthy processes of socialization and the collective endeavors of numerous generations. Racialized individuals cannot escape the status attributed to them, even though entire groups can move their position in racial hierarchies, as was the case for Asian Americans in the second half of the twentieth century. Like social capital, racialized symbolic capital is a collective resource, which can, however, be emphasized and utilized by individuals as representatives of a group (Bourdieu 1991, 203–19). Assuming that racial classifications are at least partially institutionalized (e.g., in national citizenship and the differentiated legislation applying to migrants and refugees), it is possible to treat them as capital and introduce them systematically into a theory of social inequality.[7]

If a given society is structured by racialized symbolic capital, this will affect objective class formation. For racially dominated groups, racialized symbolic capital will be a central and explicit dimension of their class position. For members of the racially dominant class, the situation is less clear. Inside a dominant culture aspects of racism that have developed into symbolic power are viewed as self-evident and natural, as "what goes without saying and what cannot be said for lack of an available discourse" (Bourdieu 1994, 165). Therefore members of the dominant group tend to find the possession of racialized symbolic capital so natural and at the same time so implicit that they cannot even put a name to "white privilege" (Frankenberg 1993). Therefore the empirical relevance of the concept of symbolic power is best understood when looking at other societies from a distance (see part 5).

3. THE RACISM OF GLOBALIZATION

We can now distinguish between two different ways in which universalistic institutions like the nation-state limit access. On the one hand, functionally differentiated subsystems and organizations expect specific types of cultural and social capital. It is harder for nonnationals to command this kind of capital. Therefore nonnationals are excluded as a by-product of the "normal" functioning of nationally specific subsystems and organizations (side-effect exclusion).

If this were the only form of closure, it would be difficult to uphold national institutions in a globalizing world. Side-effect exclusion is supplemented by a negative symbolic bias. The right of persons to participate as equals is put into doubt referring to a wide range of contingent criteria. In the long run, symbolic delegitimation results in divergent action strategies and in a racialized form of symbolic capital (structural racism).

Both forms of particularist closure differ in content and function. Side-effect exclusion is linked by content to the functioning of subsystems and organizations. A hospital will only accept medical school graduates as doctors. Structural racism, on the other hand, serves the sole goal of limiting the number of potential participants. Therefore it is based on contingent criteria, which are institutionalized through symbolic power. These criteria can be racist in the narrow sense of the word. They can also refer to national group membership, culture, religion and so on. My case study of Germany shall show that the exact content of racist closure can be extremely variable and contingent.

The functioning of structural racism is specific to all forms of symbolic domination. It is characterized not by content but by form, that is, by a dynamic interrelation of symbolic power and symbolic struggle. "The dominant class has only to *let the system they dominate take its own course* in order to exercise their domination, but until such a system exists, they have to work directly, daily, personally, to produce and reproduce conditions of domination which are even then never entirely trustworthy" (Bourdieu 1994, 184). Symbolic power is self-perpetuating and stable as long as objective and subjective structures coincide. Symbolic struggle results if the fit between subjective and objective structures undergoes an objective change. In that case actors who want to dissolve domination try to make symbolic power visible, to give a name to oppression.

During the first wave of nation-state formation—which often went hand in hand with colonialism—center states succeeded in establishing defined and generally accepted criteria that could distinguish between those who were citizens on an equal standing and those who were not. As a result of globalization processes these criteria have started to shift. Migrants increasingly cross the racialized barriers of center states and often both migrants and established citizens refuse to "melt" into a new nation. This is not just a change in identity formation, but also an effect of transnational markets and technologies which make repeated (trans)migration more likely and feasible than in the nineteenth century. At the same time many tacit agreements that were institutionalized during the violent phase of nation building are in a process of change. It is not self-evident anymore that an alien does not belong or that a person of African decent must have a blue-collar job. Neither can all of us share the belief that citizens can be held hostage by their genocidal governments or that basic rights do not apply to noncitizens.

I have suggested that modern institutions cannot close their borders with reference to legitimate and convincing criteria and that structural racism steps in where legitimate closure fails. The problem of particularist closure and the answer of structural racism are specific to modernity. As globalization threatens the existing balance between objective closure and subjective assumptions, we can observe a resurgence of symbolic struggles about racialized classifications. This "racism of globalization" is not a relic of the past, but a flexible and efficient answer to the border problems of modern institutions in a globalizing world.

4. THE GERMAN CASE

As far as globalization is concerned, the situation in Germany is not very different from that of other welfare states embarked on a neoliberal path of trade liberalization and deregulation. The particular German type of racism is interesting, however, in that it has undergone enormous shifts in content without changing the way it functions. This is relevant to the theory of race relations favored by the English-speaking world, as this theory has emphasized content over structure.

Scholars of race relations usually think of racism as racial prejudice or racialized discourse (Van Dijk 1987; Miles 1989). They acknowledge that the content of the adjective "racial" varies greatly across time and location. Nevertheless they insist on a definition focusing on content, thus stimulating a lively debate about the advantages and disadvantages of narrow versus open definitions of racism. According to Miles (1989) an analytically convincing concept of racialization processes should focus on constructions of race that are closely linked to physical difference. Others have argued that racist discourse adapts to antiracist criticism (Balibar 1991). Thus it would seem that racism disappears, when in fact it is replaced by a "new" racist discourse that constructs groups as essentially and irredeemably different and argues for social distance between them (Balibar 1991; Barker 1981; Kalpaka and Raethzel 1990).

In Germany this argument has taken an interesting turn. Traditionally the term "racism" has been applied to violence against groups targeted as racially inferior by the national socialist genocides— Jews, Sinti and Roma, and to some lesser extent Africans.[8] Few of them survived and even fewer stayed in Germany. Despite some immigration of Eastern European Jews and Roma in the past decades, these groups constitute small minorities in German society today.

After 1945 West Germany experienced two large waves of immigration. In the founding years of the republic, refugees of German decent arrived from former German territory and Eastern Europe. In some states they constituted between a fourth and a third of the population, thus causing enormous integration problems. Yet the German postwar industry needed workers and everyone agreed that these migrants were part of "our people." As a result tensions between established and outsiders (Elias 1994) were overcome in the long run.

When East Germany closed its border in 1961, the immigration of Eastern European ethnic Germans was largely replaced by a recruitment of so-called *Gastarbeiter* (guest workers) in the Mediterranean. They were supposed to return after a while and a high proportion of them did so. After 1973 Germany stopped recruitment. Nevertheless the immigration of these groups continued as a result of existing migration systems, the reunification of families, a growing number of refugees in the 1980s, and the increasing mobility allowed by European unification.

After the wall came down, ethnic Germans from the newly independent states came to Germany in increasing numbers. Officially they are considered citizens. In practice their ethnic identity differs from that of the autochthonous Germans. This means that they are treated as citizens by the state but experience social problems similar to those of "guest workers" and refugees.

As a result of the National Socialist atrocities, the term "race" is no longer used in Germany referring to human beings. Everyday and scientific concepts of "racism" tend to be limited to violence against visible minorities. Visible minorities constitute only a small number of "foreigners," however, and quantitatively speaking hostility and discrimination against the much larger Muslim and especially Turkish minorities is a more important problem. In this situation mainstream scientific discourse argues that anti-foreigner violence should be regarded as a xenophobic form of interethnic conflict (Althoff 1998; Dollase et al. 1999; Stolz 2000; Wahl et al. 2001; for a critique, see Koopmans 2001). As the Turkish are not characterized referring to biological criteria, actions against them would not be viewed as racism. This position coincides with Miles's argument for an analytically precise definition of racism, which draws a strict line between ethnic and racial conflict.

Viewed in a historical perspective, it seems unlikely that the racist ideology that pervaded German society before 1945 should have vanished between 1945 and the 1960s, while a new phenomenon, "xenophobia," suddenly appeared in the 1960s and has remained important ever since. In Germany we can distinguish different phases of immigration, which were accompanied by changes in discourse. But it is not plausible to assume that racism as such vanished and was replaced by a different problem. Instead the structural racism described above is referring to a variety of criteria, such as citizenship, looks, ethnicity, religion and language. It targets Caucasian ethnic minorities and even German citizens of German descent. I will now give an impression of the varying borders separating the people who live in Germany.

Until the year 2000 German politicians stressed that "Deutschland ist kein Einwanderungsland" [Germany is not a country of immigration] and catered to right-wing populism. The *ius sanguinis* treated ethnic Germans as citizens even when they had not lived in Germany for several generations. Children of noncitizens stayed noncitizens as long as they did not actively seek citizenship. This means that they can remain noncitizens even if their parents and grandparents were born in Germany. The law on citizenship was reformed on January 1, 2000, and supplemented with provisions for children born in Germany. Yet the reform impacts only slowly on established structures of inequality. Of the German population, 8.9 percent still are noncitizens, of which 21.4 percent were born in Germany. Fifty-five percent of the "foreign" population has lived in Germany longer than ten years. This population lacks political citizenship, and many live without a secure residence and/or work permit (Beauftragte der Bundesregierung für Ausländerfragen 2002, 300).

The official ascribed criterion in Germany is *"Ausländer"* (foreign citizen). There are no statistics of ethnic and/or racial identity or of physical features such as black or Caucasian. However (children of) migrants who do not "look German" continue to experience social discrimination, even when they have become citizens and when they are completely integrated into "German" social networks and institutions (Mecheril and Teo 1994). Violent attacks have targeted people who "look different." In the year 2000, 64 percent of 998 violent crimes committed in a right-wing extremist context targeted people who were perceived as aliens (Beauftragte der Bundesregierung für Ausländerfragen 2002, 264).

In other cases religion appears to be the relevant criterion. In June 2001 a Mannheim court ruled that the state of Baden-Württemberg did not have to employ Fereshta Ludin as a teacher because she wore a headscarf for religious reasons. Teachers are public officials and thus obliged to appear as neutral employees of the state. The court ruled that this obligation is more important than Ludin's right to religious freedom.[9] Considering that the separation of church and state is not common in Germany, this ruling has been very contentious.[10]

In the German school system language seems to be the main reason for the inequality of migrant children (Gomolla and Radtke 2002).[11] In 1999 every tenth (9.7 percent) alien pupil left school with the right to attend a university as compared to every forth German child (25.5 percent). Twenty percent of the alien children leave school without any diploma (as compared to 8 percent of the Germans) (Beauftragte der Bundesregierung für Ausländerfragen 2002).

These few selected examples show that physical criteria for discrimination in Germany can hardly be distinguished from ethnic, religious, legal, language and other differences.[12] While all of the examples parallel racialized social phenomena, only the criterion of "looks" can be interpreted as "racist" in the traditional sense of the word. In sum they add up to a structure of inequality, a system of domination (Wacquant 1997) guaranteeing that a complex of stable and flexible, of material and socially contingent ascribed criteria are held to be self-evident reasons for discrimination and inequality.

Case studies on the effects of ethnic identity, xenophobia, citizenship, racist discourse, group-focused enmity and so on offer relevant insights into specific discourses of delegitimation. In order to understand the importance of and the interconnections between them, we need to show how culturally flexible and arbitrary criteria for differential treatment can develop into a stable system of domination.

Sadly the scientific debate about the definition of racism mirrors the arbitrariness of selection criteria in processes of social closure. If the *selection* of personnel is justified referring to individual achievement and formal citizenship, it is viewed as legitimate. If persons are *discriminated* on the basis of their looks, accent, friends, or habits, we may talk about racism or ethnic conflict. But how can sociologists distinguish between legitimate and illegitimate types of hierarchy? It may be possible to show that a clear-cut biologist statement, such as "blacks are innately stupid," is definitely considered racist by a majority of people. And we can also assume that a majority of citizens in the Organization for Economic Co-operation and Development (OECD) countries feels legitimized in closing or selectively opening "their" nation-state borders to migrants. The examples differ in content and evaluation, but sociologically speaking they both exemplify collective closure referring to arbitrary criteria. The debate about narrow or wide definitions of racism tries to solve a normative question by developing clear-cut content-oriented definitions. This is impossible and sociologists should rather shed light on the complex processes by which arbitrary classifications develop into social facts.

5. SYMBOLIC POWER AND SYMBOLIC STRUGGLES IN GERMANY

The fact that I am writing about these issues shows that they have already become issues of contention. Structural racism is not limited to symbolic struggles, however. Mostly relations of symbolic power are the problem, which veil domination by making it appear as self-evident. Therefore the empirical relevance of the concept of symbolic power is best understood when looking at other societies from a distance. A German audience will find the one-drop rule in U.S. society amazing. Under the one-drop rule every person who had any African ancestry at all was considered "black." What was once an institution allowing slave owners to profit economically from raping their slaves and then selling their children, over time grew into a generally accepted classification (Davis 1992; Wacquant 1994). The black community started to feel solidarity and in fact demand solidarity from every person with any African heritage at all. In a situation of symbolic power the strategies of both the dominant and the dominated are conceived in a common context, despite the fact that the dominant groups control this system, while the dominated groups adapt to it in an effort to empower themselves.

An American audience may likewise find the German school system's practice of educating children irrespective of their native language amazing. Children who have not learned German from their families either acquire German in voluntary and costly kindergarten (and not from professional language teachers) or they are left to their own resources in school. As the path for higher education diverts from general education in grade 4 (i.e., at age 10), an extremely high proportion of migrant children ends up in the lower echelons of a hierarchically segmented school system (Gomolla and Radtke 2002). Recently this has been publicly discussed under the header "intercultural problems of migrant children." Still the "German only" practice of German educational institutions is considered to be self-evident.[13] The language skills of six-year-olds are viewed as their private affair and their parents are criticized by the public for talking to their children in their native tongue.

Often the content of symbolic struggles hints at symbolic power and the objective conflicts of interest on which the symbolic struggles are based. I will now describe a specific antiracist struggle in Germany, arguing that this struggle—and its blind spots—is typical for the kind of racism that deals with border regulation. In 1998 I observed five white German antiracist groups, as part of a research project on the unintended reproduction of racialized inequality.[14] I have worked with antiracists because they actively oppose racism and do not just conform superficially to antiracist values. If we can observe phenomena among them that are apt to reproduce racial hierarchies, we must assume that the observation is not a result of individual racist intentions, but a symptom of a racially structured society from which not even antiracists can escape.[15]

One of the six groups I observed was a radically leftist volunteer group organizing an antidiscrimination hotline and documentation center, a journal and political protests. Among the thirty group members was one non-white migrant—an obvious underrepresentation of migrants when compared to the population average in the city the group operated in. Therefore the group wondered whether they were discriminating against migrants despite their antiracist intentions. As part of a weekend meeting the group tried to reach an agreement about the definition and causes of "the problem" and to develop solutions.

> Regine: If I am working on the topic "refugees in Germany" I cannot learn 150 languages in order to speak with all of them in their language. . . . This is a specific thematic focus, which does not imply me loving to learn languages.
>
> Alex: But I think that one should start to differentiate between the people who are forced under one conceptual roof all the time. . . . The majority of migrants in the FRG [Federal Republic of Germany] speaks rather good German. They work and live. . .
>
> Birgit [interrupts]: (. . . and write . . .) dissertations.
>
> Alex: Excuse me?
>
> Birgit: And write dissertations.
>
> Alex [?]: Hm?
>
> Birgit: They are even writing dissertations.
>
> Alex: Yes.
>
> Birgit: They are even writing dissertations.
>
> [Laughter][16]

The group was debating reasons why migrants were underrepresented in the group. Half of the group believed that this was due to the migrants' lack of language skills. This argument was exemplified by Regine. She explained that it was impossible for her to communicate with all of the migrants in their language: "If I am working on the topic 'refugees in Germany' I cannot learn 150 languages in order to speak with all of them in their language." During the discussion all kinds of structural impediments to desegregation were mentioned. Most of these obstacles were presented as deficits of migrants: They are not sufficiently integrated into German society. And the antiracist group cannot be expected to overcome all those barriers to integration.

The other half of the group found this discourse racist because it generalized incorrectly and attributed a deficit to migrants and not to those who excluded them. Alex's statement contained two parts: First he argued against any kind of generalization. Second he showed that part of the migrants did know German. Thus in the second part of his argument he used a generalization himself. So far the interaction exemplified a typical symbolic struggle: Is exclusion the migrants' fault or should the majority change their hostile and false concepts about the minority?

In this situation something strange happened. Birgit interrupted Alex and added "and write dissertations." The group members asked three times, what she said and she repeated it three times and added the adverb "even": "They even write dissertations." Finally the group understood her and laughed. Birgit succeeded in showing the absurdity of a discourse fantasizing about the "true" qualities of migrants. Her statement was organized like the other general statements about migrants. It also is true, since some migrants do write dissertations. But as not all migrants write dissertations she created a contradictory statement that finally made the group laugh. Birgit's intervention can be read as an ironic critique of the patronizing discourse Alex and Regine shared.

The interaction also shows a lot about the class position of the antiracist groups. Since the observed groups were members of the middle class, whose main capital is cultural, it was no problem for them to feel solidarity for migrants with inferior cultural capital.[17] They did have a problem envisioning educated migrants however. Even though Birgit's statement was acoustically clear, it took four times until the rest of the group even understood it. In fact, the assumption that migrants are uneducated was so strong that two other groups interrupted their conversation completely after a group member introduced the image of a migrant who is more educated than the majority of the group.

In Germany the educated middle classes need not fear direct competition of migrants as they are protected by the threshold of inequality and by institutional barriers. For example, laws regulating professions usually include clauses which discriminate against aliens even more than the "normal" regulations for residence and work permits.[18] In this setting the educated middle classes can easily support multiculturalism (and look down upon lower-class right-wing extremists who do not understand the beauty of a diverse world). As a result of globalization people who know several languages and cultures and who identify with transnational entities are more marketable in the middle classes than national chauvinists. If, however, migrants turn out to be culturally rich in larger numbers, they could challenge the privileged position of the German middle classes. In this context it makes sense that the antiracist groups whom I have observed tend to view migrants as an unequal oppressed group which can be patronized. Or they ignore the migrant origin of some members of the educated middle classes. Once migrants are presented as migrants *and* culturally rich, the groups do not understand what is said and then work hard at making this fact invisible. Structural racism is not only reproduced through discourse but also through habitualized distinction practices which make it difficult for migrants to be included as migrants *and* equals.

The lines of argument in the observed group can be related to Michel Wieviorka's distinction between two logics of racism: Inegalitarian racism developed during colonialism and it "believes that there is only one universal, that of the dominant race, to which other races can only be subordinated in relations of domination" (Wieviorka 1995, 43). Differentialist racism, on the other hand, "postulates that there are as many universals as there are cultures and, behind each culture, races. It is not possible to rank or compare universals, and each of these represents so many potential threats to the others. Racism, in this case, no longer means relations of domination, but rather the setting apart, the exclusion, and, in the extreme case, the destruction of races which are thought to pose a threat" (Wieviorka 1995, 43). According to Wieviorka the inegalitarian and the differentialist logic of racism go hand in hand empirically.

By relating racism to the border regulation of modern institutions we can explain how both logics of racism connect. The differentialist logic of racism serves to construct "races" in the first place and to keep "different races" at a physical distance. Part of the observed antiracists, e.g., believe that most migrants speak a different language and have other integration deficits that keep them from participating in the group. Their position can also be seen as a discursive response to side-effect exclusion. Once racialized "others" enter the markets of a nation-state, the inegalitarian logic of racism gains importance. Those who "do not really belong here" can be present, but only at the price of inferior status and resulting exploitation. In this case they are disadvantaged by structural racism. The two logics of racism are like the two sides of a coin. By doubting the right of persons to participate as equals, they are either kept at a distance or included as inferiors. Structural racism is different from other forms of domination in that it delegitimates actors inside a social space by referring to their possible exclusion from this space.

If the position of migrants changes (e.g., as a result of globalization) or if it becomes difficult to patronize them (e.g., because they are writing dissertations), we will observe symbolic struggle. The lines of distinction shift and a group that was formerly patronized may now be viewed as "white."

CONCLUSION

When nation-states create a "threshold of inequality," when economic organizations select their employees according to economic, cultural, social and symbolic criteria, when people feel hostile towards "foreigners," we are observing complex systems of domination, which are partly rational, partly traditional and partly hostile. They cannot be characterized by a common content. But they do address a widespread problem: the particular closure of universal modern institutions. I am arguing that structural racism comes in, where official and legitimate reasons fail to justify social closure. Structural racism is a system of tacit domination, which can stabilize barriers to mobility in a globalizing world.

The new racism in Germany can be treated as a testing case for this assumption. It is rarely based on biologist criteria and in fact uses varying concepts, such as citizenship, language, religion, group membership and so on. Nevertheless it offers a social mechanism which can distinguish on a long-term basis between those who interact as equals and those who are either kept at a distance or forced to accept lower status.

I am not proposing that every kind of nationalism is by definition racist. One could imagine shifting limits to the nation-state and criteria for closure which are related in content to the goals of the nation-state. Instead I am suggesting a continuum of closure ranging from benevolent nationalism to outright racist closure. The difference is not in content, but in the form and rigidity of closure and the contingency of criteria. Structural racism works through the tacit and long-term assumptions of symbolic power and it can refer to a wide range of varying criteria. This kind of racism becomes more important when borders are crossed by increasing numbers of migrants and when groups change their status, for example, from colored to Asian to white. By creating stable borders out of contingent criteria, structural racism addresses one of the major problems of modern institutions in a globalizing world: the particularist closure of universalizing institutions.

NOTES

1. Gellner (1993) argues that nation-states emerged *because* they could guarantee a generalized education and a market for that education within their territory.

2. Research on workplace diversity shows that pluralistic employment practices may improve outcomes (Bhawuk et al. 2002) under certain conditions.

3. Citizenship can guarantee stable and legitimate distinctions to some extent (Marshall 1950; Mackert 1999). Nevertheless contradictions between different forms of citizenship abound. Some people are political citizens, but socially excluded or delegitimized. This is very often the case with visible minorities. Soysal (1994) has shown that the Turkish minority in Germany is socially included, but lacks political rights. By itself citizenship cannot guarantee clear and legitimate distinctions in a time of flux either. It must be supplemented by concepts like structural racism, which can show that and how arbitrary criteria can develop into stable inequalities.

4. Bourdieu uses the concept of "doxa" mainly for traditional societies (Bourdieu 1994). In class societies he talks of a dominant culture, which is not self-evident, but forces all other cultures to define themselves as subcultures in relation to their distance from the dominant culture (see Bourdieu 1991, 167).

5. Tilly (1999) describes the diffusion of "durable inequalities" in a similar manner. His model is compatible with the one suggested here, but he puts less emphasis on the dynamic relationship between symbolic struggles and symbolic power, which will be discussed below.

6. By adding social and cultural capital to economist theories of social inequality, Bourdieu developed a culturalist approach to social inequality. His concept of capital is very general: "Capital is accumulated labor (in its materialized form or its 'incorporated,' embodied form" (Bourdieu 1986, 241). The resources which actors own are a result of prior accumulation strategies, and they limit the potential for future action. And Bourdieu argued that apparently disinterested "non-economic" exchanges of symbolic goods (Bourdieu 1998) can mask and reproduce inequality, thereby introducing the concept of symbolic capital.

In spite of this "cultural turn" Bourdieu fails to integrate male domination into his theory of social inequality. He shows how a symbolic classification can develop into a stable difference between people. It becomes part of those institutionalized beliefs which are taken for granted by (almost) everyone, and it changes the life chances of actors. His approach to inequality lacks compelling arguments against the "capitalization" of symbolic delegitimation. Nevertheless Bourdieu does not attribute capital status to this relation of domination. Instead he remains in the Weberian tradition which treats classifications such as age, gender and ethnicity as allocative inequalities within existing class relations.

7. While the United States is characterized by a dualistic black–white racial structure, the social system in Germany offers a continuum of very specific legal and social statuses, which can be compared to the elaborated "mixed-race" systems in Latin America.

8. As national socialist Germany wanted to be a colonial nation, policy toward potential "colonial subjects" was contradictory (Oguntoye 1997).

9. Another case was decided similarly in 2002. Recently the constitutional court has ruled that states have to weigh the importance of religious freedom versus the importance of religious peace in schools. States are allowed to prohibit religious symbols of *all* denominations in order to promote the latter goal. This has resulted in conservative states proposing new prohibition laws, exempting Christian symbols from the prohibition as they are part of "our" cultural heritage. Whether these laws are constitutional is an issue of contention.

10. Social services and many schools follow the principle of subsidiarity—they are often organized by religious organizations, but financed by the state. In this system the state subsidizes social self-organization. However, once a social institution is organized by a church, the church has the right to employ only believers. And since a large proportion of social institutions are organized religiously, this results in a high level of discrimination against nonbelievers. For example, many kindergartens employ only Catholics (including nuns wearing headscarves) even though they are the only institution in a village and mainly paid for by the state.

11. The OECD PISA Study 2000 asked whether both, one or no parent was born in Germany. So far causal links can not be proven, but contextual evidence and other studies point in the direction of language skills as the main reason for disadvantage.

12. A large project researching hostile attitudes avoids this problem altogether by introducing a new concept *"Menschenfeindlichkeit"* (group-focused enmity) "meaning an anti-humanist political attitude which manifests itself especially as a rejection of minorities, such as e.g. foreigners, immigrants, homosexuals, homeless people, handicapped people etc." (Heitmeyer 2002, 3).

13. Additional education in the native tongue is offered to some groups of students in the hope that their parents will return with them to their native country. This education is not enabling them to succeed in the German system, though.

14. Many, but not all, antiracist or multiculturalist groups in Germany consist of a majority of white nonmigrant members. Racism is seen as closely connected to fascism by some Germans and thus is an issue of political contention among white German nationals.

15. A comparison with two other groups did show that the antiracist groups are very skillful in avoiding open racism and even some subtly racist discourse.

16. This quotation and the following ones were translated by me from the German original:

Regine: Wenn ich zum Thema Flüchtlinge in Deutschland arbeite dann kann ich keine 150 Sprachen [lacht] lernen, um mit allen in ihrer Sprache zu sprechen, sondern . . . das is n anderes Thema das nichts damit zu tun hat, dass ich gern (ne) Sprache(n) lerne.

Alex: Aber ich finde, man muss dann schon mal anfangen, die Menschen, die hier immer begrifflich über einen Kamm geschoren werden, des ein bisschen aufzusplitten. . . . Die Mehrheit der Migranten äh Migrantinnen in der BRD, die sprechen ziemlich gut deutsch, die arbeiten leben usw. nichtsdestotrotz [Unterbrechung]

Birgit: (. . . und schreiben . . .) Doktorarbeiten.

Alex: Bitte?

Birgit: Schreiben Doktorarbeiten.

Alex: Hm?

Birgit: Die schreiben sogar Doktorarbeiten.

Alex: Ja.

Birgit: Die schreiben sogar Doktorarbeiten.

[Lachen]

17. Bourdieu has argued that the conflict between the culturally "rich" parts of the dominant classes and the economically rich is structurally homologous to that between the lower and the upper classes. Thus he explains why a cultural avant-garde tends to sympathize with the oppressed (Bourdieu 1984).

18. See sections 2 and 4 of the law on the psychotherapeutic profession (Psychotherapeutengesetz—PsychThG), which was implemented on January 1, 1999.

REFERENCES

Althoff, Martina. 1998. *Die soziale Konstruktion von Fremdenfeindlichkeit.* Wiesbaden: Westdeutscher Verlag.

Balibar, Etienne. 1991. "Is There a 'Neo-Racism'?" In *Race, Nation, Class: Ambiguous Identities,* ed. Etienne Balibar and Immanuel Wallerstein, 17–28. London: Verso.

Barker, Martin. 1981. *The New Racism: Conservatives and the Ideology of the Tribe.* London: Junction Books.

Beauftragte der Bundesregierung für Ausländerfragen. 2002. *5. Bericht über die Lage der Ausländer in der Bundesrepublik Deutschland August 2002.*

Beck, Urich. 2002. *Macht und Gegenmacht im globalen Zeitalter: Neue weltpolitische Ökonomie.* Frankfurt/M: Suhrkamp.

Bhawuk, Dharm, Astrid Podsiadlowski, Jen Graf, and Harry Triandis. 2002. "Workplace Diversity: Emerging Corporate Strategies." In *Human Resources Management,* ed. G. R. Ferris and M. R. Buckley, 84–96, Englewood Cliffs, NJ: Prentice Hall.

Bommes, Michael. 2000. "National Welfare State, Biography, and Migration: Labour Migrants, Ethnic Germans, and the Re-ascription of Welfare State Membership."

In *Immigration and Welfare: Challenging the Borders of the Welfare State,* ed. Michael Bommes and Andrew Geddes, 90–108. London: Routledge.

———. 1999. *Migration und nationaler Wohlfahrtsstaat: Ein differenzierungstheoretischer Entwurf.* Opladen: Westdeutscher Verlag.

Bourdieu, Pierre. 2001. *Masculine Domination.* Stanford, CA: Stanford University Press.

———. 1998. "The Economy of Symbolic Goods." In *Practical Reason: On the Theory of Action,* 92–123. Stanford, CA: Stanford University Press.

———. 1994. "Structures, Habitus, Power: Basis for a Theory of Symbolic Power." In *Culture/Power/History,* ed. Nicholas B. Dirks, Geoff Eley, and Sherry B. Ortner, 155–99. Princeton, NJ: Princeton University Press.

———. 1991. *Language and Symbolic Power.* Cambridge, UK: Polity.

———. 1986. "The (Three) Forms of Capital." In *Handbook of Theory and Research in the Sociology of Education,* ed. John G. Richardson, 241–58. New York: Greenwood.

———. 1984. *Distinction: A Social Critique of the Judgment of Taste.* Cambridge, MA: Harvard University Press.

———. 1977. *Outline of a Theory of Practice.* Cambridge, UK: Cambridge University Press.

Bourdieu, Pierre, and Loïc J. D. Wacquant. 1992. *An Invitation to Reflexive Anthropology.* Oxford: Blackwell.

Davis, James F. 1992. *Who Is Black? One Nation's Definition.* University Park: Penn State University Press.

Dollase, Rainer, Thomas Kliche, and Helmut Moser, eds. 1999. *Politische Psychologie der Fremdenfeindlichkeit: Opfer, Täter, Mittäter.* Munich: Juventa.

Elias, Norbert. [1977] 1994. "A Theoretical Essay on Established and Outsider Relations." In *The Established and the Outsiders: A Sociological Enquiry into Community Problems,* 2d ed., ed. Elias Nobert and John L. Scotson, xv–lii. London: Sage.

Essed, Philomena. 1991. *Understanding Everyday Racism: An Interdisciplinary Theory.* London: Sage.

Frankenberg, Ruth. 1993. *White Women, Race Matters: The Social Construction of Whiteness.* London: Routledge.

Gadlin, Howard. 1994. "Conflict Resolution, Cultural Differences, and the Culture of Racism." *Negotiation Journal* 10, no. 1: 33–47.

Gellner, Ernest. 1993. *Nations and Nationalism.* Oxford: Blackwell.

Giddens, Anthony. 1990. *The Consequences of Modernity.* Stanford, CA: Stanford University Press.

Glick Schiller, Nina, Linda Basch, and Cristina Blanc-Szanton, eds. 1992. *Towards a Transnational Perspective on Migration: Race, Class, Ethnicity, and Nationalism Reconsidered.* New York: New York Academy of Sciences.

Gomolla, Mechtild, and Frank-Olaf Radtke. 2002. *Institutionelle Diskriminierung: Die Herstellung ethnischerDifferenz in der Schule.* Opladen: Leske & Budrich.

Habermas, Jürgen. 1996. *Die Einbeziehung des Anderen: Studien zur politischen Theorie.* Frankfurt/M: Suhrkamp.

Heitmeyer, Wilhelm. 2002. "Group Focused Enmity and Processes of Social Disintegration." Paper presented at "Xenophobia in Central and Eastern Europe" workshop, Budapest, June. www.ceu.hu/cps/eve/eve_xenophobia_heitmeyer.pdf (accessed November 22, 2002).

Kalpaka, Annita, and Nora Raethzel, eds. 1990. *Die Schwierigkeit, nicht rassistisch zu sein.* Leer: Mundo.

Koopmans, Ruud. 2001. "Rechtsextremismus und Fremdenfeindlichkeit in Deutschland: Probleme von heute Diagnosen von gestern." *Leviathan* 29, no. 4: 469–83.

Kriesi, Hanspeter. 2001. "Nationaler politischer Wandel in einer sich denationalisierenden Welt." *Blätter für Deutsche und Internationale Politik* 46, no. 2: 206–13.

Mackert, Jürgen. 1999. *Kampf um Zugehörigkeit: Nationale Staatsbürgerschaft als Modus sozialer Schließung.* Opladen: Westdeutscher Verlag.

Marshall, Thomas H. 1950. *Citizenship and Social Class and Other Essays.* Cambridge, UK: Cambridge University Press.

Mecheril, Paul, and Thomas Teo. 1994. *Andere Deutsche: Zur Lebenssituation von Menschen multiethnischer und multikultureller Herkunft.* Berlin: Dietz.

Miles, Robert. 1989. *Racism.* London: Routledge.

Nassehi, Armin. 1997. "Inklusion, Exklusion, Integration, Desintegration: Die Theorie funktionaler Differenzierung und die Desintegrationsthese." In *Was hält die Gesellschaft zusammen? Bundesrepublik Deutschland: Auf dem Weg von der Konsens- zur Konfliktgesellschaft,* ed. Wilhelm Heitmeyer, 113–48. Frankfurt/M: Suhrkamp.

Oguntoye, Katharina. 1997. *Eine afro-deutsche Geschichte: Zur Lebenssituation von Afrikanern und Afro-Deutschen in Deutschland von 1884 bis 1950.* Berlin: Hoho.

Pries, Ludger, ed. 1999. *Migration and Transnational Social Spaces.* Aldershot, UK: Ashgate.

Sartre, Jean-Paul. 1965. *Anti-Semite and Jew.* New York: Schocken.

Soysal, Yasemin N. 1994. *Limits of Citizenship: Migrants and Postnational Membership in Europe.* Chicago: University of Chicago Press.

Stolz, Jörg. 2000. *Soziologie der Fremdenfeindlichkeit.* Frankfurt/M: Campus.

Tilly, Charles. 1999. *Durable Inequality.* Berkeley: University of California Press.

Urry, John. 2000. *Sociology beyond Societies: Mobilities for the Twenty-first Century.* London: Routledge.

Van Dijk, Teun A. 1987. *Communicating Racism: Ethnic Prejudice in Thought and Talk.* London: Sage.

Wacquant, Loïc, J. D. 1997. "For an Analytic of Racial Domination." *Political Power and Social Theory* 11: 221–34.

———. 1994. "Who Is Black? One Nation's Definition." *Theory and Society* 23, no. 6: 902–8.

Wahl, Klaus, Christiane Tramitz, and Jörg Blumtritt. 2001. *Fremdenfeindlichkeit: Auf den Spuren extremer Emotionen.* Opladen: Leske & Budrich.

Wallerstein, Immanuel. 1974. *The Modern World System: Capitalist Agriculture and the Origins of the European World-Economy in the Sixteenth Century.* New York: Academic.

Weiss, Anja. 2001a. *Rassismus wider Willen: Ein anderer Blick auf eine Struktur sozialer Ungleichheit.* Westdeutscher Verlag: Opladen.

———. 2001b. "Rassismus als symbolisch vermittelte Dimension sozialer Ungleichheit." In *Klasse und Klassifikation: Die symbolische Dimension sozialer Ungleichheit,* ed. Anja Weiss, Cornelia Koppetsch, Oliver Schmidtke, and Albert Scharenberg, 79–108. Opladen: Westdeutscher Verlag.

Wievorka, Michel. 1995. *The Arena of Racism.* London: Sage.

9
TOWARD AN ANTIRACIST AGENDA IN EDUCATION: THE CASE OF MALTA

Carmel Borg and Peter Mayo

⌖

One of the main features of the present historical conjuncture, the intensification of globalization, has brought in its wake not only the mobility of capital but also mass mobility of potential labor power across the globe—two types of mobility that do not occur on a level playing field. In a mode of production always characterized by uneven levels of industrial development (see Marx and Engels 1998), people in the subaltern part of the North–South axis move up north in search of pastures new. The specter of the violent colonial process the old continent initiated has come back with a vengeance to haunt it. This process is exacerbated by the fact that highly industrialized countries require certain types of labor and that this requirement cannot be met via the internal labor market, despite high levels of unemployment in these countries (Apitzsch 1995, 68). The process of mobility of persons from South to North is therefore great.

With southern Europe witnessing mass immigration from North Africa, the Mediterranean plays an important role in this process, serving, in the view of many, as "a kind of Rio Grande" (Richter-Malabotta 2002, 73). Like other countries of the Mediterranean, Malta is firmly caught up in the throes of this mobility process. Sharing with many countries of the region a history of having been an exporter of labor power to several parts of the world, ironically including North Africa but, most particularly, former British colonies of settlement (Attard 1983, 1989, 1999), Malta has been witnessing an influx of immigrants from different parts of Africa and, most particularly, North Africa. Racism against blacks and Arabs, previously played down in the media, is now here for all to see.

Racism has hitherto been given lip service in the discourse, concerning oppression, throughout the islands forming the Maltese archipelago. This can be seen from the fact that the literature dealing with different forms of privilege and oppression in Malta rarely deals with the subject. Class and gender analyses feature prominently in sociological texts produced in Malta (see Sultana 1992, 1997; Sultana and Baldacchino 1994; Darmanin 1992; Baldacchino and Mayo 1997), but in-depth studies on racism are few and far between. In fact, the only monograph-length text to date appeared a few years ago (Calleja 2000). This text certainly fills a void concerning Maltese analysis of social difference and identity. As far as educational literature is concerned, the only article on antiracist education to date appeared in a professional journal (Borg 2002).

ISLAMOPHOBIA

A recent extremely popular television program tackled the issue on two occasions, one in 1999 and one in 2003, both sparking considerable debate in a section of the Maltese press. This debate was characterized by the expression of a particular form of racism—Islamophobia—which is rampant worldwide and has traditionally been a feature of the southern European, or "Latin arc," context. This phenomenon has to be viewed against a southern European historic backdrop featuring periods of Arab domination, which left indelible marks on the culture of these places, and long periods of European colonization marked by Christian wars against the Saracen other. This is true of the Maltese islands, which were under Arab domination for at least three hundred years. This process of domination naturally had its effect on the islands. One of its most tangible legacies is the native Maltese language, which is a derivative of Arabic with an influx of romance words. It is also written in a European script. The legacy is also evident in several Maltese surnames (e.g., Abdilla, Caruana, Saliba) and in most place-names (Rabat, Marsa, Zebbug, Mdina). The period of Arab domination was followed by a lengthy process of European rule, which consolidated Catholicism as the dominant belief system throughout the islands. This process includes (1) the Sicilian period, (2) the period when the islands were ruled by the Order of St. John of Jerusalem and, finally, (3) the British period (which followed two years of French occupation under Napoleon). Catholicism was consolidated during the first two periods. The British period of colonization started in 1800 and officially came to an end in 1964 with the country's independence, though British forces remained in Malta until 1979.

THE SARACEN OTHER

The period of European colonization left a strong Eurocentric imprint on the islands and its inhabitants. A substantial part of this period was characterized by war between European powers, acting as the bulwarks of Christendom, and the Ottoman Empire. Malta was caught up in these wars, especially during its period of rule by the Order of St. John (often referred to as the Knights of Malta), who had settled in Malta after losing the island of Rhodes to the Turks. The events of 1565, when the islands successfully repelled an invasion by Turkish troops, are commemorated every year. Images and anecdotes connected with these events are an important feature of Maltese popular lore. The iconography in works of art commissioned by the Order of St. John also reflected an antagonism toward the Saracen. This type of iconography is nowhere more apparent than at St. John's co-Cathedral in Valletta, one of the island's major artistic attractions that was also the order's church. The Ottoman adversary is represented, in this iconography, as the other (Borg and Mayo 2000 a,b). As always, and using Edward Said's (1978) terms, the iconography reflects an assumption of positional superiority, in the construction of alterity, by those who commission the work. Each sculpted figure of the Saracen other, at St. John's, constitutes an integral feature of the cathedral's ostentatious high baroque setting. The figures referred to here are specifically those of the Turkish slaves supporting the ornate wooden pulpit and the marble slaves shouldering the weight of Grand Master Nicholas Cottoner's monument. One of the latter slave figures brings to mind the typically Western construction of Caliban, the Shakespearean figure which, in conventional Western literary criticism, often prompts commentators to refer to the nature–nurture debate. What we come across here is an exotic representation not only of the Saracen other but, more generally, the non-European. The figure fits the popular Western construction of the non-European, the African in particular, represented as a deficient figure ripe for European missionary intervention. This type of image is a recurring one in the predominantly Roman Catholic country that is Malta. It features prominently in holy pictures and much of the Church's other iconography.

The baroque marble figure of the young Turkish slave, in the Cottoner Monument at St. John's, is reproduced on the front cover of Calleja's book, *Aspects of Racism in Malta*. Given the argument (centering around the issue of Islamophobia) that Calleja carries forward in this book, the choice of such an illustration strikes us as being very apt. In these artistic representations, the Saracen is also demonized, rendered the personification of all that is dark and therefore evil or irrational. This distortion has all the features of the (mis)representation of the other, "based on scientific proof" (Fanon 1963, 296)—decried by Frantz Fanon in *The Wretched of the Earth*. Of course, in Fanon's text, it is the colonized Algerian subject who constitutes alterity.

Given such a racist and Islamophobic representation of the other in both high and popular culture, not only in Malta but throughout southern Europe (e.g., the Sicilian marionettes featuring the Crusader and the Ottoman "predator"), it is not surprising that anything associated with Islam becomes the object of repudiation in the Maltese psyche. As a result, the much-despised Turk is replaced by the feared neighboring Arab, Islam being the common denominator. As Calleja (2000) points out:

> Apart from the international media's systematic campaigns against Arab interests, there is some popular Maltese cultural mythology that compounds these prejudices.

Maltese have been nurtured . . . to associate the Arabs and Islam with hostility and oppression. We have popular myths about Count Roger who liberated Malta from the Arabs and numerous other myths about Arab raids on Malta. This continued with the Knights of Malta who annihilated all historical evidence of our Arab culture and Islamic religion. We thus construe an image based on a variety of stereotypical assumptions that Arabs are hostile, violent, untrustworthy and totally incompatible with our standards and values and must hence be "kept out" both physically and attitudinally. (44)

MISCONCEPTIONS

One point that emerges from this type of racism, predicated on Islamophobia, is an astounding lack of basic knowledge concerning Islam and the Arab world. The two are conflated, when it should be common knowledge that Islam is a world religion that knows no ethnic, racial or geographical boundaries. It makes its presence felt everywhere (Shaykh 'Abd al Wahid Pallavicini 1998). One can find Islamic communities in Malta, the United Kingdom and Italy, just to give three examples. These communities do not consist exclusively of people who would be referred to as "migrants" but also include people coming from families who have been, say, British or Italian for several generations. Ahmed Moatassime underlines that the Arabs, strictly speaking, constitute a minority (approximately one-fifth) among millions of Muslims (Moatassime 2000, 113).

Lack of basic knowledge of the culture of those constructed as other is manifest in the Maltese media, which constructs Arabs as either terrorists or drug dealers. In the latter case, the media focuses exclusively on those caught, at Malta's International Airport, importing drugs, without going beyond the surface to investigate such matters as who really lies behind the operation. Furthermore, such media as school textbooks are often guilty of distorting the culture of *alterity*. We come across distortions as serious as that found in a much-used secondary school history textbook (Education Department of Malta 1976, 129). We are shown the picture of a man sporting a beard and wearing a turban purporting to represent the prophet Mohammed. Distortions such as these border on ignorance of and lack of sensitivity toward the religious values of others. It should, after all, be common knowledge that the Qu'ran prohibits representations of the Prophet and God.

Of course, these distortions are found not only in Malta but elsewhere, as Mahmoud Salem Elsheikh (1999, 47) clearly demonstrates with regard to school texts used in Italy.

While such distortions are reprehensible per se, they become all the more offensive given that the Maltese school population is increasingly becoming multiethnic as a result of the influx of foreigners in Malta. For instance, an Arab community has been present in Malta since the early 1970s, when the then Labor government forged strong ties between Malta and certain Arab states, Libya in particular. Furthermore, in addition to the presence of

Muslims in Maltese schools, there was a period between the 1970s and mid-1980s when a number of Arab teachers, many of whom were Muslim, taught Arabic in Maltese state schools. The Arabic language was rendered a compulsory subject in schools by the then Labor government. It is reasonable to assume that the more multiethnic an environment becomes, the greater the contestation that takes place with respect to the politics of representation. It was, in fact, an Egyptian colleague, a teacher of Arabic, who first brought the distortion in the history textbook to the attention of one of the chapter authors when this author was a teacher of English in a Maltese secondary state school.

Distortions are also found in early Maltese literature, where the term "Turk" is often used interchangeably with Muslim. The imagery generated by the eighteenth- and nineteenth-century literature dealing with the "traditional enemy" (read: Turks) is that of "sons of Mohammed," who regarding the Maltese as "wicked," were bent on "enslaving" Malta to convert it to Islam and to replace the Bible with the Qu'ran. They are also depicted as rapists bent on destroying whatever they found in the villages (Cassola 2000). This reflects the pervasive image of the predator in southern European culture. For many years, this literature was compulsory reading for students at different levels of the Maltese educational system.

EUROCENTRIC CURRICULA

Of course, there is much to argue about the politics of representation in texts used in Maltese schools. One rarely comes across texts in Maltese schools which provide illustrations revealing an ethnic mix. This is often compounded by the fact that, in the case of English language reading texts, the state is still using textbooks (e.g., the graded Ladybird reading books) published in England several decades ago. These textbooks are therefore not reflective of the multiethnic and multiracial contestation and ferment that characterized British society in later years. Furthermore, little seems to be done in the way of rendering courses at Maltese educational institutions less Eurocentric. A classic example here would be *Systems of Knowledge,* introduced as a compulsory area in 1987 at sixth form level. It was originally criticized for attaching little importance to the writings of authors who do not fall within the male Eurocentric framework (and this despite the presence of a huge corpus of African literature available in English). *Systems of Knowledge* was also criticized for being similar in conception to the Great Books and the process of cultural literacy advocated in the United States by Allan Bloom and E. D. Hirsch, respectively (see Borg et al. 1995). A reviewer of the current *Systems of Knowledge* official textbook provides a very positive appraisal of the work. He nevertheless makes the point that the book "could usefully have devoted more systematic attention to the implications of its own boundaries, and to the fact that its orientations are exclusively Eurocentric" (Grixti 1996, 210). He goes on to state, "More could have been made of the fact that other cultural, artistic, intellectual and technological traditions were developed in non European contexts, and that some of the most stimulating developments in art and thought often resulted from contact between different cultural traditions" (Grixti 1996, 210).

ARAB AND ISLAMIC CONTRIBUTIONS

There is often a tendency, when dealing with the Mediterranean, to concentrate exclusively on the southern European and particularly the Greco-Roman traditions, ignoring the other civilizations that have emerged in the African part of the region. These civilizations have also made tremendous contributions to the development of European civilization (see, e.g., Lê Thánh Khôi 1999, 444; 2000, 58), a point stressed by Predrag Matvejevic, who states that one cannot construct a Europe without reference to its "infancy and adolescence," namely, the formative influence of the Mediterranean (Matvejevic 1997, 119). The Mediterranean, of course, comprises the Arab and Islamic civilizations. Elsheikh (1999) regards the antagonism shown in Europe toward these civilizations as indicative of what he calls "the debtor's syndrome": "the person to whom one is indebted is constantly a hated person; particularly if the creditor, as in this case, is a strange body, rejected by the collective consciousness, hated by the political, social, cultural and religious institutions. If anything, the rage against the creditor, in these circumstances, becomes an almost moral duty and a necessary condition for the survival of that society" (literal translation by one of the authors, from Elsheikh 1999, 38).

In misrepresenting Arabs and Islam, Maltese texts and mass media obscure Western culture's indebtedness to those other civilizations that are often denigrated in Western regimes of truth. Of course, this denigration becomes a feature of "common sense" that is manifest in a variety of ways.

There is much to be said, in this context, about popular Maltese expressions. These include such expressions as "Am I black?" *(Mela jien iswed?)* uttered to express resentment at being excluded or overlooked. Other expressions represent Jews and Arabs in a pejorative light.

The ever-increasing presence of Arabs in Malta has also led to expressions of fear concerning the "threat" they are supposed to pose to the preservation of the "Maltese identity," the "Maltese culture" and the country's "Catholic values." As is often the case, we are confronted with an essentialist and totalizing discourse that negates the existence of multiple cultures and identities within a single society. There seems to be little recognition of the fact that there are no fixed identities, a point painstakingly underlined by the Vietnamese author Lê Thánh Khôi (1999, 2000) through a detailed historical overview of the intermeshing of cultures in the Mediterranean. It is a point that underscores the problematic nature of the term "race" itself. As Robert Miles has argued, "owing to interbreeding and large-scale migrations, the distinctions between 'races,' identified as dominant gene frequencies, are often blurred" (quoted in Virdee and Cole 2000, 52–53).

As Carlos Alberto Torres (1998) eloquently states, "Recognition of the complexities posed by the process of hybridization and the notion of multiple identities in the social and the psychological construction of the pedagogical subject should challenge any attempt to essentialize differences based on race, gender, class, nationality, ethnic, religious and sexual preferences" (254).

XENOPHOBIA

Columnists and opinion leaders often express the fear that the Arab population in Malta would grow to such an extent that Malta would eventually become an Islamic state, and therefore lose its "identity" in the process. The following excerpt from an opinion column, entitled "Slay the Infidel," which appeared in the *Malta Independent,* is typical of this position:

> History has taught us that Islam has always spread at the cost of the culture of the people whose lands it has occupied. In larger countries, it would take centuries for Muslim proliferation to make a quantifiable impact. Thus the political aim would not be identified for a long while yet. But Malta is a drop in the ocean where ramifications will be felt much sooner because of its limitations. The race for conquest, if such a conquest is intended, will be quick. Worse, like a stealthy predator, it will be upon us before we know what has hit us. (Zammit Endrich 1999)

Reference to the situation of women in certain parts of the Arab world is often made to justify this xenophobic attitude toward Arabs and Islam. Furthermore, the fear of Arabs and blacks has often led to very blatant and obscene acts of racism that take the form of shops and bars occasionally displaying notices barring Arabs from entering. There have been allegations that bouncers at entertainment spots have been discriminating against certain potential patrons on the grounds of race. It was reported in *The Times,* a Maltese English-language daily newspaper, on November 25, 1999, that a "man of Nigerian origin is considering filing a constitutional case, claiming racial discrimination against the owners of a Paceville [Malta's main entertainment center for young people] night club after black people were allegedly turned away on two occasions recently because of their skin colour" (Galea Debono 1999a, 4). The *Malta Independent on Sunday,* of August 8, 1999, reported a similar incident concerning blacks (Balzan 1999, 1) while *The Times* (Malta) reported a similar complaint by a French professor of Arab origin who felt that he was being discriminated against, when denied entry to a Paceville nightclub, because he was "Arab-looking" (Galea Debono 1999b, 14).

Furthermore, a section of the Maltese broadcasting media has given prominence to the publication, in 1999, of a book by Norman Lowell, a far-right candidate for the 2004 European parliamentary elections, entitled *Credo.* We are not in a position to go into the details of this book since, in keeping with our political convictions, we deliberately refuse to look at its contents. The evidence from the TV discussion programs suggests that this book expounds concepts, on a range of subjects, including race and disability, that smack of neo-Nazi "master race" theories. The author's ideas were, for the most part, decried in the course of the programs. This notwithstanding, the prominence given by TV stations to this book suggests that authors of outrageously racist works constantly prove attractive to the media in its search for the sensational and the "provocative."

LACK OF ANTIRACIST LEGISLATION

The foregoing is indicative of the fact that the gradual development of Maltese society into a multiethnic and multiracial one is marked by tensions that generate a racism which assumes different forms, some subtle and others not so subtle. These acts of racism have occurred with impunity for a long time given that it is only recently that there has been legislation allowing for the prosecution of those inciting racial hatred in Malta, even though there has been pressure for the enactment of antiracist legislation emanating from left-wing groups such as Graffiti.

Furthermore, the former Maltese prime minister is on record as having said that, although Malta's "constitutional principles do not allow racism and there are measures against it," he believes that "The time has come for racism to be made a criminal offense" (Chetcuti 1999, 1). The Graffiti group took the prime minister up on his word and, apart from organizing an activity against racism on July 22, 2000, wrote a letter to the prime minister (signed by the group's general secretary and circulated through e-mail), dated July 19, 2000, expressing their concern at the growing racism and xenophobia in Malta. The group refers in this letter to the publication of *Credo* and the allegations that Africans are being denied access to nightclubs in Paceville. There is also reference, in the letter, to one specific case involving an African who was allegedly beaten up by bouncers at a particular locality in the area. The group also refers to a study by Anthony Abela (forthcoming), from the University of Malta's Department of Sociology, which demonstrates empirically that "intolerance" is rife in Malta in various aspects of life including attitudes toward foreigners. They cite statistics from this study which indicate that 28 percent of Maltese do not want to live in proximity to Muslims, 21 percent consider the presence of Jews to be undesirable, 19 percent are averse to the presence of people of other races, while 16 percent do not want immigrants or foreign workers in the country. The letter calls on the government to introduce legislation against racism and xenophobia.

While there is a pressing need for further antiracist legislation, there is an equal need for progressive transformative action concerning race and ethnicity in different spheres and sites of practice. This chapter focuses on education, the area being conceived of here in its broader context. We argue for an antiracist agenda in education. We now attempt to identify the elements that make up an antiracist agenda in education in Malta and Gozo.

TOWARD AN ANTIRACIST AGENDA IN MALTESE EDUCATION

Two major characteristics of recent media debates on racism were the misuse and abuse of terminology and the lack of understanding of the complex nature of the subject. Panels that included educationists showed limited understanding of the language associated with antiracist projects. With sporadic exceptions, lack of familiarity with the terminology restricted the discussions to commonsense knowledge and spontaneous outbursts, rather than deep analysis. Moreover, different forms of racisms were rendered banal through a totalizing discourse, thereby defrauding the public of a serious debate on the different facets of and routes to racism.

A learning community that is committed to resisting racism cannot afford to refrain from gaining familiarity with the glossary concerning this type of oppression. Educators who have a good grasp of the terminology will automatically understand the complex nature of racism and will be in a position to comment in a complex way on the multiple nature of this form of oppression.

ANTIRACIST EDUCATION: KEY CHARACTERISTICS

Effective antiracist educational programs reflect the perspective that racism is socially constructed and therefore can be reversed. Since most racisms are manufactured within particular contexts, good antiracist programs are sensitive to the particular demographics of the geographic area in which the programs are situated. This means that it is important to address the complexities of racism by including all targeted groups within a given context. It also means that antiracist pedagogies should be reinvented within a lived space to include indigenous knowledges.

Another element that normally characterizes good antiracist programs is their praxial stance. Praxis-oriented programs consider advocacy, action and mobilization as complementary to analysis. Finally, good antiracist programs shun insularity. There is a link between racisms and global capitalism. As a result, participants need to understand how racisms come packaged in cheap products and services.

THE NEW NATIONAL MINIMUM CURRICULUM FOR MALTA: A GOOD START

The new National Minimum Curriculum (NMC), published by the Ministry of Education in December 1999, is inspired by an educational agenda that sets out to socialize students into a pluralistic, democratic and socially inclusive society. As a result, the document, which provides a framework for compulsory Maltese education from the first year of kindergarten (age 3) to the end of the secondary years (age 16), constitutes a good reference point for local educators and learning communities interested in developing an antiracist pedagogy within a scholastic environment.

The National Minimum Curriculum is sensitive to the fact that multicultur-alism and therefore diversity and difference are facts of Maltese life. The term "multiculturalism" is here used in its broader sense (see McLaren 1997; Torres 1998). This immediate and concrete social reality demands that "the educa-tional system should enable students to develop a sense of respect, coopera-tion, and solidarity among cultures" (Ministry of Education 1999, 24). According to the NMC, the development of such crucial skills should help students "better understand individual, local and regional differences and should enable them to live a productive and meaningful life in a context characterized by socio-cultural diversity" (Ministry of Education 1999, 24).

For the above project to materialize, the local educational community should discard methods of teaching built on the illusion that classrooms constitute homogeneous groups. According to the NMC, the community should embrace "a pedagogy based on respect for and the celebration of difference" (Ministry of Education 1999, 30).

Awareness, respect, affirmation and celebration of differences, including bio-differences (see O'Sullivan 1999), are not abstract concepts but con-crete experiences that have to be accessed very early in a child's life. The National Minimum Curriculum asserts that, from an early age, children should participate in an educational process which helps them "identify, appreciate and celebrate the physical, intellectual, emotional and social char-acteristics as well as their differences; enable children to develop a sense of co-operation; promote respect for human rights and the rights of other species" (Ministry of Education 1999, 74). The technological infrastructure is conceived of as an important asset in the antiracist agenda. According to the NMC, "communications technology and information technology can help draw our students closer to other students located in different parts of the world" (Ministry of Education 1999, 27–28).

An educational program intended to imbue students with an antiracist mentality cannot distance itself from historical analysis of how racisms are created, reproduced and hegemonized by privileged groups/communities/ nations. Moreover, the acknowledgment of and high regard for different cultures depends on the appreciation of the different facets of life within different countries and regions. The National Minimum Curriculum recog-nizes the need for students to enrich their cultural capital in this regard. In a section dealing with educational objectives (Ministry of Education 1999, 47–70), the document encourages schools to familiarize students with "the culture, history and different religions of the Mediterranean and Malta's history viewed within this regional context . . . [and] with the culture, history and different religions of Europe" (50).

In addition to this Euro-Mediterranean dimension, the NMC under-scores the need to "ensure that the country can avail itself of a nucleus of people who have a mastery of languages deemed strategically important. These include Chinese, Japanese, Russian and Arabic" (Ministry of Educa-tion, 1999, 82). Also stressed is the need for students to know more about "the characteristics of the most important religions and how each one of them attempts to answer the same fundamental questions concerning human existence" (Ministry of Education, 1999, 52). The areas of knowledge, among many others, provide the informative backdrop for the promotion of greater interest in, understanding of, and empathy and solidarity with societies and cultures.

Educators in Malta who are willing to help in creating an educational context that is culturally pluralistic and antiracial in character should find, in the National Minimum Curriculum, the basic ingredients for a pedagogy that can lead students to confront cultural territorialism. The drafters of this document were particularly sensitive to the fact that the previous National Minimum Curriculum, published between 1989 and 1990, smacked of Eurocentrism (for an analysis of this document, with respect to issues concerning race, class, gender and disability, see Borg et al. 1995). Eurocentrism contradicts the commitment toward genuine and critical multiculturalism, and destroys the possibility for students to understand racism and oppression within themselves and society. In fact, a Eurocentric curriculum supports, in an active or passive way, the perceived "superior" qualities of Western thought and traps students within a cultural fortress. This is an offshoot of or variation on what is often termed "Fortress Europe" centering around an essentialist and outdated fixed notion of what constitutes the "European," a notion that does not reflect the contemporary reality of a Europe characterized by multiracial/ethnic difference.

This cultural fortress breeds in students the mental attitude that whatever is good, advanced, progressive and sophisticated originates in the West. It keeps them trapped within their perceived and preset cultural boundaries, not allowing them to cross the racial and ethnic divides. To adapt a sentence from Henry Giroux, we would argue that, in crossing these borders, they can begin to "challenge" the white and Eurocentric racism to which their "body has grown accustomed" (Giroux 1998, 150). The challenge here is that of moving from a Eurocentric toward a "multicentric" curriculum, to borrow George Sefa Dei's term (Dei 1997). The traditionally subaltern would thus be encouraged to move, in the words of bell hooks (1994), from "margin to centre" (Dei 1997, 81–82). The traditionally subordinated ethnic groups would be allowed possibilities to become major actors in the curriculum and not simply adjuncts to a cast formed of people from the dominant ethnic group (Dei 1997, 83).

EDUCATIONAL PROGRAMS IN SCHOOLS

A genuine antiracist project in schools does not create new subjects. Where there is a commitment toward this pedagogy, all stakeholders within the learning community are perceived as responsible for the concretization of the project. In this way, the school avoids creating "cultural islands" that are incompatible with and/or contradict each other.

An educational program, characterized by an avowedly antiracist stance, needs to be sensitive to the process of human development. In the context of early childhood education, the program should be concrete in orientation, that is to say, it should be close to the immediate life of the children. The development of self-esteem helps individual pupils appreciate friends and adults who form part of their lives. Through the promotion and development of self-esteem, the emotional infrastructure weaves itself with the concrete and visible experience of difference. The concrete experience in this phase of the human continuum manifests itself physically, as well as in different national costumes, cuisine, traditional celebrations, music, dance and other forms of expressive arts. This is only an initial step and we recognize that a genuine antiracist education requires much more than this. We must ensure that all ethnicities, including those of the dominant groups, are included in this process. Furthermore, we must constantly oppose the tendency to exoticize minority ethnic group cultures. As Blair and Cole (2000) point out, with respect to "multicultural" education in Britain:

> The exoticization of minority ethnic group cultures and customs merely served to reinforce the notion that these cultures were indeed "Other" and drew the boundary more firmly between "Them," the "immigrants" or "foreigners," and "Us," the "real" British. Needless to say, this approach itself came under severe criticism as a form of education that was said to be tokenistic and failed to address the real problems of schools and of communities within them. (Blair and Cole 2000, 70)

The aesthetic and tactile environments, which are so crucial at the early childhood level, should be particularly sensitive to the issue of difference. Accurate information about racial and cultural differences and similarities should be evident in the visuals, stories and activity tables and corners, made available to children as part of the learning experience.

At the primary level (ages 5–11), the educational program should continue to build on the process initiated in early childhood. At the primary level, children familiarize themselves with international children's literature and with the history and development of local and regional traditions. Exposure to this literature would, hopefully, enable children to learn how different cultures, societies and communities respond to fundamental human needs. A primary-level program should also help students develop: a positive attitude toward cultures; the will to learn from the experiences of different cultures; and the will to resist different forms of prejudices, intolerance and discrimination. This attitudinal change, together with the basic knowledge, should facilitate the process of developing the necessary skills in cooperation, dialogue, critical thinking, problem solving, conflict resolution and empathy, among other skills. Without the development of these skills, the antiracist project at the primary level will remain a mere academic exercise.

At the secondary level (ages 12–16), concrete experience remains the focal point around which an antiracist pedagogy revolves. The strengthening and consolidation of critical and reflective thinking should lead to the program becoming more praxis-oriented in nature. This means that the personal and social experience of students is scrutinized in the hope that such self-reflection would lead to personal transformation and concrete action. In more specific terms, an antiracist pedagogy at the secondary level should help students:

- Realize how a racial/ethnic identity is created
- Reflect on how they may be unconsciously or actively participating in the racist project
- Understand how they are introduced to and socialized in the racist cultures
- Familiarize themselves with the basic terminology used in describing and arguing against racism
- Familiarize themselves with the experience of ethnic and racial groups present in Malta
- Realize the historical and current link between racism and imperialism
- Realize how racism can intersect with other forms of oppression
- Realize their role as change agents and cultural workers
- Engage in concrete action

At different points of the scholastic journey, students affirm their own identity, confront themselves, analyze and problematize their prejudices, intolerance and cultural ignorance, celebrate difference and become actively engaged in antiracist action.

TEACHER EDUCATION

Teachers who fail to admit the problem of racism in Malta and/or do not think that the means of confronting this problem should include educational intervention will most probably resist attempts to develop an antiracist project in their school. In a context marked by initial resistance or outright rejection, a dialogical approach is key.

A good way for one to start an antiracist project in a school is through action research. This type of research would enable teachers to examine their knowledge of and attitudes toward different ethnic and racial groups and their level of awareness with regard to the different facets of Maltese racism. The results should provide an ideal context for dialogue with teachers.

A school community that feels that there is the right cultural infrastructure to initiate an antiracist project can regard the school's development plan as its initial point of departure. The antiracist project should form an integral part of the school's overarching vision and strategy. The inclusion of an antiracist agenda in the school's development plan accords the project a sense of permanence.

The program of teacher preparation should be inspired and informed by the data obtained through action research and by the dialogue that ensues. While the program should target the specific needs of the educational community, international literature that reports on such projects generally suggests that teachers should be helped to:

- Develop greater awareness of their identity
- Examine their personal knowledge, attitudes and experiences
- Study the link between personal experience and systemic racism
- Examine the link between personal and institutional racism
- Realize how different forms of oppression intersect with and complicate the problem of racism
- Examine how racisms are rationalized
- Examine how Eurocentrism defines what is best
- Analyze different models of multicultural and antiracist pedagogies
- Engage in antiracist projects

Teacher antiracist education should not stop at the end of the aforementioned program. Ongoing preparation, in the form of dialogical and reflective meetings, should sustain the project. Simultaneously, schools need to invest in books and materials that address the foregoing issues.

CONCLUSION: REDEMPTIVE MEMORY

In all the above programs of antiracist education, one can make use of reflective and redemptive (in Walter Benjamin's sense) memory work (Simon 1992; McLaren and Da Silva 1993). This work can possibly encourage a dialectical relationship between reminiscences of a past characterized by massive Maltese emigration (involving members of the teachers' and students' families) and a present marked by increasing immigration. The program can provide historical accounts and evoke memories of the perpetration of racist attitudes toward Maltese migrants who, together with other Mediterranean people and Asians, were often regarded by the receiving authorities (see, for example, what occurred in Canada as the result of a 1910 immigration act) as "undesirable aliens" (Attard 1989, 68).

This aspect of antiracist education can take different forms. This pedagogy can take the form of theater, especially community theater or "theater in education." The inspiration for this idea derives from a dramatic presentation, by a troupe from the Laboratorio Interculturale Comune di Genoa, which took place at Sestri Levante, Liguria, Italy, during an international conference on multicultural education in the Mediterranean (October 22–24, 1998). It involved a juxtaposition of situations reflecting the harsh realities of migration both past and present. The plight of Italians who had migrated to the United States, Argentina and elsewhere, and of Italians from the south moving to the peninsula's northern regions, was juxtaposed against that of Africans (including Arabs) and eastern Europeans, with their personal narratives, moving into Italy (Mayo 2000). Theater and other cultural work along these lines can help develop a dialectical relationship between past and present that can have a redemptive effect on the participants, in the hope of fostering interethnic and interracial solidarity.

NOTE

This chapter draws material from Borg 2002 and Mayo 2000.

REFERENCES

Abela, A. M. Forthcoming. *Values 2000: European Values Studies (Malta 1984–1999)*. Summary of preliminary report submitted to the Government of Malta, September 13, 1999. http://staff.um.edu.mt/aabe2/Report99.htm.

Apitzsch, U. 1995. *Razzismo ed Atteggiamenti Verso gli Immigrati Stranieri: Il Caso della Republica Federale Tedesca* [Racism and Attitudes toward Foreign Immigrants: The Case of the German Federal Republic]. Messina, Malta: University of Messina.

Attard, L. E. 1999. *L-EMIGRAZZJONI Maltija: Is-seklu dsatax u ghoxrin*. Pieta, Malta: pin.

———. 1989. *The Great Exodus (1918–1939)*. Marsa, Malta: PEG Ltd.

———. 1983. *Early Maltese Emigration (1900–1914)*. Valletta, Malta: Gulf Publication.

Baldacchino, G., and P. Mayo, eds. 1997. *Beyond Schooling: Adult Education in Malta*. Msida, Malta: Mireva.

Balzan, S. 1999. "Racism Is Not a Criminal Offense in Malta: 'No Blacks' Rule Imposed in Popular Paceville Bar." *Malta Independent*, August 8, 1999, 1.

Blair, M., and M. Cole. 2000. "Racism and Education: The Imperial Legacy." In *Education, Equality and Human Rights: Issues of Gender, "Race," Sexuality, Special Needs and Social Class*, ed. M. Cole, 58–77. London: Routledge/Falmer.

Borg, C. 2002. "Lejn agenda anti-razzista fl-edukazzjoni" [Toward an Anti-Racist Agenda in Education]. *Education 2000*, 7: 27–29.

Borg, C., J. Camilleri, P. Mayo, and T. Xerri. 1995. "Malta's National Curriculum: A Critical Analysis." *International Review of Education* 41, no. 5: 337–56.

Borg, C., and P. Mayo. 2000a. "Malta." In *Museums and Adult Learning: Perspectives from Europe*, ed. A. Chadwick and A. Stannett. Leicester, UK: NIACE.

———. 2000b. "Museums, Adult Education, and Cultural Politics: Malta." *Education and Society* 18, no. 3: 77–97.

Calleja, M. 2000. *Aspects of Racism in Malta*. Bormla, Malta: Mid-Dlam Ghad-Dawl (Daritama).

Cassola, A. 2000. *The Literature of Malta: An Example of Unity in Diversity*. Sliema, Malta: Minima.

Chetcuti, S. 1999. "Plans to Make Racism a Criminal Offense." *Malta Independent*, August 17, 1999, 1.

Darmanin, M., ed. 1992. "Gender and Education." Special issue of *Education (Malta)* 4, no. 4.

Dei, G. S. 1997. *Anti-Racism Education: Theory and Practice*. Halifax, Canada: Fernwood.

Education Department of Malta. 1976. *Grajjiet Malta,* book 1; Valletta, Malta: Education Department.

Elsheikh, M. 1999. "Le omissioni della cultural italiana" [The Omissions of Italian Culture]. In *Islam nella Scuola* [Islam in Schools], ed. I. Siggillino and Franco Angeli, 30–45. Milan: Franco Angeli.

Fanon, Frantz. 1963. *The Wretched of the Earth.* New York: Grove.

Galea Debono, F. 1999a. "Man on Mission to Fight Racism in Malta. Considering Filing Case against Paceville Night Club—But Club Management Denies Any Form of Discrimination against Blacks." *The Times* (Malta), November 25, 4.

———. 1999b. "French Professor Complains of Inhuman Discrimination: This Is Worse Than Racism.'" *The Times* (Malta), November 23, 14.

Giroux, Henry. 1998. "Critical Pedagogy as Performative Practice: Memories of Whiteness." In *Sociology of Education: Emerging Perspectives,* ed. C. A. Torres and T. R. Mitchell, 143–53. Albany, NY: SUNY Press.

Grixti, J. 1996. Review of J. Giordmaina, ed., "Systems of Knowledge: A Guide, Book 1: Antiquity and Early Middle Ages, Middle Ages and Renaissance." *Mediterranean Journal of Educational Studies* 1, no. 2: 209–11.

hooks, bell. 1994. *Feminist Theory: From Margin to Center.* Boston: South End.

Lê Thánh Khôi. 2000. "Il Mediterraneo e il Dialogo fra le Civilta" [The Mediterranean and Dialogue among Civilizations]. In *Un mare di opportunita: Cultura e educazione nel mediterraneo del lll millenio* [A Sea of Opportunity: Culture and Education in the Mediterranean of the Third Millennium], ed. G. Pampanini. Rome: Armando Editore.

———. 1999. *Educazione e civilta: Le società di ieri* [Education and Civilization: Yesterday's Societies], trans. G. Pampanini. Rome: Armando Editore.

Marx, Karl, and Friedrich Engels. 1998. *The Communist Manifesto.* New York: Monthly Review Press.

Matvejevic, P. 1997. Address to the Civil Forum EuroMed. In *Obiettivi e mezzi per il partenariato euromediterraneo: Il forum civile euromed* [Objectives and Means for a Euro-Mediterranean Partnership: The Civil Forum Euromed], ed. Laboratorio Mediterraneo. Naples: Magma.

Mayo, P. 2000. "Globalization, Postcolonialism, and Identity: The Role of Education in the Mediterranean Region." Paper presented at the international course Redefining Cultural Identities: The Multicultural Contexts of the Central European and Mediterranean Regions, Inter-university Centre, Dubrovnik, May 16.

McLaren, Peter. 1997. *Revolutionary Multiculturalism: Pedagogies of Dissent for the New Millennium.* Boulder, CO: Westview.

McLaren, Peter, and T. T. Da Silva. 1993. "Decentering Pedagogy: Critical Literacy, Resistance and the Politics of Memory." In *Paulo Freire: A Critical Encounter,* ed. Peter McLaren and P. Leonard. New York: Routledge.

Ministry of Education [Malta]. 1999. *Creating the Future Together: National Minimum Curriculum.* Floriana, Malta: Ministry of Education.

Moatassime, A. 2000. "Mediterraneo fra plurilinguismo e pluriculturalita" [The Mediterranean: Between Linguistic Pluralism and Cultural Pluralism]. In *Un mare di opportunita: Cultura e educazione nel mediterraneo del lll millenio* [A Sea of Opportunity: Culture and Education in the Mediterranean of the Third Millennium], ed. G. Pampanini. Rome: Armando Editore.

O'Sullivan, E. 1999. *Transformative Learning: Educational Vision for the Twenty-first Century.* London: Zed.

Richter-Malabotta, M. 2002. "Toward A Multicultural Italy." *Journal of Postcolonial Education* 1, no. 2:69–79.

Said, Edward. 1978. *Orientalism.* New York: Random House.

Shaykh 'Abd al Wahid Pallavicini. 1998. "Identita'e differenze" [Identity and Differences]. Paper presented at the international conference, "Il mare che unisce: Scuola, Europa e Mediterraneo" [The Sea That Unites: School, Europe, and the Mediterranean], Sestri Levante, Italy, Oct. 22–24.

Simon, R. I. 1992. *Teaching against the Grain: Texts for a Pedagogy of Possibility.* Toronto: OISE Press.

Sultana, R. G., ed. 1997. *Inside/Outside Schools.* San Gwann, Malta: PEG Ltd.

———. 1992. *Themes in Education.* Msida, Malta: Mireva.

Sultana, R. G., and G. Baldacchino, eds. 1994. *Maltese Society: A Sociological Inquiry.* Msida, Malta: Mireva.

Torres, C. A. 1998. *Democracy, Education, and Multiculturalism: Dilemmas of Citizenship in a Global World.* Lanham, MD: Rowman & Littlefield.

Virdee, S., and M. Cole. 2000. "'Race,' Racism, and Resistance." In *Education, Equality, and Human Rights: Issues of Gender, "Race," Sexuality, Special Needs, and Social Class,* ed. M. Cole. London: Routledge/Falmer.

Zammit Endrich, S. 1999. "Slay the Infidel." *Malta Independent,* July 24, 8.

10
GLOBALIZATION BETWEEN UNIVERSAL SAMENESS AND ABSOLUTE DIVISIONS: CREATING SHARED PEDAGOGICAL BORDER ZONES AS AN ANTIRACIST STRATEGY

Anna Aluffi Pentini and Walter Lorenz

ᴥ

> The river succours and impedes native and foreigner; it limits and it en-
> ables, it isolates and it joins. It is the highway of commerce and it is a
> danger and a nuisance.
>
> —*Timothy Mo,* "An Insular Possession," 1986

Globalization has a profound effect not only on the economic and political world order but also on the development of social relationships. "Globalization can thus be defined as the intensification of worldwide social relations which link distant localities in such a way that local happenings are shaped by events occurring many miles away and vice versa" (Giddens 1991, 64). For pedagogy this poses profound challenges as to how to shape these new social relations by utilizing the learning spaces opening up within these developments.

Much has been written about the significance of economic globalization. Some argue it marks a quantum leap of capitalism that transforms all previous economic relations into something new, bewildering and potentially dangerous that breaks the established rules of capitalism (e.g., Lash and Urry 1987). Others see it merely as bringing to fruition a well-known tendency within capitalism that seeks to transcend national boundaries and release the self-steering capacity of individual choices from the ideological constraints of national policies and interests (e.g., Ohmae 1999). Equally, the accompanying effects at a social and cultural level are regarded in starkly polarized terms. For some they mark the failure and demise of the agenda of modernity. The relativity of subjective positions revealed in the free-for-all of global exchange is said to expose the promise of the "grand narrative" of emancipation, progress and civilization as an elaborate piece of deception and technological power posturing (Rosenau 1992). Others portray them as the completion of the project of modernity, a welcome rallying of its liberating, boundary-transcending agendas through a radical process of reflexivity (Giddens 1990; Beck et al. 1994). Accordingly, practical conclusions are drawn for strategies designed either to ward off the effects of globalization in a retrenchment behind such certainties as can be salvaged in the maelstrom of change or to accommodate to the new conditions and opportunities.

Much less attention is being paid to the contribution that a pedagogical perspective can make both to the analysis of these current economic and social conditions and to the tackling of the extant social implications for individuals and societies (cf. Pease and Fook 1999). This is not to claim that pedagogy can and should take it upon itself to offer economic or political solutions to problems arising from these fundamental changes, which it clearly cannot without exceeding its mandate. Nor should pedagogy limit itself to ease and smooth the "adjustment symptoms" arising from these changes. This has been its traditionally allotted role within nation-state agendas, and all too often pedagogy contributed to the division between public/structural/political processes and principles invested with "real power for change" on the one hand and private/personal/cultural issues where only accommodation seems possible, on the other. Rather, we want to propose that pedagogy can make a critical contribution to the current uncertainties by fostering vital "boundary-crossing competences" at both the personal and the structural levels. Competences in negotiating the spaces of social relations near and far, within a context of globalization, are a vital factor in regaining a human agenda from the dictates of global economics. These are all the more necessary today as individuals and communities have to negotiate their identities, their livelihood and their hold on society in an unprecedentedly complex social and political environment.

In order to face up to this responsibility, pedagogy has to first develop a good understanding of the economic and political changes that are driving globalization. It then has to examine critically the culture-specific assumptions implied in its methods which were often hidden behind a façade of scientific neutrality and "color-blindness" in the various contexts of school and social work (Khan and Dominelli 2000; Penna et al. 2000; Pugh and Gould 2000). The issue of identity was rarely raised before it was posed as an inescapable challenge by women's groups and ethnic minorities who felt misunderstood and often oppressed by the prevailing standards of "normality." Globalization forces the social professions to take the issue of identity very seriously and to include it in its parameters for action.

Globalization, as has been observed frequently, thrives on a fundamental discrepancy, if not deception. On the one hand, it heralds the disappearance of boundaries and places the totality of human interactions within one boundless field of action, highlighting the relativity, arbitrariness and ultimately the absurdity of all still remaining boundaries and barriers ranging from those of nation, culture and class to those of gender, age and ethnicity (Isin and Wood 1999). In this sense it is the manifestation of a "world society" of which Luhmann says (1993) that it supersedes the distinction and contrast between *Gemeinschaft* (community) and *Gesellschaft* (society). Everybody is functionally connected to everybody else yet ultimately responsible only for herself or himself. On the other hand, globalization manifestly creates new divisions and boundaries. It does this sometimes overtly as references back to "old certainties" which are invoked to structure the otherwise featureless landscape of tastes, fashions, and allegiances with, for instance, ethnic food, subcultural tribes, and national sports icons. At other times new divisions and pronounced inequalities emerge covertly as "accidental" by-products of competition, freedom of choice, and global readjustment of opportunities. "Neo-tribal and fundamentalist tendencies, which reflect and articulate the experience of people on the receiving end of globalization, are as much legitimate offspring of globalization as the widely acclaimed 'hybridization' of top culture—the culture at the globalised top" (Bauman 1998, 3).

Sociological perspectives portray these changes as a massive reordering of time and space in all societies. New means of travel and communication make space available to a world elite of eternally mobile rich and powerful who cover the globe with their virtually simultaneous presence via those "connections." At the same time they are running out of time, are driven by a world clock that supersedes and obliterates all "natural" time rhythms of day and night, winter and summer, young and old. The losers from this "redistribution" (which is in fact an occupation), the poor of this world find public spaces ever more restricted through these private claims, find themselves "out of place" and are left with an overabundance of time, "time to kill" through lack of resources, lack of opportunities, lack of jobs (Bauman 1998). These divisions emerge not so much between countries and regions, but within countries, contributing to the further erosion of "traditional boundaries."

We hypothesize that it is precisely within this ambiguity contained in globalization that new boundaries and divisions can become established. Furthermore, through the subterfuge of the ostensible denial of the existence of such boundaries suggested by the cultural side of globalization (and particularly the denial of their social and political character) the human capacity to recognize, negotiate, transcend and eventually to accept boundaries becomes seriously impaired, and this at a psychological as well as at social, cultural and political levels. In a "world society" as diagnosed by Luhmann (1993) the characteristics of *Gemeinschaft* (of which Tönnies [1988] says that in it people live together regardless of differences that exist between them) merge with that of *Gesellschaft* (in which, following also Tönnies, people live separated regardless of everything that unites them). Consequently differences within and between social units like families, schools, neighborhoods, cities and nations can no longer be understood and dealt with constructively. It is the fostering of the ability to deal with boundaries in all their manifold functions and meanings, individually and collectively, that constitutes today the core task of pedagogy (Aluffi Pentini 2001).

Or to put it the other way around: the "logic" of globalization becomes highly deceptive when it is seen and condoned as a quasi-evolutionary process that determines our fate and our future by transcending and suspending given boundaries and certainties quite inevitably while in fact creating new divisions (Bauman 1998). The anxiety this deception creates opens the door to new (but in fact old) ways of structuring and ordering the human world that operate with the same logic of inevitability, "naturalness" and essentialism. Once the great "chemical mixing and blending" of human ingredients has taken place on a global scale to produce the inhabitants of the global village, what remains are seemingly irreducible boundaries over which no further argument is allowed (Husband 2000). These categories and divisions are said to reveal human nature stripped to its essence, void of all cultural and traditional ties and values, unassailable to political negotiation and change (Malik 1996). Those people who "don't make it" (i.e., the transition to a global world), who fail to adjust, to seize the opportunities, who remain wedded to a world of the past are placing themselves outside the boundaries of this world society of successful opportunists and also outside any claim to the protection of collective solidarity. They are the "no-hopers," the "backward people" who at best serve as exhibits in the exotic human theme parks of tourism, and at worst need to be corralled in the segregated spaces of new urban ghettos, overflowing prisons and detention centers for illegal immigrants. The more "we" become "the same," the more "they" become "essentially different" (Guillaumin 1995).

This boundary drawing and defining along absolute lines is the device of racism, recast on a global scale in all its original, scientific, "value-free" neutrality and logic. The resurgence of racism in all societies riding the wave of globalization can only be understood fully in the context of the opportunities globalization affords it to thrive. An understanding of this connection therefore lends the intended pedagogical project an immediate antiracist character and direction, and this not primarily as a moral stance against proponents and followers of far right and neo-Nazi political ideologies and movements or as a moral cleansing of all racial prejudices in oneself. Globalization necessitates a pedagogical project that is antiracist at its core and in all its details because without this pedagogical space globalization will crush the very possibility of pedagogy and with it the possibility of founding and maintaining human societies. Nothing less is at stake. Nothing less is demanded of pedagogy but to reconstitute the conditions for human societies.

We want to describe antiracist pedagogy, including intercultural pedagogy (for their relationship, see Aluffi Pentini 1996), as a project that negotiates boundaries, or rather as a process that turns the notion of the boundary as a one-dimensional line into one of a multidimensional "boundary space" (which also includes a time dimension). The boundary thus becomes something that is negotiable, that can expand, that makes exchanges and the creation of new identities possible. But antiracist pedagogy does not aim at doing away with all boundaries; instead it holds on to and reconstitutes the vital functions that boundaries have for human individuals and societies. Boundaries are the precondition for community and for solidarity particularly in a featureless, boundary-less world.

Expanding this boundary space means revising the concept of time within a pedagogical discourse. By considering time as the element that widens the boundary and makes it "inhabitable," it turns it into a zone where identities can be negotiated. The lack of time, associated with the acceleration of time perceptions in the wake of globalization, makes boundaries instead absolute and inhospitable. By time, understood in this sense, we mean the possibility of devoting energy and creativity to developing pedagogical interpersonal and intergroup relations. Such pedagogical relations allow us to analyze where exclusive and unique belonging is appropriate and where it is appropriate to share it with others (Aluffi Pentini 2001).

Only within this wide and comprehensive agenda is it justified that pedagogy as antiracist and intercultural pedagogy applies itself to specific tasks pushed in its path by contemporary "moral panics" in the form of work with minority groups, with immigrants, refugees and asylum seekers, the integration of individuals labeled deviant, the nurturing of tolerance toward other cultures. These are not the only areas in which the pedagogical competence in transforming a linear, taken-for-granted boundary into a creative space is required. It is equally demanded, if not more, in the context of gender relations, for instance, of changing sets of relationships within families, of defining the needs and rights of children, of perceived threats of the breakdown of law and order in inner cities, of finding reference points for acceptable forms of expressing sexual identity and preference. And on the horizon of scientific and medical advances, epitomized by the human genome project, loom as yet unimaginable pedagogical tasks like screening and counseling people for potential hereditary diseases, of assisting in decisions over the life and death of patients with diseases that are treatable but only at enormous cost, of identifying people who are a potential danger to their children, their neighborhood, their society. The common denominator of all these scenarios is the finding or drawing of a boundary, a boundary between acceptable and unacceptable behavior and between people "deserving" of assistance and solidarity and those to be placed outside the bounds of that public responsibility and solidarity.

The danger is that as a scientific perspective becomes the unquestionably given framework for decision making, the moral, cultural and political dilemmas involved become reduced to a matter of "facticity." Absolute boundaries become established with reference to scientific facts, when their actual complexity would require a discursive unraveling of many strands of conflicting and at times incompatible meanings. It is again in this reductionist "facticity" that the conceptual figure of racism reemerges with the effect of stifling debate and argument, of narrowing and eliminating any space on the boundary (Lorenz 1996). And not only that, it recasts the question of collective, negotiated responsibility to one of essentialist affinity and proximity: I care for those whose interests are "quite obviously" linked with my own, through family relations, shared ethnic characteristics, nationality, business and insurance interests. The rest are "none of my business."

We want to illustrate these points first with the case of Ireland, a country of the European Union which until recently had the image of a traditional, homogeneous society unaffected by globalization and its associated immigration phenomena. But in the course of a spectacular reversal of its economic position during the late 1990s and the beginning of the new millennium, all the dangers of racism emerged in Ireland at the same time as globalization became an everyday reality. What was most alarming to observers was the fact that a country with a culture known for its easygoing, inoffensive social life generally and for its hospitality to visitors particularly could have come to show the same expressions of racism and xenophobia as other European countries toward certain categories of foreign nationals (Hargreaves and Leaman 1995). In the late 1990s militant groups formed to demand an end to immigration, to "reclaim Ireland for the Irish" and to protest against the dispersal of asylum seekers in different parts of the country (Cullen 2000). Furthermore, foreigners were being verbally and physically attacked at a growing rate and in a manner that seemed to draw wider and wider circles—from black people to asylum seekers and often to foreign nationals who visited Ireland as students and tourists (ERC 2000, 24–29).

This is all the more bewildering since until very recently Ireland had been distinguished by one of the highest emigration rates in Europe and more or less every family has a personal memory or story of the lived experience of emigration. The experience of being an emigrant was frequently associated with the encounter with anti-Irish racism manifesting itself in well-rehearsed scenarios of discrimination, stereotyping and exclusion from the full enjoyment of human, social and cultural rights. Admittedly, manifestations of racism against a minority population within Ireland, the so-called Travellers, have been around for a long time demonstrating that having experienced racism as a national group did not "immunize" Irish people against turning racist themselves. But anti-Traveller racism had a distinct (though unacknowledged) history, fed on extended direct experiences and encounters and operated on lines of discrimination and social boundaries that had been well established (MacLaughlin 1995). The racism against foreigners seemed "unrehearsed," spontaneous, "un-Irish," and, above all, featureless and volatile. It turned people into vilified enemies who shortly before had been seen as heroes, as in the case of refugees from central and eastern Europe. At other times it ceased quite suddenly and turned into generosity and hospitality toward asylum seekers in a remarkable case in a village where a local protest meeting had earlier on tried to prevent their arrival. Once face-to-face contacts had been established, many local inhabitants offered their assistance and made the "visitors" welcome (*Irish Times* 2000).

Table 10.1. Number of Asylum Applications in Ireland

1992	1993	1994	1995	1996	1997	1998	1999	2000	2001
39	91	362	424	1,179	3,883	4,626	7,724	10,938	10,325

Source: Courtney 2000 and Office of the Refugee Applications Commissioner, Dublin (http://www.orac.ie/pdf/PDFStats/Annual%20Statistics/2001%20Annual%20Report%20statistics.pdf; accessed April 20, 2005).

It is tempting, and it is indeed part of popular perceptions and their endorsement in sections of the Irish media, to blame this sudden manifestation of racism against foreign nationals on the steep increase in the volume of refugees and asylum seekers that arrived in Ireland since about 1995. Before then numbers of individual asylum seekers were so small that the government never took care to develop an asylum policy, thereby enforcing an impression of "generosity" and openness which was quite false. When official policies had to be declared, as in the case of the so-called program refugees when the government committed itself to taking set numbers of people displaced by major political events such as the Vietnam War and its aftermath, they showed a general reluctance to offer safety and shelter in Ireland and were accompanied by a strong emphasis on measures for the integration of the people received into this country. But the increase in the number of "unplanned" arrivals of refugees (see table 10.1) hit the country quite unprepared and gave rise to the use of an imagery of Ireland being "flooded" by immigrants and asylum seekers.

For a brief period in 1999 the picture looked very different. The Irish government, while insisting on its traditional defense policy position of military neutrality, demonstrated its humanitarian aid role in the Kosovo war by accepting the relatively high number of about 1,000 refugees from this conflict. They were accommodated in different locations around the country and local welcoming committees sprang up, extending the "traditional" Irish warmth and hospitality. These refugees were seen as "genuine," attracted sympathy and even solidarity; they belonged to "us" for the relatively brief period they were here (for everybody knew, once the conflict was over, they would have to go back). In relation to them the picture was unambiguous, the lines were clearly drawn, everybody knew where they stood.

But subsequently the continuous arrival of asylum seekers caused nothing but confusion. The government, after hastily amending an act that had originally foreseen an elaborate and balanced process of assessing the situation and needs of each applicant, was intent on putting up as many obstacles to their arrival and their stay in Ireland as possible. Policies in other European countries and the Dublin Convention of the EU itself as a reference point for a harsher treatment of asylum seekers played an important part in the development of these policies. At one point, in the absence of new legal provisions, the minister for justice resorted to signing deportation orders under an antiquated law from 1935, a procedure that was challenged in the courts and found unconstitutional (Carolan 1999). A new act was hastily passed to give the procedure proper legal backing. Further legislation in the form of the Illegal Immigrants (Trafficking) Act gave the police new powers to detain asylum seekers for up to eight weeks whose case had been rejected and who are awaiting deportation, when there is the suspicion that they would disappear or forge or destroy their identity documents. These measures were condemned by the opposition parties and by the Irish Refugee Council, which deemed such extensive powers to detain "excessive, especially as the decision to detain is not instigated by a member of the judiciary" (quoted in Haughey 2000).

At the same time the booming Irish economy began to register an acute shortage of labor at all skill levels. A government agency once charged with the task of creating jobs for long-term unemployed Irish people now puts its efforts into recruiting workers abroad to deal with the shortfall in many sectors of the economy. It was a total paradox that at the same time that protests were staged in some Irish villages against the arrival of asylum seekers under a government dispersal scheme, farmers complained that a contingent of eastern European farmworkers had not arrived due to complications over their immigration papers and that their agricultural products were in jeopardy. A senior tourism manager in the south of Ireland is quoted as saying, "A number of employers in Cork and Kerry have recruited Filipino staff and they've worked out very well. They speak excellent English, are very well trained and settle in Ireland very well" (*Irish Independent*, 2000).

All these measures are aimed at creating clear boundaries and unambiguous criteria for allocating people on either side of such boundaries. What is more, they imply that it would be best if people were to fall "automatically" into one of the two categories: the "bad" ones who show themselves deceitful, devious, exploitative, and therefore undeserving of our sympathy and solidarity; they can be left to get caught up in the policing measures, in the strict working of the law, but also in the perils of their voyages, if they are stupid enough to still want to come to Ireland or the west of Europe. Or they would turn out to be the "good" ones who have either "really suffered," are "genuine" refugees and deserve our sympathy and kindness, or who are willing to work here temporarily without claims to permanent residence.

Where such clear distinctions do not establish themselves, the help of specialists has to be invoked, among them social workers and social pedagogues, who assist in deciding on the merits of individual cases. Otherwise these professionals are asked to use their pedagogical skills to turn undesirable traits into acceptable ones, on a whole scale of measures from learning the language ("properly") to personal hygiene, public behavior and other forms of "civilized" behavior. These pedagogical tasks, if performed without a critical awareness of their boundary-maintaining function, have the effect of lifting individuals across an absolute boundary and into the realm of the acceptable. The pedagogy of integration often aims at making the crossing of the boundary smooth and less painful, not realizing that this practice can imply much violence against the identity of individuals and groups, and this on both sides.

The Irish government, reacting to the physical limits at reception centers in the main arrival areas and to the demands by local residents, soon embarked on a policy of dispersal. Unused buildings around the country, such as army barracks, holiday centers, and unprofitable hotels, were being identified, but plans also included the use of ships as "floatels" (ships converted to hostels). Significantly, little preparation and above all little consultation went into this scheme, presumably in order to preempt any adverse reactions that could have been voiced in the process. But, inevitably, the policy did spark off vigorous public reactions and in the various attempts to delineate the "dangers" posed by asylum seekers to local communities racism became a strong direct and indirect element (ÓhAodha 2000).

Racism manifested itself in three basic forms. First there were organized campaigns like the Immigration Control Platform, reminiscent of those well known in other European countries, which pronounced foreigners appearing in such numbers a danger to the indigenous culture, warning that their arrival would lead to overt violent resistance and conflict (ERC 2000). In a reversal of cause and effect typical of such movements, asylum seekers and refugees were made responsible for causing racist sentiments. Limitations on their access to Ireland as well as repatriation were portrayed as measures "for their own protection." Second, in more spontaneous expressions of concern by local residents in the designated dispersal areas, the "threshold of tolerance" metaphor featured prominently. This form of racist boundary drawing affirms the "good nature" of Irish people but invokes a (fictitious) numerical limit beyond which the stability of minority and majority relations were threatened and indigenous culture would be in danger of disappearing. The third modality of racism that manifested itself in organized and spontaneous protests and also very visibly in the media, created the scare of "contamination," both medically and socially. In a number of leaflets and reports, the alleged prevalence of diseases among asylum seekers, especially HIV and AIDS is given prominence and leads to demands for compulsory testing for infectious diseases. HIV and AIDS are portrayed as "foreign diseases" with their "African origins" endorsing their particular alien and threatening nature (Chiwangu 1998). Parallel to this, the involvement of asylum seekers in drug trafficking and other crime is being highlighted against the background of a growing fear of street crime in urban areas.

These various manifestations of racism have several features in common. As is characteristic of "post-Nazi racism," its imagery is more diffuse and incorporates some antiracist concerns inasmuch as it purports to prevent "real racism" and overt violence. But it shares the same appearance of "reasonableness" with the "old racism," it still feeds on fears distilled from a superficial gathering of current social problems, and it operates predominantly with quantitative images and limits as if this quantification was scientific, absolute and indisputable.

The "reasonableness" of racist ways of framing the situation of asylum seekers is lent spurious credence by the very policies the government pursues. Numbers play an important role in these official policies, as do measures designed only for a specified "class of people," which would not be acceptable for national constituents: asylum applicants can be subjected to lengthy detention and compulsory fingerprinting whereas Irish nationals are protected by much stricter human rights safeguards. Asylum seekers can be dislocated as whole groups of populations to different parts of the country without their consent, a measure that would otherwise be seen as an infringement of liberty. And since the year 2000 the social subsistence benefits they receive are only partly paid in cash and otherwise in "direct provisions" of food and clothing (Haughey 2000), an arrangement reminiscent of welfare measures for the indigenous poor in the past when it was assumed that they could not be trusted with cash, that they were too devious to use payments for the intended purposes and would spend them instead on drink and gambling. The spatial segregation of asylum seekers in designated areas and as an entity that could be easily removed from the territory therefore corresponds also to a temporal segregation: these "aliens" are being prevented from living in the present, are being treated as if they were remnants of a past age. Ironically, and by way of endorsing the link between spatial and temporal segregation, these divisions can also be reversed to place Ireland on an island of the past, floating happily on a sea of modernity that stops at its shores. The idyllic Ireland promoted by the tourist industry in this case makes the "remoteness" from the present a marketable asset. But ambivalence about identity in relation to space and time has always been a feature of Irish history, politics and culture (Kearney 1997).

This "coalition" between policies and popular sentiments in the case of immigration is indicative of a pervasive approach to social divisions as a threat to a version of "Irish identity" that is being constructed in a monolithic fashion through such policies and practices. Irish emigration had served the same purposes politically as well as socially. While it was officially being deplored as a sign of the impoverishment of the country under colonial rule or of its rural and peripheral geography, it was politically being exploited as a means of keeping the country "homogeneous" and thereby deliberately "backwards" and "pure." Those who did not fit, either on account of their religious or political views or because of their behavior, would find emigration a viable alternative to being stigmatized. Emigration functioned, in the words of Alexis Fitzgerald, as an influential adviser to the government in the 1950s, as a safety valve to release pressure arising from changes and innovations. He pronounced in Malthusian terms: "High emigration, granted a population excess, releases social tensions, which would otherwise explode and makes possible a stability of manners and customs which would otherwise be the subject of radical change" (quoted in Lee 1989, 381). What this amount-ed to was that Ireland was exporting and externalizing some of its social problems beyond its borders, from unemployment to abortion. It was no-ticeable, for instance, that initial government responses to the AIDS crisis still played on the mechanism of "deterrent," implying that people with HIV/AIDS did not "really belong," and due to the lack of care and medical provisions in Ireland, to say nothing of the prevailing moral attitudes, many of them indeed preferred to live abroad (Chiwangu 1998).

Contemporary pedagogical and social work tasks need to be located within such a political and social analysis. In discussing them we want to draw more specifically on one of the author's (AAP) research and practice experience in pedagogical work with immigrant groups in Italy, a country that, in contrast to Ireland, has a longer history of immigration (the number of foreign school pupils has reached 140,000 there) and where some of the implications of pedagogical responses have been evaluated more systemati-cally. An antiracist pedagogical response first of all has to uncover any racism implied in the way boundaries are drawn in the social landscape of a country and make these taken-for-granted boundaries problematic. Any uncritical spontaneous compliance with a seemingly obvious task, like that of further-ing the integration of migrant children into a school community or of asylum seekers into village life, brings the danger of thereby legitimizing the boundaries as they have been drawn in popular perceptions. Such interven-tions can be seen as measures aimed at the blocking of questions concerning the interests behind the drawing of such boundaries. Well-meaning multi-cultural intentions such as getting children from other countries to talk about life in their cultures may, while purporting to foster awareness and tolerance, in fact relegate the children from those countries to an irrelevant "past" and implicit "backward" status, thereby hindering their arrival in the present.

This poses controversial questions, for instance: Up to what point can young people of the second generation of immigrants be made to study the language of their parents at school when they or their parents no longer express the wish to do so? Up to what stage can a cultural mediator be made available to them as a professional who, apart from having the respon-sibility of assisting with translations, also promotes the encounter between two cultures (Aluffi Pentini 2004)?

The proposal of an intercultural educational approach is complex. It needs to take cognizance of the possibilities and opportunities that present themselves in any given situation but without imposing itself. This often implies unspecific budget allocations and policies and the risk of denying these opportunities to the very people who could benefit from the mea-sures. Conversely, the decision on the participation in courses in the mother tongue is tied in with the "boundary" question in the sense that the deci-sion can depend on the psychological and temporal distance that separates the immigrant from the experience of crossing a border. In a crucial phase during the migratory experience the need to integrate might prevail, dictated by the necessity to learn the language of the host country. But in a second moment the whole orientation might change in the other direction. It is therefore an extremely complex question that in any case cannot be made once and for all. However, as soon as this decision is considered to have been made finally and irrevocably, the immigrant becomes fixated in a fossilized image which no longer corresponds to the actual developmental process. The decision therefore concerns indirectly the boundary between the host society (of "autochthones," as they are often referred to) and newly arrived groups (as the equivalent "allochthones") which it may accentuate. In a country like Italy, where teaching of foreign languages in school is already problematic, the offer of learning the mother tongue in the second generation can easily become a weapon in the hands of demagogic agitators of the political right. They accuse immigrants of having privileges not afforded to Italians, and public institutions of acting "unfairly" by operating the principle of positive discrimination.

This is why it is important that offering such educational opportunities to immigrants should also mean improving the language learning opportunities for "autochthonous" students. This is an example of working from both sides of the boundary toward the optimization of communication and understanding.

As far as services of "cultural mediation" are concerned, which are now available in Italy and are often seen as a solution to problems of integration (Aluffi Pentini 2004), they give rise to a similar series of questions: Why do we not credit immigrants with the capacity of communicating directly with the autochthones once the quality of appropriate translations has been guaranteed? Why do we want to find a standardized solution to such a complex question of intercultural interaction? In the field of cultural mediation it would be equally appropriate to initiate a reciprocal pedagogical process around the boundary instead of delegating to a third party the task of understanding and representing meanings. The capacity to mediate should be understood as the competence to listen and as such be promoted across the whole range of professions in contact with immigrants. Language differences do indeed pose enormous problems but what needs to be avoided is that mediation becomes merely an institutionalized, mechanical tool which could dehumanize immigrants and turn them into mere "illustration material."

The pedagogical approach requires, second, the ability to involve learners in the articulation and formation of boundaries of identity. One basic element of an intercultural pedagogical approach which applies to all ages is that it identifies and analyzes the moments in a person's biography when boundaries were being crossed. The aim of this approach is to discover an existential line of continuity that connects the life stages and to validate every individual's very own living space along this line. During pedagogical consultancy at a multidisciplinary service center for immigrants in Rome (Aluffi Pentini 1999), the team emphasized that educational projects for children had to involve their immigrant family members. The intercultural dimension of this work was based on the collaboration between Italian and nonnational staff on the one hand, and the immigrant parents on the other. In the sessions with couples of parents, the question of "boundaries" had a central place in the conversations (or indeed in the periods of silence), albeit often only implicitly. Invariably this revealed problems in relation to such boundaries as they exist between different family roles or between different generations, but this also concerns the boundaries between "newcomers" and "indigenous" groups of people. The intercultural dimension of these themes was then made explicit and led to the search for an equilibrium appropriate for each particular family. The actual journey the family had undertaken as a change of geographical place crossed one type of boundary, but linked to this journey were other boundary crossings regarding the fact, for instance, that different family members undertook the journey at different chronological or biographical stages. The differences in such experiences were often never raised in the internal family interactions and the chance of arriving in the same "living space" is directly related to the symbolic reworking of the differences between such encounters with boundaries (Aluffi Pentini 1996). For instance partners might never have reflected on the time during which they were physically separated by a boundary when one of them emigrated earlier or on the significance of this experience.

At the same time, fear of reprisals accounts for a reluctance on the part of members of immigrant groups to admit to having experienced discrimination and makes it almost impossible for them to share with anyone incidents when they had suffered racism. This can therefore lead to a kind of removal from awareness of what had happened and to further divisiveness either within the family circle or on the outside between allochthones and autochthones.

Opening up the telling of episodes of racism that a person might have experienced takes time. It becomes particularly difficult to relate them while sufficient trust has not yet been established. In pedagogical consultations these episodes reveal themselves normally very hesitantly and rather late in the course of a series of interviews dealing with issues relating to the education of children. It is important to keep these oriented toward a common objective shared by the two parties on both sides of a cultural divide, an agreed goal on exploring the boundary to establish a pedagogical project as the actual meeting point (Aluffi Pentini 1996). This project will therefore have to be aimed at the future and not remain wedded to the past whereby it can achieve the gradual widening of the boundary to yield an open space. Giving space and time to experiences and emotions is linked to having different ways of encountering the boundary, a boundary which would otherwise be in danger of becoming ever more rigid. This space opens up through questions like: How did each family member experience the migration? How did the family communicate about it? At what stage of the process of translocation was the child born? From which side of the boundary do the parents or the couple together see the experience and their future plans? This can lead to further questions like: How does a couple position itself with regard to the linguistic boundaries encountered and what was their impact on its social integration? Who played or should have played the role of translator or mediator for the other family members? All this requires a slowing down of the retrospection of the experiences, a deconstruction of prevailing hard and fast meanings in order to create a softer, more playful space around these boundaries in which the new future can be planned as a project (Aluffi Pentini 1999).

Third, the pedagogical approach needs to relate these reminiscences and the competences to articulate an individual identity back to the notion of a community. This is where we suggest that the boundary, in the retelling of experiences in spatial and temporal terms relating to cultural and collective conventions, be reworked as a new time-space in which belonging to other groups of significant persons becomes possible. It is totally unrealistic to presume that any immigrant community could recreate their former cultural identity in a host country without taking into account the changed "sur-roundings." Equally, it is inappropriate for the host community to offer their prevailing cultural and social conditions as a fixed entity which newly arrived people would have to take on in their entirety and which will remain unaffected by the presence of people with different traditions and identities. If a meeting of different traditions is taking place, if communication over those differences is starting to work, it cannot but transform the space in which this is happening to create the conditions under which a new com-munity can form that accommodates elements that might at times conflict.

Fourth, evoking "community" in this still quite abstract sense can easily become dangerous idealism. The space in which the encounters take place and that needs to be transformed itself requires structure in the form of procedures for the exchanges and above all the security of civil and legal rights that participants can resort to and that protect their vulnerability. Disclosing details of one's identity, particularly where this identity has a reputation for being socially inferior and where elements of this identity have been used to reinforce a feeling of superiority on the part of the majority, is a dangerous undertaking. It is simply naïve to appeal to a "celebration of cultural difference" when identification can lead to exclusion and discrimination, to violent and racist attacks. Pedagogically speaking, if the space is to be created and expanded into something that can give rise to a community, the participants in the process need to feel the protection of the law that gives them equal rights and that makes accountable those who use cultural differences for racist purposes. This agenda points beyond appeals to tolerance and mutual understanding and includes, even in a classroom situation or in defining the scope of a family counseling service, references to rights that everybody involved can invoke, to sanctions that can be applied if rules are transgressed, to effective protection of privacy and dignity (Aluffi Pentini 1996).

This raises the question, What is the affective line that connects the concept of citizenship to the person's biographical trajectory? This undoubtedly constitutes the development of a sense of belonging. When creating a pedagogical sense of belonging, we are conditioned by rituals in each educational tradition that can often be perceived as impositions rather than invitations to belong. For instance, every kind of rule in an educational context that does not allow for the possibility of being discussed risks becoming such an imposition, regardless whether the sense of belonging is at the core of any of the pedagogical discourses of community education or cooperative learning. The presence of immigrant groups also forces the autochthonous population to question anew what constitutes and secures their own sense of belonging, and pedagogy cannot back out from posing this often uncomfortable task. Otherwise there is a risk that addressing the need for belonging in the era of globalization gets left to extremist groups, which then offer models of belonging uncritically that are ahistorical, purely utilitarian and exclusionary (Lorenz 1996). Without creating a sense of belonging in the context of community, our cities also risk becoming accumulations of ghettos with their own jungle of implicit, unwritten rules that further the dominance of the groups wielding the most power. It is in the presence of people from diverse backgrounds and with diverse interests that the formation of tangible rules and procedures of citizenship at the base becomes constitutive of a meaningful sense of belonging.

It is very important that all members of a group are involved in defining those rules, even if they are relatively small children, because it is in the defining of such shared rules that community in a concrete sense comes about. Through such sets of rules account can also be taken of the fact that people live in different communities simultaneously, that rules within a family, influenced by one cultural tradition, might be different from rules in public arenas or in religious settings. There are also bound to be conflicts between those sets of rules which cannot be harmonized, which cause dissatisfaction, unrest, and disaffection, but it is only through participation in the rule making and in acquiring the skills involved in negotiating conflicting needs and demands that any structure and thereby any community acquires legitimacy, permanency, and thereby a basis for further identity formation.

These processes also require time, not just for the encounters to take place (which in a hectic, efficiency-driven organization of services is often hard enough to achieve), but also for the reminiscing to happen. "Memory work" under time pressure is more likely to confirm stereotypes and categories that are assumed to be well known than to lead to an authentic telling of different stories, stories that do not match, that do not add up, that are full of unresolved pieces, broken by the frequent boundary crossings (Benmayor and Skotnes 1994). The pedagogical space we advocate is immediately associated with the time it requires, the time it needs to be built into this space, time in which clocks might indeed run at different speeds and not be dictated to by the impersonal quantifications of a digital order. The slowing of the flow of time and the creation of a sense of belonging are therefore two preconditions for all forms of resistance against the unbridled acceleration of globalization.

This can now be applied to the paradigmatic case of Ireland, where much of this pedagogical work has yet to be developed and where learning from the experience of other countries is crucial. The denial of space implied in the tightening of border controls and in the linear understanding of a border itself, that only conceives of an "in" or "out," not only happens in relation to immigrants but is vividly exemplified by the treatment of indigenous Irish Travellers. The social conundrum they pose always relates back to their nomadic traditions. In a society that attributes such central significance to land ownership and where social stability rests on the fact that people have fixed addresses so that they can be traced and fitted into a social order, nomadic people represent an inherent threat and acquire the whole cluster of attributes that label them deviant and dangerous. The whole point of territorial nation building was to set up an alternative to nomadism, no matter how much that traditional lifestyle might in fact be romanticized as an extrapolated fantasy of the newly formed and "settled" nations (McVeigh 1997). Nomadic habits became expelled from the territory and from the present, an elimination that became a gruesome final reality under the racist policies of the Nazis. In Ireland today the drawing of a fixed line between "traveling" and "settled" people sets up mechanisms that ensure the closure of "normal society" to Travellers. They are constantly being moved on from halting site to halting site as nobody is responsible for them. And by having to keep on the move they are perceived as endorsing all the stereotypes attached to them. Even where they are "settling," under housing schemes or in specially designed camps, their presence is tainted with the image of "not belonging." "Travellers literally find no place in Irish society" (MacLaughlin 1995, 82).

Similar mechanisms of mutual exclusion are very much at issue in the continuing conflict in Northern Ireland, even after the political settlement seems to have brought relative peace and stability. Everything will depend now not on how the communities define their social and cultural boundaries and defend their identities, but how much common space can be created over common causes and concerns (Cassidy and Trew 1998). In this process it is again vital that boundaries do not become blurred, that identities and traditions are not being denied, but that encounters expand a shared space for the creation of a shared sense of citizenship.

The racist rejection of asylum seekers in Ireland therefore is not a transfer of the established anti-Traveller racism to a new group of people. Rather, it molds itself anew in different circumstances into the same pattern because the same mechanisms apply that draw the line between settled and migrant people. It is not "ethnic difference" that causes racism, it is racism that defines ethnic difference in such absolute, unbridgeable terms. It is at this border where travelers, aliens, outcasts are constantly being produced and reproduced only to then be endowed with alleged "intrinsic qualities" as if these were part of an inherited ethnicity rather than the product of the specific circumstances of the encounter. It is racism that denies the time and space at the border in which encounter and negotiation over belonging can happen.

But racism manifests itself not just in the treatment of ethnically defined minority populations. It is a looming danger in all situations where the boundaries of social solidarity are at issue (which is virtually in all areas of social services and welfare), and this not on account of racist attitudes by social service and pedagogical personnel, but as a result of the prevailing "framing" of these encounters in a wider political context (Lorenz 1998). The case of Ireland and its traumatic encounter with globalization belies its "peripheral" and "marginal" image. What is happening in Ireland today connects this island to developments in most other countries around the globe and can only be understood and tackled with reference to these international events. But in applying their specific pedagogical skills against the background of a critical analysis of this context, social and educational service staff can make a significant contribution towards quite literally the establishment of a "new world order." It is one thing to let this new order be dictated by "economic necessities," it is quite a different matter to negotiate this order around basic human needs and around the principles that make communities possible. This work requires special attention to the dimensions of time and space as qualitative units instead of mere quantitative measures. It is in the encounter with difference that the conditions for identity get created, not as abstract psychological processes, but as social realities that demand material resources, social skills, and political and legal rights.

REFERENCES

Aluffi Pentini, Anna. 2004. *La mediazione intercultural—dalla biografia alla professione.* Milan: Angeli.

———. 2001. "Leben und Zusammenleben jenseits der Grenzen." In *Geschlechter,* ed. H. Hierdeis. Bozen, Italy: Universitätsreihe der Freien Universität Bozen.

———. 1999. "La consulenza pedagogica in un centro per famiglie immigrate: Contesto di lavoro, riferimenti teoretici, esempi e significativi." In *Come si è stretto il mondo,* ed. F. Susi, 197–232. Rome: Armando.

———. 1996. "The Specific and Complementary Nature of Inter-cultural and Antiracist Pedagogical Approaches." In *Antiracist Work with Young People,* ed. A. Aluffi Pentini and W. Lorenz. Lyme Regis, UK: Russell House.

Bauman, Zygmunt. 1998. *Globalisation: The Human Consequences.* Cambridge, UK: Polity.

Beck, Ulrich, Anthony Giddens, and Scott Lash. 1994. *Reflexive Modernization: Politics, Tradition, and Aesthetics in the Modern Social Order.* Cambridge, UK: Polity.

Benmayor, Rina and Skotnes, Andor. 1994. *Migration and Identity.* Oxford, UK: Oxford University Press.

Carolan, Mary. 1999. "Deportations Suspended after Part of Aliens Act Is Found Unconstitutional." *Irish Times,* January 23, 7.

Cassidy, C., and K. Trew. 1998. "Identities in Northern Ireland: A Multidimensional Approach." *Journal of Social Issues* 54, no. 4: 725–40.

Chiwangu, Paulina. 1998. "HIV/AIDS Discourse: The Symbolic Resonance of a Disease." Ph.D. diss., National University of Ireland, Cork.

Courtney, Damien. 2000. "A Quantification of Irish Migration with Particular Emphasis on the 1980s and 1990s." In *The Irish Diaspora,* ed. A. Bielenberg, 287–316. Harlow, UK: Pearson.

Cullen, Paul. 2000. *Refugees and Asylum Seekers in Ireland.* Cork: Cork University Press.

ERC, European Race Bulletin. 2000. A Special Report on the UK and Ireland, Bulletin 33/34, Institute of Race Relations, 24–29.

Giddens, Anthony. 1991. *Modernity and Self-identity: Self and Society in the Late Modern Age.* Cambridge, UK: Polity.

———. 1990. *The Consequences of Modernity.* Cambridge, UK: Polity.

Guillaumin, Colette. 1995. *Racism, Sexism, Power, and Ideology.* London: Routledge.

Hargreaves, Alec G., and Jeremy Leaman. 1995. "Racism in Contemporary Western Europe: An Overview." In *Racism, Ethnicity, and Politics in Contemporary Europe,* ed. A. G. Hargreaves and J. Leaman. London: Edward Elgar.

Haughey, Nuala. 2000. "Refugee Groups Disappointed with Court Ruling." *Irish Times,* August 29, 5.

Husband, Charles. 2000. "Recognising Diversity and Developing Skills: The Proper Role of Transcultural Communication." *European Journal of Social Work* 3, no. 3: 225–34.

Irish Independent. 2000. "20,000–Plus Immigrants on Way to Ease Staff Shortages." August 7, 12.

Irish Times. 2000. "Refugees Are Made Welcome by Locals in Clonakilty." January 25, 8.

Isin, Engin F., and Patricia K. Wood. 1999. *Citizenship and Identity.* London: Sage.

Kearney, Richard. 1997. *Postnationalist Ireland: Politics, Culture, Philosophy.* London: Routledge.

Khan, Parves, and Lena Dominelli. 2000. "The Impact of Globalization on Social Work in the UK." *European Journal of Social Work* 3, no. 2: 95–108.

Lash, Scott, and John Urry. 1987. *The End of Organized Capitalism.* Madison: University of Wisconsin Press.

Lee, Joe. J. 1989. *Ireland 1912–1985: Politics and Society.* Cambridge, UK: Cambridge University Press.

Lorenz, Walter. 1998. "Social Work, Social Policies, and Minorities in Europe." In *Social Work and Minorities: European Perspectives,* ed. C. Williams, H. Soydan, and M. R. D. Johnson. London: Routledge.

———. 1996. "The Education of the Nation: Racism and the Nation State." In *Antiracist Work with Young People,* ed. A. Aluffi Pentini and W. Lorenz. Lyme Regis, UK: Russell House.

Luhmann, Nikolas. 1993. *Soziale Systeme: Grundriss einer allgemeinen Theorie,* 4th ed. Frankfurt: Suhrkamp.

MacLaughlin, James. 1995. *Travellers and Ireland.* Cork: Cork University Press.

Malik, Kenan. 1996. "Universalism and Difference: Race and the Postmodernists." *Race and Class* 37, no. 3: 1–17.

McVeigh, Robbie. 1997. "Theorising Sedentarism: The Roots of Anti-nomadism." In *Gypsy Politics and Traveller Identity,* ed. T. Acton. Hertfordshire, UK: University of Hertfordshire Press.

ÓhAodha, Micheál. 2000. "Immigration Policy in Ireland: Coping with a New Diaspora." *Social Work in Europe* 7, no. 1: 58–61.

Ohmae, Keinichi. 1999. *The Borderless World: Power and Strategy in the Interlinked Economy.* New York: HarperBusiness.

Pease, Bob, and Jan Fook. 1999. *Transforming Social Work Practice: Postmodern Critical Perspectives.* London: Routledge.

Penna, Sue, Ian Paylor, and John Washington. 2000. "Globalization, Social Exclusion, and the Possibilities for Global Social Work and Welfare." *European Journal of Social Work* 3, no. 2: 109–22.

Pugh, Richard, and Nick Gould. 2000. "Globalization, Social Work, and Social Welfare." *European Journal of Social Work* 3, no. 2: 123–38.

Rosenau, Pauline. 1992. *Post-modernism and the Social Sciences.* Princeton: Princeton University Press.

Tönnies, Ferdinand. 1988. *Community and Society.* New Brunswick, NJ: Transaction Books.

11
AUSTRIA: RIGHT-WING POPULISM PLUS RACISM AT A GOVERNMENTAL LEVEL

Peter Gstettner

↝

The lack of any clear political identity in its parties has encouraged the spread of a populism with racist undertones in Austria. Populism, in the age of digital capitalism and the incredible speed at which symbols are changing, has to orient itself toward those at the top, those "up there"—since, once spokesmanship has been won, a lot of power and money are at stake as well. How life really is for those at the bottom arouses, at most, marginal interest, or is an issue only brought up before the next election. It should, therefore, come as little surprise that the reality of everyday racism and anti-Semitism has become an all-too-familiar backdrop, against which attacks on foreigners, Jews, Sinti and Romani Gypsies; brutal police raids; deportations with gagging and bonds (in Omofuma's case, with fatal results for the victim); inflammatory articles in the media (especially the *Kronenzeitung*); stigmatization; social exclusion; and racist invective have aroused, at best, narrowly limited and short-lived surges of indignation. For this reason, the negative foreign press after the last national parliamentary election had a very important effect on the perception of Austrian-style racism and anti-Semitism.[1] The mirror which was held up to Austria aroused unpleasant feelings and sentiments which people would much rather have continued to repress. Buried emotions came to the surface, and times long relegated to the past once again cast their shadows across Austria.

A first consequence of this development could be put like this: one should not turn a blind eye to racism and anti-Semitism just because both these ideologies may no longer be expressing themselves in traditional, consistent and obvious forms. The current conglomeration of verbal attacks, social exclusion, national stereotypes and legal discrimination has long ago, and very subtly, infiltrated the day-to-day consciousness of the broad political center and now determines the corresponding behavior. Structural measures to combat racism and anti-Semitism are hardly to be expected from the government, as the populist approach to their own institutionalized racism has already become an integral part of the practical politics of all the parties.[2]

The negative response abroad to the electoral success of Jörg Haider's FPÖ (Austrian Freedom Party, classed as extreme right wing in the European political spectrum) continued vociferously throughout the entire period of negotiations over the formation of the new government. It was, not least, these warnings and apprehensions which stirred the "other Austria," after one month of speechlessness, to call for a nationwide demonstration. "No coalition with racism" was the motto of the large-scale demonstration that took place in Vienna on November 12, 1999. There was talk of "the highly questionable attitude to the Nazi past," and of it being to "Austria's shame" that so many people had fallen for Haider's "demagogic rabble-rousing" against foreigners and the socially disadvantaged. After the Waldheim affair, Austria was now confronted with the reality of being back in the international headlines as "a land of Nazis." It did not help matters that, a few weeks later, a party in Switzerland was able to gain votes by means of very similar xenophobic demagogy: at the end of October 1999, Christoph Blocher led the Swiss People's Party (SVP) to spectacular electoral wins, whereby he was able to raise their proportion of the votes from 15 percent to 22.5 percent.

A second consequence can be formulated as follows: The fact that the globalization of the migration problem became the ideal lever for right-wing European antiforeigner politics, which has engulfed Switzerland as well, still provides no conclusive explanation for the FPÖ electoral success, when one compares Haider with Schönhuber, Le Pen, Blocher, or other extreme right-wing politicians.[3] Anyone seeking possible alternative social solutions to right-wing populism cannot avoid conducting a discriminating, ideologically critical analysis of the local/regional and historical conditions surrounding the Haider syndrome—whereby such an analysis has to take place in the context of the day-to-day political behavior of all party representatives. Analyses that focus solely on striking comparisons between the FPÖ and neofascist movements in other countries as well as drawing parallels with neofascism have created for FPÖ voters a mechanism of self-defeat through a process of emotionalized defense.

CARINTHIA'S SCARCELY NOTICED TRAILBLAZING FUNCTION

After the national parliamentary elections in the autumn of 1999, it was obvious that now, more than ever, tactical relations were being cultivated with the FPÖ by the other parties, and that people were generally far from clear about the consequences of the shocking electoral success of Jörg Haider, the extreme right-wing populist. The aim of the November 12 demonstrators—to prevent the FPÖ from participating in the government—came to nothing. Evidently, those in Vienna had gotten too accustomed to the idea that the Haider party's spectacular gains up to that time were an exclusively Carinthian affair. The prevailing opinion was, apparently, that this movement, which had now spread all over Austria in this astounding way, could be geographically localized and thus banished: Carinthia had been regarded as lost, as far as Austrian democracy was concerned, ever since the Carinthian SPÖ (Austrian Social Democratic Party, once oriented toward socialism) was, largely through its own fault, forced to successively cede its monopoly of power and high-handedness to its smaller partner, the FPÖ. The fact that, in the spring of 1999, the Carinthian FPÖ stepped into the shoes of the governmentally experienced SPÖ, the fact that now another party was in power in Carinthia—even this was not enough to cause a shift in the thinking of the other political parties in Austria. As long as the Carinthian FPÖ merely made use of the accepted principle of cronyism in filling posts and giving promotions, this was met with general tolerance, since, evidently, no one had ever expected that a governing FPÖ would really change the structures of power. For many people in Carinthia, a change of color at the top was change enough, seeing that over the past few years red had also been unable to keep the promises it had once made concerning posts, flats and other privileges. Many must have thought to themselves, let's just see whether the FPÖ can fulfill what it promises.

As a long-standing observer and "sufferer" of Carinthian politics, I therefore come to a third conclusion: the shock over the present Austrian government comes at least ten years too late because no attention was paid to the dialectic of the political periphery and the political center. The consequence of a lack of analytical insight into southern Austria is now upon us with a vengeance. Surprised and helpless, one searches for a new distribution of political roles, in order to as much as possible cover up the fact that no one ever perceived the developments in Carinthia, culminating in the FPÖ's assumption of power, as an alarm signal for Austrian democracy. In analysing the situation, any counterstrategy must, therefore, start from the premise that Carinthia was, and is, the drill ground and stage for the drama in which, once more, democratic Austria finds itself deeply involved.

Actually, there was no lack of forewarnings of the drama. In the autumn of 1989, after Jörg Haider had, with the help of the ÖVP (Austrian People's Party; Christian social orientation, conservative), been appointed Governor of Carinthia for the first time, he announced that he would "wind up" the "old parties' proportion system" [the Austrian system, whereby posts in the civil service are divided between supporters of the respective ruling parties in the same proportion as those parties' representation in parliament.—Translator].

His home political program, which he likewise summed up that same autumn in the saying, "The Carinthian way could help Austria get well," was either not noticed by the governing parties in Vienna, or else merely attributed to the proverbially "brown" Carinthian autumn. It was hoped that such slogans were merely seasonal phenomena and would soon disappear by themselves.

In fact, Haider's first Carinthian governorship was a passing phenomenon, since he was removed from his position due to his praise for the "well-organized employment policies of the Third Reich," and relegated to the penalty bench—demoted to vice governor—an event which was wrongly regarded by many as the "fall" or "voting out of office" of Haider. Whereas in other countries such a statement made by a member of government would have led to the loss of all political offices, Haider, in second rank, was merely presented with a welcome breathing space in which to modernize his party and get it into shape for an aggressive opposition course.

It is interesting to take another look at the Carinthia of ten years ago and ask just what was emerging from the FPÖ provincial leadership at that time. What is this FPÖ "Carinthian way" which was invoked by Haider as the cure for Austria's ills? Is it the same one that is being applied throughout the country today?

Critical analyses carried out in Carinthia in 1989 showed that the "renewal of the political system" propagated by Haider will not only lead Austria to the extreme right margin of Europe but could also unite with other extreme right-wing European movements. It was wholly in tune with the Zeitgeist that, engaged in the poker game to win the maximum votes, all European right-wing populists played the national ace so as to trump "multicultural society" with the "national patriotism" card (cf. Gstettner 1993). At that time, what counted was winning points on a very central and controversial European issue—stirring up feelings against "foreigners" by employing racist slogans with respect to migration and asylum policies. This was precisely the area where basic and civil rights could be most easily cut back and continuing democratization prevented, since any line of action defending foreigners and their rights would never find a strong lobby. Even then, such tendencies were part of the FPÖ's modernization trend, in that Haider was loudly propagating "regionalism" in Carinthia. His favorite idea, ridiculed in Vienna, was the "Free State of Carinthia." This concept, not unlike that of the Italian separatists from the "Lega Nord," was meant as a countermovement to EU centralism, and also as a threat to the party headquarters in Vienna, should it stand in the way of his "renewal programme."[4] This propaganda did not provoke any significant opposition in either of the two other parties. On the contrary, everyone wanted to join in: social elites were encouraged in areas where the withdrawal of state control had already successfully begun—in the area of once politically controlled public institutions. The retreating state, with its discredited institutions, opened the way for the neoliberal principle to foster a new, apparent freedom of the individual: the go-ahead was given to the hard-working and respectable, to the flexible and the conformist. Thus, the "homeland" became the fine-meshed territory of the restrictive politics of regimentation and control. On the other hand, politics' global obligation to develop a more humane and fair distribution of economic and ecological resources, and to enable peaceful cohabitation in a multicultural society, was gradually abandoned. The emotionalization and privatization of public affairs were, on the contrary, encouraged politically—for example, the envy of any personal advantage on the part of one's neighbor, fears connected to maintaining one's own standard of living in the face of increasing economic migration, and the concern over "identity" when faced with a sustained "overforeignization" of one's homeland.

In this way, the FPÖ succeeded in rechanneling the prevailing political disenchantment into as many fear and protest votes for its own party as possible, and to let the "old parties" know that they were no longer conducting their policies in the public interest, or, in other words, "in the interests of the man on the street." Yet the private sphere was neither presented in a positive light nor given a forward-looking perspective. It was regressively cut off from the world, focused on the past and shown as negatively confronting the challenges it faced. Thus, Carinthia under Haider has not, up to now, had any successes at all, either in tourism or industry, or in its educational, cultural, media, or scientific policies. The much-advertised "renewal" has been revealed as being merely a state of stagnation, in which ever-changing announcements and political gags represent the only real movements. Paul Virilio (1992) would call this a state of "breakneck standstill."

MODERNIZATION IN THE ZEITGEIST OF POPULISM

Today, the FPÖ presents itself as the second-strongest national party in the postmodern, de-ideologized guise of a conventional medium-size or large party. The party's "right-wing extremism" has dissolved. Although the classical elements of extreme right-wing movements, like racism and anti-Semitism, continue to exist in the FPÖ, their contours have been blurred, due to their flexible implementation and the globalization of all processes.[5] They have been elevated in a general trend toward the neoliberal opening of the markets (including markets of symbolic politics), and toward the deregulation of traditional political systems. To sum it up: the conductors and orchestras have left the stage, and the managers of the playback specially put on for the media are now calling the tunes (cf. Anselm, Freytag, Marschitz, and Marte 1999, 9–22). An FPÖ modernized along these lines is well advised not to oppose these trends too openly. As the "center party," it is easier for the FPÖ to coolly look on whenever neo-Nazi groups form again on the extreme right.

The FPÖ may continue to promise its followers renewal, but its perspectives and policies are constantly and swiftly changing. They too are subject to the speed of "digital capitalism" and to signs of wear and tear—witness

Haider's self-stylization as the people's tribune, Robin Hood, champion of families and children, supporter of minorities, regionalist or ethno-pluralist. The only important thing here seems to be to maintain the image of a role model who stands for opinion leadership, for diffuse protest and direction-less change.

Renewal and change have thus become ideologies in themselves, since no one now asks in which direction and for whose benefit anything should be changed. Moreover, the fact that "change" consists merely of the exchange of one elite for another, and that the FPÖ is now pressing forward to gain those centers of control over power and capital hitherto occupied by the other parties, is thereby disguised. It is precisely when everything is set in motion, stirred up, and when traditional systems lose their orientational function, that calls for a strong leader, a *Führer,* a new force for law and order, get loud again. There are no calls, in times like these, for increased democracy, since the greater flexibility and availability (even disposability) of the individual, and a more eager and obliging attitude on the part of the masses, who are also capable of supporting a party leader in their party and individual interests, is all in harmony with the trend toward denationaliza-tion and with the axioms of neoliberal capitalism. In times of globalization, this means the concentration of power without centralization, flexible pro-duction while maintaining higher work levels, and the abrupt laying-off of workers without considering age and qualifications (cf. Sennett 2000).

The omnipresence of a ruthless, go-getting mentality and a self-centered nonculture must inevitably lead to a new, more brutal confusion, a social and psychodynamic unease—self-made, yet nonetheless far-reaching—which has, evidently, been manipulated and politically used most successfully by Haider's party. As far as that is concerned, Haider-style populism can be described as an anti-intellectual, irrational, predemocratic movement that seeks to bring in a *Führer* state, as well as a deregulated economy and the mobilization of the racist discourse.

Since Haider's populism propagates the (evil) Nazi past as a (better) future system offering "well-organized employment policies," counterstrat-egies must begin with that central theme, and consciously link the past and future together through the work of remembering and planning. This project should be set up from the perspective that the sight of, and responsibility for, the past century of barbarism can give us the security we need for the establishment of a "citizens' society." Democracy and the protection of human rights must guarantee that this project should not fail due to lack of freedom, since it

> leads to the incapacity to stand up for one's rights and to put up any resistance. Lack of security leads to the loss of the courage necessary to form the basis for resistance and to join together in the name of a society which is more open-minded where human needs and desires are concerned. In both cases, the results bear a striking resemblance to one another: democratic pressure becomes weaker,

one sees a growing incapacity to deal politically, and a massive increase in the urge to escape from politics and responsible citizenship. (Bauman 1999, 32)

Finally, a fourth conclusion: it is only through gaining freedom and security that it will be possible to defeat the "populism plus racism" concept because right-wing propaganda is still making use of people's fear and anxiety, the defamation of education as "reeducation," the denunciation of antifascism as "left-wing fascism," the denigration of international solidarity as a relic of "self-righteous do-goodism," contempt for intercultural education as "left-wing nonsense," and so on. An open "civil society," conversely, requires the freedom of a democratic culture that accepts the necessity of conflict and the struggle for human dignity and rights as an object of public and, if necessary, controversial politics.

NOTES

1. The EU center for monitoring racism and hostility toward foreigners in Vienna (EUMC) published a report at the end of 1999 showing that racism and hostility toward foreigners have increased more sharply in Austria and Switzerland than in other EU countries, although it is precisely in these two countries that unemployment is relatively low and the level of affluence comparatively high. Evidently, though, good political capital is to be gained through the fears of the affluent, just as promises and uncovered checks can be used to stir up the envy of those who have supposedly or actually come off worst economically. The inflammatory "art" of demagogues and populists consists in being able to address the winners as well as the losers, and to place themselves on the side of the anxious and frustrated. As far as all that goes, one has to agree with Peter Glotz, when he writes: "The readiness of many people to defend what they have with bitter ferocity and brutality is quite incredible, and is always underestimated by emancipatory strategists" (Glotz 1999, 129).

2. Cf. the relevant analyses and proposals for antiracist educational strategies by Aluffi Pentini, Gstettner, Lorenz, and Wakounig (1999) and Fassmann, Matuschek, and Menasse (1999).

3. Apart from Haider, none of these party leaders, however unequivocal and clear the signals showing their sympathies toward Nazi ideology, can boast of Haider's steady rise to power since taking over leadership of the FPÖ in 1986. The political results of his career are unprecedented in Europe's right-wing party landscape. And, if one can believe forecasts, the rise of right-wing extremism to become an "extremism of the centre" (Lohmann 1994) has not yet reached its peak with the FPÖ's electoral success on October 3, 1999.

4. My enumeration of these trends is based on the results of analyses collected and published by my colleague Gero Fischer and myself (cf. Fischer and Gstettner 1990).

5. The following classical elements of right-wing extremism are enumerated in the relevant scientific literature (e.g., Schwagerl 1993): the systematic defamation of parliamentary democracy, the authority of the state under a strong leader, the creation of "bogeymen," racist agitation and aggression toward foreigners, anti-Semitism, the reinforcement and exploitation of feelings of fear, nationalistic-biological versions of

history, the ideologization of national identity, and deceptively innocent depictions of the Nazi period.

REFERENCES

Aluffi Pentini, A., P. Gstettner, W. Lorenz, and V. Wakounig, eds. 1999. *Antirassistische Pädagogik in Europa: Theorie und Praxis.* Klagenfurt, Austria: Drava.

Anselm, E., A. Freytag, W. Marschitz, and B. Marte, eds. 1999. *Die neue Ordnung des Politischen: Die Herausforderungen der Demokratie am Beginn des 21. Jahrhunderts.* Frankfurt am Main: Campus.

Bauman, Z. 1999. "Freiheit und Sicherheit: Die unvollendete Geschichte einer stürmischen Beziehung." In *Die neue Ordnung des Politischen: Die Herausforderungen der Demokratie am Beginn des 21. Jahrhunderts,* ed. E. Anselm, A. Freytag, W. Marschitz, and B. Marte, 23–34. Frankfurt am Main: Campus.

Fassmann, H., H. Matuschek, and E. Menasse, eds. 1999. *Agrenzen, ausgrenzen, aufnehmen: Empirische Befunde zu Fremdenfeindlichkeit und Integration.* Klagenfurt, Austria: Drava.

Fischer, G., and P. Gstettner, eds. 1990. *"Am Kärntner Wesen könnte diese Republik genesen": An den rechten Rand Europas: Jörg Haiders Erneuerungspolitik.* Klagenfurt, Austria: Drava.

Glotz, P. 1999. *Die beschleunigte Gesellschaft: Kulturkämpfe im digitalen Kapitalismus.* Munich: Kindler.

Gstettner, P. 1993. *Die multikulturelle Gesellschaft: Ein neues Feindbild? Pädagogische Herausforderungen durch Rechtsextremismus, Deutschnationalismus und Ausländerfeindlichkeit.* Klagenfurter Universitätsreden, vol. 24. Klagenfurt, Austria: Carinthia.

Lohmann, H.-M., ed. 1994. *Extremismus der Mitte: Vom rechten Verständnis deutscher Nation.* Frankfurt am Main: Fischer.

Schwagerl, H. J. 1993. *Rechtsextremes Denken: Merkmale und Methoden.* Frankfurt am Main: Fischer.

Sennett, R. 2000. *Der flexible Mensch: Die Kultur des neuen Kapitalismus.* Munich: Goldmann.

Virilio, P. 1992. *Rasender Stillstand: Essay.* Munich: Hanser.

12
GREECE: XENOPHOBIA OF THE WEAK AND RACISM OF THE MIGHTY

Georgios Tsiakalos

⊷

"PROGRESSIVE" RHETORIC AND REACTIONARY PRACTICE

Scholars who engage in the state of minorities and racism in Greece are faced with an interesting phenomenon: the harmonious coexistence of a "progressive" rhetoric with a reactionary practice. The inconsistency between rhetoric and practice has become the canon for both individuals that represent state institutions and authorities and certain organizations in society.

It is not a form of institutional schizophrenia removed from logic. On the contrary, it is a form of systematic and to a large degree successful handling of an existent network of racist discriminations. A handling, which, after all, aims at the unobstructed reproduction of this network and the timely absorption and assimilation of every reaction as well as the expulsion of alternative radical suggestions to the social and political margin.

This is the kind of handling that the ruling political class has attempted after the fall of the fascist regime in 1974, since:

1. It has incorporated in its rhetoric elements of the progressive discourse simply as rhetoric schemata; consequently, it has incorporated the antiracist discourse as well.
2. It has supported by all possible means (e.g., by offering university positions and funds) the advancement of scholars who are willing to serve any political leadership participating in multiple mechanisms of manipulation.
3. It has created with the assistance of these scholars a virtual reality in order to present issues relating to minorities and racist discrimination.

For the construction and acceptance of this virtual reality, in particular, there are networks that function with the participation of government executives and local authorities, as well as university members, educators and social workers, leaders of temporary nongovernmental organizations, media staff, and others. This collaboration offers participants personal gain and also constitutes the necessary framework of agreement for the coverup of racist phenomena. Of course, it would be wrong to consider that all individuals involved in such intricacies have a clear understanding of contributing to the reproduction of social injustice. Apart from the self-interest that prevails in these intricacies, another decisive factor is the influence of a powerful ideology of cultural racism and colonialist paternalism on at least certain of the social actors involved.

In the era of mass and uncontrolled immigration from countries that starve to countries that prosper, consequently to Greece as well, these phenomena are accompanied by

1. An augmentation and multiplication of forms of exploitation of the poor and the weak, the peak of which are the almost slave possessive relations in the sector of paid work.
2. An escalation of the chasm between the official discourse on the respect of human and social rights and the reality experienced by immigrants, refugees, and members of many minorities.

At the same time, with the harmless handling of the social problem that racism is recognized to be, there has been an intensification of the use of theories through which a "natural" interpretation of negative phenomena is offered.[1]

The introduction above seemed necessary in order to illuminate the framework in which some facts of the Greek reality concerning racism should be comprehended.

IMMIGRANTS IN GREECE

Impressive economic growth in the past twenty-five years has converted Greece from a traditional country of origin to a host country of immigrants. From the time of deep political changes in Eastern Europe, Greece—a country of about 10 million citizens—has accepted more than a million immigrants. Most of those immigrants crossed the Greek borders illegally. Some of them legalized their status later but many have remained illegal.

The continuous illegal mass entry of immigrants is documented daily in a tragic way: with deaths at the steep mountainous areas at the north borders of the country with Albania and Bulgaria, deaths at mine fields that cover part of the east borders with Turkey, deaths by drowning at frequent wrecks on the Aegean Sea.[2] There are no detailed elements, but the number of people who enter Greece illegally is the biggest among the countries of the European Union. This is due to the fact that Greece has broad borders with three of the countries of the former eastern bloc and it also has hundreds of islands, which neighbor with the Asiatic coast and thus lend themselves to illegal landing.

The reference to Greek islands neighboring with Asia does not exclusively concern geography: it also concerns the political and economic situation that prevails in the countries of this area and forces millions of people to become refugees or immigrants. Thus thousands of Kurds from Turkey, Iraq and Iran; Afghans; Pakistanis; Indians; Palestinians; Filipinos; and people of other Asian countries seek shelter in Greece. To those, refugees from various African countries are added.

The biggest number of immigrants and refugees, however, come from countries of Eastern Europe: mainly from Albania, the republics of the former USSR, Bulgaria, Poland, and Rumania. Among these, members of native Greek minority groups in the former USSR and Albania represent a particular case as they become legal rather easily. Individuals coming from Greek minorities of former USSR countries acquire Greek citizenship quickly.[3] On the contrary, many limitations apply in the case of all other immigrants and refugees, the result being that many hundred thousands live in Greece illegally.[4]

It is a common belief that the Greek economy has greatly benefited from the work of immigrants, particularly illegal immigrants.[5] Indeed, it is considered that Greece managed to reach the economic indicators that were required for its participation in the united European currency due to their work. Their low wages, which by violation of the law are by far below the legal limit, allowed the Greek economy development rates much higher than its inherent possibilities and mainly allowed its growth in sectors, such as agriculture, tourism, and construction, which would have stagnated without the cheap workforce of immigrants.

This reality is obvious not only in the economic indicators but also in the everyday life of even the most distant villages. With their work, immigrants revitalized economic units that had been threatened with extinction and contributed to the creation of new ones, thus producing surplus value and consequently prosperity. Moreover, many middle-class Greek families have been given the opportunity to improve their standard of living by taking advantage of the cheap services offered by immigrants (house cleaners, house maintenance and repair, etc.) that under different circumstances these families could not afford.

Nevertheless, it is also true that parallel to the many people who have benefited from the illegal work of immigrants, there is also a smaller number of the Greek population that has suffered economic damage. According to Sarris and Zografakis (1999), the illegal occupation of immigrants in the Greek economy has contributed to an increase of the income chasm between the poor and the rich. The same scientists estimate that 37 percent of the Greek population that live in urban households and whose head is one inexperienced worker suffer loss from the illegal work of immigrants, while all other groups of the population benefit.[6]

THE PUBLIC DISCOURSE ON RACISM

The question, Is there racism? raised in Greece is usually related to the question, What should or has to be characterized as racism? The answer offered by Greek society is not different from other European societies—where often the question about the existence of racism is answered negatively due to the choice of a very limited definition of racism.

In Greece, the spontaneous response is that there is no racism. This is a common response despite the large number of attacks against immigrants—attacks justified by the offenders on the ground of the victims' origin.[7] The refutation of even the suspicion of the existence of racism is usually based on a simple deliberation: racism is incompatible with Greek civilization. The arguments offered in support of this deliberation are:

1. "Traditional Greek hospitality" has never in the history of the Greek nation allowed racism to appear.
2. Racism has long been condemned as a heresy by the Greek Orthodox Church, to which most Greek people belong.

Of course, everyone can judge if the above arguments justify the deliberation on the basis of which the existence of racism is refuted. It is true, however, that such a deliberation often obstructs processes of collective self-knowledge and obliges to a state of censorship and self-censorship all those who do not want to risk a clash with their social environment by declaring the opposite.[8]

Contrary to denying the existence of racism, the view that the Greek society is characterized by strong "xenophobia" is widespread. This fact may surprise as controversial but it is easily explained if we consider that for Greek-language users the two words are differently charged—both semantically and emotionally.

In the case of racism, the concept is exclusively associated with negative facts that happened abroad: such facts are mainly the racism of Nazi Germany, the apartheid of South Africa, the racial discrimination of past times in the American South. In all cases the concept is associated with unfair, aggressive behavior exclusively originating from victimizers.

On the contrary, the word "xenophobia" is a neologism even for Greeks. Although it is made up of two Greek words, it does not draw its origin from the Greek language but it is a loan from abroad. As a neologism it does not bear any historical luggage and is understood by Greek-language users only etymologically: "the fear caused by strangers." In this case, if there is any aggressive behavior, it comes from the individual who causes the fear and not from the individual who feels fear. It is, in other words, a concept in which both victims and victimizers are not defined in the same obvious way as in the case of racism; indeed, in some cases the roles appear reversed. In the case of xenophobia, the xenophobe may be accused of unjustified fear. However, the proof of the fact that the fear is not justified falls as the obligations of other individuals. This proof is usually the responsibility of strangers themselves, of those who support the presence of strangers, and finally of those who allow the entry of strangers.[9]

From the above, it becomes obvious that in the Greek context, the choice of the word "xenophobia" as opposed to the word "racism" is not innocent but has a particular function, which goes hand in hand with the function the concept has acquired in the rest of Europe. Indeed, one can hardly deny the significance the concept of xenophobia has acquired in the European political and scientific discourse—to a large degree as a result of the fact that in most texts of the European Union and the European Council as well as in the official political discourse it almost always accompanies the term "racism." Nevertheless, the use of the two terms as an unbreakable pair—racism and xenophobia—evokes the impression that racism is a result, almost the "next phase" of fear caused by the presence of strangers.

Thus in an almost self-evident way two forms of racism become inferior or are completely abolished in the frame of public discourse:

1. Racism resulting from self-interest as a behavior consciously chosen because it yields profit.
2. Institutional racism: the racism of the state and its services.

These are very significant omissions with serious repercussions in the study of racism and its confrontation. This is particularly true of the second case because (1) institutional racism is the strongest and most painful form of racism and (2) it nourishes and legalizes the xenophobia of simple people.[10]

These omissions are not random. They are the result of the prevalent view concerning the bearers of racism, according to which racism concerns just individuals who have no correct knowledge of the facts associated with a particular group of people (e.g., immigrants and those who have a socially unacceptable attitude toward this group). According to this view, this incorrect knowledge and the socially unacceptable attitude results in a negative behavior of the particular people, which in terms of the dominant perspective is conceptually identified with racism. Consequently, in this framework, prevention and confrontation of racism restricts the modification of incorrect knowledge and the alteration of attitudes individuals hold for the particular group.

One realizes that to the degree this theoretical framework is inadequate or incorrect, as it does not include institutional racism and racism born out of self-interest, the corresponding activities for handling racism will be equally inadequate and ineffective.

RACISM, XENOPHOBIA, AND THE CONCEPT OF THE OTHER

The attempt to describe the extent and nature of racism in Greece with the assistance of scientific research studies that have been conducted to this day reveals the absence of relevant studies. In addition, there are not any reports by governmental services about racist discrimination in everyday life, neither about assaults with racist motives against immigrants and members of minority groups—despite the fact that the media often report incidents[11] like the following one:[12]

> In a village of 5,000 people, in Kriekouki, Attica, two dozen villagers took wood and iron clubs and rifles and took it upon themselves to "correct" the economic immigrants. On the night of May 17th the "army" assembled as if in a conspiracy. "Twenty to twenty-five people," says Thanassis G., and another villager adds: "They took a fifteen year old boy with them to show him how they beat people." They ran wild to the old houses where Albanians sleep and began to hit whoever they happened upon. "They broke the jaw of a 17 year-old Albanian, the heel of another one." . . . On the next evening, 18th of the month, the incidents were repeated but to a smaller extent. The commander of the police station did not have evidence in his hands so he could not move the procedures. "If they press charges, I will start the preliminary investigation," he said.[13]

The practice of governmental authorities of not documenting racist attacks and consequently not publishing relevant reports is in complete opposition to the practice applied in the case of documentation and publication of crime. Crime is reported and publicized on the basis of the ethnic origin of suspects. This is also true of Gypsies, who are Greek citizens and who in educational matters are denied ethnic distinctiveness by the Ministry of Education and the educational authorities, thus being denied the right to be taught in their mother tongue.[14]

Consequently, it is impossible to draw conclusions about the extent of racism in Greece based on official data. On the contrary, there are many reports concerning xenophobia—in reality, certain views and attitudes. These are usually "asserted" through questionnaires including hypothetical questions of the type, Would you like your child to attend the same class with foreign children? or spurious questions of the type, Which of the following groups don't you trust?[15] There are numerous such research studies, which fill newspapers and trigger comments by government officials. These comments usually include an appeal for tolerant behavior and a reassuring statement confirming the will and ability of the government to check every possible danger caused by foreigners.

A characteristic example is a research study conducted by Eurobarometer (funded by the European Union) in the fall of 2000. The media publicized in the strongest possible way (e.g., front-page coverage, TV and radio shows) the results of this study, according to which Greece had 38 percent, the highest percentage of xenophobia in Europe, the average being 15 percent. According to the study, 21 percent of Greek people are bothered by the presence of people with different religion (Belgium: 26 percent, Denmark: 31 percent, Ireland: 8 percent); 24 percent are bothered by the presence of people of different race (Belgium: 27 percent, Denmark: 23 percent, Ireland: 20 percent); 38 percent are bothered by the presence of citizens of different nationality in their country (Belgium: 24 percent, Denmark: 24 percent, Ireland: 17 percent).[16]

Equivalent coverage was given to other similar research studies, which yielded similar results. A good example is the discovery that only 36 percent of the Greek people agree to the statement: "It is positive for a society to be made up of different races, religions, and cultures" (Austria: 52 percent, Germany: 53 percent, Belgium: 56 percent, Sweden" 77 percent).

An engagement with the inevitable contradictions of the results of these research studies, which would definitely yield much more interesting results than the mere presentation of percentages, does not concern this chapter.[17] Xenophobia is recorded by the media and political leaders in Greece as a negative phenomenon that needs to be confronted. A proof of the relative interest of political leaders is the funding of intervention programs and the support of NGOs that are active in this field.

However, it is self-evident that a disturbing phenomenon cannot be dealt with on the basis of a simple record of answers to certain questions. For this purpose, a theory is required, which would help interpret facts and reveal the reasons underlying the disturbing phenomenon. In the face of a public denial of the existence of racism, on the one hand, and public disturbance by xenophobia, on the other, there is such a theory.

A review of literature and of public discourse unfolding in the media promotes a theory that interprets racism and xenophobia as products of a problematic relationship of an individual with the Other. Most representatives of this theory locate the beginning of the problematic relationship in a strong distrust toward strangers as a result of their education or of their personal inability to reject classifications that applied only in the past. Serious studies within this framework lead to identification of the role that central ideological constructions of the Greek ruling class have played, the most prevalent of which is the central significance given to the concept of the Greek nation and the particular religion in all ideological institutions and especially in school. Other studies locate the problem in the absence of personal experience with the Other or inadequate knowledge about the Other.

All studies, given that in relevant polls the percentage of disturbing answers is higher among people with low educational level and is reduced as the educational level of interviewees increases, point to the same conclusion: handling the problem is just a case of certain changes in education aiming at the proper information about the specific groups of strangers who are the target of xenophobia. These changes would center on the school with the advent of intercultural educational programs and also on the wider society with corresponding intercultural activities of "educational character."

Indeed, closer observation reveals that the concept of the Other does not correspond to a distinct representation in people's minds. On the contrary, when people think of the social categories and groups against which xenophobia is directed, they use exclusively special and distinct terms ("Albanians,"

"Turks," "Blacks," "Muslims," etc.). They resort, that is, to social classifications using certain features that have acquired specific content in their lives, such as ethnicity, religion, or skin color. These are both real features and social constructions that have acquired a character of real features. Nevertheless, the Other as a distinct concept does not exist in their minds. Social scientists are the people who for their own purposes (e.g., economy of language) put the common umbrella Other over the above terms. In other words, the Other does not exist as a social construction but only as a sum of social categories without, however, characterizing an entity with new qualities. That is why social actors use it just as a synonym of its parts (Other means "the Albanian," "the Gypsy," "the Muslim," the "foreigner," even "the stranger" in the sense of the unknown or the one not belonging to the particular group.)

These observations have practical value. In the past, new and refined terms without real content were often used in social sciences simply to impress. Most of them have disappeared without any consequences for science or society. There have been, however, cases, and this is one of them, where the use of such a term is pregnant with danger.

The use of the concept of the Other in a way that refers to something self-existent allows certain representatives of this theory to locate the start of this problematic relationship in the very nature of the human being. In other words, it allows them to consider disbelief, fear, even aggressiveness in the relationship with the Other as a biological disposition. In this framework, it is quite characteristic that the bibliography recommended for intercultural and antiracist education in Greek schools includes the book *On Human Nature* by the founder of sociobiology, E. O. Wilson.[18] The same book holds a distinct position in the small library of the "FORUM of Social Organizations ALL DIFFERENT—ALL EQUAL," which has been funded by the Greek government and the European Community and in which governmental services and antiracist NGOs participate.

The prevalence of the concept of the Other in Greece follows trends in the relevant public discourse in almost all other countries in Europe. Indeed, attempts to define racism as a product of erroneous views and unacceptable attitudes and to locate the reasons for its existence in a problematic relationship with the Other seem to be common in most European countries.

A characteristic example is the insistence of politicians who participated in the International Holocaust Conference in Stockholm (January 2000) to describe the Holocaust as an example of lack of tolerance and understanding of the Other, the "Different," the "Stranger." Obviously this is a case of an unintentional effort to reconcile the historical facts with today's predominant theory about the origin of racism.

However, the Holocaust itself contradicts the views that at the beginning of the process toward racism lies a problematic relationship of the individual with the Other or inadequate knowledge of the "stranger" and the "different."

A closer look at the experience of the Holocaust reveals that the victims were "next-door neighbors." People who, until the appearance of the racist propaganda and the establishment of the racist regime, nobody had considered strangers or Others. They were neighbors, fellows at school or work, colleagues, fellow players in orchestras and in athletic groups, comrades-in-arms in the German army, decorated national heroes. They were often spouses.

In other words, the moral we can reach from the study of racism of that period is that it is not some different, some strangers, some Others who are the target of racists and become first victims of discrimination and later victims of genocide. It is not particular characteristics of the victims that cause the racist brutality but, on the contrary, it is the racist brutality that constructs often nonexistent and invisible differences and turns "our people" to "other people."

It is characteristic that racist scientists recorded as "the most dangerous biological feature" of Jews "their adaptability to the people of the country they lived, so that they did not differ from them." Thus the "certificate of Aryan origin," which was considered a prerequisite for a marriage license or professional practice, was given after investigation of the origin of ancestors up to seven generations back—because nothing visibly different, strange, or Other existed to justify the racist discriminations and the racist crime, it had to be discovered in the distant past.

An argument of our time against the theory that xenophobia is the result of an a priori rejection of the Other constitutes the spontaneous reaction of Greeks to boat people: in every case of mass landing, the residents with their reaction of solidarity obliged authorities to provide hospitality and permanent stay. In other words, what is an illegal immigrant for the authorities and what is the Other for social scientists, for common people are human beings in danger, who cause spontaneous feelings of solidarity.

Despite all the relevant facts, it seems that ruling political classes and the scientists who share their views like to blame the responsibility for racism and xenophobia either on human nature or on innate human inadequacy to experience the "Other," the "stranger," the "different." Greece does not seem to deviate from the prevalent trends.

However, experiences until now, and in particular those of the Holocaust and apartheid, oblige the adoption of a perspective that takes into consideration all forms of racism and the ways racism associated among them.

FORMS OF RACISM AND XENOPHOBIA

Historical experience forces us to understand racism as a network of views, attitudes, behaviors, and/or established measures that obliges people in subordination only because they belong to a distinct social category.[19] As an excuse for the discrimination, the distinctiveness of the group is often used, to which it is often attached a supposed inferiority and/or dangerousness.

In relation to the above definition of racism, three points need to be stressed:

1. Racism is detected in the discriminations that result in subordination. Consequently, a basic element is the behavior against the distinct social category and not the views about it and the attitudes toward it. Even if there is usually a harmonious relationship among views, attitudes, and behaviors, it so happens that racist behavior does not necessarily presuppose the existence of negative views and attitudes, and conversely, negative views and attitudes do not always lead to negative behavior.

2. A necessary element for the appearance of racism is the ability of exercising power against a distinct social group. Thus, racism may emerge only in conditions of unequal distribution of social and/or political power and it is exclusively initiated by the mighty. On the contrary, members of socially and politically weak groups may develop racist behaviors only against members of weaker groups and only on the condition that they do not face the opposition of a stronger form of power, such as the state authority.

3. The spectrum of subordination is wide: it ranges from derogatory expression to murder. In social life, however, its very core is always exclusion from public and social goods or unequal participation in them.

On the basis of this perception, careful observation reveals that racism appears in Greece, as well as in other European countries, in three different ways:

1. Racism = negative views + negative attitudes + negative behavior + power, the result being the subordination of the group subjected to the negative behavior.

2. Racism = personal profit + negative behavior + power, the result being the subordination of the group subjected to the negative behavior.

3. Racism = institutionalized measures of discrimination + exercise of power on the part of authorities, the result being the subordination of the group subjected to the negative behavior.

In Greece, when in the public discourse there is reference to "xenophobia and racism," as a rule the first form of racism is meant. Nevertheless, the other two forms of racism are more frequent and more intense. Moreover, they constitute the basis for the construction of negative views and attitudes and the framework of tolerance of the racist behavior of individuals and groups.

The examples that follow may illustrate the way in which the institutional preservation of many immigrants in an illegal status and the "self-evident" unequal distribution of power foster racism.

Case 1: Status of Illegitimacy and Subordination to the Employer

The way in which employers exploited the illegal status of immigrants to avoid paying wages for months was already reported in the 1980s. On October 17, 1984, the newspaper *AVGI* reported:

> There is a large network of employers-policemen that jointly exploit illegal workers from Pakistan and India. Certain employers employ these illegal foreign workers with ridiculous payment and when payday approaches, the employers call the police. The unprotected and illegal foreigners, well aware of their precarious status (they have no work permit), flee to the mountains and gorges to hide and the last thing they care about is their payment.

Immigrants today face similar problems. This applies more in the case of female illegal immigrants who are forced into prostitution. When they turn to the police they are the first ones to be punished with deportation for their illegal entry into Greece. Their deportation means the following:

1. They will never be given the right to enter Greece or any other European Union country legally.
2. They cannot testify as witnesses against their procurers at the trial that follows.
3. They usually fall back in the hands of the procurers of their country and after an exemplar punishment for their insubordination they are sent back to the same or another country.

In other words, the illegal status becomes a framework in which coercion develops, which in turn perpetuates subordinate and undignified living conditions.

Case 2: Unequal Distribution of Power and Subordination to the Local Community

Since 1991, approximately 150 Albanian workers with their families have lived and worked in the village of Loutra in Lesvos. The coexistence of Greeks and Albanians presented no problems until June 29, 2001. On that day, a group of young Albanians, irritated at being denied entrance to a disco, beat and wounded four Greek peers. At once the police deported the Albanians who participated in the incident, and the local authorities decided to expel all Albanians and their families from their village (even though they had no legal right to do it).

The municipal council of Lesvos, to which the community of Loutra belongs administratively, "despite their reservations for the decision, characterize the reactions justified and deem the decision worked positively since no outrages were committed on the part of the indignant villagers."[20]

A few days later, the president of the Greek Republic expressed the view that the discrimination committed by institutional members against a whole group of people not only does not constitute a racist act but, on the contrary, functions as a shield against racism. During his visit to the island, he stated that the group expulsion of 150 people on the mere grounds that they were Albanians "was not an expression of racist sentiments. If it were for such feelings, [the villagers] would not have accepted [the Albanians] from the beginning. It was merely the expression of a reaction and indignation for an action which was considered an insult against local people and their kind behavior."[21]

The assessment of the above action by the president of Greek Republic is characteristic of the prevalent view for the concept of racism: racism, as it follows from the above statement, is for the ruling political class the expression of negative sentiments that exist in the relationship of groups before their first meeting and manifest themselves with negative behavior and rejection from the first moment.

With this in mind, one can understand the phenomenon described in a previous section, that is, to reject the view that there is racism in Greece and at the same time, to admit that there is strong xenophobia.

Indeed, if such a conceptual framework is acceptable, it makes sense that cases such as the following are not labeled racist:

1. "Armed residents in Gianitsohori, Ilia, beat, wounded, threatened and humiliated 25 young Albanians, because, according to information, some of them asked a decrease of working hours (they worked from dawn to dusk, i.e., 12–13 hours a day) and better wages."[22]
2. "The communal council of Poulitsa, Korinthia, decided to forbid the selling of alcohol to Albanians and fixed the highest wage for them at the amount of 5,000 drachmas (i.e., much lower than the legal limit)."[23]

From these examples, one can easily realize that through unequal distribution of power within the boundaries of a local community, Greek people profit and immigrants are condemned to subordinate living. It is a relationship that is condemned in words, but in practice it obviously enjoys the acceptance of the ruling political class.

The fact that the contradiction of rhetoric and practice is a political choice becomes evident with the third example.

Case 3: Legalization of Immigrants' Residency and Award of Employers' Illegal Action

The process of legalization of the thousands of illegal immigrants is used for the returns of social security contributions, which were lost since the immigrants' work was illegal. In order to acquire a green card, one of the conditions was to have collected a certain minimum number of social security stamps, very difficult for those working "off the books." However, for legalization purposes, the immigrant is entitled to buy stamps by paying the equivalent, without having to prove that he or she actually worked and without having to name certain employers.[24] The process has particular significance because the equivalent that the immigrant pays in order to buy stamps is mainly paid by the employer in the case of legal occupation. Thus immigrants are not only paid by employers far below the legal ceiling but at the same time they are charged with the employer's contribution to social security.

The above procedure essentially secures the influx of contributions in the social security fund but at the same time, for employers, it secures that the cost of work remains exceptionally low. Consequently, from the particular form of legalization, profits ensue for the social security fund and the Greek employers of immigrants, while on the contrary, the economic cost is awfully high for immigrants. In essence, the illegitimacy of employers is prescribed and resources are transferred as a kind of fine from immigrants to the social security fund.

The question raised is why immigrants are interested in this form of legalization. The answer is simple: mainly in order to avoid a sudden deportation that may occur any time they are in the status of illegal residency.[25] Indeed, illegal immigrants commonly stay and work, the police being in the know, but they are not arrested or deported. Police officers who decide to act of their own accord are usually opposed by employers of illegal immigrants. Employers, through networks of clientele relations with local authorities and politicians, usually manage to escape punishment as well as to impose complete inertia on the part of police and consequently, the de facto recognition of illegal occupation. This, however, is overthrown from time to time, because the police proceed to extended operations of discovery, arrest and deportation of illegal immigrants after a decision of the central administration, usually the Ministry of Public Order. These operations have an exclusive goal: to create the impression that the state fights illegal immigration. Thus, immigrants who are arrested, are taken by buses back to the borders and are deported from the country—always accompanied by TV crews and with public statements by governmental executives for the harsh punishment of illegal immigration.

All the above illustrate the ways in which the following significant but contradictory goals are reconciled in practice:

1. The interest of Greek employers and the Greek economy in general for the illegal occupation of immigrants.
2. The need to avoid large deficits in the social security fund.
3. The interest of the state to appear powerful, competent and determined to protect the law and to fight illegal immigration.

The blend of these contradictory goals may satisfy many targets of the economy and the state, but it also has a significant collateral consequence:

the creation of feelings of fear and insecurity among a part of the indigenous population.

STATUS OF ILLEGITIMACY AND EMERGENCE OF XENOPHOBIA

As actions of power display, police operations of mass arrests and deportations of illegal immigrants usually occur as a reaction to incidents of criminal acts in which foreigners appear involved. In addition, in everyday language these police operations are called "operations sweep," and they largely contribute to the formulation of views, attitudes and behaviors in relation to immigrants. For a part of the population, indeed the part that formulates views under the influence of the media and in harmony with the behavior of the state authorities, the police operations constitute an indication of the dangerousness of immigrants. Moreover, their arrest and deportation in a mass way establishes the impression that immigrants as a social category constitute a direct threat, which justifies emergency measures.[26] Consequently, the source of fear of strangers, which occupies a part of the Greek population, may be located very easily: it is the activity of the state against illegal immigrants.[27]

This fear coupled with the fact that several indigenous workers are actually affected by the illegal occupation of immigrants—they are affected by the fact that many employers can occupy workers with very low wages and without proper social security—constitutes the basis of what several research studies define as xenophobia.

CONCLUSION

A closer look at racism and xenophobia in Greece makes us realize the significance of the distinction between the racism of the rich and mighty and the xenophobia of the poor and weak. The former grows and is preserved because of self-interest and it enjoys the protection of the state in many ways. The latter is the fear born and fed out of the former and can turn into racism in state-provided conditions.

It is obviously significant to gain an insight of nature of racism and its function at a time when profit constitutes the first and foremost criterion by which social phenomena are assessed. In this way we may explain, without resorting to an alleged deficit of human beings, why racism exists and is sustained despite its moral condemnation.

NOTES

1. The origin and spread of such theories follows a characteristic route from the center of power to the periphery. They are born in places and countries where political authority is powerful and they are carried to areas and countries where political power is reinforced with the support that such "valid scientific theories" bring to bear.

In relation to this, it could be proven very useful to read anew, to reformulate and adjust to new data the model proposed by Galtung (1971) about the types of imperialism associated with center–periphery relationships, in which special emphasis is given to the significance of communication and culture.

2. See Tsiakalos 2000, where many such incidents are recorded. The number increased radically in 2001, particularly after the beginning of military operations in Afghanistan.

3. Greek-origin immigrants from Albania are not treated in the same way as Greek-origin immigrants from the former USSR, who acquire Greek citizenship easily. The ulterior motive of the Greek government to maintain a large number of Greek minority residents in Albania confronts these immigrants with the following paradox: on the one hand, they are entitled to legalize their stay in Greece and acquire a status that gives them a privilege in relation to foreigners; on the other, however, it is much harder for them to acquire Greek citizenship (and therefore to become "Greek") compared to other groups of immigrants. Thus they remain "foreigners" with significant negative consequences in their lives. Unlike Greek citizens, they are not entitled to freely immigrate to more prosperous countries of the EU.

4. A publication of the Jesuit Refugee Service Europe (Barrett 2001, 37) refers to the ways and difficulties of legalization: "The regulation campaign in Greece started in 1998. The first phase was that of recording the foreigners and lasted for 5 months. Anyone missing the deadline was not allowed an extension. Those recorded were allowed to stay, work legally, and proceed to the second phase, that of acquiring the 'limited duration residence permit,' or 'Green Card.' In order to acquire the Green Card, one of the conditions was to have collected a certain minimum number of social security stamps, very difficult for those working 'off the books.' The Green Card is issued usually for 1 year, but considerable delays in the process meant that not all applications were considered within a year of being made. In order to renew [it] a much higher number of social security stamps were needed. Few migrants are able to provide that, and so very many were expected to fall back into irregularity once more."

5. See Sarris and Zografakis 1999.

6. The above speculation refers to illegal occupation and not to the occupation of immigrants in general.

7. See Tsiakalos 2000.

8. That this is not just a matter of speech becomes obvious from the following incident: On February 2, 2001, the three-member trial court of Athens sentenced the architect Sotiris Bletsas to fifteen months in prison and a fine for "dissemination of false news." His "crime" was distributing a chart of languages spoken in Europe issued by the European Bureau for Less Used Languages (EBLUL), an EU institution that functions due to a decision of the European Parliament and funded by the Commission. In this chart there is a reference, which is false according to the plaintiffs and the court decision, to the fact that in Greece, "except Greek and parallel to it" the native population also speak Turkish, Slav Macedonian, Arvanitika, and Vlahika. A member of the Greek parliament, among others, had lodged the complaint.

Of course, the existence of these languages is known not only to linguists but also to all Greeks and the thousands of people who speak them as mother tongues.

9. In everyday language, people use the word "stranger" as a synonym for "foreigner."

10. See Tsiakalos 1983.

11. See Tsiakalos 2000. An effort for systematic report of racist discriminations and assaults is made by certain NGOs (e.g., Greek Helsinki Watch), which are funded for this purpose by international organizations, including the EU Commission.

12. See Tsiakalos 2000.

13. *Eleftherotypia*, May 21, 1993 (a daily newspaper with the largest circulation in Greece).

14. The view of the person in charge of special programs for the education of Roma children is quite characteristic. To the question of educators if Roma constitute a minority and consequently if they have the right to their mother tongue (Romane), he answered, "Greek Gypsies are a part of the Greek people and the Greek nation both through time and at present. They are not a minority. Therefore, we do not talk about a minority. . . . Some of the Greek Gypsies are Muslims in their religion. Muslim Gypsies are officially protected by the known treaty, which defines minority educational matters in Greece" (Ethnicity and Intercultural Education 1998, 67–68).

With the last sentence, reference is made to the Treaty of Lausanne between Greece and Turkey, in effect since 1923. This treaty determines, among other things, that "Muslim minorities" in Greece and "Christian minorities" in Turkey have the right to be taught in their mother tongues. The executive of the Ministry of Education considers that when Gypsies are Muslims they are a minority and therefore have the right to their mother tongue. On the contrary, Christians or atheists belong "through time and at present to the Greek nation." Since they are not "protected" by international treaties, it is not possible to be considered by either scientists or educators a distinct cultural, social language minority with a distinct mother tongue.

Then again, the same people are considered and are automatically recorded as minorities when they are involved in crimes.

15. It is difficult to claim that this method succeeds in recording true attitudes. What it records is the subject's view about his or her attitude.

16. Obviously in the presentation of the study results, the media identify xenophobia with the negative assessment of the presence of other nationalities in the country.

17. The complete lack of such a discussion is a sign of limited interest in the real phenomena, which could be revealed through comparison, analysis, and interpretation of data of all relevant studies.

Similar studies during the same period of time detect different attitudes when the question concerns the personal relationship of the interviewee with foreigners. Thus in a study conducted by KAPPA Research in February 2001, to the question, "Would it bother you to associate with people of different nationality," 92.1 percent replied they would not be bothered and only 6.2 percent claimed the opposite. Similar were the results concerning religion and people of color (87.4 percent vs. 11.5 percent, and 91.2 percent vs. 8.1 percent, correspondingly).

18. For a criticism of an alleged biological basis of xenophobia, see Tsiakalos 1982.

19. A distinct group is not the same as a visible group, and its existence does not assume the existence of a real feature. The distinct group is often a construct.

20. *Ta Nea*, August 18, 2001.

21. *Eleftherotypia*, August 16, 2001.

22. *Metro*, May 1998.

23. *Metro*, May 1998.

24. For the legalization process of 2001, stamps equivalent to 250 wages within 12 months were required. A figure, which in reality is never reached by any worker.

25. In a poll conducted by the Ministry of Internal Affairs, to the question "What problems does legalization solve in your everyday life?" 43.9 percent of the immigrants answered "I will be able to move freely, without fear," 32.9 percent "I will be able to work legally," 28.9 percent "I may come and go to my country as I please," 16.7 percent "I will have social security/health care," 13.2 percent "I will be able to live with my family" (*Eleftherotypia*, July 6, 2001).

26. This behavior on the part of authorities offers socially acceptable arguments to racist and fascist organizations so that they can consciously develop their activities. The latter will reinforce the activity of the state and contribute to rekindling a sense of insecurity and xenophobia.

27. With reference to the way that public discourse for immigrants, even in the case of good intentions, may cater to fear and reinforce negative attitudes and racist behaviors, see Tsiakalos 1983.

REFERENCES

Barrett, Lena, ed. 2001. *Voices from the Shadows: Stories of Men and Women Living with Irregular Migration Status.* Brussels: Jesuit Refugee Service Europe.

Ethnicity and Intercultural Education. 1998. Proceedings of the Roundtable Religion and Cultural Identity: A Model for Intercultural Education for Greece of 2000. Project 37188–CP-3–97–1–GR-COMENIUS-C2, 1998. Ioannina, Greece, December.

Galtung, Johan. 1971. "A Structural Theory of Imperialism." *Journal of Peace Research* 8, no. 2: 81–118.

Sarris, A., and S. Zografakis. 1999. "A Computable General Equilibrium Assessment of the Impact of Illegal Immigration on the Greek Economy." *Journal of Population Economics* 12, 155–82.

Tsiakalos, Georgios. 1982. "Ablehnung von Fremden und Aussenseitern." *Unterricht Biologie*, August–September, 49–58.

———. 1983: *Ausländerfeindlichkeit: Tatsachen und Erklärungsversuche.* Munich: Beck.

———. 2000: *Handbook of Antiracist Education.* Athens: Ellinika Grammata. In Greek.

13
VIOLENCE IN THE NEW GERMANY: REFLECTIONS ABOUT THE CONNECTION BETWEEN BLOCKED IMMIGRATION, POLITICS, AND PEDAGOGY

Franz Hamburger

Immigrants in Germany, especially eastern Germany, can no longer live safely. In public places and in broad daylight they are chased, harassed, beaten, and sometimes even killed. The police and the local authorities are not able to guarantee safety, appropriate education, or criminal prosecution for those who perpetuate hate crimes. In some sensational cases, the Federal Prosecutor's Office has taken over the investigation of murder cases, an unusual procedure authorized by the Federal Court despite the resistance of local authorities. Another example of this fearful situation is the action of a prosecuting attorney in Thuringen, who, without any evidence, blamed a left-wing extremist for the arson attack on a synagogue in Erfurt until the facts proved otherwise. This unusual procedure of the Federal Prosecutor's Office taking over investigations was used before and after 1993, but at that time Jews were not harassed and killed in broad daylight as is the case today with foreigners in eastern Germany.

IMPENETRABILITY OF THE VIOLENCE STATISTICS

The year 1995 began with positive news for the "New Germany": "The number of xenophobic acts of violence and crime in the past year distinctly decreased." This information in the *Süddeutsche Zeitung* (February 3, 1995) was given the political "all-clear" signal because it meant a drop of 50 percent, compared to 3,100 xenophobic acts of violence in the year before.[1]

The expression "New Germany" has a double meaning and strange flavor. The state newspaper with the name *Neues Deutschland* of the former DDR (German Democratic Republic) used this title with the claim of the expression, but pathetically gambled it away during its existence. The current New Germany defines itself mostly through having overcome the DDR—except for the economic potential of the Big Germany, there have been no further attempts to connect the demanding elements of the weak democratic tradition with the current political tendency. Only by linking history with current developments can these points find any legitimacy—a legitimacy that can be achieved only when the everyday economic challenges are met instead of the usual lip service stirred up during election campaigns.

The birth of the New Germany was followed by an explosion of xenophobic violence. Between 1990 and 1993, the Federal Criminal Police Office registered 15,000 acts of violence against immigrants. The actual number, however, is probably much higher. Many acts of crime—even when directed against immigrants—are not always classified as hate crimes if there is no explicit xenophobic connection or xenophobic motive. Therefore the statistics of xenophobic acts of violence include only crimes that are easily recognizable as such.

Recently there have been more and more occasions when police investigation takes the acts of violence out of the xenophobic context and explains them as private revenge. A report from March 10, 1995, illustrates this point:

> Two arson attacks were committed on houses with mostly Turkish tenants in Gladbeck, North Rhein-Westphalia. The house occupants were able to put out the fire, according to the Criminal Police Office in Recklinghausen. A nineteen-year-old Turkish woman was brought to the hospital with suspected smoke inhalation. There were no obvious suspects. The house occupants including the injured woman would be questioned, said the police spokesperson, though the motives of the attacks were unknown. Around 2:45 A.M. strangers threw flammable material—probably gasoline—in the wooden hallway of those two houses located in Brauck district. The house occupants noticed the fire because of the strong smoke and put it out. The police ruled out the possibility of a xenophobic act of violence in all likelihood.

As this type of incident occurred more frequently, the claim that these incidents are not xenophobic crime continued even after the theory of general revenge was proven wrong. The statistics of the xenophobic crime are therefore much closer in number to the entire police crime statistics because they are interest-manipulated in order to show evidence of progress in the area of security. The police authorities are not interested in having these crimes increase, because the police department already holds many pro–nation-state biases.

Data about the political and ideological orientations of police officers suggest that their closeness to Republicans is an important issue, especially when this orientation is coupled with the old right blindness of police and law and order. The attempt to promote a positive image of the German nation is not easily compatible with a special investigation strategy for xenophobic crimes. Many crimes are not being reported mainly because victims are frightened or because the offenders are protected by connections with those in power.

The temporary climate of public concern also should not be used as a point of reference for political manipulation to the degree that, in the long run, it could damage the image of Germany as an export power in the world. A short notice in the *Süddeutsche Zeitung,* December 21, 1994, unveiled the issue and its respective connections. The Federal Criminal Police Office received, in the first three-quarters of the year, 937 reports of anti-Semitic acts of violence as informed by the federal government on request of the Party of Democratic Socialism (PDS) in the Bundestag.[2] The Grünen (Green Party) in Rhineland-Pfalz's *Landtag* (state parliament) initiated a research study that showed that a majority of the suspects were between eleven and fourteen years old—not even of the age of criminal responsibility—and most of the other suspects were between fifteen and eighteen years old. Thus we find high levels of youth violence, which is extraordinarily political, being depoliticized by certain interest groups.

XENOPHOBIC YOUTH VIOLENCE

Four towns symbolically express the terror of the New Germany: Hoyerswerda (September 1, 1991), Rostock (August 22, 1992), Molln (November 23, 1992), and Solingen (May 27, 1993). At the same time, they mark two different categories of events, which, when considered together, show the dimension of violence. In Hoyerswerda and Rostock, groups of youth and adults attacked and hurt groups of immigrants, especially undocumented aliens, with the approval of the watching crowd. The aggression in eastern Germany is rather obvious and legitimized by politics and the public. In Molln and Solingen, so-called individual offenders, from a milieu of violent youth, harassed and killed foreign families, mostly Turkish aliens.

According to the statistics of the Department of the Interior regarding violence of right-wing extremists, the number of reported crimes has increased as follows.

1988	73
1989	103
1990	270
1991	1,483
1992	2,285
1993	2,323

Clearly, the year of reunification of East and West Germany—1991—was a year of greatly increased violence. The term "youth violence" needs to be clarified. The age structure of the suspected offenders with proven or highly possible right-wing extremist motivation is indicated as follows.

16–17 years	20.3 percent
18–20 years	47.5 percent
21–30 years	29.0 percent
31–40 years	2.5 percent
41+ years	0.6 percent

I would like to take a critical look at this situation, including reactions to the violence, explanations and illusionary explanations, as well as demands on pedagogy.

ETHNICITY IN POLITICS

Violence against aliens—especially against Roma (Gypsies), who were victims of hate crimes in Germany—is connected to the politicized view of ethnicity as it is becoming increasingly visible. This form of politicization of ethnicity channels the potential violence, the proportions of which are shaped by many other factors as well. Through the politicization of a social problem—often intensified by media and the public—a group of people becomes the object of aggression. Wars and pogroms are always rooted in latent violent potential. Xenophobic aggression develops first through the political propaganda blindly embraced by young people who have friendly contacts with international youth groups that practice violence against foreigners. Therefore, what needs explanation is the direction of violent acts, not the latent propensity to violence.

In order to discuss this more general issue, a more comprehensive theory would be necessary in which the actual media-reinforced phenomena of public attention should not be included as empirical basis. Therefore, the issue is not, as it has been argued, that foreigners increasingly reject immigrants, but, instead, the political exploitation of the immigration process for the sake of preserving power.

The problem started with the "discovery" of immigration at the end of the 1970s. Its political interpretation can be illustrated in a randomly chosen news report from December 1, 1981: "Berlin's Turks' Decree. Immigrants—influx—time bomb. The immigrants' amendment proposed by the Berlin senator of the interior Lummer, who limited the influx of immigrant family members, albeit controversial, will be accepted because the other states in Germany struggle with the same problems. The difference is that in crowded Berlin the problems become more apparent sooner than anywhere else in Germany. The Christian Democratic Union Party (CDU)–ruled states Schleswig-Holstein and Baden-Württemberg have already expressed their approval."

The publicity surrounding the number of immigrants is a conspicuous cause that already unveiled its ideology in Schleswig-Holstein (as the state with the lowest percentage of immigrants). Since the beginning of the 1980s, the rejection of the immigration process has been a political pathology that invariably involves political interests, and violence is the price to be paid. This violence is not new—it was only repressed in public memory during the 1980s, through, among other things, the glossing over and playing down of such violence by the police public service. The ethnicization of politics began long before the violent predisposition problems of the youth, long before German unification, long before the disintegration of the eastern bloc and the ensuing east–west migration. The prepolitical xenophobia was transformed during the national unification while the politics of social inequality have had a continuous impact on it. However, it is not a combined strategy of both the national state and the society, marked by inequality that is directed against immigrants who are simply used as scapegoats. There are also some conflicting interests, which is why the historical comparison to fascism doesn't lead very far in uncovering the root cause of the current state of xenophobia. Policy makers would like to pretend that the economy is color-blind and can be exported to whomever, which partially holds back the state through competing political parties and their interests.

POLITICS OF SOCIAL INEQUALITY

The framework for the analysis of violence is complicated because of a specific combination of both immigration and social politics. Politics of social inequality has led to a considerable redistribution of social resources. Within the middle class of German society, the average income has decreased, while in the upper echelons of society the net income from business and property has grown continuously. If we look closer at the lower sector of society, we can easily see how the number of people receiving welfare has increased. However, even above this threshold, new forms of poverty have spread, creating a new class of working poor.

A quarter of German society is at least periodically threatened with poverty. If one is negatively affected by this social reality of the widening of inequality that reaches deep into the middle class, one has to have a deep political awareness to be able to explain the situation through something other than a scapegoat mechanism. The politics of inequality heightens the political contradictions of immigration. The social groups that are threatened with or affected by social decline support the legally structured exclusion of immigrants. In order to have a pariah class beneath the lowest social class, the weakest group of immigrants, asylum seekers, is particularly discredited and its membership in society is reduced to a status of bare existence. Immigrants are systematically included in the restructuring of the social inequality (although they themselves can be divided into further categories); in a restructured hierarchical society, immigrants are usually put in a precarious status at a precipice where they can easily be pushed over when the economy bursts due to the inherent design that produces inequalities.

MIGRATION AND IMMIGRATION POLITICS

By these processes it is not a question simply of social issues but also of political events. Years ago the "silly season" was filled with news about the Loch Ness monster—now, in election years, the immigrant problem is publicized. The explicitly right-wing extremist parties are not the only ones who try to win over voters by raising this issue. Instead, the parties compete to obtain approval by manipulating the mobilization of feelings about "us." Since communists or similar groups and systems are no longer a factor, the central element in the right-wing election campaign is the strategic link to the latent and manifest anxiety about foreign infiltration, fear of modernization, and national awareness.

However, since the majority of German society has grown accustomed to the presence of legal immigrants and the "asylum seeker flood," they cannot seriously complain about it; therefore the connection between immigrants and crime becomes very appealing. The crime anxiety and the fear of immigrants, which is not inherent but, rather, a result of an intensive media campaign, represent two forms of fear covered under one category. At least in the election campaigns, immigrants are also used for political purposes, and this way of using them has been economically worthwhile.

This "immigrant politics" is in conflict with a widely held assumption that Germany is a country of immigrants, and this fact constitutes a political issue. But even apart from the fact that immigration had been identified and accepted as a social issue by the end of the 1970s, the continuous presence of immigrants (9 percent of the population) has required relevant policies. However, for the last two decades these policies have failed to appear in every part of the country. Since 1979 the main claims included in the report of Heinz Kuhn, the first immigration representative in the German government, have not been addressed. This report analyzed from a sociological perspective the immigration process, formed the adequate educational and sociopolitical consequences, and did not yet require changes in state and naturalization laws in the way they are necessary today. Furthermore, the Immigrants Law of 1990 merely refined the defense mechanism and linked the few immigrants' rights with many requirements.

At the same time, continuous migration is, and has been, a part of society throughout human history. The intensity of migration and its forms vary, but there hasn't been an immobile time yet. Futile attempts to stop migration through the use of power are also part of the history of migration. Experiences such as the current situation on the border between Mexico and the United States, which is protected with a metal fence, or on the German eastern border, which is protected electronically, make clear the impossibility of building a European fortress. This fortress cannot exist because the Europe of the future relies on a cheap workforce, and Europe does not want production costs to increase. Europe will build walls against the unwanted influx, but it will open many gates for the influx it needs.

MIGRATION SOCIETY

For more than ten years Germany has had a migration measure of approximately 1.5 million people annually. The term "migration measure" includes the totality of migration, not just short-term immigration (e.g., tourists). The migration measure is the yardstick for the fluctuation at the borders of a society; in Europe, Germany is a comparatively restless country because it does not have any calming strategy, for example, in the form of naturalization politics. The extent of the annual migration measure is surprising also because of the continuously increasing portion of the foreign population living permanently in Germany. The problems caused by the permanent residence of immigrants and the continuous fluctuation need to be dealt with politically.

Considering fluctuation, internal European mobility has only just begun. The rules of liberality in the European Union are slowly becoming visible in social and cultural practices. The inclusion of the trans-nations status will speed up this process, which in general will lead to immigration to large European cities. The future will therefore be structured according to the pattern of the past. The migration of the highly qualified workforce will concentrate in the metropolis, where unskilled immigrants are also looking for jobs. This leads to the current, albeit paradoxical, situation: the number of poor people increases in the wealthy areas of Europe.

In view of the current level of refugees, containment politics is partially successful, but it cannot prevent approximately one hundred thousand people from entering Germany annually. In regard to immigrants, the situation was similar; stricter immigration requirements reduced the number of immigrants considerably. Even German embassies in other countries have broadcast the disadvantages immigrants face in Germany in order to reduce the desire to emigrate. In the history of migration, this strategy has often been more successful than physical barriers and walls.

The hindering of legal migration automatically increases illegal immigration. From the early to mid-1990s, the number of illegal entries and deportations grew five times higher, the number of police suspects without residence status doubled, and the number of proceedings against immigrants who were employed illegally was three times higher (Vogel 1996). This is where, in a way, the immigration political vicious circle closes. The presence of aliens who, just because they are aliens, are included in suspect statistics makes them easy prey for all populists and for a considerable crowd of politicians who request the tightening of immigration control. At the same time, the requests to the population from politicians suggest a solution to the problems that does not really work. The increase of illegality and its manipulation before elections is being used to intensify all kinds of fear. And this, again, can be used in politics.

Yet the reasons for the continuous immigration can be found within Germany. The demand for a cheap labor force, especially during particular seasons of the year, is easily addressed with an immigrant labor force. The expansion of unskilled services, the tax system supporting a service society, and the decrease of the price of labor in general create jobs for immigrants. Prostitution, private nursing, and subcontracted cleaning services require female staff, who are mostly requisitioned abroad. In this case the status of illegality is easily accepted or cleverly used, although it is connected with a beneficial dependence. Economically, the illegality and status without rights is worthwhile. Therefore the deregulation of the labor market has increased the incentives for migration within Germany.

The migration incentives are also being intensified abroad, albeit in a different way. Even if so-called globalization can be diagnosed not as a sudden jump into disaster but more as an argument prop in a battle for a share, the continuous process of the integration of the international economy is unstoppable. Increasingly more countries in the world (this is true also for Europe on a different level) are included in a world economy based on a division of labor, and they develop very specific sectoral concentrations, making them susceptible to crises. The mobilization of labor forces and their being laid off in crises cause migration pressure. The elimination of travel barriers by a worldwide flow of immigration traffic and the promotion of migration by an international mass communication system with its suggestive advertising campaigns do the rest to vitalize migration.

The role of migration is finally recognizable by the fact that this political reality is a conflict that threatens Middle Europe with a mass migration that not only has the support of NATO but also the whole sympathy of German foreign policies—no matter what their political intentions are.

NO STRUCTURING OF IMMIGRATION

The standstill in immigration politics was expressed by the *Süddeutsche Zeitung* on March 12, 1998, with the front-page headline "Children of immigrants still remain immigrants." This article was written at the end of the PDS's attempt to defeat the coalition through the fact that the differences between the Liberal Party of Germany (FDP) and the Christian Democratic Party and Christian Social Party (CDU/CSU) in terms of naturalization rights for immigrants' children are being used as scapegoats setting the stage in preparation for a parliament vote. Also the FDP gave up its plans (at least until the next preelection campaign) to support the issue that all children born in Germany should be able to acquire German citizenship. Bear in mind the fact that approximately one hundred thousand immigrants move annually to Germany. The paradox logic is to expose an undesirable group of immigrant children born in Germany who, in an extreme case, will never see the ascribed home country of their parents. Immigrants are not only an economical good as a labor source but also a political good. Immigration policies are used by politicians to demonstrate their liberality (minority position) or their loyalty to the native population through the unequal treatment of immigrants (majority position). The immigrant population, which is not entitled to vote, is exposed to this political manipulation.

Especially in times when the strengths of the nation-state control the politics of mainstream society, economics soften, and immigration as a wedge issue gains in importance, which, in turn, can ensure the increase of loyalty of voters to different political parties through symbolic action. In such a context, the trivial and at the same time audacious requirement of CSU, that immigrants who want to stay in Germany should learn to speak better German, can become a political argument.

The fact that immigrants are used as a political tool to increase the loyalty image of political parties diminishes the remaining chances for a structured integration politics. Even the continuous and consistent transformation from immigrants to nonimmigrants, which in Sweden, for instance, reaches a 5 percent rate of naturalization per year, is not possible in Germany with its 0.3 percent rate given the immigration restriction due to politics. Every discussion and reflection about culture, multiculturalism, and interculturalism must fit in the frame of immigration politics because the main argument in the culture discourse about difference and differences appears totally different under the circumstances of the fundamental inequality of immigrants and nonimmigrants than under the circumstances of equal rights.

POLITICS IN A TRANSNATIONAL SPACE

Two circumstances have a specific impact in the field of migration politics: the creation of transnational social spaces and the Europeanization of the political *instrumentarium*. The development of transnational social spaces through migration has been practiced as a research approach in the United States and contains ideas also for the European situation (Pries 1996). This concept has been developed specifically for the analysis of the migration between Latin America and North America. It clarifies that career biographies of many people cannot be sensibly assigned to national spaces. The premises of the national states perform biographies, but so does the opportunity structure for labor and life chances in an international space.

> By transnational social spaces are meant ordinary life realities, which develop mostly in context of international migration, and which are geographically—spatially diffused or deterritorialized. At the same time, they create not only a transitional social space, which is an important reference structure of social positions and positioning, as well as structures the ordinary life practice, career-biographic projects and identities of people and simultaneously points out the social connection of national societies. (Pries 1996, 24)

The reality reflected in this concept is remarkable through liquefaction of the previous orientation model, while the thinking in previous and present countries and the assignment of "identity" is usually linked to the nation-state.

Conversely, new structures develop, which can be analyzed in the following dimensions:

- political-regulative frame (support, tolerance, illegalization, prevention of migration; connection between residence permit, access to labor market, and social insurance system);
- material infrastructure (communication media provide for presence; transport media provide for exchange of products, money, persons; social nets, professional organizations, culture);
- social structures: positions, institutions, career backgrounds; and
- transnational identities.

In Europe, the strong ideological orientation toward the nation-state—despite or because of the integration of Europe—has blocked the development and adaptation of the concept of transnational social spaces (it does not overlook but demands the nation-state). In any case it requires separate summary observations. For instance, in many ways, the observed and problematized "migration pendulum" has been "normalized" as an element in this context. Also the differentiation, destandardization, and deregulation of European migration processes become easier to interpret. State-regulated social security systems lose their relevance for the immigrants because of the lack of importance of standardized labor relations. That is the reason the individualization impetus, which is usually connected to migration, becomes powerless for the sake of social integration—something that is typical for the second generation and encourages self-identification with ethnicity.

VIOLENCE

The research on violence in the past decades has been described as oppressor centered (Nedelmann 1997). If we take the victim's perspective into consideration, then the violence will be easily recognizable as a connections-and-relations characteristic. There is a difference between crime in relationships among "friends" (people who know each other and live together) and crime in "relations" among strangers. The analysis of violence has a different emphasis in these two cases; in the first, much attention is paid to the dynamic and history of the relationship; in the second, the offenders' and victims' characteristics are individually analyzed. Public attention is strongly concentrated on violence among strangers; the study of violence in relationships—even after the creation of women's shelters and despite unambiguous experiences of child caretakers—remains taboo. Violence against old people in elderly homes is at least occasionally discussed, but violence in private home care is not a common topic. By rejecting those discussions, society protects its structures and institutions; for example, if violence in the family were discussed publicly more often, the family as an institution would lose its legitimacy and a demand for political control of the family might arise.

Violence against strangers instead of relationships with strangers is a phenomenon that has concerned German society for years, at least a large part of it. At the same time, it is important to note that it is not solely a German problem; reasons for concern turn up in other European countries and outside Europe. While arson attacks on refugee shelters and homicides with immigrant victims are not discussed as a social priority, people should not deceive themselves by the common impression that violence is increasing explosively. The presentation of violence in the media is in itself a reality level just like the police work report expressed in suspect statistics: when we talk about violence, we need a clear definition of the level of reality construction we are discussing.

At the same time, we should take into account the expansion of the term *violence*, which now describes not only physical actions but also psychological and verbal ones. This expansion of the term is a result of an increasing sensitivity to hidden violence that invariably harms human relationships and adversely affects the development of the individual.

Conversely, acts of brutal crime, physical wounding, or even murder are being handled in the same way as a much more minor offense, such as swearing. That calls for a limitation of the use of the term *violence* and for a possible differentiation between the terms *harm, exercise of excessive power,* and *repression.*

In the end, these citizen groups, which stylize themselves as intense fighters against violence, profit from the inflation of the term *violence.* The violence of right-wing extremists is mostly against strangers, who are labeled as strangers; that is, being identified as strangers becomes a crucial precondition to becoming a potential victim. Describing people as strangers places them in opposition to the in-group and is a premise for unrelated aggression. The action follows the legitimization of the process designed to target the victim in a particular case that later leads to the general construction of the victim category.

Our recent history shows an example of this fatal process: how Jews and the Roma, through increasing agitation and propaganda, were first symbolically and then in reality excluded and forced out of existing social relations, so that they could then be labeled as unlimited objects of hate. Politics plays a big part in legitimizing the category of victim because it declares publicly the affiliation and nonaffiliation of different ethnic groups and offers a variety of problem-solving views that could lead to a more harmonious coexistence among these groups. Politics can also create scapegoats. Delegitimizing the presence of immigrants combines with an ethnic-centered ordinariness of justification of the victim category. It is also used in the legitimization of counterviolence, which wants to justify itself as violence against potential offenders. It looks also for other legitimate victims, who are easy to find in the latest immigrant group (for example, refugees).

Violence against immigrants is—at least publicly—disapproved of and condemned. The moral judgment is important; otherwise the floodgates would open, as was the case with the violence against Jews through National Socialism. This aspect, however, is only one of many aspects of these events. There is also a functional aspect, in which violence against immigrants is useful. The reports about violence against strangers—shown on TV or told as a personal story—deter further migration. This deterrence is an important factor in migration politics. Since reports about "milk and honey" in the promised land of Germany dominate, the defense against unwelcome migration must be adequately armed technically, politically, and militarily. But if the desire to migrate can be negatively influenced, the costs of the defense are lower; hence deterrence through violence is functionally useful.

Violence against strangers also legitimizes deportation policies, which argue that increasing migration will lead to even more violence against immigrants; therefore, a strict deportation policy is needed for the immigrants' own benefit. The meaning of this argument cannot be explained without a context; it can be meant in a humanitarian sense, or it can be a case of doing a thief's own bidding. And finally, the extent of right-wing extremist violence is used as an argument to legitimize violence against the right wing.That violence against immigrants is useful in many ways is one reason why it has lasted for such a long time.

Nowadays we not only morally condemn violence against immigrants but also develop a politics against this violence. The ramifications of these actions are decreasing in the continuing conflict, even if reports about the negative migration balance in 1997 signal a short-term loosening. The price for this "success" was very high. If not for the sake of this short-term effect, the existing possibilities should be used for naturalization, granting of rights safely in another form, antidiscrimination politics, and democratic integration. For example in *The Manifest of the 1960s* (Bade 1994), such possibilities were presented; it is not that we do not know what should be done.

CRITIC OF THE PEDAGOGIC DISCOURSE OF VIOLENCE

Violence cannot be seen only in a context of migration and politics. Talking about violence, especially in educational institutions and among youth, has become autonomous and is marked by a diffuse increased rhetoric. Although comments about both the quantitative and qualitative changes in violence lack comparative data, the research refers mostly to self-assessment; the term *violence* is defined differently, and its definition has changed in principle. Criminal statistics show only the long-term changes, but even those do not show the changes in report procedures, perception of the faculty on the classification of violence, and the transfer of violence from private into public spaces.

The common perception of the strong increase of violence remains stable. The interests connected with talking about violence and the functions that the discourse of violence undertakes in social contexts are easier to understand than changes in the violence itself. Violence is a product, and it is easy to sell. However, violence is also a good of the ethical evaluation of actions, motives, persons, and situations. The offender is discreditable and the prosecutor of violence reserves for himself the right to discredit others. The discourse of violence is therefore a social discourse of exclusion and separation. The discourse of violence contains a social differentiation strategy that, especially in education, maintains the resignation of the opposition toward the integrational aims and objectives of education reform. The reform of education in the 1960s and 1970s not only criticized the theories of meritocracy as legitimating a socially hierarchical school system but also wanted to replace the culture of difference with a culture of similarity. In the social theory of Norbert Elias, this hypothesis can be interpreted as a discussion about assigning of ethnic traits by the filling of a social rank. Oppressors must have a place on the fringes of the "social space" (Bourdieu 1982).

These reflections present only one side of the discourse of violence. The exclusion of violence as an option in social interactions is rightfully considered to be progress, a humanization of social relations. In this context, the differentiation of the term *violence* (that is, personal/structural violence) is progress that, measured on people's well-being as well as on the norms of justice and freedom, gives an exact analysis pattern for violence relations and arguments for the practical critic of violence. It is possible that discussion of the increase of violence is the price we must pay for progress in the analysis of violence.

For pedagogy, the resulting dilemma is constitutive. On the one hand, it is connected to the social context of the discourse of violence and is involved through the public theorizing of violence. On the other hand, it is the genuine role of pedagogy to contribute to the cultivation of human relations through its educational influence. The internalization of morally motivated thresholds of aggression, especially against those who are weaker and vulnerable, the transformation of the potential for violence into nonviolent forms of dialogue, facilitates safety and the reduction of fear in social relations.

Pedagogy can deal with this dilemma only if it strictly connects its own methods with its self-presented goals. The creation of fear as motivation for learning, the withholding or threatening with withdrawal of acceptance, and the use of discrediting as a discipline method do not cultivate pedagogical relations but, rather, develop circumstances for violent opposition. The fact that they are justified under certain circumstances as a necessary method for self-preservation is also an indication of the circular form of violence relations.

DEFINITION OF PEDAGOGICAL GOALS

The level of discourse is not irrelevant to the analyzed issues. If "violence" is a problem of a daily dialogue in a youth community, or if it is articulated in the reports of a supervisor, if it is an issue in a pedagogical interaction, if it is theorized in an academic discussion or in public discourse—it will change the nature of violence itself. These categories of discourse are related to each other; in theorizing the actions of an individual, the texts and contexts of the different categories are connected to each other. Especially if sociopolitically hot topics are directed to pedagogical praxis, a professional discussion on a certain level of discourse about who undertakes which roles is required. Because violence is defined as a youth problem, it has been automatically linked to pedagogy. At the same time, pedagogy had a chance to declare its responsibility for the cultivation of interaction and socialization. To clarify the confusing connection between social expectations and a self-defined area of responsibility, it is necessary to define the structure of pedagogical actions, so that the limits and possibilities of such actions become clear. The "social framing" of these actions is constructed in such a way that by undertaking one part of the obligation, another part can be rejected. The range of "transformation obligations" must be arranged with the methodological range of pedagogical interaction. This range is markedly differently in kindergarten than in a youth community or in vocational school, but it is always determinable concretely. However, provided that the political and economical circumstances have an impact on the situation, the first limit of pedagogy becomes visible. "This limit is where social problems are being constituted in complex interdependence construct of economical, social and political destabilization, inequality and power relations" (Helsper 1993, 237).

The second limit of pedagogical actions develops from simultaneous demands to understand young people's actions and to attempt to change them; without the attempt to change the violent behavior against other people, we cannot talk about pedagogical actions. At the same time, these actions contain the risk of going "too far" and of intervening in an illegitimate way in those children's lives. Practically they are becoming more dependent on pedagogical help instead of receiving support that is linked with the students' potential for learning and exceling.

The third limit can be defined as a "de-emphasis of the subject matter" (Helsper 1993, 240), which limits educators' individual action competence. In the "client" this limit marks the sociologically acquired range of actions and changes that can be broadened only in therapy.

Specific pedagogical action possibilities open up within these structural limits. But what are they concretely?

If pedagogy wants to approach violence through "reeducation," it will achieve an effect opposite to pedagogy's stated goals. There are two reasons for that: In antiviolence programs, education is usually designed as technology. One actor tries to influence another, to drive out a certain kind of behavior. A symptom should be made to disappear, but without addressing the circumstances that caused it. This technique overlooks the fact that in the totality of sociological environment the single intention can with the same probability come true or, under certain circumstances, produce the opposite results. Such possibility emerges from the second reason, which reflects the recipient's perspective on education. One person is rejected and becomes the reason for intervention, so that the acceptance of exertion of influence demands devaluation of one's own actions. The probability that this occurs in a confrontational climate is very small and can only be expected in a context where other important parts of a person have been accepted, so that a clear look at the problem of one's actions is possible. The smaller the change in the situation of young people's lives, the bigger their interest in presenting their opinions in a dialogue with an educator, which again would be an "interesting" experience for the educator. Therefore, in a sense of technological knowledge we cannot know what our pedagogical actions should be.

With this critique, pedagogy has no basis yet. It has to come up with an "even better" reaction to violence and respond to the differentiated legitimization requirements. The form of action posed by pedagogy as an alternative to the sociotechnological control model is communication. This aims at the need for discussion, wants to offer and create reasons for socially appropriate behavior, encourages changes in behavior, and involves communication itself in the dialogue. The interest in understanding requires recognition and acceptance of the others and cannot undertake any actions against their will. The effects will develop proportionally to the actual structure that embraces as a goal the politics of ethnic understanding.

These characteristics describe only one interaction structure. As pedagogical actions, the general communicative actions require concrete persons who would represent action standards in a particular situation and who would present them to teenagers and children in an argumentative way. Behaviors that will not be developed for the sake of instrumental experiments can be learned only in a culture that recognizes and practices this kind of behavior. As a learning condition for developing communicative behavior, children and teenagers need not only the information about the existence of such values but also the practical experience and the experience of an emotional certainty that will allow them to take the risk of self-transformation.

Pedagogical actions are also necessarily connected to a living space that is structured in a meaningful way, even if it is linked to system structures. It is possible even in communities created for this purpose, if somehow they can go beyond the production of knowledge. While persons are somehow able to act in produced arrangements as authentic persons, they make in fact the reference to reality possible. The less they concentrate on a direct changing of behavior and the more they simply engage in the negotiating of situational demands, the sooner they can expect to rely on the results of the social interactions. Pedagogy does not exist only within this paradox.

Pedagogical actions are reflected in the production of the public violence debate, which recognizes the concrete responsibility of the specific field and creates through interactions a "microcosm" of the exertion of influence. This interaction can be structured through the competence of people who practice social rules and expect the same from others. Only under these circumstances—this is my hypothesis, at least—can closely defined concepts become methodologically revelant.

DEALING WITH RACISM

The racism we have to deal with, like anti-Semitism, is not just an aspect of the attitude of certain individuals but part of social knowledge. The term *social knowledge* refers to a social behavior developed as a collective certainty of the society not connected to an individual experience but passed on in the socialization process—at least in rudimentary form—to every member of the society. This kind of knowledge is part of the self-evident truth of the society, which, at the same time, separates itself negatively from other societies.

The separation of "us" from the "others" has been fulfilled for the past two hundred years, especially during the nation-state period. During the wars of the nineteenth and twentieth centuries this separation model, reinforced through the *identification* of a people and its nation-state, caused violent excesses and still has not been discredited. The differentiation between "inside" and "outside," between "local" and "foreign," is in fact a harmless differentiation only if it is used for ideological orientation, if it can be reflected and made relative, if the identity of an individual does not depend on it, and if it is in practice not relevant. In the nationalist reality, however, this harmless differentiation becomes incredibly dangerous.

Anti-Semitism and xenophobia refer not to a single, isolated prejudice but to a structure of thinking that is defined as "racism." By that we mean a structured perspective on perception and judgment that had been developed historically and is acquired in the socialization process. Such handicaps can be reduced, reinforced, or replaced with other perception models, but in times of crisis they can also be politically manipulated.

The core of the racist way of thinking refers to the opinion that differences between people are biological or culturally fixed along physical traits—an explanation referring only to a biological basis. Second, the racist way of thinking involves the devaluation of other groups and nations, which, in turn, justifies discrimination and extermination. These facts make clear the great pedagogical challenges and the need to work against racism. It is not enough to confront xenophobia with kindness to foreigners, because both of them strongly refer to the special character of the object of perception. Philo-Semitism, for example, is understandable as an antithesis to hostility toward Jews, yet it does not treat Jewish people as subjects like all other people. That is exactly what matters in democracy and pedagogy.

CONCLUSION

The reflection about changes in pedagogical actions must first call to mind the differentiation among prevention, pedagogy, politics, and the police.

Prevention refers to the structure of socialization processes, preventing the catalyst for violence from emerging. *Politics* refers to the balance of interests so that unavoidable conflicts can be solved without violence. *Police* represents the violence monopoly of the state and may be used only for protection against violence. As for pedagogy, the action cannot develop in situations of actual violence (in these situations police or mediation is needed) but refers to it.

In its structure the action is ambivalent because it treats the oppressor or the person of racist attitude with refusal and acceptance at the same time. It refuses violence but accepts the person. The ambivalence becomes a paradox because both of these positions should be expressed at the same time. To be able to do that, the educator must differentiate between the dimensions of cognitive communication and affective relation. If the racist person experiences both, his or her emotional and social safety is granted, and in the best case that will allow the constructive analysis of the cognitive dissonance. This is only possible if the educator contradicts the racist comments of the youth. In order to be able to fulfill the paradoxical intervention, the educator needs professionalism and reflexivity.

NOTES

1. National daily newspaper.
2. The lower house of the German parliament.

REFERENCES

Bade, K. 1994. *The Manifest of the 1960s: Germany and Immigration.* Munich: Beck.

Bourdieu, Pierre. 1982. *Die feinen Unterschiede.* Frankfurt am Main, Germany: Suhrkamp.

Helsper, W. 1995. "About 'Normality' of Youth Violence: Socialization-Theoretical Reflections about the Relation of Acceptance and Violence." In *Pedagogy and Violence,* ed. W. Helsper and H. Wenzel, 113–54. Opladen, Germany: Leske & Budrich.

———. 1993. "(Socio-)pedagogical Programs against Youth Violence: Theoretical Reflections in Practical Purpose." In *Desire of Rioting: Youth Violence against Foreigners,* ed. W. Breyvogel, 213–51. Bonn: Dietz.

Nedelmann, B. 1997. "Violence Sociology at Crossroads: The Analysis of the Current and Ways to the Future Violence Research." In *Violence: Special Edition 37 of the Cologne Journal for Sociology and Social Psychology,* ed. Trutz v. Throta, 59–85. Opladen/Wiesbaden, Germany: Westdeutscher Verlag.

Pries, L. 1996. "Transnational Spaces: Theoretic-Empirical Drafts Based on Labor-Immigration Mexico-USA." *Journal for Sociology* 25: 456–72.

Vogel, D. 1996. "Illegal Immigration and Social Security System: An Analysis of Economical and Socio-political Aspects." Zes working paper no. 2/96, Bremen.

14
EQUALITY OF DIFFERENCES VERSUS POSTMODERN RACISM

Ramón Flecha, Lena de Botton, Iñaki Santa Cruz, and Julio Vargas Clavería

༚

THE RISE OF NAZISM IN EUROPE

Politicians and intellectuals have expressed surprise at the recent growth of Nazism throughout Europe, triggered by Austria's FPÖ (Freedom Party) members joining the country's current coalition government. Jörg Haider, the party's leader, had previously vindicated Hitler's labor policy and proclaimed that Austria belonged to a Greater Germany. The old ghost of the 1930s was at large again. It set off all the political alarms and led the European Union to impose sanctions.[1] The report's findings provided more surprises: The Austrian government is implementing the same kinds of policies other EU governments are applying in their own countries with respect to the rights of minorities.[2]

Many of those who were so shocked by both Haider's ascent and the report's conclusions have made their own ethnocentric and relativist interpretations of the situation. A more ethnocentric view holds that European democracy is so solid that even a party like FPÖ has to act in a way that is neither Nazi nor racist in order to enter government. To fight the rise of Nazism, ethnocentrists propose to strengthen European culture and institutions against any kind of questioning that may weaken them.

A relativist stance argues that every country has the right to freely choose its own government without the restrictions imposed by allegedly universal values. Relativists also point out that European interference has increased FPÖ's influence in that this party can now play a role as Austria's defender against foreign attack.[3] Their proposal is that antiracist actions, policies and movements should be curbed because they promote what they attempt to fight: racism.

In contrast to the ethnocentric stance, many Romà[4] and Arab associations and other antiracist organizations warn that Haider's ideas and goals are a radicalization of some aspects of European culture generated by Nazism and still present in European institutions and thinking.[5] Unlike the relativist view, many Romà and Euro-Arab associations stress that Europeanist attitudes that generate racism are not to be seen as universal values in the same way human rights are. European ethnocentric racist views favor the exclusion of some peoples and cultures from the definition and the exercise of those rights. These groups make a dialogic proposal: They aim to strengthen universalist principles of human rights by redefining them in accordance with an open dialogue among all cultures in order to ensure all people's enjoyment of such rights.

The Romà are not surprised by the recent rise of Nazism. Romani associations have been consistently warning people about this danger, even when ethnocentric intellectuals and politicians have deemed these warnings alarmist and even counterproductive. Those associations are now warning that Haider's rise is not a fluke but grew out of European culture and society, whose racist elements are the basis for the ascent of Nazism. Nazism can reach new cabinets unless determined action is taken to deal with the matter (Flecha 1999).

In the meantime, neo-Nazi forces have been growing in a number of European countries. FPÖ came in second in the 1999 Austrian general election, garnering 26.9 percent of the vote. It formed a coalition with ÖVP (People's Party), which ranked third in the election, to topple the longtime ruling socialist party. FPÖ's electoral manifesto proclaimed, "Austria is not a country of immigration" (FPÖ 2000, 25). In the October 2000 local and provincial elections in Flemish Belgium, far-right Vlaams Blok increased its already high electoral support, winning one out of three votes in Antwerp.[6] Prior to the election, the Vlaams Blok had stated that Flanders should be an immigrant-free country. In 1997, Norway's neo-Nazi Progress Party (Fremskrittspartie) came in second in the general presidential election with 15.3 percent of the vote. In the 2001 elections it still earned 14.6 percent of the vote, earning twenty-five representatives in the Parliament. In France Jean Marie Le Pen won 15.1 percent of the vote in the 1995 presidential election. The National Front (FN), led by Le Pen, got 14.9 percent of the vote in the 1997 legislative election. In the last elections (2002) its support was maintained: The FN won 17.8 percent in the second round of the presidential election and 11.1 percent in the legislative. Furthermore, it elected seven representatives to the European Parliament in the 2004 European elections. The FN's manifesto proposes barring all nonnationals from French citizenship and reforming naturalization and citizenship laws in accordance with *ius sanguinis*.[7] Analysts have been shocked by the success of the National Front among former left-wing voters, who are discouraged by the crisis of the industrial age and welfare society or politically orphaned by the demise of communism.

Many European intellectuals and institutions are horrified at such growing support, but they do not seem to realize that these parties introduce themselves to their constituencies as the staunchest and most consistent defenders of policies and ideas already put forth by those intellectuals and institutions themselves. In Germany, some institutions that have proposed to ban the far-right National Democratic Party sponsored a campaign called Children instead of Indians (*Kinder statt Inder*).[8] Unfortunately, in the presence of traditional parties that allow or foster the idea that immigration is a problem, neo-Nazi parties and racist mobilizations appear to be pursuing merely the same endeavor.

The apparent lack of significant vote shares for far-right parties in some European countries does not mean that the problem does not exist there. Often racist opinions and votes underlie more prevailing (and more democratic) positions in the ideology of the main parties. One such case is Spain, where populist outbursts of racism occur despite the low percentage of votes received by openly racist parties. For example, in El Ejido, a wealthy town in Almería (southern Spain), a series of attacks on Arab immigrants, their businesses and their families and the NGOs that tried to help them followed one after another for five days in February 2000.[9]

Not long before, in late 1999, the Spanish House of Deputies had passed a reform of the Spanish immigration law that went far beyond what the Popular Party (PP), the ruling conservative party at the time, had envisaged. The PP was forced to gather the support of centrist parties and accept their amendments to the proposal of law because it had only 44 percent of the seats in the House of Deputies. The proposal had been sponsored by the Ministry of Labor, which saw an urgent need for more foreign labor in the country. When the proposal came before the Spanish Senate for a vote, the PP senators used their majority in the Senate to reject the earlier proposal and introduced restrictive amendments that needed further approval by the House of Deputies in order to become law. Lacking a majority in that chamber, the PP lost the support of Catalan and Canary Islands conservatives. This meant the original, less restrictive version of the reform was enacted, to the dismay of the main officials in the ruling party, who then promised to pass a much stricter version right after the upcoming election if they obtained a majority of the seats in both houses of parliament.

The El Ejido events occurred in the midst of that electoral campaign in which the PP wanted to offer a tougher stance on immigration. The general climate was that Spaniards had been too lenient with immigrants, and only those who were necessary to Spain's economy and ready to become integrated should be allowed to enter and/or stay.

Greenhouse agriculture had experienced rapid growth in El Ejido. About 15,000 Arab immigrants had been hired, most of them (about 11,000) illegally; they lived in poor conditions and were isolated from the rest of the population. In 1999, the expansion into new markets clashed with the competition posed by Moroccan agricultural products. Spanish agrarian associations called for demonstrations against Morocco and against the Arab population. Agrarian associations in El Ejido asked for the replacement of

Arab laborers with Eastern European workers and offered the latter 8,000 jobs.

During this period, the response to two incidents reflected the tone and consequences of the racist political and social reality with respect to Arab immigrants in El Ejido. This was preceded by rising tension between Spaniards and Arab immigrants and the general lack of acceptance of these immigrants in the community, which led to a series of altercations that exacerbated the hostile climate. A few weeks after the killing of two agricultural workers, a young woman was murdered, and this set off a full-blown racist outburst in El Ejido. Those who took part in the subsequent demonstrations to condemn these acts, as well as the local government and some in the media, did not blame the presumed killer for the death but instead extended culpability to all "Arab immigrants," which resulted in subsequent attacks on the general Arab immigrant population.[10] The European Commission president harshly criticized this racist outburst while Spain's ruling party, the PP, tried to curb a racist display by El Ejido's mayor—a PP member—when he downplayed racist attitudes of the people in his village. However, the Spanish prime minister eventually gave in to pressure as he resorted to relativism to vindicate racist demonstrations and the mayor's position, claiming that one must live there to be able to judge it. In the March 2000 general election, two months after the conflict, the ruling party went from holding 46.2 percent of the vote in El Ejido to 63.6 percent. Only a few months later the new PP government, backed by a majority of the seats in both houses of parliament, submitted a more restrictive proposal to parliament for the reform of the immigration law.

FROM MODERN TO POSTMODERN RACISM

Present-day racism has significant differences from the kind of racism associated with Nazism in the past. Neo-Nazi party leaders do not endorse Hitler's extermination of Jews and Romà. Most of their voters profess not to be racists and not to consider Romà or Arabs inferior. The most radical ones point out that non-Europeans should live in their countries of origin rather than on European soil, but most would even accept them as long as their numbers do not become too high and they adopt European culture and norms. However, this purportedly nonracist mentality justifies and even prompts physical assaults on Romà and Arabs in their homes. Far from being nonracist, it is a new kind of racism that merely displays different features from the traditional kind.

The factors that characterized the modern racism that prevailed in the primarily industrial society of the past do not explain what is happening in today's information society. In this chapter we argue that we are witnessing the rise of postmodern racism, which has new social, cultural and intellectual foundations (Flecha 1999). Therefore we present important reasons for concern, explaining how this new type of racism is immune to antiracist positions developed after World War II and how the new discourses of diversity in Europe today hide postmodern racist ideas. We finally argue that in order to stand up to the new forms of racism and Nazism, we need to develop new orientations for our antiracist policies and institutions.

Modern racism was shaped during the industrial age, coinciding with the traditional modernity school of thought. Traditional modernity backed Western universalism, which involved inequality among ethnic groups, cultures and people in general. European and non-European cultures could live together in the same European countries, but the latter would always be subordinated to the former. Europe accepted immigrants because they took the worst jobs in industrial societies, which were reaching levels close to full employment. Inequality between cultures legitimized the subordination of non-Europeans to Europeans—the former were tolerated but experienced worse living conditions. Their members were considered a necessary labor force in the economies of the industrial society, but they did not have the same rights as Europeans.

This situation was made all the more evident by the February 2000 attacks in El Ejido, Spain. A few days later, there were several meetings among different groups. Moroccan workers and NGOs for the defense of immigrants and human rights denounced the attacks and the social and working conditions these immigrants had been subjected to. However, agricultural employers consequently became uneasy about hiring Moroccans, and 40 percent of Moroccan workers were fired. The reason given was that they generated too much social conflict. Such a statement denies Moroccan workers their role as social agents of development and their subjectivity and ignores their important economic contribution.

The current rise of racism and Nazism in Europe is taking place in a new social and cultural context constituted by the information society and dialogic modernity. Informational capitalism imposed an early phase in the information society in which a social Darwinist model was hegemonic— according to which only a part of the world population was selected for the development of the information revolution while the rest was excluded (Castells et al. 1999; Touraine 2000). While the European metropolis specialized in informational media, Africa found itself entering a new era of poverty. Considerable numbers of Africans set out across the Strait of Gibraltar, risking their lives aboard barges *(pateras)* to partake in the West's wealth.[11]

Traditional modernity included a series of egalitarian objectives. Social movements that fought for them were gradually overcoming racist, class-based, sexist and ageist obstacles throughout the industrial age until reaching their peak in the 1960s. Such progress had the support of progressive social movements and the opposition of reactionary political and social forces that aimed to maintain and extend old privileges.

In the second phase of the information society, radical social movements are reinforcing egalitarian goals and redefining them by taking different collectives and people into account. In this way they are gradually leaving behind traditional modernity (in which a dominant minority of people imposed their values on the rest) and bringing in dialogic modernity (in which values and measures need egalitarian dialogue and consensus among different parties to be approved). Romani and Arab associations are taking a more radical stance in conceiving and defending their equality of rights in all domains of social life, as well as exercising them from their own identities. Not only do Romani associations, for example, claim their right to education, but they also want schools to change their current ethnocentric practices as well as take Romani culture into account. Arab associations demand new school menus to accommodate Muslim religious prescriptions (since Islam is the majority religion in the Arab culture) and courses on Muslim culture and religion and the recognition of already existing elements of Arab culture in European societies (e.g., intellectuals such as Ibn Jaldun and Averroes).

Dialogic modernity overcomes traditional modernity's ethnocentrism and relativism and the logical racist, sexist, class-based and ageist limitations to traditional modernity's egalitarian goals. Dialogic modernity overcomes ethnocentrism by establishing egalitarian dialogue as a principle according to which the arguments of every person involved in that dialogue have equal weight. It leaves relativism behind in that all arguments on which a consensus is gathered are to be respected in all circumstances. That would be the case, for instance, of the equality of rights among people from different ethnic backgrounds.

In this dialogic modernity, nobody wants to be labeled a racist or an antiegalitarian. The new opposing reaction would not have any future if it openly defended the superiority of the European "race" over the Romà or the Arab race. However, saying that people from non-European cultures are different (rather than inferior) earns political leaders votes and support. So does saying that these people would therefore be better off if they lived in their own territories rather than in the unfamiliar environment of European society.

NAZI INTELLECTUALS' NEW RISE

There is an elitist prejudice that takes for granted intellectuals' denial of all responsibility for Nazi movements. Thus Nazism is seen as the responsibility of politicians, military commanders, members of the bourgeoisie or even the desperate lower classes, but not of those who occupy the highest ranks in the world of culture and art. However, intellectuals are not above right and wrong. Some intellectuals determinedly fought Nazism just as others actively collaborated with it. English historian David Irving, for example, argues that there was no Holocaust, that not even half of what has been reported about concentration camps ever took place and that gas chambers never existed (Gausa 2000).

Racism is present not only in political parties, the media or peripheral neighborhoods but also in universities and academic environments. The same proposals that are launched by some parties have been made by some intellectuals as well. The antiracist fight must be taken to all relevant spheres. In the cultural domain, there must be room for contrasting ideas in a context of free discussion.

Within Europe, the selection process has created a situation in which excluded social sectors have been seen as an unnecessary burden by those who hold better social positions. In the presence of unemployment and underemployment among people considered to be autochthonous Spaniards, those who are seen as nonautochthonous, even if they are second-generation Arabs or have been in Europe for as many centuries as Romà have, are considered the source of new social burdens, dirtiness and conflict.[12] The new Nazism has found its main source of strength in a popular position to limit the entry of new immigrants and even expel some of those who already live and work in Europe.

Most in favor of expulsion say they are not racist, they do not consider Romà or Arabs to be inferior at all and they do not want to harm them in the least. On the contrary, they say, they wish a better life for them in those territories where they can live with their own kind. Le Pen's FN manifesto proposes that the "return of third world immigrants to their countries of origin will be complemented by a generous aid policy to those countries. France will help foreigners, but in their homes." The legitimizing force behind this new postmodern racism lies in its nonracist appearance and its nondefense of inequality.[13] Postmodern racism does not use inequality to justify why Turks should be subordinated to Austrians; instead it uses difference to legitimize why Turks would lead happier lives if they stayed in their own country.

Postmodern racism promotes concepts such as difference and territory in order to defend the notion that Austrians and Turks cannot live together in the same space, since conflict is allegedly unavoidable. Such statements allow some to hold that all "peoples" should live in their own territory: Austrians in Austria, Turks in Turkey. New Nazism voters may be European citizens who understand the Turks so well that they want to spare them from exploitation in Europe by repatriating them to their country.

Contact between different communities awakens fears of acculturation in some sectors. An example of the fear that the presence of other cultures may cause is offered by recent events in Terrassa, a city near Barcelona. Terrassa went through two phases of rapid expansion, both closely linked to immigration: In the 1960s, many newcomers were immigrants from other parts of Spain; later, in the 1990s, a wave of non-EU immigrants, mostly Moroccan, enlarged the city. Currently these two communities live together in neighborhoods such as Can'Anglada, but with occasional conflicts. The conflicts reached their height in July 1999. The Moroccan collective was rejected by nationals, as it was considered to be a source of insecurity, sexism and problems in general. Older Can'Anglada inhabitants would not tolerate this new collective's cultural manifestations. Arabs, they said, should keep their cultural peculiarities private—these were never to be seen in the neighborhood's public life.

An earlier "Darwinist" phase in the information society is now opening the way for a second phase in which the main goal in Europe is to achieve an "information society for all." Many social movements and organizations have succeeded in the fight against exclusion and succeeded in imposing a criterion according to which all European citizens have the right to participate in the new information society without being discriminated against on the basis of class, ethnic background, gender or age. In this second phase, the idea of equality is being strengthened and reconsidered in light of diversity and pluralism, far from the discourses that defend difference without equality and justice.

The growth in postmodern racism has been complemented by an intellectual postmodern fad that has restored the reputation of the main Nazi intellectual to date: Martin Heidegger. The strategy pursued in this endeavor is similar to that of postmodern racism: to make him appear nonracist in the same way new Nazism appears to be non-Nazi. Its main purpose has been to present Heidegger as a non-Nazi author.

First, there were attempts to conceal or deny his personal and public involvement in the defense and promotion of the Nazi project. However, clear proof of his involvement can be found. Heidegger even asked German professors to vote for Hitler. Two days before the November 1933 plebiscite, he made a speech that began: "German teachers and comrades! My fellow Germans! The German people has been called to vote for the Führer, but the Führer asks the people for nothing, on the contrary, he gives the people the chance to make the highest of free decisions: [knowing] if the entire people wants its own existence or not. Tomorrow the people will not demand anything but its future" (Farias 1989).[14]

Once his implication was made evident, attempts were made to depict his differences with Hitler and other Nazi leaders as opposition to Nazism itself. However, even though Heidegger did not die until 1978, he never said or issued any word of self-criticism regarding his collaboration with Nazism, and he never made any public defense of democracy or human rights. His posthumous letter disappointed those who hoped he would.

Even though Heidegger's personal acts made it all too obvious that he had been involved in Nazism, his followers have aggressively asserted that only unintelligent analysts can draw Nazi overtones from his work. This is where the debate is now. However, there is no need for much debate, as Heidegger himself established the connection between his work and Nazism, for instance, when he wrote that Hitler was the people's *Dasein*.[15]

In fact, both Heidegger's work and that of his most vindicated (by postmodernism) followers attempt to destroy or deconstruct the same universal values Nazism did: democracy and equality (see Derrida 1967; Foucault 1975). Such deconstruction weakens cultural workers' commitment to the fight for human rights for all people.[16] Cultural workers and Romà and Arab associations that carry out an antiracist task struggle to secure the same human rights for all people. Such a utopia is deconstructed by Heideggerian postmodernism, which clears the way for the influence of a postmodern racism that resists the universalization of citizenship, labor markets and social welfare rights. Through dialogue and exchange of ideas, people from different cultures can collectively fight for equality while maintaining their own cultural specificity. In this sense, the Spanish Muslim women's association, Insha Allah, condemned the book *La mujer en el Islam* (*Women in Islam*), written by a Muslim imam in the town of Fuengirola, as well as his subsequent comments when he intended to justify women's mistreatment on allegedly religious grounds. This shows how within each of those cultural communities groups and collectives are fighting for a more egalitarian society (Utrera 2000).

NEGATIVE AND AFFIRMATIVE CRITICISM

Some radical people sympathize with Heideggerian ideas and authors. Such intellectual confusion is one of the factors that weaken the ideas of the antiracist. It is mainly due to two causes: many people tend to read secondary sources rather than original works, and no distinction is made between negative and affirmative criticism. Among the poor secondary sources, for example, one can find literature that mentions Heidegger's antiauthoritarianism or Foucault's opposition to power.[17]

Negative criticisms mention only whom or what the author is against and ignore whom or what the author is in favor of. This results in contradictions that weaken critical movements. If we claim to be against capitalist democracy without saying what we are for, we may be favoring such diverse positions as those of Nelson Mandela and Haider, or Paulo Freire and Heidegger.[18] Negative criticisms may lead us to make mistakes such as saying Haider's policy proposals for intercultural relations are critical because they pose a radical critique to the system, or considering Heidegger's contribution as a good theoretical basis for intercultural relations because it also postulates a radical critique.

Affirmative criticisms combine a critique of what one opposes with an affirmation of what one supports. In this way, those who are in favor of Mandela and Freire are against Haider and Heidegger. Affirmative criticisms are made by those who are against capitalist democracy because they want a deeper and more universal democracy not hijacked by large corporations. Taking this perspective, we must ground antiracist orientations not in the contributions of those who are against capitalist democracy (such as Haider and Heidegger) because they long for dictatorship but rather in the contributions of those who struggle for a better democracy (such as Mandela and Freire).

DIFFERENCE WITHOUT EQUALITY AS A LEGITIMIZATION OF POSTMODERN RACISM AND NAZISM

Literature on racism over the past decade has been rife with such confusion. The result has been rather consistent with a neoliberal system that, at the peak of the Darwinist phase of the information society, worked against the goals of equality and the universalization of human rights for all people regardless of origin.

Heidegger, Derrida, Foucault and their postmodern followers deconstructed the idea of equality. As their influence grew, literature about intercultural relations moved the goal of equality aside, right when prevailing social Darwinism and neoliberalism were staging their fiercest attack on the egalitarian goals of progressive social movements. This joint offensive facilitated a growing inequality and left the floor open for postmodern racism. Neoliberalism has been interested in defending and using the discourse of difference or diversity, without mentioning equality. These ideas were introduced in the critical literature by Heidegger's postmodern followers and are the basis of postmodern racism, which constitutes the social ground of the vote for and the adherence to neo-Nazi groups in Europe. Their policies are fully consistent with a Heideggerian affirmation of one's own identity and difference (Heidegger 1962, 1974).

From a relativist approach, whereby every culture can only be understood and judged from within, there is room for the appearance of some authoritarian groups that strive to impose their own view on the rest of the members of that cultural group. However, the lack of legitimacy (according to relativism) of all external criticisms would leave large sectors of the population in a given community defenseless and voiceless. This was the case of the Afghan population subjected to the Taliban rule. Women, for instance, experienced repeated violations of their rights and had become mere shadows. International denunciation and solidarity could help Afghan women's organizations in their own struggle for social justice.

Haider and other neo-Nazi politicians claim to be friends of Turkish and Moroccan immigrants. It is not unusual to see them with people from these cultures in their campaign appearances. They never say these groups are inferior—only that they are different. They claim the best way for them to affirm their own identity is by doing it in their own national territories. They accept and actively defend difference. The postmodern deconstruction of equality and all universal values (including democracy and human rights) helps neo-Nazi politicians advance their proposals. They do not accept equality, that is, the goal of universally extending the same rights to all people and the exercise of the same voice in the active definition of such rights, whether they are autochthonous Austrians, Romà, or Turks. They radically oppose this because it is the main enemy of their own proposals.

EQUALITY OF DIFFERENCES TOWARD OVERCOMING RACISM AND NAZISM

Many Romani and Arab associations and other progressive antiracist movements resort to the following motto: *We are all equal, we are all different.* They thus assume the equality-of-differences principle, also defended by renowned contemporary authors in the social sciences (Beck 2000; Freire 1997; Habermas 1998; Touraine 2000) under different concepts and nomenclature. This is due to a dialogic turn in society and in the social sciences, whereby social agents claim to have their voices included both in the decision-making spaces of their lives and in the research and theoretical debates of the social sciences. Some authors discuss the move toward a dialogic modernity (Flecha et al. 2003).

When Romà discuss equality of differences, they talk about achieving equal rights without giving up their own culture. They oppose both the ethnocentric orientation of traditional modernity focused on a homogenizing equality and the relativistic orientation of postmodernism that promotes the maintenance of cultural and structural difference—thus leaving the door open to a Nazi reaction against modernity.

Traditional modernity proclaimed equality as a goal, but it based this exclusively on Western cultural premises, without allowing for dialogue with other cultures. If citizenship was granted to an immigrant, for instance, it was in exchange for his or her acceptance of the dominant culture while giving up his or her original culture. When human rights were proclaimed, they were elaborated from the ethnocentric perspective of those who dominated the world at the time. Not so long ago, Spanish Romà had to choose between "passing" as *payo* (mainstream Spanish non-Romà) or suffering different types of persecution and exclusion. The modern homogenizing equality did not solve the social problems of European Romà and Arabs and did not contribute to overcoming their exclusion.

In the European countries we often forget that within the Romà and Arab communities, among others, are also voices that fight for a more egalitarian society while upholding their cultural difference. Many Turkish women know that emancipation is a matter of gender equality, female recognition and visibility, and to fight for this is far from integrating Western women's values. In Istanbul women organized demonstrations when female students wearing the *hijab* (veil) were barred from university or denied graduation. In the demonstrations some wore the *hijab* and some short skirts; all were defending equal rights. They were being asked to choose between their education and their culture, which should not be incompatible (De Botton et al. 2005).

Nazi rebellion against modernity was much more aggressive to the Romani community than traditional modernity, denying them any possibility of living in Western societies, not even as integrated or excluded individuals.

Hitler achieved that by exterminating Romà in countries like Germany and Poland. Today, postmodern racist manifestations are forcing Romani families to leave town or burning immigrants' houses (as in the El Ejido riots). These demonstrations of rebellion proclaim we are no longer equal, but different. They make a relativist defense of *difference* and diversity that refuses equality. In Haider's FPÖ manifesto (FPÖ 2000, 12) one can read the following: "It is thus diversity which guarantees the future intellectual and cultural development of Europe and it must be preserved from current tendencies of leveling down and egalitarianism."

Postmodern intellectuals tried to convince us of this very idea. They argued that ethnocentrists had made people believe we were all equal, and now we realize how different we actually are. Romà and other cultural minority groups know how mistaken the former affirmation is. Difference is not a new conquest of social or political movements; it is the oldest human value. When Europeans set out to colonize other continents, they never considered native inhabitants as their equals. For centuries they have not considered the Romà traveling across Europe as their equals, but as different people.

The new value for which social movements have fought for centuries is equality. This was the value of the U.S. civil rights movement in the 1950s and 1960s, and it is still the value for which Romani and Arab social movements continue to fight. In current dialogic modernity, Romani people no longer accept whatever *payos* decide equality to be. They insist that the diversity of voices be heeded and participate in an egalitarian dialogue that defines what is equal and what is fair, and how equality will be realized. Romani women's associations, for instance, are struggling to transform schools so that their culture is represented in a quality educational provision and their girls do not fail and drop out. Equality in education cannot take mainstream schools for granted; it needs to be redefined by involving all stake holders (Vargas and Gómez 2003). These women thus claim equality of differences.

POLITICAL VEIL AND PERSONAL VEIL

Ethnocentric inequality stems from a belief in superior and inferior cultures, languages or ethnicities and requires the adoption of mainstream values and behavior as a necessary condition to exercise established rights. Romà and Arabs in Europe must give up their identity and their culture to exercise such rights. This is a form of modern racism. Defense of relativist difference becomes a form of postmodern racism through denying universal values such as human rights. Equality of differences from a dialogic perspective opposes both types of racism, defending equality of rights for all people and groups who share the same territory and standing for a multicultural definition of rights.

The *hijab,* one of the most characteristic elements in Arab-Muslim culture, has set off intense debate in different European countries. The practice of wearing the *hijab* has been commonly identified with backwardness and sexism. Not to deny the obvious inequality that exists among members of the Arab culture, this conclusion should not be drawn about the whole collective. In the Arab world there are many positions. This can be seen in the everyday use of the veil. There are two types of veil: a political one and a personal one (De Botton et al. 2005). The political one can manifest in different ways, but they all share a reaction against the imposition of a given social model on Arab women (either the Western model of emancipation or the model of religious fundamentalism). Both the prohibition and the imposition of the veil silence women's voices. An example of this fact are the disparate situations of Afghan women and Istanbul demonstrators.

However, there is also the veil that comes from a woman's free decision (a personal veil), regardless of whether the reasons that lead her to such a choice are cultural, religious, intellectual or nationalistic. Women from different cultures, including those who have been silenced or who are still at the margins, can fight for a better world against the many current forms of racism, sexism and discrimination, from the dialogic power based on equality of differences (Beck-Gernsheim 2003). In the words of Moroccan sociologist Fatima Mernissi (1993), "Women's solidarity will be global when interclass and intercultural barriers are brought down."

NOTES

1. The EU imposed a diplomatic blockade on Austria in February 2000, when the ÖVP entered a cabinet coalition with FPÖ. Later, on September 12, the EU lifted all sanctions because they were deemed counterproductive.

2. The report's general conclusions start with point 108, where the authors write, "The impression we have is that the Austrian government is compliant with its commitment to common European values. The Austrian government's respect for the rights of minorities, immigrants, and refugees is not less than that of other EU member states" (Ahtisaari et al. 2000).

3. The report specifies in point 116 that "in our opinion, if the measures passed by the other 14 EU member states are maintained, the effect would be counterproductive and thus they should be put to an end. The measures have already generated widespread nationalist sentiment in Austria, especially since in some cases sanctions have been mistakenly interpreted as aimed at Austrian citizens" (Ahtisaari et al. 2000).

4. "About Denomination of Gypsy People in Official Documentation of World Conference Against Racism," Romà International Organization, www.union romani.org/new2001–09–03.htm.

5. Philosopher of science Karl Popper said Haider would like to do the same as Hitler did.

6. Vlaams Blok's rise has been uninterrupted since the 1980s, as electoral support for traditional parties has decreased. From 1978 to 1999 it increased its share of votes in national elections from 1.4 percent to 16.5 percent of the

total vote in Flanders. Christian Democrats decreased from 43.5 percent to 26.8 percent.

7. This is a descent-based attribution of citizenship for expatriates' children who, upon returning to their parents' country of origin, receive automatic access to citizenship. It is one of the legal ways of acquiring nationality in different countries, including France.

8. In view of a demand for 75,000 computer experts by the German information technology industry, German corporations set their sights on India, where some 350,000 software professionals work. In an attempt to emulate U.S. immigration policies, the Schroeder cabinet issued special work permits to foreign experts in order to lure them to Germany. Schroeder announced that 20,000 green-card-type visas would be issued, allowing these experts to settle in Germany for a five-year period. The conservative opposition of the Christian Democratic Party made use of the *Kinder statt Inder* motto while showing their opposition to green cards and calling for more high-tech education for German children.

9. Events in El Ejido are not unique. Similar assaults on immigrants' groups, homes and businesses took place repeatedly throughout the same year, for instance, in Can'Anglada (Terrassa, near Barcelona) and in Lepe (Huelva, in southern Spain).

10. Language is full of ideology. At about the same time, another horrible killing took place in Spain and nobody accused a generic "Spaniard" of this murder but a specific person with a name and a personal and social context.

11. The Strait of Gibraltar is the point where the waters of the Atlantic Ocean and the Mediterranean Sea meet. It separates Africa's northern coast from Spain's southern shores. Given their proximity to the African coast (some 15 kilometers), the Andalusian towns of Tarifa and Algeciras receive the largest number of clandestine immigrants, many of whom, traveling in precarious overloaded launches, drown before reaching the shore. From January to October 2000, more than 12,000 immigrants were arrested while trying to disembark on the Andalusian coast. Algeciras Acoge (a nongovernmental association in Cadiz, Spain, that provides services to immigrants coming by boat to this coastal area of Spain) and the Association for Human Rights calculate that in 1999 some 500 immigrants died while trying to cross the Strait of Gibraltar (Bejarano 2000).

12. According to Le Pen's FN manifesto, one of the effects of immigration is "the aggravation of crime. More than one-third of those imprisoned in French penitentiaries are foreigners. As for those indicted for drug traffic, according to deputy dell Angola's report, 60% are foreigners" as well (www.front-national.fr/programme/changement/immigres.htm, October 17, 2000).

13. Vlaams Blok's racism is a postmodern and xenophobic kind of racism. Flemish racial or cultural superiority over immigrants or the need for the latter to become assimilated or eliminated is never openly stated. Instead, VB proposes a strict cultural separation under the appearance of cultural relativism. It defends sending non-EU immigrants back to their countries of origin.

14. This quote is found on page 224 in the Spanish edition of Farias 1989.

15. *Dasein* is defined in the German language as life or existence. Heidegger uses this term as one of his fundamental concepts in *Being and Time* (1962). He broke the word down, separating *Da* and *sein*, relating it to who the human being is, the question of being itself and the potentiality-for-being (Heidegger 1962).

16. Derrida (1967) developed the concept of *différance*, a neologism that is

distinct from the French concept of *différence*. Derrida combines two meanings: to differ in space and to defer in time.

17. We have mentioned elsewhere (Flecha 1999) examples of the intellectual confusion and the prejudice against the antiracist fight entailed by such misreading.

18. One of the most common banners in neo-Nazi demonstrations reads "Against the EU and Large Corporations" (Val 2000).

REFERENCES

Ahtisaari, M., J. Frowein, and M. Oreja. 2000. "Texto completo del Informe de los tres 'sabios' sobre el Gobierno austriaco." *El Pais* (Barcelona, October 10).

Beck, U. 2000. *What Is Globalization?* Cambridge: Polity Press.

Beck-Gernsheim, E., J. Butler, and L. Puigvert. 2003. *Women and Social Transformation*. New York: Peter Lang.

Bejarano, J. 2000. "Más de veinte inmigrantes desaparecen frente a la costa de Taria al unirse otra patera." *La Vanguardia* (Barcelona), May 1.

Castells, M., R. Flecha, P. Freire, H. Giroux, D. Macedo, and P. Willis. 1999. *Critical Education in the New Information Age*. Lanham, MD: Rowman & Littlefield.

De Botton, L., L. Puigvert, and M. Sanchez-Aroca. 2005. *The Inclusion of the Other Women: Breaking the Silence through Dialogic Learning*. Dortrecht, Netherlands: Springer.

Derrida, J. 1967. *De la Grammatologie*. Paris: Editions de Minuit.

Farias, V. 1989. *Heidegger and Nazism*. Philadelphia: Temple University Press.

Flecha, R. 1999. "Modern and Postmodern Racism in Europe: Dialogic Approach and Anti-Racist Pedagogies." *Harvard Educational Review* 69, no. 2:150–71.

Flecha, R., J. Gomez, and L. Puigvert. 2003. *Contemporary Sociological Theory*. New York: Peter Lang.

Foucault, M. 1975. *Surveiller et punir: Naissance de la prison*. Paris: Gallimard.

FPÖ. 2000. *Program of the Austrian Freedom Party*. http://194.96.203.5/englisch/Program.htm.

Freire, P. 1997. *Pedagogy of the Heart*. Lanham, MD: Rowman & Littlefield.

Gausa, M. 2000. "Un tribunal inglés condena a David Irving por racista y por negar el holocausto." *La Vanguardia* (Barcelona), April 17.

Habermas, J. 1998. *The Inclusion of the Other: Studies in Political Theory*. Cambridge, MA: MIT Press.

Heidegger, M. 1974. *Identity and Difference*. HarperCollins.

———. 1962. *Being and Time*. New York: Harper & Row.

Mernissi, F. 1993. *El poder olvidado: Las mujeres ante un Islam en cambio*. Barcelona: Icaria-Antrazyt.

Touraine, A. 2000. *Can We Live Together? Equality and Difference*. Stanford, CA: Stanford University Press.

Utrera, J. 2000. "El imán de Fuengirola explica formas de pegar a las mujeres." *El Pais* (Barcelona), July 17.

Val, E. 2000. "Los neonazis desafían la amenaza de prohibición y marchan por Berlín." *La Vanguardia* (Barcelona), November 5, 14.

Vargas, J., Gómez, J. 2003. "Why Romà Do Not Like Mainstream Schools: Voices of a People without Territory." *Harvard Educational Review* 73, no. 4:559–90.

15
PORTUGAL WILL ALWAYS BE AN AFRICAN NATION: A CALIBANIAN PROSPERITY OR A PROSPERING CALIBAN?

João Menelau Paraskeva

⊸⊝

In one of his more provocative remarks, the Portuguese dictator António Salazar claimed that "Portugal will always be an African nation." Such a despotic statement requires cautious consideration of two things. First, it is important to understand why Salazar and his regimes of truth claimed such an identity; second, one has to analyze how schooling has perpetuated what one might call a bizarre reracializing policy.

Since we will consider schooling's judicial record in this reracializing political framework in the following section, I invite the reader to adopt a radical critical perspective toward the arguments that underpin such a repressive policy. A good way to start this radical critical analysis is to clarify political particularities of the Portuguese dictatorship epoch. In this section I will unveil how and why António Salazar's political regime wisely attempted to frame Portugal beyond the Portuguese borders, an attempt that was anchored in the idea that "we" are a "nonracial" community of people, which is to say that "we" are all Portuguese.

An accurate way to understand the arguments over such autocratic and repressive appropriation is to rely on the approaches suggested by radical critical scholars Boaventura de Sousa Santos, Michael Omi and Howard Winant, David Gillborn, Frantz Fanon and Donaldo Macedo, among others.[1]

In a remarkable analysis of the Portuguese repressive position in what "used to be peacefully understood" as a natural extension of the "Portuguese Iberian territory," Boaventura de Sousa Santos highlights the differences between the Portuguese colonizing posture and the way many other Western countries, such as England, position themselves within the colonial ministry.[2] Since it is precisely on this difference that he based his radical arguments of Portugal as a colonial and postcolonial reality, I will address the complexity of his analysis.

According to Sousa Santos, any serious debate over Portuguese colonial and postcolonial cartography requires a careful analysis of "the identity processes within 'space-time' of the Portuguese [culture and] language."[3] There is an immeasurable zone of contact during many centuries that involved both the Portuguese people and other people from "América," Asia and Africa. In order to understand this specific zone of contact, Sousa Santos put forward four ways through which one can understand the Portuguese empire: (1) Portugal has been a semiperipheral country within the modern capitalist system since the seventeenth century; (2) this semiperipheral condition has continued to be reproduced and is based on both the colonial system and the way Portugal joined the European Union; (3) there is analytic value in the world system theory concerning the conditions that have been "imposed" by globalization; and (4) the Portuguese culture is indisputably a border culture, without any content.[4] In other words, while it is a culture with form, its form is that of a border, a perimeter zone.

As Sousa Santos argues, Portugal's idiosyncratic status as a semiperipheral country has developed over the years, with the particular characteristics of (1) having medium economic development and, consequently, a mediating position between world economic centers and peripheries and (2) being a state that, by and large, was never able to lay claim to the more vital characteristics of a modern state found in the countries at the center of the capitalist colonial project.[5] The Portuguese colonial empire had a vastly different progression from other colonial empires, particularly the British Empire.

This particular (political) aspect points to another peculiarity. This semiperipheral condition has been reproduced until today, anchored in a disturbing colonial framework, albeit covered with the mask of democracy, that greatly influenced the way Portugal joined another imperial stratum in forming the European Union. One has to understand that "since Portugal is a semiperipheral country, the Portuguese colonialism should be seen as semiperipheral also."[6] In this sense, we are before a "subaltern colonialism," with a double colonial subaltern position based on colonial discourses and practices.[7] Since the seventeenth century the history of colonialism has been written in English, and Portugal was and still is an English subaltern dependent empire, a position that made Portugal "England's informal colony."[8]

If the Portuguese colonial empire was created as a subaltern informal colonialism, influenced by England, one must ask what took place in the Portuguese processes of colonization. Following Sousa Santos's approach, it is important to understand whether the colonized people of a subaltern colonial country were subcolonized or overcolonized.[9] One must pay attention to what he calls the "mirror games" to understand Portugal's multifaceted dual-subject positions both in Europe and within the "colonies."[10] In so doing, we will perceive how Portuguese subject positions within the cartography of Western imperial colonialism were quite explicitly Calibanian, while Portuguese subject positions within its colonies were de-Prospering, gradually assuming a Calibanian position. By unveiling such intricate subject positions, which are rooted in multiple issues of identity, we begin to understand the real basis of António Salazar's claim.

The Portuguese subject positions within the Western imperial colonialism platform were those of a Caliban. As Sousa Santos argues, the Portuguese empire "was never able to comfortably accommodate itself within the original space-time processes of the European Prospero."[11] This argument becomes even clearer if one pays cautious attention to how Portugal was seen from the outside. By anchoring his radical critical arguments in the analyses of the Portuguese empire made by important authorities like Lord Byron, Frère Claude Bronseval, Castelo Branco Chaves, Richard Crocker and Charles Adam, Sousa Santos makes his position even stronger.[12] In fact, Portugal was seen in quite a negative way.[13]

Despite its colonial position Portugal was never acknowledged by its imperial counterparts as a rightful member of the Prosperian platform. This particular imperial position must be understood within the complex sphere of eugenic issues, issues that were deeply intertwined with economic, cultural and political influences. To be more precise, the Portuguese empire—and its skewed subject positions—must be viewed within the interplay between a capitalist and a colonialist framework. Again, Sousa Santos's claims deserve to be highlighted:

> If modern capitalist power has always been colonial, in the case of Portugal and its colonies, that modern capitalist power was much more colonial than capitalist. [That is to say], while the British Empire was based on a dynamic balance between capitalism and colonialism, the Portuguese empire was based on a deeply unbalanced relation between an excess of colonialism and a huge lack of capitalism. Thus, the specificity of Portuguese colonialism clearly shows a political economic reason. Portugal's semiperipheral condition was a direct result of its capitalist deficit. Such condition was also overtly latent, not only within the political, social, juridical, and cultural platforms, but also on the survival, oppressive, resistance, proximity and distance logics of the socializing daily life practices.[14]

This point is crucial. Some reductive analysis tends to divorce race from gender and from economic categories within capitalist colonial political practices, as though the economy were the only reason for the genocidal processes described above. As Walter Rodney argues, people mistakenly connect inhuman slavery practices only with racial issues, even though eugenic racist policies were implicated in imperial governance:

> European planters and miners enslaved Africans for *economic* reasons, so that their labor power could be exploited. Indeed, it would have been impossible to open up the New World and to use it as a constant generator of wealth had it not been for African labor: There was no other alternative: the American [Indian] population was virtually wiped out and Europe's population was too small for

settlement overseas at that time. Then having become utterly dependent on African labor, Europeans abroad found it necessary to rationalize that exploitation in racist terms.[15]

Barbara Fields, "a relative orthodox Marxist," challenges radical critical approaches that contextualized "race as a historical explanation" by claiming race to be an ideological construct.[16] She pushes her approach to a kind of dead end (thus arguably falling into a contradiction) by understanding race "alone" to be at the core of capitalist and colonial exploitation "scientific" projects. The word *scientific* here is crucial. Capitalist colonial scientific exploitation must be seen as a set of strategies bumping against each other in dynamic ways. By highlighting just race or just economics, we will not uncover the real relational platform of capitalist colonial scientific exploitation processes of profiting from "golden goods" such as cotton, sugar, rice and tobacco, among many others. Obviously, in order to achieve its purposes, the capitalist colonial strategy was based on race policies that are derived from so-called scientific arguments. Despite their antagonistic positions, both Steven Selden's and Richard Herrnstein and Charles Murray's analyses can serve as a credibility check for our arguments.[17]

While the former accurately denounces the sickening eugenic racist policies developed in the United States, processes based on "scientific reason," the latter had the audacity to claim white superiority based on purportedly scientific arguments. Thus the word *scientific* has paved the path for capitalist colonial exploitation practices. To borrow from David Gillborn's insightful analysis and terminology, while Selden denounces racism as a social construction, Herrnstein and Murray disgracefully defend race as a biological fact. According to William Tate IV's description about racial tensions, "low intelligence is at the root of society's social ills, and policy formulation must take that in consideration."[18] As Donaldo Macedo argues, "Oppressive dominant ideologies have throughout history resorted to science as a mechanism to rationalize crimes against humanity that range from slavery to genocide by targeting race and other ethnic and cultural traits as markers that license all forms of dehumanisation."[19] Undeniably, and as Gillborn also stresses, one "cannot understand life in multi-ethnic comprehensives without reference to the economic, gender and 'race' inequalities at work in society as a whole."[20]

To sum up, Portuguese colonial positions among other colonial empires—such as England—were also "scientifically" based. As it was "far from a link within a global hierarchy, [this] became a way of being both in Europe and overseas."[21] Curiously, this particular sub-Prosperian position exhibited by the Portuguese empire was elaborately overdetermined, a position deeply related to a Portuguese Calibanian Prospero within its very colonies. The weakness of Portugal in assuming a fully powerful Prosperian position among its counter-Prosperian colonial allies was due to its inability to conceptualize, design and foster a well-built, balanced bond between capitalism and colonialism, and to Portugal's power in avoiding a Calibanian subject position within its colonies. Any radical critical analysis of capitalist colonial discourses and practices will show that those discourses and practices are deeply overdetermined by race, class and gender categories. These categories do not exist in a social vacuum but are the product of socially constructed segregation, instigated by those who maintain economic, cultural and political power.

From this perspective, one can identify the irreversible de-Prospering processes within Portugal's colonies. One of the main issues for these processes was *cafrealização* (from *kaffir*, an offensive word used especially in southern Africa as a disparaging term for a black person) and *miscigenação* (miscegenation), an embarrassing set of discourses and practices for Portugal's capitalist and colonialist allies. Given this colonial reality, Sousa Santos put forward the concept of proto-Calibans.[22] As he states, not only the repressive Portuguese colonial discourses and practices were "based in a non-stop disqualification of, say, the African people, but simultaneously, those discursivities and practices were thoroughly and meticulously incapable of avoiding also a disqualification of a Portuguese's fully capitalist position, since they mixed with the African people, adopting and incorporating their way of living and above all 'creating new beings.'"[23] Again, this double incapability demonstrated by the Portuguese empire had its roots in the unbalanced (and thus damaging) relation between capitalism and colonialism. As Sousa Santos explicitly shows, the "apparitional character of [Portugal's] colonial power" has to be understood within the frames of a pale colonial state, unable to fully capitalize [on] their colonies, a fragile position that is crucial to perceive the interidentity itineraries that gradually emerged based on the interplay of the political, cultural, economic, ideological spheres and race, gender, and class categories.[24]

I am not claiming that the Portuguese colonial empire did not commit real genocide or was less sanguinary than other colonial capitalist empires. It was, however, deeply incompetent and unable to win political, cultural, economic and social recognition from its close allies, simply because of its inability to derive the maximum possible results from capitalist and colonialist practices. This placed Portugal in an uncomfortable colonial position: a Prospero assimilated by Caliban in its colonies, and a sub-Prospero or a real Caliban among its close colonial allies. Both of these situations were unavoidable, resulting in a painful paradox for a pretentious colonial power.

Those complex practices of *cafrealização* and *miscigenação* were not necessarily based on superior human qualities such as respect, love, passion, admiration, equality and freedom. Frantz Fanon's analysis posits that they were.[25] By allowing into his analysis the real voice of Mayotte Capécia's *Je suis martiniquaise* history, Fanon strengthens his approach. According to Capécia's own experience, "A woman of color is never altogether respectable in a white man's eyes, even when he loves her."[26] Frantz Fanon's radical critical interpretation of Capécia's relation with the white man saw that that relation was based on a complex stew of submission, "lactifica-tion," and physical attraction. As he argues, "Mayotte loves a white man to whom she submits in everything . . . he is her lord . . . she asks nothing, demands nothing except a bit of whiteness in her life."[27] Mayotte Capécia's understanding of this relation is solely anchored in the physical: "All I know is that he had blue eyes, blond hair, and a light skin, and that I loved him."[28] It is clear from Fanon's analysis that the relation between the wom-an of color and the white man not only exhibits a kind of cult of submis-sion, deeply ingrained in economic, racial, gender and power relations, but also shows an extraordinary attempt to subvert "the two poles of the world."[29] To be more precise, this "genuinely Manichean concept of the world . . . white or black" had to be challenged. And this was a kind of agenda for all "Mayotte Capécias of all nations."[30] In bringing Michel Foucault's ideas to our argument, this dangerous dichotomy creates a powerful and intricate interplay, resulting in "the body of society [that is] a social body that needs to be protected" and challenged.[31]

In this context, and complexifying Sousa Santos's approach, the Portu-guese capitalist colonial empire was always in transition within a trinity composed of Prospero's and Caliban's positions and a third sphere.[32] The fight for a Prosperian recognition was doomed to fail since the Portuguese people were always seen by their capitalist colonial associates as a particular nonwhite race, with an amalgamated heritage based on Jews, Arabs, Blacks and French, a disgusting eugenic combination that incorporates the worst characteristics of those races.

Along with Sousa Santos, one might say that the Portuguese capitalist colonialist empire was fueled by such a remarkable paradox.[33] It is precisely this idiosyncratic capitalist and colonialist illogic that allows one to refute colonialism on the basis of a set of binary processes: that is, Prospero acting according to his superiority on one side and a bunch of nonhuman, clumsy, disorganized, inferior Calibans resisting this superiority on the other side. As Macedo accurately maintains, "one has to realize that ignorance is never innocent and is always shaped by a particular ideological predisposition."[34]

In opposition, I claim that Portugal, given both its paradoxical capitalist colonialist position and the powerful capacity of the colonized people to subvert Portuguese colonial predispositions, allowed for the emergence of a set of intricate interidentity processes that were not merely a combination of opposites—Prospero and Caliban—and this was a singular achievement. In these processes, as Fanon reminds us, "the last *sequele* of a titanic struggle carried on against *the other* have been dissipated."[35]

By showing its inability to act as a major player within Western colonial processes, the Portuguese capitalist colonial empire opened the door for the emergence of counterhegemonic forms of agency, forms that the empire was not ready to deal with. In a way, the Portuguese capitalist colonial empire in its colonizing processes ended up being painstakingly and thor-oughly colonized as well.

It is precisely in terms of this paradox that António Salazar's repulsive statement has to be understood. And, in fact, the tyrannical Salazar was well aware of this paradox, fabricated from his own despotic dictatorship.

One of the factors that undergird this repressive position is based on the interplay between Portugal—as a sub-Prosperian intervenor within the capitalist colonial imperial exploitative logic—and the rest of its allies, particularly England, which was a full Prosperian actor in the colonialist exploitation project. Portugal's paradoxical position on the capitalist chessboard drove this sub-Prosperian country to another paradox, that is, its odd, tenacious resistance to starting decolonizing processes along with its close allies. Salazar's dictatorship was quite slow to understand the urgent economic need to take the next step, which was giving up the colonies and concentrating all possible resources—ideological, political, cultural, economic and religious— on a new form of colonialism: neocolonialism. Salazar's tyrannical regime became a fatal obstacle to this exploitation upgrade. Oddly enough, this embarrassing obstacle was a result of Portugal's semiperipheral position. The Portuguese empire was not yet ready for that step.

Its paradoxical position—a sub-Prospero among its European capitalist colonial counterparts and an assimilated Caliban within its own colonies—prevented Portugal from fully capitalizing on its colonies as its closest partners did. In fact, the Portuguese capitalist colonial empire was taken by surprise, and its reaction was a bizarre political strategy to reframe its capitalist colonial position within the colonies (in this particular context, it is interesting to remember the hilarious speeches made by Salazar's minister of foreign affairs, Franco Nogueira, at the United Nations, as he tried to (re)frame Portugal outside the capitalist colonial political project).

Unsurprisingly, this strategy of proudly carrying on with an outdated model of capitalist colonialism led Portugal to another political dead end, and attempts to whitewash the Portuguese capitalist colonial judicial record were also unsuccessful. However, in attempting to do so, Portugal reracialized its own discourses and practices. Ultimately, what we have is a sub-Prosperian semiperipheral anemic capitalist colonial state hitting its closest allies with new strategies and extending compulsory invitations to Portuguese people from the main land, but also all the people from its colonies. In so doing, Portugal was surrendering to such a paradox, which, in turn, Portugal later became entrapped by it.

In this manner, it attempted to rebuild a racial framework and wipe out racial segregation categories that had been highly valuable for the capitalist colonial empire but were "quite embarrassing now." It also created a new common enemy—the true Prospero. Ultimately, this new political strategy extended well beyond the wiping away of "the other" (the people from its colonies), and created a new "other" (real European Prosperian) common enemy. In so doing, Portugal was expressing "identity difficulties within its own essence."[36]

It is precisely in this context that Salazar's outrageous remark that "'Portugal will always be an African nation" must be understood. What is really interesting is that Salazar's despotic regime not only was deeply aware of Portugal's sub-Prosperian, semiperipheral anemic capitalist colonial position but was also conscious of being "the other" within its closest allies' eyes. As Peter Rigby brilliantly stresses, "the dominant white, male culture is never placed as 'the Other,' whose peculiar 'differences' need to be explained to anyone . . . it is only 'minorities' that constitute the Other."[37] Peculiarly enough, the Portuguese capitalist colonial empire was always much closer to the other, yet pretentiously refused to admit it.

This odd reracializing process offers evidence of what Macedo straightforwardly denounces as the capacity of those who have power to constantly align and realign their position on a particular issue.[38] The Portuguese government was attempting to secure its position but also to open a political space to build and crystallize the (common) sense that there was no such thing as racism in Portugal, since "we" symbolize the distinguished, well-off product of a univocal political and cultural legacy. This inheritance derives from the concept judiciously coined as "Portugalidade" (by Portugalidade I mean a common cultural platform based on the Portuguese language and culture), which in essence is perpetuated by political and cultural discourses and practices. There is no space for the other, since there simply is no other: We are a nonracial community. Consequently "we" becomes a peaceful—yet putrid—commonplace as a concept of agency and practice, evidence of a reracializing political project.

Two other issues make Salazar's remark even more sordid and outrageous. First was his arrogance in co-opting the other, a category that was immediately in use the first time the Portuguese white man touched African soil, for his own political gain, as if this characterization described an actual monolithic racial group. Such a pompous reracializing process has to be seen as an effort to wipe out economic, cultural, gender and class dynamics—all at once. As Deborah Youdell reminds us, it is a terrible mistake to assume that there is no "hierarchy within the other."[39] In a powerful and insightful radical analysis, she tries to "understand the continued inequities of school experiences and outcomes experienced by African Caribbean students."[40] She blatantly argues for the need to see such a palpable hierarchy that "appears to be concerned, not only with the relationship between Black and White race identities, but with hierarchical relations between race and ethnic identities other than White."[41]

A second outrage was Salazar's attempt not only to build such a despotic subject position—a new synthetic "we"—but also to try to gain legitimacy within the international sphere. In fact, we were and still are incorporated in the "new synthetic 'we,'" but this was based on what we could call the first-person dictatorial singular. The capitalist colonial segregation and exploitation processes created a new syntax form that introduced a new way of using the pronoun, which was in fact the only way.

This reracializing policy is strongly denounced by Michael Omi and Howard Winant, who point out that one must be deeply cautious in recognizing that race is a dynamic category.[42] They deserve to be quoted at length:

> The main task facing racial theory, in fact, is no longer to problematize a seemingly "natural" or "common sense" concept of race—although that effort has not been entirely completed by any means. Rather our central work is to focus attention on the *continuing significance and changing meaning of race*. It is to argue against the recent discovery of the illusory nature of race; against the supposed contemporary transcendence of race; against the widely reported death of the concept of race; and against the replacement of the category of race by other, supposedly more objective categories, like ethnicity, nationality, or class. All these initiatives are mistaken at best, and intellectually dishonest at worst.[43]

According to David Gillborn, Salazar's reracializing despotic strategy provides conspicuous evidence that "race changes, [that is] it works differently through different processes, informs and is modified by diverse contemporary modes of representation, and changes with particular institutional contexts."[44] Unsurprisingly, this ostentatiously political construction—"despicably by law"—of a new "we" challenging and challenged by a new "other," is another instantiation of an old capitalist colonial imperial strategy of silencing the voices of all the African people who were subjected to the barbaric policies of capitalist colonial exploitation.

This is not a minor issue if one is deeply committed to nonnegotiable antiracist education. Dwight Reynolds's insights concerning an autobiographer's approach in the Arabic literary tradition can teach us a great deal here.[45] As he shows, the Western literary tradition made a political effort to build and propagate the idea that autobiography—as a literary tradition—did not exist in the Arabic world, and also the pale forms of texts closest to what the Western imperial intellectuals "condescendingly" coined as autobiographical were based in the cult of individual identity. Drawing from the earlier works of Georg Misch and Franz Rosenthal, Reynolds challenges the idea that there is no such thing as autobiography outside Western culture.[46] Moreover, he dismisses this arrogant position as intellectually dishonest, since it deliberately neglects not only the powerful secular scholarship in Arabic literature in which autobiography has a strong literary tradition, but also ample autobiographical material that was deeply influential in the Western literary tradition. In fact, it was an attempt to "portray the autobiography as a product of the West," but this, as Dwight Reynolds claims, is an example of "the fallacy of Western origins," a fallacy that is anchored in three misconceptions.[47] First, there is the "assumption that autobiography is extremely rare in Arabic literature," despite the real evidence showing precisely otherwise—as documented by Albert Hourani's work.[48] Second, and based on the first mistaken assumption, is that those few (autobiographical) texts "have been presumed to be, and have therefore been studied as, anomalies rather then as a part of a literary genre or historical tradition."[49] Finally, there is the Western judgment that "these Arabic texts do not constitute 'true' autobiographies."[50]

Such an arrogant Western position is currently visible in the English-only movement in the United States, which has to be seen "as a form of colonialism."[51] Macedo's insightful analysis can teach us a great deal here. "Colonialism imposes 'distinction' as an ideological yardstick against which all other cultural values are measured, including language. On the one hand, this ideological yardstick serves to overcelebrate the dominant group's language to a level of mystification and, on the other hand, it devalues other languages spoken by an ever-increasing number of students who now populate most urban public schools."[52] Capitalist colonial segregational, exploitative discourses and practices in fact did (and do) commit real genocide, a genocide that not only crosses language issues but also, as Macedo fiercely argues, "rests on a full understanding of the ideological elements that generate and sustain linguistic, cultural, and racial discrimination, which represent, in my view, vestiges of a colonial legacy in our democracy."[53]

The reader might claim that Reynolds is addressing a different world—the Arabic literary world. However, the same analysis can be applied to the African literary tradition. Taking Portugal as an example, until very recently African literature was viewed in Portuguese academia as "minor literature," or not even that. Until recently, the history of Portuguese capitalist colonial genocidal practices was written from a white man's perspective. The West persists in positioning Africa as a continent without human political solutions, and the mainstream media depicts Africa as a "red cross" problem. That is, there is no political solution for the African continent. Those who are profoundly committed to subverting this situation have to hear the real voices of the real African people, talking about their real lives, asking about their real struggle for survival, talking about the need to "make babies to sell" in order to relieve inhumane living conditions. Before such a reality—a result of capitalist colonial scientific exploitation processes—we still must deal with some scholars talking about a postmodern era, while arguably more than two-thirds of the world does not have the chance to participate in the modern era, despite their direct contribution to the construction of wealth for a tiny minority in the modern era.

One of the insidious residues of capitalist colonial discourses and practices in Portugal is cultural protectionism enforced via a national curriculum. As I have challenged elsewhere, "the national curriculum is a deplorable, unforgivable and a predatory historical mistake," a lethal mechanism that barbarously multiplies cultural and economic segregation.[54] The Portuguese national curriculum must be viewed within the context of the capitalist colonial epoch, an epoch that "tried to eradicate the use of African languages in institutional life by inculcating Africans through the educational system in Portuguese, only with the myths and beliefs concerning the savage nature of their cultures."[55] In fact, the current Portuguese curriculum is not that different from the one used during the Portuguese colonial epoch, at least with regard to its poisonous content.

In applying this analysis to Salazar's arrogant statement, I can claim that it was a reracializing strategy that not only co-opted colonized, exploited people but also used the old capitalist colonial strategy of silencing their voices. Summing up, the pragmatic political strategy was devised to challenge the pressure that Portugal was facing from its closest allies to give up its colonies and to maintain its hegemonic power within its colonies as well. This was a suicidal political strategy, which regrettably remains in fashion.

Actually this reracializing set of processes is still very influential today. As Sousa Santos argues, Portugal's latest pretentious attempt to re-Prosperize its position—exhibited in its economic fervor to join and stay in the European Union—provides real evidence that this is a nation deeply influenced by this intricate interidentity paradox, and the paradox has been refurbished for the contemporary world. Claiming that "we" always will be an African nation creates space to claim that "we" always belonged within the European world. It is a pathological fear of the Calibanian position that ironically ends up in a Calibanian situation. In the next section I will resume a radical critical analysis of the way schooling has intentionally helped perpetuate such illogic. A good way to do this is to consider the way a particular part of the history of the capitalist colonial empire (for example, the discoveries) has been taught in schools in most Western nations, among which Portugal proudly maintains a sub-Prosperian seat.

SAYING THE UNSAYABLE: HOW SCHOOLS PARTICIPATE IN A CONVENIENT COMMONSENSICAL COMMONSENSE

I have attempted to challenge and interrupt in a noneuphemistic way a commonsensical, supercilious and profoundly dangerous claim, unfortunately among too many others, found throughout Portugal, namely, that there is no such thing as racism in Portugal since "we" symbolize the distinguished, well-off product of a univocal political and cultural legacy. Let's try to understand how this peculiar position has been perpetuated in Portuguese society with the connivance of schooling practices. We can begin this analysis by examining the distorted way particular discovery heroes have been portrayed in Western history, especially U.S. history.

We should first consider critical analyses by Howard Zinn, Noam Chomsky, Tzvetan Todorov and bell hooks concerning the way Columbus is presented in schools. I will rely also on the analyses of James Loewen, Jean Anyon, Patrick Brindle and Madelaine Arnot.[56] I will close this argument by comparing Michael Apple's and Bruno Latour's approaches.[57] In so doing I will be able to trace clear similarities in the way the history of capitalist colonization has been portrayed in Portuguese history textbooks.

For centuries, Columbus has been portrayed as *the* discoverer, a real hero for Western civilization, and this is the message that dominates U.S. textbooks.

However, as Zinn, Chomsky, Todorov and hooks stress, this message is a fallacy. In *Legitimacy in History*, Chomsky refutes the Columbus hero concept, arguing that the American continent was really a stage for genocide. As he claims, "Here in the United States, we just committed genocide. Period. Pure genocide. Current estimates are that north of the Rio Grande, there were about twelve to fifteen million Native Americans at the time Columbus landed; [however,] by the time Europeans reached the continental borders of the United States, there were about 200,000 [which means] mass genocide."[58]

The shocking reality Chomsky reveals is that "throughout American history this genocide has been accepted as perfectly legitimate," notwithstanding the fact that Columbus "was a mass murderer himself."[59] It is precisely this critical challenging of the legitimacy of history that one can trace in both Zinn's and hooks's perspectives. However, while for Chomsky it constitutes a process of historical engineering, for Zinn and hooks we are embedded in a process of obliteration that tends to perpetuate "white supremacist capitalist patriarchy."[60]

Zinn views the American past as a gendered history, mostly "done" by rich white men. As he maintains, U.S. history is a process of "sort of leaving 'it' out," an insidious process of obliteration in which the schools are not innocent.[61] As Zinn highlights, one can notice this process of obliteration in the way textbooks have portrayed the Vietnam War—a "central event for our generation in the US [since] as I've often commented, we only dropped seven million tons of bombs on 35 million people, and we only have two insipid paragraphs in the textbooks on the war in Vietnam."[62] It is this process of obliteration that Zinn identifies in the way the Columbus legacy has been reproduced, not only in society at large but also in school curricula.

As Zinn highlights, Columbus's history is one of "masculine conquest."[63] Despite the fact that the indigenous people greeted Columbus and his armada in a friendly way (as one can see in Columbus's own account: "they are the best people in the world and above all the gentlest—without knowledge of what is evil—nor do they murder or steal . . . they love their neighbors as themselves and they have the sweetest talk in the world . . . always laughing [they] are very simple and honest and exceedingly liberal with all they have, none of them refusing anything he possesses when he is asked for it"), this attitude was perverted (since Columbus saw the Indians "not as hospitable hosts, but as servants [they] could subjugate [and] make them do whatever we want").[64] Furthermore, the native Indians could not escape the cruel process of genocide, murder and rape of women and children who were "thrown to dogs to be devoured."[65] One can conclude from Zinn's words that glorifying Columbus is nonsense, since Columbus's legacy is one of conquering and subjugating native people. In fact, the very idea of conquering and subjugation suggests an assumption of the native Indians' inferiority. Thus Columbus's history is based on a racist and gendered (women was especially victimized by Western brutality) rationale that perpetrated genocide. Moreover, and based on Todorov's analysis, Columbus demonstrated eugenic arrogance in his contact with the Indians. According to Todorov, who based his analysis on a study of Columbus's letters conducted by Andrés Bernaldez, the Indians were portrayed by Columbus as "although physically naked [they are] closer to men than to animals," yet one should not minimize the ideological meaning of the word *although* here.[66] Oddly enough, Columbus was incapable of recognizing the diversity of languages used by the Indians and accepting them as real (obviously quite different from Latin, Spanish or Portuguese). Thus "already deprived of language [according to Columbus, they are also] deprived of all cultural property [by] the absence of costumes, rites, religion."[67] This particular race–gender vision of Columbus's legacy is also made explicit in bell hooks's approach.

According to hooks, "the nation's collective refusal to acknowledge institutionalized white supremacy is given deep and profound expression in the contemporary zeal to reclaim the myth of Christopher Columbus as patriotic icon."[68] As she bluntly remarks, "embedded in the nation's insistence that its citizens celebrate Columbus's 'discovery' of America is a hidden challenge, a call for the patriotic among us to reaffirm a national commitment to imperialism and white supremacy."[69] According to hooks, this fallacious message is transmitted in the classroom:

> When I recall learning about Columbus from grade school on, what stands out is the way we were taught to believe that the will to dominate and conquer folks who are different from ourselves is natural, not culturally specific. We were taught that the Indians would have conquered and dominated the white explorers if they could have but they were simply not strong or smart enough. Embedded in all these teachings was the assumption that it was the whiteness of these explorers in the "New World" that gave them greater power. The word "whiteness" was never used. The key word, the one that was synonymous with whiteness, was "civilization." Hence, we were made to understand at a young age that whatever cruelties were done to the indigenous peoples of this country, the "Indians," were necessary to bring the great gift of civilization. Domination, it became clear in our young minds, was central to the project of civilization. And if civilization was good and necessary despite the costs, then that had to mean domination was equally good.[70]

As hooks argues, we must not forget Columbus's murderous history, and it is precisely this horror that one "must reinvoke as [we] critically interrogate the past and rethink the meaning of Columbus."[71] She continues: "in our cultural retelling of history we must connect Columbus's legacy with the institutionalization of patriarchy and the culture of sexist masculinity that upholds male domination of females in daily life; [that is to say] the cultural romanticization of Columbus's imperialist legacy includes a romanticization of rape."[72] In fact, as she bluntly asserts, "white colonizers who raped and physically brutalized native women yet who recorded these deeds as the perks of victory acted as though women of color were objects, not the subjects of history."[73] It is in this context that hooks reminds us that "any critical interrogation of the Columbus legacy that does not call attention to the white supremacist patriarchal mind-set that condoned the rape and brutalization of native females is only a partial analysis [since] it subsumes the rape and exploitation of native women by placing such acts solely within the framework of military conquest, the spoils of war."[74] Whether it is "historical engineering," a "process of obliteration" or a process that prizes "white supremacist capitalist patriarchy," the fact is that Chomsky, Zinn and hooks are questioning precisely the kind of knowledge that has become legitimate—the central concern in Michael Apple's intellectual process. In so doing, they are actually challenging the social and political legitimacy of particular segments of history. In fact, as Chomsky argues, "there can't be anything more illegitimate; [that is to say] the whole history of this country is illegitimate."[75] He writes,

> A few thanksgivings ago, I took a walk with some friends and family in a National Park, and we came across a tombstone which had just been put in along the path. It said: "Here lies an Indian woman, a Wampanoag, whose family and tribe gave of themselves and their land that this great nation might be born and grow." Okay, "gave of themselves and their land"—in fact, were murdered, scattered, dispersed, and we stole their land, that's what we're sitting on. . . . Our forefathers stole about a third of Mexico in a war in which they claimed that Mexico attacked us, but if you look back it turns out that that "attack" took place inside of Mexican territory. . . . And it goes on and on.[76]

Chomsky, Zinn, Todorov and hooks claim there is an intentional fallacy based on the erroneous portrayal of Columbus as a hero. In so doing, they basically assert that U.S. society is based on a secular lie that has been reproduced in the school curriculum through its textbooks. This charge is substantiated by sociologist James Loewen, who spent two years at the Smithsonian Institution surveying twelve leading high school textbooks of American history. Loewen also challenges the way Columbus has been presented in school textbooks.

He notes that the twelve textbooks surveyed "leave out virtually everything that is important to know about Columbus and the European exploration of the Americas."[77] Loewen stresses that Columbus's legacy is so broad and pivotal that mainstream "historians use him to divide the past into epochs, making the Americas before 1492 'pre-Columbian.'"[78] Notwithstanding Columbus's insidious motivation, the fact is that "textbooks downplay the pursuit of wealth as a motive for coming to the Americas."[79] Following the same line of thought pursued by Chomsky, Zinn, and hooks, Loewen argues that "the way American history textbooks treat Columbus reinforces the tendency not to think about the process of domination [when in fact] the traditional picture of Columbus landing on the American shore shows him dominating immediately." Actually, as Loewen highlights, "Columbus claimed everything he saw right off the boat."[80] However, "when textbooks celebrate this process, they imply that taking the land and dominating the Indians was inevitable if not natural."[81] The fact is that "Columbus introduced two phenomena that revolutionized race relations and transformed the modern world [through] the taking of land, wealth, and labor from indigenous peoples, leading to their near extermination, and the transatlantic slave trade, which created a racial underclass."[82] Columbus's mark within the Americas is, in essence, one of murder, exploitation and rape—genocide.

As Jurjo Torres Santomé reminds us, the official culture in the vast majority of Western countries that is perpetuated through a common curriculum only validates specific knowledge portrayed by a masculine world, and as the Galego scholar highlights, a brief glance through the textbooks reveals silence and occultation of the working class.[83] Torres Santomé, like hooks, argues that textbooks promulgate a biased vision of society that prizes a white, middle-class, heterosexual, blond male.[84]

It is in this context that both Jean Anyon's *Workers, Labor and Economic History, and Textbook Content* and Patrick Brindle and Madeleine Arnot's *England Expects Every Man to Do His Duty: The Gendering of the Citizenship Textbook, 1940–1996* exhibit their pertinence.[85] In an empirical study of seventeen well-known secondary-school U.S. history textbooks approved for use, Anyon argues that the content expressed in the textbooks "despite the claim of objectivity serve[s] the interests of some groups in society over others."[86] As the author stresses, a mark of U.S. textbooks is their "omissions, stereotypes, and distortions" with regard to Native Americans, blacks and women, "which reflect the relative powerlessness of these groups."[87] Thus, as Anyon argues, "the school curriculum has contributed to the formation of attitudes that make it easier for those powerful groups whose knowledge is legitimized by school studies to manage and control society."[88] That is to say, "textbooks not only express the dominant group's ideologies, but also help to form attitudes in support of their social position."[89] In the same line of analysis, although more focused on gender issues, Brindle and Arnot identified three textbook frameworks: "exclusionary, inclusionary, and critical engagement."[90] They claim the exclusionary is the most common approach and "exclude[s] both the private sphere and women from its construction of the political domain."[91] In this set of textbooks, there is clearly "general inattention and lack of interest in the position of women; it is not unusual for women to receive no attention at all."[92] A very small group of textbooks "sought to include women and the private sphere in various different ways."[93] That is to say, a small minority of texts attempted to include representations of women as citizens; however, with one exception, none of them portrayed women "within the polity of active [agents]."[94] In this kind of textbook women are presented as mere add-ons. And finally there are textbooks with a critical engagement approach in which the women highlighted are in both the private and public spheres.

It is precisely this "wisely peculiar" vision of Columbus that we can find if we pick up a Portuguese history textbook in any bookstore or library. In the textbook sections that deals with the discoveries, one can notice a resemblance between Columbus and Vasco da Gama, and Pedro Álvares Cabral's heroic discoveries are also described. In the Portuguese school curriculum, these men are all treated as the great heroes of Western civilization. This politically perverted discourse needs to be challenged.

First, in Portugal, students must learn (or they fail) that the discoveries constituted a great moment in world history and that they were undertaken for two reasons: to expand the territory and to Christianize the barbarian indigenous people. To invite Michael Apple into this discussion, these are the two official reasons in the past five hundred years that every student in Portugal has had to memorize. After all, the discoveries were a colossal enterprise—one that only the great Western white male was able to accomplish—but quite simple to justify and learn. Yet the "official" reasons that students must learn hide some crucial issues. One issue is language. Instead of a debate between teachers and students over the discoveries as a critical arm of the capitalist colonialist empire's exploitation project, and the way that genocidal political project was conceptualized and developed, students are taught that the intention was to expand the territory—quite a natural desire. In fact, this official reason not only becomes legitimized but simultaneously displaces the political reason(s): power, an uncited desire that pumps up the capitalist colonialist machine, one that relies on segregation, exploitation and genocide.

Another vital issue is the elimination of discourses concerning race, gender and class segregation. Expanding the territory is presented as a natural desire totally divorced from practices of exploitation and genocide or categories of race, gender and class. Thus, this official reason not only has nothing to do with these things but also was a peaceful event; the great Portuguese heroes like Vasco da Gama had only to consult some divinities to certify that they were ready for the enterprise.

Second is the religious issue. Here again we have the same strategy. The discoveries had another grand motive—to Christianize the so-called barbarian indigenous people. Once more, language plays a key role, in legitimizing the barbarity inherent in the Christian crusades. There is no debate between teachers and students over this arrogant religious position—for example, why the tyrannical need to Christianize? Why the dichotomy of Christians versus barbarians? What happens to the religious beliefs of the indigenous people? What is the connection between Christianizing and slavery and exploitation? Why, five hundred years later, out of ten million Mozambicans are close to nine million Muslims? Were "the indigenous people" Muslims before? What we really have is students being taught the official, legitimate religious reason, one that pretentiously took civilization to a barbarian point of the world. Vasco da Gama and Pedro Álvares Cabral and Columbus and their laudable armadas brought light to that dark part of the globe. In fact they put that part of the world on the map—the map of capitalist colonial exploitation.

The third and critical point is that the textbook version of the history of the discoveries is narrated exclusively by Portuguese voices. In fact, there is no space for concern about this. Instead of a powerful discussion of this issue by teachers and students, we have students "learning" about a praiseworthy Portuguese historical epoch—an epoch that forcefully established an antagonistic relationship between the Portuguese people and indigenous people—without any access to the voices of the indigenous people. Teachers and students are given a particular set of official Portuguese voices, and the stories of the admirable Portuguese era are told in those voices. I am not claiming here that one cannot find other kinds of analysis. What I am denouncing is that this nonmainstream analysis does not have space in the school curriculum, since students do not need to know anything but the "official reasons" for the national tests.

Language plays a critical role in the vast capitalist colonial project, a project that conceptualized and developed an egotistical cult of the "Westernization" hegemony, a cult that was (and still is) portrayed as the best manner of human existence. Such a cult was (and still is) deeply rooted in an elaborate set of predatory discourses and practices.

Even the way the decolonization process appears in history textbooks is erroneous. Students are taught that this process was the result of a coup d'état in Portugal. Wisely and intentionally, no connection is made with, say, the African liberation movements, which were seen as outsiders in the process. Thus, it is quite normal to hear (from teachers, students, politicians) in Portugal bizarre statements such as, "When we gave independence to Mozambique," "When we gave up Angola," "When we negotiated the independence of Cabo Verde or Guiné Bissau." Actually, this is the official curricular discourse in the vast majority of Portuguese schools. There is no legitimate space for teachers and students to resume a serious debate over the real reasons that instigated the revolution in Portugal in 1974. "We" (Western capitalist colonial male) expanded the territory and Christianized the indigenous people; "we" decolonized because "we" were tired of António Salazar and Marcelo Caetano's tyrannical regime; "we" gave up our land; and "we" neocolonize now, because "they" (poor people) are not ready to govern themselves yet. The stories of Portuguese history continue to be told by the same glorious, undefeatable narrators. Oddly enough, this self-aggrandizing "we" was also (and still is) a major asset in helping Portugal become a member of (and cement its position in) the European Union—"we" have a surplus of cultural capital in the relations between the African continent and Europe. Fairly diachronical, palpably synchronical, this belabored "we" is an endemic lethal practice, to say the least.

Carefully reading a government-approved textbook borrowed from a twelfth-grade student, we noticed the total absence of such words as *genocide* and *human exploitation*. Conversely, easily found are such terms as *acculturation, cultural integration, discoveries, expansion,* and so on. We do notice the use of phrases like *slavery traffic, commerce monopoly, colonial empire,* and *colonization*; however, such words appear in the text in a way that precludes the reader from making historical connections. For example, the traffic of slaves is treated not as a disgusting capitalist colonial practice but as something that did huge damage to capitalist colonial intentions, since it "causes the de-population of vast territories"; slavery—and its traffic—"was not a problem for the slaves, but actually a dilemma for the Portuguese regime."[95] Another peculiar perspective is the official use of words such as *acculturation* and *cultural integration.* Such practices are treated as "important [phenomena] that created profound alterations in the populations' way of life, since they were facing a much more powerful culture."[96] So, instead of *colonized* we have the *populations,* and *acculturation* and *cultural integration* do not describe genocidal practices but notorious phenomena driven by a superior culture—What can "we" do? We are superior. It is interesting to observe that students and teachers not only have to consider such an epoch in a wisely distorted way—regrettably reproducing it—but also have to address Portuguese empire expansion problems. The total absence of any analysis of the damage that such an epoch caused to those "populations" is truly despicable. This is pure intellectual dishonesty. Moreover, this particular textbook—which has a circulation of 17,000 copies, a remarkable number for a small country like Portugal—is undeniable evidence of the way the capitalist colonial era is authored and narrated by Portuguese voices.[97]

Michel Foucault's study of fearless speech is towering. Anchoring his analysis in the etymology of the word *parrhesia,* he argues "the one who uses *parrhesia,* the *parrhesiastes,* is someone who says everything he has in mind [and] he does not hide anything, but opens his heart and mind completely to other people through his discourse [that is to say] the word *parrhesia* refers to a type of relationship between the speaker and what he says [for] in *parrhesia* the speaker makes it manifestly clear and obvious that what he says is his own opinion."[98] So according to Foucault's understanding "in *parrhesia* the speaker emphasizes the fact that he is both the subject of the enunciation and the subject of the enunciandum—that he himself is the subject of the opinion to which he refers."[99] Moreover, the *parrhesiastes* "says what is true because he *knows* that it is true [and] he knows that it is true because it is really true [hence] the *parrhesiastes* is not only sincere and says what is his opinion, but his opinion is also the truth because it is really true."[100]

Before such an interesting analysis one might ask: Where are the indigenous "parrhesia" and "parrhesiastes"? What happen to them? By recapturing Dwight Reynolds's claims over "the fallacy of Western origins" explained earlier, we can understand the pretentious Western position that there is no such scientific (and thus credible) indigenous "parrhesia" and "parrhesiastes" tradition. By combining this arrogant position—one that has the frightening audacity to even argue that the notion of a "scientific" text, such as autobiography, was well beyond the other's imagination, let alone practices—with the hard reductive and positivistic way of allowing teachers and students to engage only in unchallenged rote learning—it is quite easy to perceive how the school curriculum is implicated in historical distortion by perpetuating an arrogant Western vision of the world. Dwayne Huebner straightforwardly illustrates the reductionism of the learning theory in this example: "For centuries the poet has sung of his near infinitudes; the theologian has preached of his depravity and hinted of his participation in the divine; the philosopher has struggled to encompass him in his systems, only to have him repeatedly escape; the novelist and dramatist have captured his fleeting moments of pain and purity in unforgettable esthetic forms; and the [man] engaged in the curriculum has the temerity to reduce this being to a single term—learner."[101]

In fact, such a dishonest understanding of students and teachers, combined with a school that wisely "shows by hiding," makes the curriculum a powerful device to perpetuate a distorted vision of history, a curriculum that "is selective with a vengeance, in other words is not a simple selection, [but] a selection that reproduces dominance and subordination."[102] Underneath such a shameful accomplishment lies a pathetic need to keep claiming the nonexistence of particular lethal realities. This argument becomes more powerful when articulated with Bruno Latour's position. In *Pandora's Hope,* he asks: Where were microbes before Pasteur? Latour bases his approach in what he calls "three trials," namely: "(a) the thing itself, soon to be called ferment, (b) the story told by Pasteur to his colleagues at the Academy of Science, and (c) the reactions of Pasteur's interlocutors to what is so far only a story found in a written text," three trials that, according to Latour, should be "first distinguished and then aligned with one another."[103] However, as Latour highlights, "despite what the metaphor of 'trials' implies, phenomena are not 'out there' waiting for the researcher to access them"; that is to say, "lactic acid ferments have to be 'made visible' by Pasteur's work."[104] Wisely he pushes the reader for a cautious understanding. That is "the optical metaphor may account for the visible but not for the 'making' something visible; [in other words] the industrial metaphor may explain why something is 'made,' but not why it has thus become visible."[105]

Thus, to the apparently simple question "did ferments exist before Pasteur made them up?" the answer must be "No, they did not exist before he came along."[106] It is important to understand that the complexity of such a question does not "reside in the 'historicity' of ferments but in the little expression "to make up.'"[107] Thus, as Latour argues, "if we meant by 'historicity' merely that our contemporary 'representation' of microorganisms dates from the mid-nineteenth century," the concern is trivial.[108] Conversely, if "we meant by 'historicity' merely that the ferments 'evolve over time' like the infamous cases of the flu virus or HIV, there would not be difficulty either."[109] The former case "entails that we should be able to say that not only the microbes-for-us-humans changed in the 1850s, but also the microbes-for-themselves [and] their encounter with Pasteur changed them as well; [in other words] Pasteur, so to speak, 'happened' to them."[110] For the latter, "like that of all living species . . . the historicity of a ferment would be firmly rooted in nature [and] instead of being static, phenomena would be defined as dynamic."[111] Clearly, according to Bruno Latour's analysis, the question "did ferments exist (or not) before Pasteur?" could really signify two distinctive things. The answer to the question depends on the articulation human–nonhuman and subjectivity–objectivity.

What can we draw from Latour's analysis? To be more precise, what is the connection between his approach and our radical critical scrutiny over (school and curriculum) knowledge? In comparing these approaches, we see that Latour's insight becomes even more fragile. Notwithstanding the fact that one can find overlapping nuances between our position and Latour's approaches (e.g., "reality" is not out there waiting to be discovered, or as Michael Apple commented, reality "doesn't stalk around with a label"), the fact is that for Latour "microbes," "phenomena" "reality," or "knowledge" only exist if one theorizes them.[112] Accepting this could lead to an intellectual ambush, since, if one does not theorize, say, poverty, segregation, racism, sexism, genderism, starvation and so forth, it means that they do not exist. To put it more bluntly, if these "particular" painful social sagas do not "happen" to someone, to use Latour's own words, this does not mean that they have no "reality." Here Apple's approach proves more powerful.[113] The very fact that textbook knowledge values specific kinds of social "phenomena," "reality," or "knowledge," while distorting and even obliterating many others, does not mean that those many others do not exist. Unfortunately, for a vast majority of the human population, realities such as poverty, starvation, racism and sexism are the underpinnings of their daily lives. For Apple—one of the most powerful radical critical scholars—reality is a social construction and the real issue is trying to understand who participates in the construction of such realities. [114] By being knowledgeable about this particular argument, one will be able to understand in a deep sense how realities such as HIV or the floods in Latin America and South Africa are social constructions, not only in the way they "happened" but also (and this is of critical importance) in the way the dominant societal power articulates the political, economic and cultural mechanisms that address those realities.[115] Notwithstanding the fact that, say, epidemics should be seen as a dynamic phenomenon, as Latour points out, the issue is not only how it is "made up" but who is being targeted and who benefits from such a reality. One would be naive to minimize the relation between pollution and floods (which belies the premise of "natural disasters") and not consider whom those floods target and what policies are put in place to address these dramatic problems. Oddly enough, for both Apple and Latour a key concern is how "phenomena," "reality," and "knowledge" are made up. For Apple they are social constructions "overdetermined" by economic, cultural, ideological and political practices, yet based on a selective tradition. For him the issue is trying to see who benefits from "particular" social constructions. One of Apple's central questions is who benefits if we believe in specific social constructions.[116] It is important to think about why racism "happened" (to use Latour's terminology), say, to Paul (from *Official Knowledge*) or Joseph (from *Educating the "Right" Way*) or Mayotte (from *Je suis martiniquaise*), why what happened affects different groups differently.[117]

The real issue is to perceive not only why the invasion of capitalist colonial segregation and exploitation practices "happened." We also should not naively neglect the media's role here. We need to question why mainstream media express particular kinds of arguments while obliterating so many others and why particular kinds of arguments happen to be prized, not only by the mainstream media but also by textbooks. To take as an example the wars in Afghanistan and in Iraq—in which Portugal again demonstrated its paradoxical nature by both denouncing and supporting Bush, Blair and Aznar's lunatic vision—one needs to challenge why antiwar positions are twisted in or absent from the mainstream media, which presented the war as something inevitable and not as an invasion. Why did the mainstream media not denounce the supposed motive for the war and instead shift the focus to, say, Laci Peterson's murder? It is precisely this kind of "happening" that makes Michael Apple's question—who the benefactor really is?—more pertinent.

The same concerns arise with textbooks. According to Apple, the issue is to understand who benefits from the fact that particular views of reality are prized while many others are continuously silenced. Why do particular events never receive notable space in textbooks but only get added as an afterthought, often in a distorted way? Why do specific happenings, such as starvation and poverty (which compose the daily life of so many individuals) only occur to particular minorities, and why are they barely mentioned in textbooks? These questions call to mind Chris Jenks's approach toward the making of (an unequal) social reality. As he stresses, "We should attempt to reject the assumption that the individual as a social being has in some way been placed into society, that consists of a preestablished static set of pattern relations, which he then comes to know [or, to use Latour's terminology, "happens" to him or her] by virtue of his common membership, that is, through the process of socialization."[118] Conversely, "we should pose as our problematic concern the possibility that the individual, through the ongoing process of 'knowing,' or being-in-the-world, has constructed and continues to construct for himself in concert with others, a 'sense' of his social existence and his social environment as patterned and ordered."[119] As Jenks argues, the task is "not to make statements about the 'real' forms of the world, but rather examine the meanings and the possibilities provided by these forms as constructed within a particular social order."[120]

In discussing how curriculum knowledge—a regulated, compromised commodity—participates in a distorted vision of the discoveries, I have scrutinized particular critical approaches (Noam Chomsky, Howard Zinn, bell hooks, Tzvetan Todorov, James Loewen, Jean Anyon, Patrick Brindle and Madeleine Arnot, Jurjo Torres Santomé, Michael Apple and Bruno Latour) with the aim of making our political and pedagogical arguments more powerful. It seems clear, as I have demonstrated elsewhere, that the notion of curriculum is not limited to a power and social control device but should be seen as a regulated, compromised commodity that participates dynamically in the construction of political, economic and cultural identities. The notion of curriculum is one of identity.[121]

CRITICAL RACE THEORY: DEBUNKING THE ENDEMIC WESTERN "WE"

In this chapter I have attempted to achieve several goals. (1) I analyzed in a radical critical way the political reasons that underpinned António Salazar's tyrannical claim, and in so doing I argued that his statement needs to be subjected to a broader analysis of the Portuguese capitalist colonial and postcolonial platform. (2) I determined that such a paradox must be seen as an overdetermined set of processes that pushed the Portuguese capitalist colonial empire into a continuing transitory position, ending up in a Calibanian position. (3) Consequently, I highlighted how such a complicated position was an assumption of Portugal's capitalist colonial semiperipheral position. (4) I also examined how school curriculum perpetuates such a puzzling identity for most people (5) which, in so doing, promulgates a set of predatory discourses and practices that produces a twisted version of historical happenings, thus participating in a social construction of reality that fosters segregation.

Now I wish to call the reader's attention to the particular discourses and practices that position themselves as antiracist radical alternatives fighting for a more democratic and just society. In so doing, I will highlight critical race theory as a powerful antiracist device to understand and destroy such dangerous racial commonsense assumptions.

One of those antiracist discourses is multiculturalism. In fact, most multicultural curriculum approaches are pale add-ons in a culture of tolerance that actually serve to silence other cultures, languages and ways of seeing and being in the world. To be more precise, most multicultural curriculum approaches—such as the ones that the national Portuguese school curriculum has adopted—are a subtle form of cultural genocide. This kind of cultural genocide is more lethal than the explicitly racist approaches portrayed, say, by Richard Herrnstein and Charles Murray or even by Jean Marie Le Pen, Jörg Haider, and Eugene Terreblanche.[122] At least these men do not hide their racist views. Although one should not minimize their explicitly racist claims—after all, they were able to galvanize support from millions of people in the United States, France, Austria and South Africa—gray approaches such as some multicultural curricula are even more lethal.

Donaldo Macedo offers one of the most powerful radical critical arguments.[123] According to him, multicultural educational platforms failed to achieve a just cultural and economic democracy, given two main critical issues: "1) the teaching of cultural tolerance as an end in itself and 2) the lack of political clarity in the multicultural education movement which, in turn, prevents even the most committed educators from understanding how the school of positivism which many of them embrace, informs and shapes multicultural program and curriculum developments, often neutralizing the possibility for the creation of pedagogical structures that could lead to an authentic cultural democracy."[124]

By assuming what Macedo calls a "paternalistic cult of cultural tolerance," most multicultural approaches not only end up "fracturing cultural identities" but sink into policies of "integration" and "acculturation," thereby participating in expunging the cultural capital of particular minority cultures. This cultural tolerance becomes one of the vital organs of the arrogant Western predatory pedagogical apparatus. As Macedo argues, "If we analyze closely the ideology that informs and shapes the present debate over multicultural education and the present polemic over the primacy of Western heritage, we can begin to see and understand that the ideological principles that sustain those debates are consonant with the structures and mechanisms of a colonial ideology designed to devalue the cultural capital and values of the colonized."[125] In essence, what most multicultural approaches seem to intentionally disregard is that, as David Gillborn reminds us, "policies based on the assumptions of assimilation/integration were . . . ill-conceived, partial and often racist."[126] In this context Macedo claims, "Before we can announce a more democratic pedagogy around multiculturalism based on a truly cultural democracy (this obviously would involve languages as factors of culture), we need to denounce the false assumptions and distortions that often lead to a form of entrapment pedagogy whereby dominant values are usually reproduced under the rubric of progressive approaches."[127]

Recapturing Gillborn's antiracist approach, what most multicultural approaches seem to neglect is that "racism changes [and] anti-racism must recognize and adapt to this complexity."[128] Race is not a monolithic category. In order to understand, interrupt and destroy racist xenophobic discourses and practices, especially in a moment characterized by an "ethnic and cultural war," we need, as many radical critical antiracist scholars suggest, to avoid the traps of most mainstream multicultural approaches and rely on critical race theory.[129] This approach views race as an endemic social issue that does not exist in a vacuum. There is a need not only to interrupt what Jeffrey Milligan felicitously calls the "idolatry of inclusion" but also to develop critical race theory lenses.[130] It is precisely this challenge that I am putting forward. Following William Tate's antiracist approaches and deconstructing António Salazar's dictatorial claim, I have challenged how such a claim has to be seen as a truthful expression of "traditional interests and cultural artifacts [that] serve as vehicles to limit and bind the educational opportunities of students of 'minorities.'"[131] I also have challenged the shameful obliteration of particular events from the Portuguese capitalist colonial era, and in so doing I have pushed for a "contextual/historical examination [that recognizes] the experiential knowledge of people of color" in analyzing society, which will help debunk the xenophobic and predatory endemic "we."[132]

NOTES

1. Boaventura de Sousa Santos, "Entre Prospero e Caliban: Colonialismo, Pós-Colonialismo e Inter-Identidade," in *Entre ser e estar: Raízes, percursos e discursos da identidade,* ed. Maria Irene Ramalho and António Sousa Ribeiro (Porto, Portugal: Edições Afrontamento, 2002), 23–85; Boaventura de Sousa Santos, *Pela mão de Alice: O social e o político na pós-modernidade* (Porto, Portugal: Afrontamento, 1994); Michael Omi and Howard Winant, "On the Theoretical Status of the Concept of Race," in *The RoutledgeFalmer Reader in Multicultural Education,* ed. Gloria Ladson-Billings and David Gillborn (London: RoutledgeFalmer, 2004), 7–15; David Gillborn, *"Race," Ethnicity, and Education: Teaching and Learning in Multi-Ethnic Schools* (London: RoutledgeFalmer, 1990); Frantz Fanon, *Black Skin, White Masks* (New York: Grove, 1967); Donaldo Macedo, "The Colonialism of the English Only Movement," *Educational Researcher* 29, no. 3 (2000): 15–21.
2. Sousa Santos, "Entre Prospero e Caliban," 23–85.
3. Sousa Santos, "Entre Prospero e Caliban," 23.
4. Sousa Santos, "Entre Prospero e Caliban," 23–26.
5. Sousa Santos, "Entre Prospero e Caliban," 23.
6. Sousa Santos, "Entre Prospero e Caliban," 24.
7. Sousa Santos, "Entre Prospero e Caliban," 24.
8. Sousa Santos, "Entre Prospero e Caliban," 26.
9. Sousa Santos, "Entre Prospero e Caliban," 26.
10. Sousa Santos, "Entre Prospero e Caliban," 26.
11. Sousa Santos, "Entre Prospero e Caliban," 53.
12. Sousa Santos, "Entre Prospero e Caliban," 23–85.
13. According to analyses of Lord Byron, Frère Claude Bronseval, Castelo Branco Chaves, Richard Crocker and Charles Adam, it is undeniable that the Portuguese people were seen in a quite dysphoric way: "The Portuguese people are slothful, lazy, indolent, do not take advantage of their rich soil, and moreover they do not know how to sell the wealthy resources of their colonies; Portuguese people live exclusively from the gold that comes from Brazil; Without a doubt, the Portuguese people are the most ugly race of Europe; Their heritage is a complex result of Jews, Arabs, Blacks and French and it seems that they have assumed and incorporated the worst characteristics of such races; Like the Jews, Portuguese people are penny pinching, stingy, dishonest; like the Arabs, they are jealous, malicious and vindictive; like the people of color, the Portuguese people are rude, false, servile; and they incorporate from the French, vanity, arrogance, superiority; There is no Portuguese book that is worth reading; and finally Portugal is a nation that is deeply fueled by ignorance and pride." In this regard please cf. Sousa Santos, "Entre Prospero e Caliban," 23–85)

14. Sousa Santos, "Entre Prospero e Caliban," 24–28.

15. Walter Rodney, *How Europe Underdeveloped Africa* (Washington, DC: Howard University Press, 1982), 88–89.

16. Barbara Fields, "Slavery, Race, and Ideology in the United States of America," *New Left Review* 181 (1990): 95–118; Omi and Winant, "On the Theoretical Status of the Concept of Race," 7–15, 8.

17. Steve Selden, *Inheriting Shame: The Story of Eugenics and Racism in America* (New York: Teachers College Press, 1999); Richard Herrnstein and Charles Murray, *The Bell Curve: Intelligence and Class Structure in American Life* (New York: Free Press, 1994).

18. Gillborn, *"Race," Ethnicity, and Education*; Selden, *Inheriting Shame;* Herrnstein and Murray, *The Bell Curve;* William Tate IV, "Critical Race Theory," *Review of Research in Education* 22 (1997): 195–247.

19. Macedo, "Colonialism of the English Only Movement," 17.

20. Gillborn, *"Race," Ethnicity, and Education,* 11.

21. Sousa Santos, "Entre Prospero e Caliban," 28.

22. Sousa Santos, "Entre Prospero e Caliban," 28.

23. Sousa Santos, "Entre Prospero e Caliban," 57.

24. Sousa Santos, "Entre Prospero e Caliban," 58.

25. Fanon, *Black Skin, White Masks.*

26. Capécia, *Je suis martiniquaise,* quoted in Fanon, *Black Skin, White Masks,* 42.

27. Fanon, *Black Skin, White Masks,* 42.

28. Capécia, *Je suis martiniquaise,* quoted in Fanon, *Black Skin, White Masks,* 42.

29. Fanon, *Black Skin, White Masks,* 44.

30. Fanon, *Black Skin, White Masks,* 44.

31. Colin Gordon, ed., *Power/Knowledge: Selected Interviews and Other Writings—1972–1977: Michel Foucault* (New York: Pantheon, 1977), 55.

32. Sousa Santos, "Entre Prospero e Caliban."

33. Sousa Santos, "Entre Prospero e Caliban."

34. Macedo, "Colonialism of the English Only Movement,"16.

35. Fanon, *Black Skin, White Masks,* 42.

36. Sousa Santos, "Entre Prospero e Caliban."

37. Peter Rigby, *African Images: Racism and the End of Anthropology* (Washington, DC: Berg, 1996), 1.

38. Donaldo Macedo, *Literacies of Power: What Americans Are Not Allowed to Know* (Boulder, CO: Westview, 1994).

39. Deborah Youdell, "Identity Traps or How Black Students Fail: The Interactions between Biographical, Sub-Cultural, and Learner Identities," in *RoutledgeFalmer Reader,* 84–102, esp. 90–93.

40. Youdell, "Identity Traps or How Black Students Fail," 83.

41. Youdell, "Identity Traps or How Black Students Fail," 90.

42. Omi and Winant, "On the Theoretical Status of the Concept of Race."

43. Omi and Winant, "On the Theoretical Status of the Concept of Race," 7.

44. David Gillborn, "Anti-Racism: From Policy to Praxis," in *RoutledgeFalmer Reader,* 35–48, 45.

45. Dwight Reynolds, *Interpreting the Self: Autobiography in the Arabic Literary Tradition* (Berkeley: University of California Press, 2001).

46. Georg Misch, *Geschichte der Autobiographie*, 4 vols. (Bern: A. Francke, 1949–1969); and Gerhard Schultke-Bulmke and Franz Rosenthal, *Die Arabische Autobiographie: Studia Arabica* 1 (1937), 1–40, quoted in Reynolds, *Interpreting the Self*, 17–35.

47. Reynolds, *Interpreting the Self*, 21, 17–35.

48. Albert Hourani, *Arabic Thought in a Liberal Age: 1739–1939* (Cambridge: Cambridge University Press, 1983), quoted in Reynolds, *Interpreting the Self*, 26.

49. Reynolds, *Interpreting the Self*, 27.

50. Reynolds, *Interpreting the Self*, 28.

51. Macedo, "Colonialism of the English Only Movement," 16–17.

52. Macedo, "Colonialism of the English Only Movement," 16.

53. Macedo, "Colonialism of the English Only Movement," 16.

54. João Paraskeva, "El currículo como prática de significaciones," *Kikiriki, Revista Cooperación Educativa* 62–63 (2001): 8–16.

55. Macedo, "Colonialism of the English Only Movement," 16.

56. James Loewen, *Lies My Teacher Told Me: Everything Your High School History Textbook Got Wrong* (New York: New Press, 1995). Jean Anyon, "Workers, Labor and Economic History, and Textbook Content," in *Ideology and Practice in Schooling*, ed. Michael Apple and Lois Weis (Philadelphia: Temple University Press, 1983), 37–60. Patrick Brindle and Madeleine Arnot, "England Expects Every Man to Do His Duty: The Gendering of the Citizenship Textbook, 1940–1996," *Oxford Review of Education* 25, no. 1–2 (1999): 103–23.

57. Bruno Latour, *Pandora's Hope: Essays on the Reality of Science Studies* (Cambridge, MA: Harvard University Press, 1999).

58. Noam Chomsky, "Legitimacy in History," in *Understanding Power: The Indispensable Noam Chomsky*, ed. P. Mitchell and J. Schoeffel (New York: New Press, 2002), 135.

59. Chomsky, "Legitimacy in History," 136.

60. Noam Chomsky, *Chronicles of Dissent: Interviews with David Barsamian* (Monroe, ME: Common Courage, 1992), 75–88. Howard Zinn, "Reflections on History," in *The Future of History: Interviews with David Barsamian* (Monroe, ME: Common Courage, 1999), 3; bell hooks, *Outlaw Culture: Resisting Representations* (New York: Routledge, 1994), 197.

61. Howard Zinn, "You Can't Be Neutral on a Moving Terrain," in *Future of History*, 47–75.

62. Zinn, "Reflections on History," 3.

63. Howard Zinn, *On History* (New York: Seven Stories, 2001), 102.

64. Columbus, quoted in Zinn, *On History*, 99.

65. Las Casas, quoted in Zinn, *On History*, 101.

66. Bernaldez, quoted in Tzvetan Todorov, *The Conquest of America: The Question of the Other* (New York: Harper & Row, 1984), 35.

67. Bernaldez, quoted in Todorov, *Conquest of America*, 34–35.

68. hooks, *Outlaw Culture*, 198.

69. hooks, *Outlaw Culture*, 198.

70. hooks, *Outlaw Culture*, 199.

71. hooks, *Outlaw Culture*, 202.

72. hooks, *Outlaw Culture*, 203.

73. hooks, *Outlaw Culture*, 203.

74. hooks, *Outlaw Culture*, 203.

75. Chomsky, "Legitimacy in History," 136.
76. Chomsky, "Legitimacy in History," 136.
77. Loewen, *Lies My Teacher Told Me,* 29.
78. Loewen, *Lies My Teacher Told Me,* 29.
79. Loewen, *Lies My Teacher Told Me,* 30.
80. Loewen, *Lies My Teacher Told Me,* 35.
81. Loewen, *Lies My Teacher Told Me,* 35.
82. Loewen, *Lies My Teacher Told Me,* 50.
83. Jurjo Torres Santomé, "The Presence of Different Cultures in Schools: Possibilities of Dialogue and Action," *Curriculum Studies* 4, no. 1 (1996): 25–41.
84. Torres Santomé, "Presence of Different Cultures in Schools."
85. Anyon, "Workers, Labor and Economic History, and Textbook Content"; Brindle and Arnot, "England Expects Every Man to Do His Duty."
86. Anyon, "Workers, Labor and Economic History, and Textbook Content," 37.
87. Anyon, "Workers, Labor and Economic History, and Textbook Content," 49.
88. Anyon, "Workers, Labor and Economic History, and Textbook Content," 49.
89. Anyon, "Workers, Labor and Economic History, and Textbook Content," 49.
90. Brindle and Arnot, "England Expects Every Man to Do His Duty," 108.
91. Brindle and Arnot, "England Expects Every Man to Do His Duty," 108.
92. Brindle and Arnot, "England Expects Every Man to Do His Duty," 110.
93. Brindle and Arnot, "England Expects Every Man to Do His Duty," 108.
94. Brindle and Arnot, "England Expects Every Man to Do His Duty," 112.
95. Marinho, Cardoso, and Rothes, *História 8* (Porto, Portugal: Areal Editores, 1999), 36.
96. Marinho, Cardoso, and Rothes, *História 8,* 36.
97. Marinho, Cardoso, and Rothes, *História 8,* 36.
98. Michel Foucault, *Fearless Speech* (Los Angeles: Semiotext(e), 2001), 12.
99. Foucault, *Fearless Speech,* 13.
100. Foucault, *Fearless Speech,* 14.
101. D. Huebner, "Curricular Language and Classroom Meanings," in *Language and Meaning,* ed. J. Macdonald and R. Leeper (Washington, DC: ASCD, 1966), 10.
102. Michael Apple, interview, in João Paraskeva, "Here I Stand: A Long [R]evolution: Ideology, Culture and Curriculum" (Ph.D. diss., University of Minho, Portugal, 2003).
103. Latour, *Pandora's Hope,* 122.
104. Latour, *Pandora's Hope,* 139.
105. Latour, *Pandora's Hope,* 139.
106. Latour, *Pandora's Hope,* 145.
107. Latour, *Pandora's Hope,* 145.
108. Latour, *Pandora's Hope,* 145.
109. Latour, *Pandora's Hope,* 146.
110. Latour, *Pandora's Hope,* 146.
111. Latour, *Pandora's Hope,* 146.
112. Michael Apple, *Official Knowledge: Democratic Education in a Conservative Age* (New York: Routledge, 2000), 43.

113. Apple, *Official Knowledge*, 43.

114. Michael Apple, *Ideology and Curriculum* (New York: Routledge, 1990).

115. Apple, *Official Knowledge*.

116. Apple, *Ideology and Curriculum*; Apple, *Official Knowledge*.

117. Apple, *Official Knowledge*; Michael Apple, *Educating the "Right" Way: Markets, Standards, God, and Inequality* (New York: Routledge, 2001); Capécia, *Je suis martiniquaise*.

118. C. Jenks, *Rationality, Education, and the Social Organization of Knowledge: Papers for a Reflexive Sociology of Education* (London: Routledge & Kegan Paul, 1977), 2.

119. Jenks, *Rationality, Education, and Social Organization of Knowledge*, 2.

120. Jenks, *Rationality, Education, and Social Organization of Knowledge*, 2–3.

121. Paraskeva, "Here I Stand."

122. Richard Herrnstein and Charles Murray are authors of *The Bell Curve*. Jean Marie Le Pen is the leader of the neo-Nazi party in France. Jörg Haider is the leader of the neo-Nazi party in Austria and the governor of Carinthia. Eugene Terreblanche is the leader of the neo-Nazi Afrikaner party in South Africa.

123. Donaldo Macedo, "Multiculturalismo para além da ditadura do positivismo," in *Políticas educativas e curriculares: Um século de estudos curriculares*, ed. João Paraskeva (Porto, Portugal: Didáctica, in press). See also Macedo, "Colonialism of the English Only Movement."

124. Macedo, "Multiculturalismo para além da ditadura do positivismo."

125. Macedo, "Multiculturalismo para além da ditadura do positivismo."

126. Gillborn, *"Race," Ethnicity, and Education*, 147.

127. Macedo, "Multiculturalismo para além da ditadura do positivismo."

128. Gillborn, "Anti-Racism," 45.

129. Macedo, "The Colonialism of the English Only Movement," 15.

130. Jeffrey Milligan, "Multiculturalism and the Idolatry of Inclusion," in *Multi-Intercultural Conversations: A Reader*, ed. Shirley Steinberg (New York: Peter Lang, 2001), 31–48.

131. Tate, "Critical Race Theory," 234.

132. Tate, "Critical Race Theory," 235.

INDEX

ABOUT THE CONTRIBUTORS

Anna Aluffi Pentini is professor at the Pedagogical Faculty of the Terza Università di Roma and has been part-time lecturer at the Universities of Bolzano, Genoa, and Innsbruck. A graduate in educational sciences and a qualified interpreter, she completed her Ph.D. in 1995 on the topic "Intercultural Education between Theory and Practice." Aluffi Pentini has conducted numerous research projects (e.g. with CENSIS and AASTER, Milan) in this and related pedagogical areas, lately with migrant infants and with cultural mediators. Her major publications deal with contemporary issues in intercultural pedagogy and action research.

Zygmunt Bauman is emeritus professor of sociology at the University of Leeds and the University of Warsaw. He is a prolific writer, and his most recent major books include *In Search of Politics* (1999), *Globalization* (2000), *Liquid Modernity* (2000), *The Individualized Society* (2001), *Community: Seeking Safety in an Insecure World* (2001), *Society under Siege* (2002), and *Wasted Lives* (2004).

Carmel Borg is senior lecturer and dean of the Faculty of Education at the University of Malta, where he teaches and researches in curriculum studies and critical pedagogy. His books include *Gramsci and Education* (coedited with Joseph Buttigieg and Peter Mayo, 2002) and *Children and Youth at Risk* (coedited, in press). He is the editor of the *Journal of Maltese Education Research* and coedits the *Journal of Postcolonial Education*.

Bill Christison joined the CIA in 1950 and served on the analysis side of the agency for twenty-eight years. From the early 1970s he served as national intelligence officer (principal adviser to the director of central intelligence on certain areas) for, at various times, Southeast Asia, South Asia, and Africa. Before he retired in 1979 he was director of the CIA's Office of Regional and Political Analysis, a 250–person unit. He is a contributor to *The Politics of Anti-Semitism* (2003).

Kathleen Christison worked in the CIA, retiring in 1979. Since then she has been mainly preoccupied by the issue of Palestine. She is the author of *Perceptions of Palestine: Their Influence on U.S. Middle East Policy* (1999) and *The Wound of Dispossession: Telling the Palestinian Story* (2001). She is also a contributor to *The Politics of Anti-Semitism* (2003).

Lena de Botton is coordinator of the Arab and Muslim Studies Group Alhiwar at the University of Barcelona. She is European of Arab decent. She is currently finishing her Ph.D. at the École des Hautes Études en Sciences Sociales in Paris. Among her latest publications is *The Inclusion of Other Women: Breaking the Silence through Dialogic Learning,* coauthored with Lídia Puigvert and Montse Sánchez.

Ramón Flecha is professor of sociology at the University of Barcelona and director of CREA, the Centre of Research in Theories and Practices that Overcome Inequalities at the Science Park of Barcelona. He has directed research projects internationally and nationally on issues related to education, multiculturalism, immigration, the labor market, and the inclusion of cultural minorities. His extensive research is dedicated to the analysis of social inequalities and how they can be overcome, focusing especially on marginalized groups. He has published "Modern and Postmodern Racism in Europe: Dialogic Approach and Antiracist Pedagogies" in *Harvard Educational Review, Contemporary Social Theory* (with Jesús Gómez and Lidia Puigvert, 2003), *Critical Education in the New Information Age* (with Manuel Castells, Paulo Freire, Henry A. Giroux, Donaldo Macedo, and Paul Willis, 1999), and *Conocimiento e identidad: Voces de grupos culturales en la investigación social* (with Michel Wieviorka and Alain Touraine).

Henry A. Giroux holds the Global TV Network Chair in Communications at McMaster University in Canada. His most recent books include *The Abandoned Generation: Democracy beyond the Culture of Fear* (coauthored with Susan Searls Giroux, 2003), *Take Back Higher Education: Race, Youth, and the Crisis of Democracy in the Post Civil rights Era* (2004), *The Terror of Neoliberalism* (Paradigm, 2004), *Border Crossings* (2005), *Schooling and the Struggle for Public Life* (2005), and *Against the New Authoritarianism: Politics after Abu Ghraib* (2005).

David Theo Goldberg is director of the system-wide University of California Humanities Research Institute. He is also professor of African American studies and criminology, law and society, as well as a fellow of the Critical Theory Institute at the University of California, Irvine. Goldberg is the author of, among others, *The Racial State* (2002), *Racial Subjects: Writing on Race in America* (1997), and *Racist Culture: Philosophy and the Politics of Meaning* (1993). He is also the editor or coeditor of, among other works, *Anatomy of Racism* (1990), *Multiculturalism: A Critical Reader* (1995), *Race Critical Theories* (with Philomena Essed, 2001), *Relocating Postcolonialism* (with Ato Quayson, 2002), *A Companion to Racial and Ethnic Studies* (with John Solomos, 2002), *Between Law and Culture* (with

Michael Musheno and Lisa Bower, 2002), and *A Companion to Gender Studies* (with Philomena Essed and Audrey Kobayashi, 2004).

Panayota Gounari is an assistant professor in the Applied Linguistics Graduate Program at the University of Massachusetts Boston. She holds a Ph.D. in cultural studies in education from Pennsylvania State University. She specializes in bilingualism, multicultural education, literacy, and technology in language education. Her primary areas of interest include language policy and linguistic hegemony, critical discourse analysis,language and the politics of difference, the role of language in social change and the construction of human agency and democratic spaces as well as its implications for critical pedagogy. She coauthored *The Hegemony of English* with Donaldo Macedo and Bessie Dendrinos (Paradigm, 2003).

Peter Gstettner has been professor for educational science at the Alpen-Andria University of Klagenfurt in Austria since 1981. He is currently the director of the Institute for Educational Science and Educational Research and cofounder and director of the Ludwig Boltzmann Institute for Intercultural Educational Research, established in 1999 at Klagenfurt-Villach. His areas of interest include methods of field research, minority studies, ethnopsychology, racism, and educational reforms in Europe.

Franz Hamburger studied sociology, educational science and philosophy in Heidelberg and Cologne (1966–1972). From 1972 to 1978 he was research assistant at the University of Heidelberg, where he earned his Ph.D. in 1975. Since 1978 he has been professor of social work at the Department of Education of the University of Mainz in Germany. He has research experience in the fields of migration and minorities and has conducted international comparative studies in social work. He is also founder and director of the ISM, Institute for Social Research, Mainz.

Walter Lorenz is professor for applied social studies at the Free University of Bolzano, Italy. Formerly he taught social work as Jean Monnet Professor at the National University of Ireland, Cork, and coordinated several European scientific networks. His research interests and publications include antiracism and comparative aspects of European social work and social policy. He was cofounder of the *European Journal of Social Work* and coedits the online journal *Social Work and Society*.

Donaldo Macedo is professor of English and distinguished professor of liberal arts and education at the University of Massachusetts Boston. He has published extensively in the areas of Creole languages, critical literacy, bilingualism, and multiculturalism. His publications include *Literacy: Reading the Word and the World* (with Paulo Freire, 1987), *Literacies of Power: What Americans Are Not Allowed to Know* (1994), and *Howard Zinn in Demo-*

cratic Education (with Howard Zinn, 2005). His work has been translated into several languages.

Peter Mayo is associate professor in the Department of Education Studies, Faculty of Education, University of Malta, where he teaches and researches in the areas of adult education and sociology of education. His books include *Beyond Schooling: Adult Education in Malta* (coedited with Carmel Borg, 1997), *Gramsci, Freire and Adult Education: Possibilities for Transformative Action* (1999), *Gramsci and Education* (coedited, 2002) and *Liberating Praxis: Paulo Freire's Legacy for Radical Education and Politics* (2004). He is the founding editor of the *Journal of Postcolonial Education,* which he currently coedits, and he is the reviews editor of the *Mediterranean Journal of Educational Studies.*

João Menelau Paraskeva was born in Mozambique. He held an honorary fellowship in the Department of Curriculum and Instruction of the University of Wisconsin—Madison in 2000–2003, and he is currently professor of curriculum and instruction at the University of Minho at Braga, Portugal. He is also the senior editor of the multilanguage journal *Currículo sem Fronteiras* and editorial board member of other international journals. His publications include *The Dynamics of Cultural and Ideological Conflicts within Educational and Curriculum Foundations* (2000), *Winds of [De]schooling: The New Threat to Public Schooling* (with Michael Apple and Jurjo Torres Santomé, 2003), *Educational and Curriculum Dialogues on the Left* (2004), *Educational and Curriculum Policies: A Century of Curriculum Studies* (2005); and *Ideology and Culture: General Tensions in the Curriculum Field* (2006).

Edward Said (1935–2003) was one of the world's most celebrated, outspoken, and influential public intellectuals. He wrote more than twenty books that have been translated into thirty-six languages including *Beginnings* (1975), *The Question of Palestine* (1979), the internationally acclaimed *Orientalism* (1979), *Covering Islam* (1980), *Culture and Imperialism* (1993), and *Power, Politics, and Culture* (2001). He began teaching in 1963 at Columbia University, where he became a professor of English and comparative literature and where he taught until his death.

Iñaki Santa Cruz is professor of economics at the University Autonoma of Barcelona. His main body of research is on immigration and the labor market, and among others is the R&D study *Amal,* on illegal Muslim immigration in Spain. Among his latest publications are "Discriminación étnica en el mercado laboral" in the Basque journal *Lan Harremanak.*

Georgios Tsiakalos has been a professor of pedagogy since 1984 at Aristotle University of Thessaloniki, where he is also the dean of the Faculty of Education. He has done research in the areas of population genetics, racism and sociobiology, social exclusion and poverty, education of migrants and minorities, educational praxis, and educational reforms. One of his first important publications was his book *Ausländerfeindlichkeit: Tatsachen und Erklärungsversuche* 1983) on the developing racism in Germany, which was based on an analysis of the implications that a prevailing cultural racism had even on the well-intentioned politics in that country. His most recent publications (in Greek) include *Handbook of Antiracist Education* (2000) focusing on everyday racism against poor immigrants in Greece, *The Promise of Pedagogy* (2001), and *Reflections of Human Society* (2004).

Julio Vargas Clavería is director of the Romà Studies Center at the University of Barcelona. He is a Rom and a person of respect in the Spanish Romaní community. Among his latest publications is "Why Romà Do Not Like Mainstream Schools: Voices of a People without Territory," coauthored with Jesús Gómez and published in the *Harvard Educational Review.*

Loïc Wacquant is professor at the University of California—Berkeley, distinguished university professor of sociology and anthropology at the New School for Social Resarch, and researcher at the Center for European Sociology in Paris. His interests include comparative urban marginality, ethnoracial domination, the penal state, bodily crafts, social theory, and the politics of reason. His recent books include *Body and Soul: Notebooks of an Apprentice Boxer* (2004) and *Deadly Symbiosis: Race and the Rise of Neoliberal Penality* (2005).

Anja Weiss, Ph.D., is a sociologist at Ludwig Maximilians University in Munich. She is currently working on a transnational theory of social inequality. Her research interests include social inequality, racism and interethnic conflict, and migration. Weiss's publications include "The Transnationalization of Social Inequality," (*Current Sociology,* 2005), "Rassismus wider Willen" [Racism without Racist Intentions] (2001), and *Klasse und Klassifikation* [Class and Classification], coedited with Cornelia Koppetsch, Albert Scharenberg, and Oliver Schmidtke (2001).